LITIGATING THE NURSING HOME CASE

THIRD EDITION

JAMES T. O'REILLY AND MARK TASSONE

ABA
AMERICAN BAR ASSOCIATION
Senior Lawyers Division

Cover design by Sara Wadford/ABA Design

Printed in the United States of America.

29 28 27 26 25 5 4 3 2 1

A catalog record for this book is available from the Library of Congress.

Contents

About the Authors xvii

Acknowledgments xix

In Memoriam xxi

PART 1
Understanding the Context 1

CHAPTER 1
Introduction 3

CHAPTER 2
Definitions 13

2:1 Key Definitions 13
2:2 Background 15
2:3 Operational Aspects of Federal Controls 16
2:4 Applying the SNF and RUG Measures 17
2:5 Federal and State Integration of Standards 18
2:6 Federal Funding Brings Control 18
2:7 Understanding the Integrated Elements of the Legal Structure 20
2:8 Interactions of Regulation with Tort Liability 22
2:9 Purposes of the Resident's Nursing Home Stay 24
2:10 Significance of the Federal Funding Source Categories 24
2:11 Integration with Tort Liability 25
2:12 Political Aspects 26

CHAPTER 3
Identifying the Defendant Nursing Home Owner 29

3:1 Who Owns This Nursing Home? 29

3:2 How Has the Home Managed to Obtain a Profit? 30
3:3 Role of the Corporate Budget Official 31
3:4 Role of the Nursing Home Administrator 32

PART 2
Responsibilities of Professionals **33**

CHAPTER 4
Roles and Liabilities of Nursing Professionals **35**
4:1 Participants 35
4:2 Staffing Levels 36
4:3 Meeting Individual Patient Care Needs 37
4:4 Allocating Responsibilities 39
4:5 Professional Responsibility 40

CHAPTER 5
Roles and Liabilities of Physicians **43**
5:1 Role of the Nursing Home Medical Director 43
5:2 Contractual Obligations 46
5:3 CMS Norms on Physician Obligations 47
5:4 Documentation of Decisions 48
5:5 Actual Supervision of Patient Care 48
5:6 Pharmaceutical Prescriptions 49
5:7 Role in Restraints 50
5:8 Malpractice Issues 50
5:9 Physician Duty and "Right to Die" Claims 51

CHAPTER 6
Supporting Staff and Their Roles **53**
6:1 Consequences of Understaffing When Presented as a Cause of Harm 53
6:2 Dietary Support 54
6:3 Pharmacy Support 56
6:4 Laboratory Support 59
6:5 Rehabilitation 61
6:6 Documentation 61

6:7 The Role of Nursing Home Administration 62
6:8 Admissions 63
6:9 Accounting 64
6:10 Staff Training and Selection 64
6:11 Support Rules of Specialized Units 65
6:12 Illustrative Case 66

CHAPTER 7
Facility Safety Issues **67**
7:1 Premises Safety Issues 67
7:2 Fire and Emergency Issues 68
7:3 Floods and Evacuations 68
7:4 Removal 68
7:5 Avoiding Preventable Errors 69
7:6 Facility Maintenance Issues 69
7:7 Stairway Accidents 70

CHAPTER 8
Liability for Neglect: Skin Ulcers and Infection Problems **71**
8:1 Overview 72
8:2 Use of Clinical Practice Guidelines or CMS Guidelines as Evidence of the Standard of Care 76
8:3 Use of Regulatory Violations to Establish Negligence Per Se or as Evidence of the Standard of Care 78
8:4 Legal Issues 81
8:5 Dividing the Causes 82
8:6 Care Must Be Continuously Supervised 84
8:7 Record-Keeping Is Essential to Defense 85
8:8 Standard of Due Care 85
8:9 Short Staffing 87
8:10 Evidence 88
8:11 Defenses 89
8:12 Damages 90
8:13 Punitive Damages 90
8:14 Burns 90

8:15 Other Infection Concerns 91
8:16 Lessons from the Cases 91
8:17 Summary 94

CHAPTER 9
Fall-Related Injuries **95**
9:1 Introduction 95
9:2 Resident Assessments by Nursing Homes 98
9:3 Measures to Avoid Fall Injuries 99
9:4 Resident Evaluation 101
9:5 Procedures and Documentation 104
9:6 Response to the Fall Event 104
9:7 Transportation Concerns 105
9:8 Fall Cases Are Not Simple 105
9:9 Legal Implications of Fall Injuries 107
9:10 Proving Nursing Home Negligence in the Fall Case 109
9:11 Assembling the Proof of Causation 111
9:12 Few Fall Cases Reach Appellate Levels 112
9:13 Evaluating Potential Litigation 113
9:14 Plaintiff's Theory of the Case 115
9:15 Policies and Noncompliance 116
9:16 Examples of Fall Injury Cases 117

CHAPTER 10
Liability for Neglect: Wandering, Elopement, and Escape **119**
10:1 Overview 119
10:2 Response When Residents Escape 124
10:3 Why Residents Wander 124
10:4 Safety versus Secure Buildings 125
10:5 Staff Responsibilities 125
10:6 Framing the Complaint 126
10:7 Lessons from the Cases 127
10:8 Summary 130

CHAPTER 11
Use of Resident Restraints **133**
11:1 Overview 133
11:2 Restraints and Uses 134
11:3 Restraint-Injury Litigation 135
11:4 CMS and State Norms 136
11:5 FDA Hazard Alerts 137
11:6 Summary 138

CHAPTER 12
Assault and Abuse **139**
12:1 Overview 140
12:2 Long-Term Care Ombudsmen Programs 143
12:3 Incidence of Abuse 145
12:4 Overview of Intentional Harm: Abuse by Caregivers 146
12:5 Overview of Neglect by Caregivers 150
12:6 Overview of Abuse by Other Residents and Nonemployee Third Parties 152
12:7 Criminal Aspects 154
12:8 Definitions 156
12:9 Sources of Assaults 158
12:10 Regulatory Duty of Care for Protection of Residents 159
12:11 Nursing Home Response to Assaults 162
12:12 Framing the Complaint for Civil Tort Liability 163
12:13 State Alternative Malpractice Remedies 166
12:14 Defending the Nursing Home's Supervision 167
12:15 Rape and Sexual Assault 169
12:16 Effects of Shock and Public Outrage 173
12:17 Allegations of Concealment of the Assault 173
12:18 Allegations of Employee Hiring and Supervision Errors 174
12:19 CMS and State Penalties 176
12:20 Punitive Damages 177
12:21 Liability Insurance 177
12:22 Evidentiary Issues 178

12:23 Governmental Immunity 179
12:24 Effect of Resident Assault on Liability to Employees 180

CHAPTER 13
Pharmaceuticals **183**
13:1 Overview 183
13:2 Medication Management 185
13:3 Inappropriate Use of Antipsychotic Medications 186
13:4 Adverse Drug Interactions 188
13:5 Polypharmacy 189
13:6 Overview of Relevant Litigation 190
13:7 What Drug-Related Problems Are Likely to Arise in Nursing Homes? 191
13:8 Shared Liability: Malpractice or Drug Problems? 192
13:9 Malpractice by Misprescribing 193
13:10 Risks of Negligent Polypharmacy 196
13:11 Overdosing of Pharmaceuticals 197
13:12 Negligent Misdelivery 199
13:13 Drugs as a Resident Restraint Option 199
13:14 Inattentive Medical Oversight 200
13:15 Medical Device Problems 202

CHAPTER 14
Food-Related Harms **205**
14:1 Food-Related Litigation 205
14:2 Why Litigation Occurs 207
14:3 Types of Harm from Food 209
14:4 Chronic Risk: Weight Loss and Wasting 210
14:5 Lessons from the Cases 211
14:6 Acute Risk: Choking and Aspiration 213
14:7 Expert Testimony 214
14:8 Tube and Pump Feeding 215
14:9 Responsibility for Care and Feeding 217
14:10 Dehydration 219
14:11 Setting the Standard of Care 220
14:12 Evaluations of Resident Nutritional Needs 220

CHAPTER 27
Damages **337**
27:1 Elders Tend to Have Low Economic Damages 337
27:2 Noneconomic Damages or "Specials" 337
27:3 Calculating Damages 338
27:4 Allocating Liability 340
27:5 Death Effects 341
27:6 Effects of Tort Reform 342
27:7 Punitive Damages 343
27:8 Statutory Damage Provisions 346
27:9 Caps as Deterrence to Litigation 346
27:10 Consequences of Large Awards for Medicaid Eligibility 347

CHAPTER 28
Defenses **349**
28:1 Overview 349
28:2 Defenses Related to Residents 353
28:3 Defenses Related to Families 356
28:4 Defenses Related to Regulators 356
28:5 State Charitable Immunity 357

CHAPTER 29
Arbitration **359**
29:1 Overview 359
29:2 The Case for Requiring Arbitration by Contract 360
29:3 Criticism of the Use of Arbitration 361
29:4 Costs and Award Limitations 365
29:5 Procedures 365
29:6 Defenses against Arbitration 366

CHAPTER 30
Motion Practice **369**
30:1 Discovery Motions 369
30:2 Failure to State a Claim 370

30:3 Summary Judgment 371
30:4 Removal to Federal Court 371
30:5 Motions after Verdict 372
30:6 Remittitur 372

CHAPTER 31
Trial Procedure Issues **373**
31:1 Voir Dire—The "Ideal" Juror 373
31:2 Presentations and Demonstrative Evidence 374
31:3 Decisions on Evidence 375
31:4 Impeachment and Response 375

CHAPTER 32
Insurance **377**
32:1 Coverage of Nursing Home Liability Cases 377
32:2 Settlement Authority at "Policy Limits" 379
32:3 Bad-Faith Litigation 380
32:4 Beneficial Role of Insurers 380

CHAPTER 33
Verdicts and Settlements **381**
33:1 Overview 381
33:2 Settlement Influences 382
33:3 Effects of Settlement and Release 382
33:4 Verdicts Allocating Percentage Fault 383
33:5 Special Verdicts and Interrogatories 383
33:6 Verdicts against Individual Actors 383
33:7 Partial Settlements with Selected Defendants 384
33:8 Releases of Selected Defendants 384
33:9 Threats of Bankruptcy 385

CHAPTER 34
After-Verdict Liens and Offsets **387**
34:1 Subrogation and the Effect of Repayment of Liens 387
34:2 Specific Steps for the Prudent Plaintiff's Counsel 391

34:3 Informing the Client Early 391
34:4 Continued Eligibility 392
34:5 Payment of Private Insurer Liens 392

Table of Cases 395

Index 417

About the Authors

Professor James T. O'Reilly taught in the College of Law and the College of Medicine at the University of Cincinnati. With this publication, he has published 57 texts and about 200 articles and previously served as Section Chair of the American Bar Association's Section of Administrative Law & Regulatory Practice. His books on elder care issues have been widely used and he has been active in legal aid programs for elders in the Cincinnati area. He is a graduate of Boston College and the University of Cincinnati College of Law.

Mark Tassone is a litigator in private practice who has focused his legal career on litigating nursing home cases on behalf of plaintiffs and their families before trial courts, appellate courts, and other tribunals. His practice spans both state and federal courts. Mark's background in litigating nursing home cases adds the insights of practical, hands-on experience interviewing families, gathering evidence, reviewing medical records, deposing nursing home staff, and resolving cases on behalf of his clients. More than anything, Mark is guided by a passion for advocating for the elderly and others who cannot speak for themselves.

Prior to entering law, Mark graduated from Hampden-Sydney College with a double major in Latin and Greek as well as classical studies. Mark obtained a master's degree in Latin from Florida State University. He then taught Latin in public schools before attending the University of Cincinnati College of Law.

About the Authors

Acknowledgments

The authors remain incredibly grateful for the love and support of their families throughout the laborious process of compiling this new edition. Professor O'Reilly thanks his family, Carol, Jessie, and C.B., for their support throughout his years-long efforts as an author. Mr. Tassone expresses his immense gratitude to his wife, Sara, for her love and support of this text and the time commitment that has come with it. He also thanks his children, Roman and Iris, for the incredible joy they bring to his life.

In Memoriam

I met my co-author, James T. O'Reilly, at a meeting of the Ohio Nursing Home Task Force. We both spoke about the challenges facing nursing home residents and were united in our desire to create better conditions for them.

Unfortunately, Jim passed away during the preparation of this text. In the year leading up to his passing, Jim devoted his energy to sculpting this third edition into what he believed would be his greatest publication.

I am endlessly grateful for the opportunity to join Jim in authoring this text. I cannot hope to repay the guidance and mentorship that he provided me during its drafting. Instead, I can only hope that these pages will guide future generations of practitioners to strive in the pursuit of justice for the elderly—a mission that forever remained dear to Jim's heart.

PART 1

Understanding the Context

CHAPTER 1

Introduction

The reader who is interested in nursing home law and policy may be surprised to learn that Las Vegas oddsmakers and nursing home owners have a great deal in common, since "the House always wins." In each situation, the owners' instinct to profitable operations leads to stacking the deck in favor of the establishment and against the player or elderly resident.

Since gambling and growing old are inevitable aspects of human society, the structures of both systems have evolved to preserve the institution against the individual. Both systems publicize their desire for fairness and universal welcoming of all customers, yet both recognize that the individual can sometimes score a windfall success against the House. Your role as plaintiff's remedial response to nursing home errors is your client's opportunity to help even the odds.

Making the situation appear to be positive and inviting, while preventing those occasional windfalls, and controlling the rules against the interests of the individual player, is a paradoxical challenge for both Las Vegas casino owners and for the nursing home industry.

The comparison may shock some readers, but the nursing homes of 21st-century America are lucrative investments largely because of their owners' ability to control the consequences of misconduct or errors in patient care.

Most of America's 17,000-plus nursing homes serve their residents very well; some homes are superior, while others are terrible. Government is both part of the solution and part of the problem; if only federal controls were the only safeguard, the state of nursing home care supervision would be far more lax than it is. The Senate Select

Committee on Aging found in 2023 that "[b]y conducting comprehensive inspections, known as standard surveys, every 15 months and promptly investigating complaints, state surveyors are the eyes and ears ensuring quality care is delivered."[1] Plaintiff counsel extend those eyes and ears by inducing better safety measures.

We start this examination of tort remedies with a tough premise: The odds are that nursing home patients would be treated worse if litigation remedies were not available to deter malpractice and deter owners' disregard for patient needs. This role of litigation is not a disputable proposition in the states with the weakest oversight of nursing home managements, and it has been well explored elsewhere.[2]

But the statistical odds are that only a tiny minority of the attorneys reading this book will take a nursing home lawsuit through to a jury verdict that brings a very profitable outcome for the contingent fee advocate. How do you earn such a status?

Unlike conventional tort disputes of highway crashes and sidewalk slips, this category of consumer decisions to "purchase a service" of residential care arises within a highly regulated system, in which occasional tort judgments are a deterrent force to the regulatory sanctions in that state.

The odds are that nursing home lobbyists will continue to fund the political campaigns of the key legislators whose state and federal budget choices and policy directions could constrain the profitability, as well as the effectiveness of regulation, of nursing homes. But perceptions are skewed by an imbalance of legislator information sources. Most legislators do not visit nursing homes, except when seeking elder write-in votes during campaign season. The odds are that the nursing home owners will continue to fund political events and continue

---

1. Press Release, Casey Pushes for Information from State Nursing Home Inspectors Amidst Staffing Shortages, Widespread Inspection Delays (Sept. 13, 2022), https://www.aging.senate.gov/press-releases/casey-pushes-for-information-from-state-nursing-home-inspectors-amidst-staffing-shortages-widespread-inspection-delays.

2. *See, e.g.*, Jeffrey Spitzer-Resnick & Maya Krajconovic, *Protecting the Rights of Nursing Home Residents: How Tort Liability Interacts with Statutory Protections*, 19 Nova L. Rev. 629 (1995).

to beg their elected friends for protection from rapacious contingent fee lawyer "sharks."[3]

The primary loser in all these political games is sound public policy. The other losers are the people who are the reader's parent, grandparent, former neighbor, or other elder whose quality of life is in the hands of the nursing home's accountants. This is a commercial business whose margins depend on control of costs, yet whose "customers" are much more at risk with each owner's cost-based reduction in protection. It takes a while to absorb this counterintuitive reality, because "buns in the beds" compared to capacity is a critical measure of whether the profitability will increase or diminish over time. Not all "buns" are alike, as state Medicaid reductions lower the income of the nursing facility and it must improve its looks to attract self-paying wealthier residents or those who can pay with higher priced long-term care insurance.

Should you become involved with nursing home problems? The nursing home "game" is stacked against the plaintiff's attorney as problem solver and protector of the weak, but the game is worth the effort. Absent a vigorous independent counterweight to the industry's collective power, society needs to have advocates for the individual patient's legal rights; if not tort lawyers, who else could deter even worse conditions within nursing homes?

Consider an analogy. Centuries ago, when great sailing warships dominated the sea lanes of Europe, a nation with a harbor full of warships could deter its neighbors from aggression without ever firing one cannon on the high seas. Tort lawyers' potential ability to seek economic punishment of the nursing home industry is a deterrent like those historic fleets. It makes the industry leaders sufficiently careful about their costs of tort liability, so that their operations should not usually descend below a reasonable standard of due care. It is paradoxical that even though well-funded industry efforts in some state legislatures seem to have hobbled the tort remedies of survivors of

---

3. John Rodgers, *Nursing Home Liability Bill Won't Pass This Year*, Nashville City Paper (Apr. 2008).

nursing home victims in some states, the victims would have been even worse off had there not been some implicit threat of liability to encourage the maintenance of standards of patient care. Regulation by a 15-month series of "surveys" alone would simply be too little, too late to make up the difference.

Why have the nursing home safety conditions in America descended to such a state of wide dissatisfaction? Why is the staffing ratio of nurses and helpers to assist tube feeding or immobilized patients so unfavorable to quality care?[4] What is the root cause of the understaffing safety problem? How did the mixture of federal and state legislative responses to the COVID-19 pandemic contain or confuse the courts on issues of immunity?[5]

Money and power are the answers. Sociologists and geriatric studies scholars can answer the collective public choice questions; political scientists can count the elements underlying elected officials' motivations. Nursing home revenues are projected to exceed $232 billion in the United States by 2030.[6]

But the cynic's response is that the statutory tort law of the states has often been stacked sharply against plaintiff tort actions for compensation from nursing homes. The avoidance of access to such tort compensation has been a remarkably successful focus of the nursing home industry's lobbying.

On the other side of the public debate are well-meaning but far less affluent interest groups of retired persons and family members seeking reforms.[7]

The conscious choices about cost cutting that have been undertaken by some members of the nursing home industry have victimized some of their patients, whose poor care has resulted in premature death or

---

4. Charles Duhigg, *In Nursing Homes, More Profit, Less Care*, N.Y. TIMES 1 (Sept. 23, 2007).

5. *See, e.g.*, Cagle v. NHC Healthcare-Maryland Hts., LLC, 78 F.4th 1061 (8th Cir. 2023).

6. https://www.grandviewresearch.com/industry-analysis/us-skilled-nursing-facility-market.

7. The National Citizens Coalition for Nursing Home Reform is the most-focused group but has a tiny fraction of the lobbying clout of the American Health Care Association and other nursing home owner groups.

extensive pain.[8] Insufficiency of public funds paying for higher-quality care for Medicare patients has meant a rise in avoidable mortality and morbidity.

The industry in turn is publicly bemoaning its fiscal "victim" status, held back from greater profitability by the fiscal decisions of the legislative appropriators to cut Medicaid and Medicare funds allocated to long-term care. They could devote their investments to other fields, of course.

Legislators who had been elected to impose "no new taxes" seem to have discounted the value of giving more public funds for institutional care of elderly Americans, those whose contributions to society are deemed to be a part of the past.

When fiscal choices about tax dollars for care of aged Americans are made, cuts in spending on Medicaid and Medicare—made so that taxes on the younger working taxpayers do not rise—drive down the rates of reimbursement payments for the great majority of nursing home patients' care. Imagine a balloon squeezed at one end; squeezing public benefits' per-bed income of the nursing home's owners, while increasing demand requires more profits to attract further investment, results in more stress on costs such as on staffing—the provision of sufficient numbers of trained care personnel.

The nursing home industry choices about caregiver staffing reflect a calculus of investment risk. As public benefit payments decrease relative to costs of quality care, it appears that cutting personnel related expenses may sometimes be considered essential to profitability. The industry has a persuasive story of future growth demand to attract Wall Street investors. Yet in order to be able to accommodate the "baby boomer" generation in the 2020s and 2030s, the rate of return on capital invested in nursing home construction and operation must be sufficient to continue to attract investors.

Somewhere deep in the fiscal mix of incentives and deterrents is the cost-savings need for the owner to avoid being hit with litigation windfalls in favor of the patients' estates and survivors. Litigation

8. *See, e.g.*, Duhigg, *supra* note 4.

follows from months of friction, airing the disappointment of the family about the incident or pattern of bad care that their elderly resident had received. Avoidance of "being sued" acts as a discipline upon costcutters' choices. So the nursing home owner *could* ideally spend more now on selection, retention, training, and quality of staff, to reduce future disappointment and to mitigate harm to patients.

But pragmatic accountants run many groups of nursing homes today. An array of corporate games with multiple shell companies is evident in some chains. Minimal compliance is deemed sufficient; minimal staffing appears to survive the loosened scrutiny of public overseers. Investing the nursing home's capital budget into a law firm's efforts at regulatory and legislative defense pays greater returns than investing in annual salaries for a dozen additional nurses. Not all homes think this way; many charitable and religious nursing homes have been paragons of good practices. The for-profit nursing home industry's legislative and appellate advocacy efforts toward the control of future exposure to litigation will have a longer-term impact on costs and especially on the reduction of catastrophic financial penalties in the form of punitive damage verdicts.

And so, it is rational economic behavior for the nursing home owners to lobby legislators for tightening constraints on suits against abuses in the nursing home. The dollars spent on lobbying return a long-term deterrence benefit that is greater than spending the equivalent dollars on night-shift nurses and training of nurses' aides. Counsel who defend nursing home companies have a great advantage in the potency and durability of their client, compared to plaintiff's counsel. By the nature of eligibility requirements, most Medicaid-funded nursing home patients are indigent. Their families could not afford the hourly rates of highly skilled litigators. Risks of loss from suing are virtually all on the side of the nursing home resident. The successful contingent fee plaintiffs' attorneys are those who turn away cases, maintaining an informal "quality control" by their examination and selectivity of cases. The defense can deduct its costs of litigation defense (or could insure against these costs), while the plaintiff's counsel is a risk-taking entrepreneur, with a high overhead cost and hopes for an extensive use of bank lines of credit to pay the costs of preparing each potential case.

Overall, as a broad generalization of its strategy, the for-profit nursing home industry appears to have opted for legal strategies for shielding its choices about cost control, instead of investing more heavily in nursing staffing and enhancement of health quality approaches. What does that investment look like?

There are four legal strategies. The first is lobbying for the state legislature's imposition of an arbitrary dollar cap on damages that an elder can incur. Reducing the amount of compensation that families can win reduces their ability to find lawyers who will risk financial burdens to take on a very expensive and lengthy battle with the nursing home insurer's advocates. This underside of tort reform is well understood by litigators yet is rarely explained in the general news media.

The second defense strategy of owners is insisting on contracts that require or seemingly require arbitration of disputes, which eliminates punitive damages and sharply curtails awards for pain and suffering. The claimed "death" of the civil jury system is still years away in American tort law, but the nursing home industry's overwhelming efforts to channel future disputes away from the possible sympathies of a civil jury in state courts have been remarkably successful.

Arbitration has been an excellent system for co-equal commercial parties to reach a negotiated end point to their commercial disputes in a timely manner. The U.S. Supreme Court has aggressively protected commercial arbitration in its decisions. But "co-equal" arbitration is not as desirable for the elderly and debilitated residents of the nursing home as it might be for an errant railroad line. Here the moment of acceptance of page 45's fine print by the elder in a wheelchair or their highly stressed family member, rapidly arranging all of the admission paperwork, is key. She or he is figuratively at the mercy of the nursing home's chief financial officer in a distant office tower.

Arbitration in the context of nursing homes is a corporation's iron shield against litigation, a virtual prescription for the patient's defeat in court, and will be a belated source of the family's frustration after an error leads to death or serious harm. Simply put, arbitration is a bad fit for resolving the compensation needs of the injured and often indigent elder.

The third strategic issue is the evolution of a pro-defendant ethos in litigation discovery. The huge expense of expert witness testimony regarding the standard of care which the defendant nursing home had failed to meet, or otherwise recast, is a formidable barrier. Few, if any, nursing home tort lawsuits can be managed for less than $50,000 in plaintiff's pretrial and trial costs, paid up front by the contingent fee attorney. In a climate of verdict caps and litigation expenses, even the most frugal plaintiff's counsel cannot hope to make an economically wise choice to accept the routine case without studying the facts in order to find very substantial prospects for financial rewards.

The final aspect of defense is the nursing home industry's use of a complex web of small corporate entities that can carry minimal insurance and some of which can be taken into bankruptcy if a major verdict is achieved by the estate or survivors of a nursing home victim.[9] If the actual recovery of the jury award is frustrated, then the pursuit of similar awards will dry up. The defense efforts to deter lawyers from nursing home suits by designing a complex structure for avoiding judgment makes eminent sense for the nursing home industry's protection of profitability.

Some readers may have expected a more upbeat introduction, and we apologize for the pragmatism shown here. The best ending for such a gloomy forecast is a paraphrase of the ancient teaching of Rabbi Hillel: If justice is to be done in the world, why not me to do justice?

And why not *now* to achieve that justice? If the lawyer is convinced that wrongs were done to the nursing home patient about whom the inquiry is made, then the lawyer should seek to help the surviving family to obtain justice. This may mean a lawsuit with expensive discovery. It may mean litigating along with others to break the arbitration clause's stranglehold on compensation; it may mean assembling a public body's evidence for that public entity's action, such as a state

9. *Id.*

attorney general injunction or a state ombudsman's condemnation of the owner; it may mean a well prepared barrage of publicity against the nursing home owner for conscious malfeasance toward the residents. If justice is to be done for the weakest of our elders, then why would you not do it?

CHAPTER 2

Definitions

2:1 Key Definitions
2:2 Background
2:3 Operational Aspects of Federal Controls
2:4 Applying the SNF and RUG Measures
2:5 Federal and State Integration of Standards
2:6 Federal Funding Brings Control
2:7 Understanding the Integrated Elements of the Legal Structure
2:8 Interactions of Regulation with Tort Liability
2:9 Purposes of the Resident's Nursing Home Stay
2:10 Significance of the Federal Funding Source Categories
2:11 Integration with Tort Liability
2:12 Political Aspects

2:1 Key Definitions

Elderly residents seeking supportive care have multiple options today. No single view could capture all the aspects of all the residential facilities in the United States. In this text we refer generically to the category of long-term residential skilled-care facilities for the elderly as the "nursing home," but we recognize that there are subcategories that are relevant to the litigator's evaluation of a potential case.

Many plaintiffs' medical malpractice counsel are familiar with lawsuits alleging that the high duty of care owed by hospitals to their patients was not met. But the facilities we discuss in this text are not treated as hospitals under regulatory systems or under state negligence jurisprudence. In many states, effective lobbying by hospitals has placed limitations on the malpractice actions that can be brought, and in some states long-term care facilities also enjoy the advantages of this statutory protection. The category of facilities addressed in this text is much broader than hospitals, and receives a different, lighter "duty of care" analysis in the courts.

We address in this book the tens of thousands of long-term care facilities that are certified to receive Medicaid and Medicare reimbursement funding for occupants of some or all of their beds. These include skilled nursing facilities that use licensed nurses; subacute or "intermediate care" units; and special care units.[1]

Facilities that do not perform or maintain higher-skilled patient care measures, such as gastric tube feeding of impaired patients, reside in the broader category of "nursing facilities." All of these are subject to state license requirements and must comply with state rules, local health rules, and local fire codes. Some of these are certified facilities, meaning that they have passed inspection ("survey") by a team of state long-term care inspectors, and these facilities can have the costs of their care of individual Medicaid or Medicare patients reimbursed by federal and state funds.

The financial power, like the "blood" that pumps through the system of nursing homes, is federally directed and state-shared Medicaid money, and if the government funding for the residents in a care facility stops, the facility will (almost inevitably) close down. Sometimes the same building or complex of buildings contains several types of facilities, from assisted living up to skilled nursing, and the licensure and funding arrangements vary within that overall facility in order to classify and to receive reimbursements for those who are deemed to be Medicaid eligible. To study a particular entity, one would consider the detail in a nursing home's Medicare annual cost reports as a useful differentiating marker of the subcategories. The federal database "Nursing Home Compare"[2] has a useful set of baseline information.

---

1. Definitions for the subcategories may be found in 42 C.F.R. § 400.200–.203.
2. Medicare.gov, Nursing Home Compare, http://www.medicare.gov/nursinghomecompare/search.html.

Counsel who consider using that federal and state data in trial would be well advised to read the website commentaries on the data, its origins, and limitations. "Long-term care" as a category includes services to elderly persons, disabled persons, mentally challenged persons, and persons undergoing extensive rehabilitation after injury or illness.[3] A separate category is "assisted living facilities," which charge far less than a nursing home and which provide fewer services.

The evolving nature of state and federal control of private in-home health care services[4] makes them interesting for study, but these situations vary so greatly that we cannot cover all of them in this text. Other texts are available on these issues.

2:2 Background

This section very briefly explains the regulatory background of the nursing home and skilled nursing home. Decisions about patient safety issues were not a part of the original 1962 Medicare system. Medicaid for low-income persons with few assets evolved later and has had a very large impact on the nursing home field.

Medicaid's regulatory controls on nursing home patient safety were included in 1987 legislation, the Nursing Home Reform Act, known by the acronym of its larger packet of legislation, OBRA-87.

The federal Center for Medicare and Medicaid Services (CMS) controls the standards for funding with which nursing homes are reimbursed for their services to indigent persons covered by Medicaid.[5] It also manages the reimbursement of the limited services, about 100 days of inpatient care, for elders covered by Medicare. The reimbursement for services and for resident care is governed by a complex federal statute[6] and a complex set of rules.[7]

---

3. Richard Kaplan, *Retirement Planning's Greatest Gap: Funding Long Term Care*, 11 Lewis & Clark L. Rev. 407, 414 (2007) (costs average $32,294 for assisted living and $71,000 for nursing homes).

4. *Id.* at 411.

5. Ctrs. for Medicare & Medicaid Servs., http://www.cms.gov.

6. 42 U.S.C. § 1888.

7. 42 C.F.R. pt. 413.

2:3 Operational Aspects of Federal Controls

The operational aspects underlying these federal and state conflicts are important for counsel to understand. Beneficiaries are eligible under Part A Medicare for care at a skilled nursing facility (SNF) after a minimum three-day covered stay in an acute care hospital. Part A covers SNF services for up to 100 days per "spell of illness." Medicare Part B covers therapy services for SNF patients who have exhausted their Part A benefits or did not have a qualifying hospital stay. Patients at SNFs are eligible for nursing care or physical, occupational, and speech therapy ordered by a physician. Therapy must be reasonable, necessary, specific, and effective for the patient's condition. The following conditions must be met:

- the therapy level's complexity and sophistication, or the patient's condition, require the skills of a qualified therapist rather than nonskilled SNF staff;
- the medical record contains an active treatment plan that includes specific and measurable treatment goals related to the patient's condition along with a reasonable time estimate of when those goals will be achieved;
- the treatment plan describes the specific therapeutic interventions to restore the patient's level of function lost or reduced by illness or injury;
- the amount, frequency, and duration of therapy must be reasonable and necessary for the patient's condition;
- therapy is provided either by or under the direct supervision of a licensed therapist; and
- therapy must be provided with the expectation, based on the assessment made by the physician or therapist of the patient's restoration potential, that the patient's condition will improve substantially in a reasonable and generally predictable period of time, or the therapy must be necessary for the establishment of a safe and effective maintenance program.

2:4 Applying the SNF and RUG Measures

SNFs use an assessment tool known as the Minimum Data Set (MDS) to assess a patient's clinical condition, functional status, and expected use of services. Based on this assessment, the SNF classifies patients into resource utilization groups (RUGs). Each RUG classification has a different reimbursement rate. There are eight RUG categories. Two are "Rehabilitation" and "Rehabilitation Plus Extensive Services." These "therapy RUGs" are for beneficiaries who need physical, speech, or occupational therapy. The other six categories, known as "nontherapy RUGs," are for patients who require little to no therapy.

Each different RUG classification has a different per diem payment rate. Medicare pays more for therapy RUGs than nontherapy RUGs. Therapy RUGs are divided into five therapy levels: ultrahigh, very high, high, medium, and low. Medicare pays the most for ultrahigh therapy and the least for low. Plaintiff asserted that the nursing home, in order to maximize reimbursement rates, purposely assigned patients to the higher RUGs, whether they needed it or not.

Lawyers who have not encountered such detailed regulatory controls in prior civil cases may be surprised by the results of their study of the CMS control on policies and practices of nursing homes.[8] Metrics of health and safety performance for evaluating the nursing homes are fixed in CMS rules.[9] Patient rights may have been violated in a particular injury case.[10] These federal rules are comprehensive standards for health, safety, and protection of the rights of the nursing home patients.[11]

8. For example, the CMS Surveyor Guidance is a 400-page loose-leaf binder, available from the states, from CMS, or from the American Health Care Association website. *See* Ctrs. for Medicare & Medicaid Servs., State Operations Manual, CMS Pub. No. 100-07, Appendix PP: Guidance to Surveyors for Long Term Care Facilities. State Operations Manual (Feb. 2023).

9. 42 C.F.R. pt. 483.

10. *See supra* note 8. CMS Surveyor Guidance is a 400-page loose-leaf binder, available from the states, from CMS, or from the American Health Care Association website. These are tied to state tort law norms.

11. 42 C.F.R. pt. 483.

The federal standards for nursing home operations are implemented by state long-term care agencies, and states operate with requirements in their programs that are in addition to the CMS rules and guidance documents.

2:5 Federal and State Integration of Standards

The federal Medicaid norms are dominant as the primary standards of care, but they are not exclusive; the state may require more actions by nursing home operators to satisfy state legislation, such as a statutory "patient's bill of rights."[12]

The private nursing home may choose to advertise and market its additional level of performance. Referencing third-party accreditation in its brochure may create an obligation to show a higher standard of behavior.

Funding sources for skilled nursing care have largely been government sources such as state/federal Medicaid, veterans benefits, or a limited amount of days under Medicare after hospitalization ends. A nursing home could survive without federal funds if it had donors or private-pay patrons who could make up for the loss of public funding. Such a home could opt not to "certify" certain bed spaces for Medicare or Medicaid patients. It could become totally "self-pay," or could be a fully not-for-profit charity institution, and thereby would be outside CMS controls, subject only to state licensure controls. It has been relatively infrequent that a nursing home has not sought and accepted Medicaid/Medicare patients.

2:6 Federal Funding Brings Control

The federal government funds Medicare and also funds a large portion of the federal-state Medicaid program.[13] (Key terminology distinc-

12. *See, e.g.*, N.C. Div. of Aging & Adult Servs., Residents' Rights, http://www.ncdhhs.gov/aging/rights.htm.

13. Ctrs. for Medicaid & Medicare Servs., Medicare Program—General Information, http://www.cms.hhs.gov/medicareGenInfo/.

tions will be essential: "Medicare" is for the elderly; "Medicaid" is for funding the health care of indigent or disabled persons.) States provide a significant share of Medicaid funding. Reimbursement of costs through these federal-state funding mechanisms is the power that fuels the regulatory authority of the government over the nursing home.

Nursing homes are intended to be places of comfort and healing. According to Centers for Medicare & Medicaid Services (CMS) data, in July 2022, approximately 1.2 million people resided in more than 15,000 certified nursing homes. "Most nursing homes in the United States are certified to serve as both skilled nursing facilities, which provide a clinically managed recovery period after a person's illness or injury, and long-term care facilities that deliver health care and services a resident needs for mental or physical conditions not rising to the level of skilled nursing care." Conformity to "Conditions of Participation" in Medicare and Medicaid is essential to the income stream of the skilled nursing facility.[14]

Historians of the ancient empire that centered around today's Turkey, the Byzantine Empire, gave that name to complex and multilayered "byzantine" designs that are virtually impossible for the lay person to understand. Legions of American lawyers have become vested in the lucrative arts of interpreting this byzantine fiscal arrangement for skilled nursing facilities and their supportive networks of companies. When we call the funding aspects of modern nursing home regulation "byzantine," we mean that its bureaucracy has grown into a jungle of rules, guidelines, exceptions, and subexceptions that defy the reader's ability to comprehend how it actually works. For that reason, if the reader wishes to delve into funding and finance issues, we recommend other resources.[15]

Our focus is on the patient injury compensation disputes that arise out of actions or omissions by the staff of a nursing home. To the extent that a plaintiff could show that an injury was due to a deliberate reduction in key medical or personal care staffing by a for-profit care facility,

---

14. Report of Off. of Inspector Gen., Nursing Homes (2023).
15. *See, e.g.*, Douglas Singh, Effective Management of Long-Term Care Facilities (2005).

the jury's decision on liability may be affected by the view that the circumstances of patient harm came from a pattern of willful neglect that was intended to maximize profitability of the nursing home.

2:7 Understanding the Integrated Elements of the Legal Structure

States have the primary role in oversight of virtually everything about long-term skilled nursing care facilities, except the financing of the nursing home, and even there, loan and aid programs may have funded the bricks and mortar of the facility. State long-term care agencies or health departments issue nursing home licenses, inspect and certify the compliance of a new facility, conduct surveys, test and give credentials to administrators and medical personnel, receive complaints, and take enforcement actions.

The federal role of funding Medicaid and Medicare comes with strings attached, and these conditions include complying with the federal norms or "Conditions of Participation" that have been set by CMS. A 2008 federal report showed that 91 percent of the 15,000 then-covered facilities that were subject to periodic survey visits had an average of seven deficiencies noted in the postsurvey reports.[16]

Because of the political power of elders, the actions of legislating about elder care are done carefully by all prudent elected officials. State statutes about nursing homes reflect the reality that elders vote and their collective anger against a state legislator could doom reelection prospects. Opposing the establishment of protections for vulnerable elders in nursing homes makes the legislator very vulnerable to criticism. As a result, societal decisions about nursing homes are taken by legislators in response to public revulsion about abusive conditions in nursing homes. The federal 1987 Nursing Home Reform Act, known by the acronym OBRA-87, is the foundation for today's federal

16. Memorandum from Daniel R. Levinson, Inspector General, to Kerry Weems, Acting Administrator, Ctrs. for Medicaid & Medicare Servs., Memorandum Report: Trends in Nursing Home Deficiencies and Complaints, Sept. 18, 2008, http://www.oig.hhs.gov/oei/reports/oei-02-08-00140.pdf.

regulation of nursing homes. Some states before OBRA-87, and many states since, have adopted state-specific norms of quality performance that are to be followed by the nursing home owners and operators.

About 23,000 nursing homes receive federal funding.[17] These are subject to inspectional "surveys" done by states under contract with the federal CMS. Chapter 23 discusses the survey process.

The nursing home quality enforcement burden falls on the states, though a particular state is arguably without sufficient federal funding to comprehensively audit all of the state's licensed facilities.[18] State budgets are tight. Investigators have been critical of the weakness of this enforcement process: "Low [penalty] imposition rates and slow and/or difficult collection efforts may minimize the effect that [CMS penalties] ultimately have on noncompliant facilities."[19] The OBRA-87 amendments empowered the federal CMS to impose penalties and, in extreme cases, to suspend new admissions or to impose receivership over the management of the nursing home.[20]

More than 1,000 appeal case precedents can be reviewed in the "nursing home" category of decisions within the U.S. Department of Health and Human Services' Departmental Appeals Board.[21] In addition, state health agencies may impose their own sanctions with their own set of appeal procedures.[22] Plaintiffs' counsel should be prepared to draw the court's attention to the comparable cases of negligent conduct that had been punished by state and/or federal enforcers. Doing so may foreclose an argument by the defense that what happened to the client was simply routine care.

---

17. U.S. Gov't Accountability Office, GAO-06-326, Long Term Care Facilities (Mar. 31, 2006).

18. *Abuse of Our Elders: How We Can Stop It: Hearing before the Senate Comm. on Aging*, 110th Cong. 6 (July 18, 2007) (testimony of Office of Inspector General, U.S. Dep't of Health & Human Servs.), http://www.aging.senate.gov.

19. *Id.*

20. 42 U.S.C. § 1396r(g); *see* Robert Hawks, *Grandparent Molesting: Sexual Abuse of Elderly Nursing Home Residents and Its Prevention*, 8 Marquette Elder's Advisor 159 (2006) (addressing remedies).

21. U.S. Dep't of Health & Human Servs., Departmental Appeals Bd., http://www.hhs.gov/dab.

22. *See, e.g.*, Calif. Health Facilities, Consumer Information System, Health Facilities Information, http://hfcis.cdph.ca.gov/default.aspx.

2:8 Interactions of Regulation with Tort Liability

The federal officials of CMS have the money to aid owners to build and equip and fuel the growth of skilled nursing facilities; but the states have the license authority and the tort liability system to discipline the homes and their owners. From the standpoint of patient safety, the four protectors against patterns of nursing home misconduct are

- state surveys;
- federal "Conditions of Participation" standards;
- plaintiffs' attorney advocacy; and
- insurance carrier "loss control" inquiries.

The size of potential tort jury verdicts deters some insurance companies from writing liability policies for operators of nursing homes. This experience induces the insurers to audit their already-insured facilities to help the owners forestall avoidable patterns of misconduct. The state tort precedents about nursing home liability are therefore quite significant as a force for self-regulatory action.

The death or serious injury cases are likely to be expensive for the site operator and for its insurer. The utilization of state tort standards of due care during highly publicized trials featuring victimized, helpless elders will "send a message" encouraging quality care. This message will augment weaknesses in state and federal supervision, as many observers including the U.S. Government Accountability Office have observed shortcomings in the operation of the public regulatory apparatus.[23]

The state tort precedents and state or federal rules are not a perfect fit; much of the state common law of duties of care will be applied to actions or omissions, while state regulatory duties apply, since the

23. Among the many Government Accountability Office reports on nursing home conditions are GAO-06-117 (Dec. 28, 2006) (serious gaps exist between state survey and federal survey results; states missed key care concerns in numerous nursing home visits); GAO-05-65 (Nov. 10, 2004) (VA spent 27 percent on community, private and state nursing homes), and GAO-04-684 (Apr. 30, 2004) (assisted living facilities).

defendant in the negligence trial is also a highly regulated facility. Publicly held data will aid the plaintiff's assembly of its case; in some tort cases, information comes out of discovery that triggers intense scrutiny by regulatory officials. One can picture the on-camera television reporter asking the state nursing home regulator why this terrible situation at XYZ Home had been "tolerated" or "ignored" by the state. The jury verdict is not the final stage of the nursing home claim.

These cases are not easy to win. A no-pay jury verdict on June 1 for the defense might be a short-lived triumph for the nursing home company, if the state's "for cause survey" team arrives one week later, armed with the exhibits used at the trial. For experienced tort lawyers who are novices in this nursing home field, appearances may be deceptive: trouble with nursing homes cannot always be detected from the public agency survey records. Whistleblowers are invaluable guides for the litigants.

Complaint files, ombudsman records, and testimony may demonstrate a pattern of ignored patient abuse. Experienced advocates know that the combination of rules and lawsuits should deter further cases of abuse and neglect, where either remedy alone—a tort trial or a wider regulation—would do less.

Nursing home rights legislation has been passed in California, New York, and other states that empowers the resident or his or her personal representative to sue for violations and to obtain punitive damages and attorney's fees in certain cases. Negligence per se can be used in tort cases by establishing that violations of the law or relevant rules were proximately causative of the patient's harm.

State contractual and tort law standards of care can be applied, in appropriate cases. The legislative picture is not one-sided in favor of the elderly residents. Nursing home industry lobbying efforts have succeeded in some states with the adoption of owner protections from liability through state law, authorizing exclusive arbitration, caps on remedies, and so on. But a pragmatic politician knows that angry picketing by elders is newsworthy and a reputation in the news media for protecting elders is more valuable than a preelection contribution from a lobbying firm for the state's long-term care association.

2:9 Purposes of the Resident's Nursing Home Stay

Experts in the nursing home field categorize the residents of nursing homes in several subcategories:

1. Short-term rehab patients who leave in a matter of weeks;
2. Physically normal persons with Alzheimer's or brain disease who need protective care for activities of daily life;
3. Mentally competent persons with physical impairments who need help with daily activities of life;
4. Very sick patients, such as ventilator-dependent persons discharged from hospitals for the nursing care available at a competent nursing facility; and
5. Patients with chronic end-stage ailments.[24]

The third and fourth categories are most susceptible to negligent care and will be most susceptible to injuries as patients in the nursing home. The second category contains persons who will "wander" and may be injured outside the home if they can escape its security.

Concerns have been expressed that the government policy for use of long-term care should be better defined in Medicaid legislation. Traditionally, policy has been based upon a step-down or devolution from hospital care, which has been called "the culture of illness and disease."[25] The only legally enforceable duty of nursing homes that provide "intermediate care" is to monitor and then to move more-diffuse patients to a skilled nursing facility where the degree of medical care will meet their needs.[26]

2:10 Significance of the Federal Funding Source Categories

The availability of long-term care usually depends upon access for the resident to individual payment sources (self-pay or insurance)

---

24. Cultural Change in Long Term Care 41 (Audrey Weiner ed., 2003).
25. *Id.* at 44.
26. Stogsdill v. Manor Convalescent Home Inc., 343 N.E.2d 589 (Ill. App. 1976).

or showing of the resident's poverty (Medicaid). The inability to pay costs of long-term care may qualify a person for Medicaid.

There is not a similar poverty requirement for Medicare, eligibility for which is age related, limited in time, and controlled by specific restrictions.

Note the distinction. Where the funding source is Medicaid, the indigent person demonstrates eligibility for one of the designated beds in the desired nursing home. These beds can be available for years, but the person could lose eligibility by receiving substantial additional funds, such as from a lawsuit verdict or an inheritance. When the funding source is Medicare, the elderly patient's short-term needs after hospital discharge are met by a stay that cannot exceed 100 days in a year. When the funding source is the resident's private long-term care insurance or the family's private-pay assets, no federal or state conditions apply.

Federal nursing home benefits legislation has been a complex part of the Medicaid/Medicare program for years. In addition, the Department of Veterans Affairs uses privately run or state-run nursing homes for about 27 percent of its veterans' needs for nursing home space.[27]

Other sources provide detailed background on these complicated regulatory and financial issues.[28]

2:11 Integration with Tort Liability

Several factors correlate with a higher likelihood of a nursing home being sued:

- nursing home deficiencies found in the survey done by state survey inspectors;
- large, for-profit chain ownership of the nursing home; and

---

27. U.S. Gov't Accountability Office, GAO-05-65, re Veterans health care, http://www.gao.gov.

28. Patricia Day & Michael McCauley, Understanding Elder Law (ABA 2002); Daniel Cody & Kathleen Scully-Hayes, A Practical Guide to Medicare Appeals (ABA 2007); The Complete Guide to Medicaid and Nursing Home Costs (Atlantic 2008); Armond Budish, Beating the Medicare Trap (1995).

- location of the home in a state that has "nursing home resident rights" legislation in place.[29]

There are useful websites for regulatory information about nursing home quality,[30] but the vulnerability of a specific nursing home or chain is almost impossible to discern from outside. The great majority of these cases are settled, and leave no precedential effects on the record.[31] The Westlaw newsletter "Verdicts, Settlements & Tactics" provides many of the settled cases and defense verdicts that do not appear in conventional reporters. Liability is well recognized among caregivers and institutions.

The risk of being sued definitely should have a deterrent effect on nursing home operations. A nursing home staff member said it best: "The threat of malpractice is by far more central to our operation than the residents' control over their own lives and property. 'Safety first' means safety from lawsuits; caring for oneself, independence, and self-esteem matter less."[32]

2:12 Political Aspects

The plaintiff's counsel in a nursing home case may be encountering his or her first conflict with the well-organized health care industry. This is a mismatch; the very effective targeting of the lobbyists has been very well organized in the state legislatures. What is "business as usual" for the industry is novel and challenging for the attorney first entering a tort case on these issues.

The attorney should not be naïve; if your state elder care agency seems to be tilted toward the interests of the defendant operator, and if it seems that the enforcement director never quite bites the vulnerable

29. Christopher Johnson et al., *Predicting Lawsuits against Nursing Homes in the United States 1997–2001*, 39(6) HEALTH SERVS. RES. 1713 (2004).

30. See Medicare.gov, Nursing Home Compare, http://www.medicare.gov/nursinghomecompare/search.html.

31. Johnson, *supra* note 29.

32. THOMAS GASS, NOBODY'S HOME: CANDID REFLECTIONS OF A NURSING HOME AIDE 151 (2005).

nursing homes, then look at the campaign money that is reported for the legislators whose committees oversee the state elder care agency. Shielded by potent but barely visible political forces, the respondent in a state proceeding will usually get the benefit of the doubt.

Plaintiffs' counsel will never have the pervasive, constant presence that defendant nursing home operators will maintain in political circles.[33] Sensitivity to political pressure is recommended.

33. *Consumer Reports: Nursing Homes Business as Usual*, 17 ABA Experience 20 (2007).

CHAPTER 3

Identifying the Defendant Nursing Home Owner

3:1 Who Owns This Nursing Home?

3:2 How Has the Home Managed to Obtain a Profit?

3:3 Role of the Corporate Budget Official

3:4 Role of the Nursing Home Administrator

3:1 Who Owns This Nursing Home?

Books about routine tort liability usually do not spend pages of effort on the identification of the defendant. A nursing home liability case, however, may teach the advocate about state partnership law, limited liability companies, offshore owner accounts, and other minutiae of business claims.

For years, efforts have been made to hide the true ownership, precisely so as to avoid patient injury liability judgments that could drain the available assets from a corporate owner.[1]

Having a limited liability company or shell company with minimum capital that is in charge of protecting the needs of vulnerable patients is a serious problem for the plaintiff who seeks to collect on a damages verdict. Some ownership arrangements are intentionally fuzzy and difficult to understand, to insulate the entity that actually

1. *See, e.g.*, J. Casson et al., *Protecting Nursing Home Companies: Limiting Liability through Corporate Restructuring*, 36 J. Health Law 557 (2003).

holds the profits at a distance from the operating corporation's potential liability to an aggressive plaintiff.[2]

Federal case law has limited applicability to the issue of inclusion or exclusion. Courts have upheld the extension of past penalties to "new" successor operators of the same facility, reflecting the view that transfer of ownership carried with it the obligation to pay off penalty orders that the U.S. Department of Health and Human Services had imposed on the preceding operator of the same facility.[3] The Affordable Care Act regulations will increase transparency concerning ownership.[4]

Further, each skilled nursing facility must have a state license, and that applicant must provide information about ownership of the nursing home as a condition for receiving Medicaid and Medicare reimbursements.[5] A good research library with an experienced research paralegal can aid the injured plaintiff's counsel who is considering how to target the liability claims upon the medical and nonmedical personnel and the subsidiaries responsible for the operations of the long-term care facility.

3:2 How Has the Home Managed to Obtain a Profit?

The corporate management of a nursing home chain is likely to make a profit by holding down its staffing costs, maximizing the enrollment of private payment residents, and assuring a steady flow of "intake," i.e., replacement applicants for the available beds as they become vacant. Many skilled nursing facilities rely on the system of income provided by Medicare in the "facility case-mix ratios,"[6] the Medicaid/Medicare certified beds that will provide a steady flow of income.[7]

---

2. Charles Duhigg, *At Many Homes, More Profit and Less Nursing*, N.Y. Times 1 (Sept. 23, 2007).

3. BP Care Inc. v. Thompson, 398 F.3d 503 (6th Cir. 2005).

4. CMS Proposed Rules, Medicare Program; Prospective Payment System and Consolidated Billing for Skilled Nursing Facilities; Disclosures of Ownership and Additional Disclosable Parties Information, 76 Fed. Reg. 26,364 (May 6, 2011).

5. CMS Proposed Rules, *supra* note 4.

6. CMS Final Rule, Medicare Program, 74 Fed. Reg. 40,291, 40,292 (Aug. 11, 2009).

7. Douglas Singh, Effective Management of Long-Term Care Facilities (2005).

In an extreme case, proof that the home's administrator had maximized profits and deliberately conserved funds by cutting staff and providing poor care that then harmed patients could support a successful criminal prosecution of the administrator for elder abuse.[8] If the entity is a nonprofit, its IRS Form 990 is publicly available[9] and plaintiff's counsel may be able to discern its financial profitability, with the help of an accountant who can deconstruct the actual numbers through understanding of the assumptions presented by the corporation in the IRS form.

3:3 Role of the Corporate Budget Official

The least visible but potentially most important representative of the nursing home owner might not have ever been inside the home. The budget officer of the corporation responsible for the profitability of the enterprise has a difficult task in dealing with complex federal and state funding and billing reimbursements. The budget officer directs the decisions about the number of skilled nurses who will be available for duty, taking into account state minimum staffing ratios, if any exist. This person has a fiscally "make or break" decision-making role in the nursing home hierarchy.[10] The same official decides how much or how little insurance to carry for potential liabilities, using what has been called "creative accounting" to set up companies that carry no insurance, and are unlikely to permit "piercing the corporate veil" to obtain compensation.[11]

As an expert on punitive damages in nursing home cases has commented: "Nothing is more helpful to the plaintiff than to have a management-level employee testify that repeated requests for more

8. State v. Serebin, 350 N.W.2d 65 (Wis. 1984), and case comment, 1986 WIS. L. REV. 339.

9. This information is available at GuideStar, http://www.guidestar.org, for example.

10. Duhigg, *supra* note 2.

11. Sara Jurand, *Lack of Insurance Hinders Recovery in Nursing Home Cases*, 42 TRIAL 14 (Feb. 2006).

staff were made to corporate [officials], but were denied because 'it wasn't in the budget.'"[12]

3:4 Role of the Nursing Home Administrator

States issue licenses to the persons who manage their state's nursing homes,[13] in an attempt to enforce some minimum requirements for careful administration. This helps with the accountability of the proper care of patients.[14] The administrator implements the budget decisions of the corporate managers and supervises the work of the nursing, therapy, dietary, and other departments. The external relations work confronts the administrator with the role of ambassador to the hospitals and state nursing home surveyors,[15] complaint responder for the families of residents,[16] sales manager to prospective self-paying customers, and spokesperson to the media after an accidental death or an escape of a wandering resident.

Internally, the role of administrator is part recruiter, part salesperson, and part family liaison with the operating staff, and "behind the curtain" acts as the manager of nurses and other professionals, the negotiator with any unions, and the disciplinarian of errant or absent workers at the facility. This is an extremely complex role for the licensee.

12. T. Patrick Ford, *Punitive Damages in Nursing Home Cases*, *in* NURSING HOME LITIGATION: PRETRIAL PRACTICE AND TRIALS 429, 456 (Ruben Krisztal ed., 2d ed. 2003).

13. States like California publicly list their licensed persons. Calif. Dep't of Pub. Health, L & C Certification Verification Search Page, http://www.applications.dhs.ca.gov/cvl/.

14. SINGH, *supra* note 7.

15. *See* Chapter 20.

16. P. Allen et al., *Nursing Home Complaints*, 47 J. GERONTOLOGICAL SOC. WORK 89 (2006).

PART 2

Responsibilities of Professionals

CHAPTER 4

Roles and Liabilities of Nursing Professionals

4:1 Participants
4:2 Staffing Levels
4:3 Meeting Individual Patient Care Needs
4:4 Allocating Responsibilities
4:5 Professional Responsibility

4:1 Participants

The director of nursing at the nursing home has a vitally important role in patient care.[1] She or he sets the tone for the professional staff who operate the home and is accountable for patient care decisions in conjunction with the medical director. If litigation results from harm to a patient, the director of nursing will inevitably be a pretrial deponent and trial witness.

The shifts of licensed nursing employees are largely composed of certified nursing assistants who have been taught the basics about nursing home patient care. Shifts are led by a supervisory nurse, sometimes called the charge nurse, and by the designated nurses who work with him or her. The categories of nurses who work at the home can include an advanced practice nurse or nurse practitioner who has additional training and added levels of authority in patient care. Regularly

1. Douglas Singh, Effective Management of Long-Term Care Facilities 273 (2005).

licensed registered nurses are typically on duty. Licensed practical nurses also provide care, and medication technicians deliver medications if they are not delivered by the nurses. Physical therapists work on muscle and bone issues and occupational therapists work on the patient's capacity to handle routine tasks. Feeding aides, administrative staff, orderlies, and cleaning crews round out the personnel needs.

Courts sometimes consider these interrelated roles when an expert is proffered in a liability case. State document requests will provide the individual licensee's background for the state certifications needed for each role when plaintiff asks the court to allow nurses as experts regarding patient care claims.[2]

Most of the actual work with patients inside a nursing home is done by a certified nursing assistant (CNA), whose tasks include helping patients with daily life activities, like dressing and toileting.[3] This is the unglamorous but necessary care role that is the base of the whole pyramid of care in the skilled nursing facility.

4:2 *Staffing Levels*

There are several norms for adequacy of staffing at the nursing home; some are set by the type of patients cared for at the home, under guidance of state and Center for Medicare and Medicaid Services (CMS) officials. The vague language of the CMS rule calls for nursing home staffing quantity that is "adequate" for the needs of the patients.[4] Recently, CMS for the first time established minimum staffing levels for nursing homes.[5] However, these levels are only the minimum and are not, per se, adequate. Nevertheless, historically nursing home chain owners have cut the nursing staff, reduced the delivery of

2. Cornerstone Hosp. of S.E. Ariz. v. Marner, 231 Ariz. 67 (Ariz. Ct. App. 2012).
3. 42 U.S.C. § 483.75(f).
4. 42 U.S.C. § 483.30.
5. *Id.* § 483.35(b); *see also* Medicare and Medicaid Programs; Minimum Staffing Standards for Long-Term Care Facilities and Medicaid Institutional Payment Transparency Reporting, 89 Fed. Reg. 40,876 (May 10, 2024), https://www.federalregister.gov/documents/2024/05/10/2024-08273/medicare-and-medicaid-programs-minimum-staffing-standards-for-long-term-care-facilities-and-medicaid.

quality care, and thereby increased their profits.[6] But the fallout from this decision is rapid turnover and more likelihood of injury. Federal and state penalties for understaffing of the patient care roles can result from study of past accidents and their connection to inadequate staff supervision of patients.[7]

Voluntary accreditation bodies like the Joint Commission also have standards that specifically cover nursing homes.[8] Plaintiffs may evaluate all of the external norms that should have been followed, and may recognize patterns of noncompliance that underlie a negligence claim.

The defense of a nursing home should be built on the continuous, regular, and appropriate gathering of patient care data in the company's paper or electronic records. Studies of the patterns of injury show the likely elements that characterize a nursing home that is more likely to be sued, including short staffing and reductions in patient care efforts within the for-profit chains of nursing homes.[9]

4:3 Meeting Individual Patient Care Needs

The director of nursing should have a leading role in the decision to admit a new resident, based on an evaluation of his or her medical condition and likely needs for special services. The liability of the nursing home would greatly increase if it made an inaccurate decision and an applicant was accepted who needed much more care than the home could provide, for example, intravenous infusion therapy requiring special pharmacy and nursing training.[10]

Each patient's individual care plan must be signed by a physician. The nursing staff is required to receive, review, and understand the comprehensive care plan for each resident. Then the staff must act

---

6. Charles Duhigg, *At Many Homes, More Profit and Less Nursing*, N.Y. Times 1 (Sept. 23, 2007).

7. Asbury Ctr. v. U.S. Dep't of HHS, 77 F. App'x 853 (6th Cir. 2003).

8. The Joint Comm'n, http://www.jointcommission.org.

9. Christopher Johnson et al., *Predicting Lawsuits against Nursing Homes in the United States 1997–2001*, 39(6) Health Servs. Res. 1713, 1724 (2004).

10. Singh, *supra* note 1, at 267.

within that plan when implementing actual patient care.[11] Plaintiff will be able to show in many cases that the impressive "comprehensive plan of care" was not met by the actual performance of the overworked nursing staff and that it was the lack of needed care or protection steps that had contributed to the injuries or death of the resident.

Nurses are key players at the admission stage for new residents. Comprehensive resident assessments must be made for all Medicaid and Medicare patients at the time of entry. This is a team effort of nurses, social worker, therapist, and the dietician,[12] which then produces the Minimum Data Set, which is the CMS documentation used in the resident assessment instrument.[13] Unlike the therapist and the medical director, nurses also have daily contact with the patient. The nurses have the most impact on patient health records, and so their validation of the written or electronic record's accuracy can be essential for depositions in tort cases asserting negligent care.

"Significant changes in condition" are to be assessed by the nurses and the medical director must be notified; then the plan must be altered according to the needs of that patient. The factor of greatest importance for the nurses is in the performing of the daily assessment and in overseeing the daily needs of patients. A large penalty can be imposed on a facility that had failed to notify a physician of a significant change in patient condition.[14] For example, a hospice patient had the right to have her family notified of changes in her condition, and failure to do so was a violation of its obligation to preserve "dignity and personal integrity" of the patient.[15]

Each certified nursing home will be inspected or "surveyed" for compliance with state rules and with the Medicare Conditions of Participation. Medicare's current edition of the Manual for Surveyors is the rulebook that prudent nursing home administrators will follow. Expectations of CMS and state long-term care surveyors are best met

---

11. 42 C.F.R. § 483.20(d).
12. Singh, *supra* note 1, at 280 (useful chart of the Minimum Data Set).
13. *Id.* at 278.
14. Batavia Nursing & Convalescent Ctr. v. Thompson, 129 F. App'x 181 (6th Cir. 2005).
15. Hendrix v. Maison Orleans I, L.L.C., 101 So. 3d 1013 (La. Ct. App. 4th Cir. 2012).

by having talented nurses give competent care, document their work, and show during the survey visit that the nurses are meeting the residents' needs in a timely manner, with attention to the requirements of the state rules. If nursing home payroll records show a sudden increase of care staff on the first day of the survey, this suggests a gaming of the survey system. This false front might be cited at trial to undercut the defense argument that staffing was adequate; such staffing gimmicks would impeach the defense's typical assertion that staffing had been deemed adequate because the surveyors had not cited the owner for inadequacies of staffing.

Nurses are very important in documentation of the patient's daily needs and medical condition. Nurses have professional obligations to respond to symptoms, such as of a stroke, that can be intercepted and dealt with effectively if the symptom is reported as soon as it is observed. The complexity of tasks that nurses perform varies greatly. But the central task for purposes of litigation defense will be the nurses' contribution to accurate records of each day's actual care.

Training of CNAs and of resident feeding aides is managed by the nurses, presuming the nursing has state approval to train and certify nursing assistants. These CNAs must be trained to retain their licensure. Continuing education credit can be claimed for in-service training obligations. It is a red flag of state regulatory action if the state suspends the nursing home from being permitted to train new CNAs. Suspension of this power reflects doubt by the state that the nursing home is acting properly. Disciplinary and licensing information may be available on the website of a state nurse licensing board.

4:4 Allocating Responsibilities

In skilled nursing homes, a feeding tube into a patient's abdomen may be inserted by a licensed nurse practitioner, though implantation of the tube is usually so specific and so dangerous that a hospital surgeon or physician will be asked to perform this as outpatient surgery. Medical licensing boards and the American Medical Directors Association, the professional society of nursing home doctors, may have set practice guidelines. Responsibility for maintenance of the tubes is restricted to nurses, not to the less-trained aides. Medical oversight of the tube is an essential element of the patient's avoidance of infection or other problems.

Responsibility for assessment of the patient after falls rests with the nurse; the physician should be called and the visibly injured patient will be sent to a hospital for testing.

Responsibility for the use of straps, vests, and other physical restraints is strictly limited under CMS rules, as discussed in Chapter 11.[16] A physician must authorize the restraint, and the informed consent of the patient or personal representative should be on file for the state survey team.

Responsibility for skin ulcer assessments also rests with the nurse.[17] The degree of response depends on the seriousness of the skin problem, as discussed in Chapter 8 of this text.

Responsibility to assess urinary infection needs begins with the registered nurse, who then involves the medical director and the care team in deciding on a written program for dealing with the problem with monitoring, medications, and patient movement. The CNA's failure to clean the resident properly can be the source of Medicare penalties against the nursing facility's violation of the Medicare Conditions of Participation.[18]

4:5 Professional Responsibility

Should the nurse report inappropriate treatment or serious violative conditions to the state long-term care agency? In the face of employer retaliation risks to careers, what should be done is not always what *is* done. "Nurses, if they want to keep their jobs, often become silent partners in poor care."[19] The extent of this phenomenon is debatable in

16. 42 C.F.R. § 483.25(h).
17. 42 C.F.R. § 483.25(c).
18. Harmony Court v. Leavitt, 188 F. App'x 438 (6th Cir. 2006).
19. Charlotte DiGregorio, Everything You Need to Know About Nursing Homes 115 (2005).

specific cases, but ethical standards for nurses in the state can be used on cross-examination at trial to elicit admissions of the nursing home's inappropriate decisions or its inactions in response to patients' needs. Whistleblower protections aid in the reporting of bad conditions and bad behaviors, but the back pay might not be a great reward; these can be combined with False Claims Act cases in which the Medicare fraud prosecution recovers money for the government and a share of the money goes to the former employee.

CHAPTER 5

Roles and Liabilities of Physicians

5:1 Role of the Nursing Home Medical Director
5:2 Contractual Obligations
5:3 CMS Norms on Physician Obligations
5:4 Documentation of Decisions
5:5 Actual Supervision of Patient Care
5:6 Pharmaceutical Prescriptions
5:7 Role in Restraints
5:8 Malpractice Issues
5:9 Physician Duty and "Right to Die" Claims

5:1 Role of the Nursing Home Medical Director

The medical care of the nursing home patient can be provided by his or her personal physician (the "attending" physician) but is more frequently provided by the medical director of the nursing home. For reasons of travel time to the nursing home, and inadequate Medicaid or private insurance reimbursement of medical fees, most private attending physicians do not make house calls; they instead pass their coverage of patients who enter a nursing home to the doctor who is employed by or selected by the nursing home.[1] "While there may be

1. Douglas Singh, Effective Management of Long-Term Care Facilities 267–68 (2005).

advantages for all parties in this type of arrangement, it means that the connection of patients to their personal physicians is lost."[2]

The medical director of a nursing home is subject to explicit federal requirements for his or her patient care activities,[3] as well as the usual array of professional care roles. The nursing home must have at least one licensed physician under contract to perform the necessary medical services for its patients.[4] The medical director reports to the administrator and should have a cooperative relationship with other departments of the nursing home. The role of nursing home doctor is in growing demand, but carries a relative "social and professional stigma" compared to other medical specialty practices.[5] A review of the website of the professional society for medical directors is helpful.[6]

Unlike hospitals, where the centerpiece of the mission is healing, the nursing home seeks to maintain the activities of residents' daily living in a secure setting, with medical care as an important but subordinate position. This means that the physician in "charge" of nursing home patients is not held to the same acute care standard as a physician practicing within a hospital setting who deals with sick and dying patients arriving at the hospital from the general population. The maintenance of nursing home residents' health, within the set of circumstances they bring into the institution, is the continuing responsibility of the medical director, nurses, therapists, and staff.

The physician in the general community often sees patients one by one, with the physician's staff integrating services with external therapists, pharmacies, and so on. Inside the nursing home, the medical director relies upon the facility's pharmacist for scrutiny of the patients' medications more than a private doctor normally relies upon

---

2. Kathryn Locatell, MD, *Physician Liability Issues, in* NURSING HOME LITIGATION: INVESTIGATION AND CASE PREPARATION 78 (Patricia Iyer ed., 1999).

3. 42 C.F.R. § 483.75(i).

4. 42 C.F.R. § 483.40; CTRS. FOR MEDICARE & MEDICAID SERVS., STATE OPERATIONS MANUAL, CMS PUB. NO. 100-07, APPENDIX PP: GUIDANCE TO SURVEYORS FOR LONG TERM CARE FACILITIES F385, F386.

5. SINGH, *supra* note 1, at 268.

6. AMDA (formerly the American Medical Directors Association), http://www.amda.com.

an external pharmacist.[7] Integrated medical services do not often exist in the community at large.

The tort litigation perspective asks about negligence compared to a standard of professional competence found in medical malpractice law. This asks whether the medical director's care job for a particular plaintiff-resident was properly aligned with the duty undertaken, and whether breach of that standard of care caused harm. The American Medical Directors Association's clinical practice guidelines are a great starting point for understanding what should have been done for a particular nursing home patient.[8]

The medical director role may be undertaken by any doctor, but even the best-intentioned and most conscientious physician would be challenged by all the oversight and active roles that the medical director position includes. Lawsuits attack the degree of care that was provided. Sometimes delays in informing the medical director of the patient's crisis are cited as reasons for penalizing the nursing home.[9] Errors made in the care of a patient falls on the physician who is acting as the medical director and may be attributable to a lack of the medical directors' attention who had been deemed responsible for 200 or more patients.

Abuse that occurs inside the nursing home is reportable under state laws. The statutory duty to report abuse or neglect falls on the physician, but often the time actually spent in that physician's contact with the patients is minimal. Changes in patient condition may trigger a need for a medical examination and a clinical treatment or hospitalization decision. But not all changes in condition come to the doctor's attention. Nor do all medically significant problems draw the speedy response and attention of reporting that is likely to be needed if the medical intervention is to make a difference in patient outcomes.

---

7. Andrew Spillane, *Negligence Liability's Role in Changing Pharmacotherapy Responsibilities*, 12 Marquette Elder Advisor 453 (2011).

8. AMDA, Clinical Practice Guidelines in the Long Term Care Setting, http://www.amda.com/tools/guidelines.cfm.

9. Cox Ret. Props. Inc. v. Johnson, 323 F. App'x 668 (10th Cir. 2009).

Classic American folklore envisions a solid trusting relationship of one family doctor with one elderly patient. Times have changed. The degree of patient-physician interaction in the nursing home context is generally minimal, if the patient does not have an acute need for attention from the busy doctor. The resident's family probably does not know the nursing home's doctor at all. This distance in professional allegiance is significant to lawyers, as this produces a lower psychological barrier to the family litigating against that physician for malpractice. There appears to be less reluctance to sue, compared to the long-standing respect given by patient and family to the private family doctor of Norman Rockwell fame. Physicians who work for nursing homes are aware of this shift of perceptions, and how it impacts on the propensity for them to be targets of litigation.[10]

The ideal is different from the reality, for economic reasons. The nursing home patient has the legal right to be treated by his or her own attending physician, so long as that physician complies with the rules of the nursing home. But reimbursement from Medicare is low, visits are not convenient, travel from office to facility and back is not well compensated, and the risks of medical regulatory and malpractice liability issues are burdensome. So most family and individual doctors hand over the care of the patient to the medical director of the nursing home.[11] An individual with sufficient wealth can afford in-home nursing care and a continued relationship with a chosen physician. Most residents of most nursing homes lack that connected relationship, though some physicians are very adept at building trusting relationships among the shifting population of the nursing homes that they serve.

5:2 Contractual Obligations

The medical director's contract with the nursing home and his or her agreement with the hospital at which she or he has admitting

10. Locatell, *supra* note 2.
11. SINGH, *supra* note 1, at 267.

privileges will be discoverable in a case asserting malpractice and negligent institutional care. In the contract, there may be incentives for certain cost savings, and there may be allocation of responsibilities of certain types. The Center for Medicare and Medicaid Services (CMS) regulations are the foundation of these contracts; knowing that state surveyor teams will examine the records, the nursing home owner probably conforms the terms of the contract to at least the minimum elements in the regulations.[12]

Counsel for an affected resident will have to decide whether to make separate demands upon the physician's own malpractice carrier and that of the nursing home. It may be that the individual scope of coverage for a physician carved out his or her role in nursing home work. Or the coverage may be silent, so that the physician malpractice carrier shares liability with the carrier who covers the potential liability of the nursing home. It may be that the physician who is sued for nursing home omissions is denied coverage by his or her "office" or group malpractice carrier, while the "employer coverage" expected from the nursing home group fails to materialize. In some cases, a major fatal error may have caused large tort liability exposure, and then a nursing home shell corporation or limited liability company dissolves, in the face of the exposure to litigation over a death or egregious injury.

5:3 CMS Norms on Physician Obligations

The CMS requirements for the medical director role are a substantial burden if they are taken seriously.[13] Coordinator, supervisor, intervenor, and approver of care are each roles for the medical director in the CMS rules. The medical director is to work with the patient's private attending physician, where one exists, and must be responsive when a change in patient condition occurs. Supervision of nursing care by a physician is required under CMS rules,[14] under state "scope of nursing

12. 42 C.F.R. § 483.40.
13. *Id.*
14. *Id.*

practice" statutes, and by the agency's Guidance for Surveyors who visit and inspect operations on behalf of state Medicaid agencies.

5:4 Documentation of Decisions

Physicians learn from the experience of peers about the importance of record-keeping for future malpractice defense. Documentation of medical decisions is especially important in nursing homes, especially since so much of the work is done remotely via a doctor's telephone consultation with the supervisory nurses and director of nursing.[15] As a physician expert has written: "The more the physician abdicates decision-making to others and minimizes the time spent with each patient, the more likely it is that he or she will at some point be at risk for bad patient outcomes and lawsuits."[16]

The terms "abdicates" and "minimizes" are powerful terms in a powerful context.

Conflicts of records sometimes occur; a variation of the physician records with those of the nurses can put both into jeopardy if the treatment or prescription has an adverse effect. Discovery requests should probe the availability of both sets of records.

5:5 Actual Supervision of Patient Care

An element that will play well for plaintiffs in a jury trial is the small amount of actual contact that the defendant physician had with the plaintiff. The actual number of hours that the physician is present at the nursing home will virtually always be less than the jurors might expect. This does not mean the care is abnormally insufficient, but it may create a perception that service to one patient in the 50-patient nursing home was a low priority for the physician—creating an inference of negligent oversight of the plaintiff's medical needs. These will be highly fact-specific debates.

---

15. SINGH, *supra* note 1, at 269–71.
16. Locatell, *supra* note 2, at 81.

CMS and state survey programs focus on how well the nursing home lived up to its care plan for the patient. Care plans are intended to be crafted at meetings of the medical team, including physicians, nurses, therapists, and others who have the duty of updating the treatment plans of individual patients. The paperwork for which the physician is responsible may be a source of some frustration, with some physicians delegating or ignoring the documentation responsibilities, in ways that future litigators will highlight to the jury. But the essential core issue will be: was the doctor told about the stroke symptoms or other urgent matters? Failure to notify the doctor violates Medicaid and Medicare requirements for a certified nursing home[17] and can result in a cash penalty against the nursing home of $800 per day.[18]

Changes in condition such as unexpected weight loss should be tracked by the nursing staff and reported to the physician. Standing orders can be given for drugs and therapy of certain types, to be available as needed in the judgment of the nurses.

5:6 Pharmaceutical Prescriptions

A physician has several vulnerabilities in covering a larger number of institutionalized patients, with so much delegation of care to nurses. The physician must have an awareness of other attending physicians' prescriptions and directives for their patients. These would appear in the chart of clinical care notes.

Although the physician and the consulting pharmacist are independent professionals under separate contracts, the physician must have an up-to-date knowledge of geriatric pharmacology, especially an awareness of contraindications for use of medications. Errors in prescribing may result from a lack of understanding of a patient's clinical needs, or a rushed visit or a lapse of memory.

The physician is presumed to have ready access to the patient's clinical record. This would presumably give the physician an awareness

17. Cox Ret. Props. Inc. v. Johnson, 323 F. App'x 668 (2009).

18. Senior Rehab. & Skilled Nursing Ctr. v. U.S. Dep't of HHS, 405 F. App'x 820 (5th Cir. 2010).

of the prescriptions that this patient is receiving from other physician prescribers, as well as the drugs delivered to the patient under the standing orders for that category of patients. Both the physician and the consulting pharmacist should be aware of any medication contraindications. If a drug prescribed for the patient is not on the state formularies (approved lists of certain drugs that can be reimbursed by state agencies), then the consulting pharmacist and the physician should discuss alternatives. Chapter 13 deals with risk issues related to pharmaceutical reactions.

5:7 Role in Restraints

Informed consent should be obtained for the use of straps or other restraints on patient movement. The physician must sign the order for restraints and there should be informed consent by the representative or the family before they are used.

If a patient is injured by a physical restraint, the subsequent investigation may ask about the physician's role in approving the use of that restraint.[19]

5:8 Malpractice Issues

The standard of care in physician malpractice is typically set at the current local standard of physician competence in that field of practice, such as geriatrics. For nursing homes, the federal CMS rules and survey guidance documents are a starting point in defining the "correct" delivery of nursing home medical director services. If the surveyors found inadequacies in their inspection of the work of the physician, that may be used as a part of plaintiff's proof. But these are minimum standards; the standard of care may be established by testimony of a plaintiff's expert who serves as a nursing home medical director elsewhere in the state.

19. 42 C.F.R. § 483.13.

The points of greatest vulnerability are the intake or admission phase, when the physician is required to evaluate the patient on the basis of his or her history and physical condition, and when a change of condition occurs that should trigger a response by the physician.[20] Did the reasonable physician have a duty to act, and how rapidly?

Particularly with understaffed nursing homes or homes with poor training and hiring practices, the physician's exposure to malpractice suits seems to be affected by the ability of the staff members to implement the physician's directives. The doctor often communicates with supervisory personnel by phone. Will the action that is directed by that physician for patient X be accurately recorded on the chart for X, and then implemented accurately and in a timely manner? More and better-trained staff would reduce errors, increase responsiveness, detect more change-of-condition moments, and reduce nursing home liabilities. A national expert in nursing home law suggested that the need for more resources had held back the use of advanced practice nurses, whose expertise would be very beneficial to the physician in carrying out treatment and care.[21]

5:9 Physician Duty and "Right to Die" Claims

This book does not address the moral quandary of assisted suicide and the right of the patient to be helped at the final hours by a sympathetic doctor. But it can be an issue.

The refusal to withdraw life support from a comatose patient, without court order, is a protected action for the treating physician, for which he or she will not be held liable in damages for continued life of the patient.[22] A patient's court-appointed conservator refused to continue paying nursing home costs after the physician refused the conservator's request to terminate the life of the ward, but the court

20. Locatell, *supra* note 2, at 85.
21. Marshall Kapp, *Legal Anxieties and End of Life Care in Nursing Homes*, 19 Issues in L. & Med. 111, 133 (2003).
22. Grace Plaza v. Elbaum, 183 A.D.2d 10, *aff'd*, 603 N.Y.S.2d 386 (2d Dep't 1992).

enforced the duty to pay.[23] The strong debates over the roles of physicians intersect with the need of nursing homes to have some certainty regarding the actual documentation of the period preceding the resident's death, to lessen potential tort exposure.[24]

23. *Id.*

24. *See, e.g.*, Thaddeus Pope & Lindsey Anderson, *Managing Risk at the End of Life: Voluntarily Stopping Eating and Drinking: A Legal Treatment Option at the End of Life*, 17 WIDENER L.J. 363, 365 (2011) (citing the previous edition of this book).

CHAPTER 6

Supporting Staff and Their Roles

6:1 Consequences of Understaffing When Presented as a Cause of Harm
6:2 Dietary Support
6:3 Pharmacy Support
6:4 Laboratory Support
6:5 Rehabilitation
6:6 Documentation
6:7 The Role of Nursing Home Administration
6:8 Admissions
6:9 Accounting
6:10 Staff Training and Selection
6:11 Support Rules of Specialized Units
6:12 Illustrative Case

6:1 Consequences of Understaffing When Presented as a Cause of Harm

Nursing homes are a service to elderly and disabled people, yet their benefits are only as good as the actions of people who operate their service. Significant problems can arise when a nursing home has too few workers who can provide the necessary health care services. A legal vulnerability arises where staffing is not funded at a sufficient level to ensure the safety of nursing home residents. Owners are looking to reduce their costs. Nursing home personnel are sometimes short-changed, with negative consequences for the patients. The role of the litigator is to discern what had gone wrong and how it could have been remediated, so that understaffing does not have negative health consequences for others. This chapter focuses on the personnel aspects of the nursing home that have safety-related consequences.

Congress has considered legislation to require more employee staffing of nursing homes, to amend titles XVIII and XIX of the Social Security Act to revise minimum nurse staffing requirements for skilled nursing facilities under the Medicare program, and to enhance nursing facilities under the Medicaid program.[1] CMS requirements for adequate staffing have been actively resisted by the investors who own groups of nursing homes and fear lost profits as costs rise.

Understaffing problems could sometimes be compounded by falsification of employment records. Corporate owners' decisions on adequacy of nursing home staffing are very significant to liability cases regarding employee back-pay obligations. In the future, corporate owners that knew of the harm that could be caused by chronic understaffing of their nursing homes might be held liable in a jury trial for the total adverse consequences of understaffing.

6:2 Dietary Support

Litigation relating to food issues at the nursing home is usually one of three types: the patient choked on food when being served; the patient did not receive sufficient food and failed to thrive as a result of the deprivation; or the liquid-format feeding tube was obstructed and not cleared, resulting in harm to the patient. Chapter 14 addresses specific details of these food issues.

Each nursing home that has been certified for Medicaid and Medicare must have a registered dietician under contract or on staff.[2] Within two weeks after admission, each new resident must be evaluated for an individual dietary plan. Counsel should study the legislative proposals for Center for Medicare and Medicaid Services (CMS) rules on nursing

1. Quality Care for Nursing Home Residents Act of 2019, H.R. 5216, 116th Cong. (2019).
2. 42 C.F.R. § 483.35.

home dietetics.[3] These federal norms and state equivalents have been in place since 1991.[4] They build upon the state licensure equivalents.

Because there often are dietary aspects to the individual patient's vulnerability to medical problems, the plaintiff's counsel should inquire about the nursing home's dietician support. The dietician's role goes beyond ordinary meal planning for a group residential facility. Beyond that, this dietary evaluation recognizes the healing aspects of delivering proper nutrition as well as the risks that might be posed by improper foods. The counsel for plaintiff who suffers from dehydration or malnutrition, and the disease problems that they can create, should prepare to depose the dietician and subpoena paperwork in the central file regarding how food service helped or harmed this plaintiff and his or her needs.

Medicaid/Medicare providers file annual cost reports that can be used to show the jury in a damages case the very small expenditures made by this nursing home for nutritious meals for the plaintiff and other residents. If the total budget for food was very low, and the population of residents has grown, the jury will understand that the quality and taste of the food will suffer.

The individual residents' refusal of food is a potential concern; these refusals should be recorded, and alternate forms of liquid nutrition should be offered.[5]

Special dietary needs of each new resident should be evaluated and a feeding program should be part of the initial evaluation and care plan. The dietician and her or his assistants should write up their evaluations of each resident's nutritional needs and should keep up the charting. The dietician should be careful in the evaluation to avoid making assumptions that would not withstand future postcrisis justification. The records of the dietician may be helpful to a future litigant.

Sometimes there can be errors in the feeding assignments for aides who are responsible for feeding diabetic residents, residents with difficulty swallowing, residents with risks of strong adverse reactions to

3. *Id.*
4. 56 Fed. Reg. 48,874 (Sept. 26, 1991), as amended at 68 Fed. Reg. 55,539 (Sept. 26, 2003).
5. 42 C.F.R. § 483.35(d)(4).

certain allergens, and so on. Training for feeding assistants is typically required by state rules to deliver adherence to the optimal patient diet.[6]

Documentation of patient assessments is important evidence in defending a future malnutrition claim.

Choking risk is a parallel concern. Liability is likely to be raised wherever a choking death becomes known to family.[7] Patient risk assessment includes ability to swallow and digest rougher foods. The physical chewing consistency of foods may be important for patients with digestion problems. An obstructed airway may cause an unattended resident to choke to death. In such a case, the dietetic record will become a centerpiece of the plaintiff's negligence claims.

"Failure to thrive" is a classic symptom of malnutrition and may be a side effect of disease, such as the wasting syndrome in some AIDS patients.[8] This merits attention in the patient records and there should be a remedial action plan for the proper care and feeding of the patient.

Liquid and supplemental nutrition alternatives to solid foods are subject to the nutritional evaluation of the nurses, physician, and dietician. The special case of tube feeding is subject to a physician's evaluation of its appropriateness, and the resulting orders for a tube to be inserted.[9]

Care for certain groups of patients is a problem; any special dietary limitations in the patient's record should be recognized by the actual dietary plan that is in place. In the worst case, shortages of staff for supervised meals might allow the choking patient to be ignored, so that the patient would be at high risk if unattended.

6:3 Pharmacy Support

Physicians prescribe drugs; nurses deliver them; in between, the selection and preparation of prescription drugs must be done correctly.

---

6. 42 C.F.R. § 483.35(h).
7. *See, e.g.*, Sharp v. Parkview Care Ctr., Inc., 940 So. 2d 724, (La. Ct. App. 2d Cir. 2006) (choked on sandwich).
8. 42 C.F.R. § 483.25(i).
9. 42 C.F.R. § 483.35(h)(3)(ii).

There is a need for accountability of this function so that the correct drug in the correct dose is delivered in the correct time period. Decisions need to be made about the appropriateness of a particular drug for a particular patient, and contraindications and warnings need to be considered by the prescriber.[10]

The failure to make proper choices and to monitor use of a drug like a potent antipsychotic drug was the basis for a wrongful death action.[11] One of the basic pharmacology limitations to be understood is that the federal CMS rules ban the use of psychoactive drugs as a chemical restraint to immobilize residents, except in specified emergency situations.[12] Constantly sedating a dementia patient to keep her or him from wandering outside the home would violate the permissible CMS norms. Chapter 13 addresses this topic.

Pain medication use for ailing patients, especially those in hospice care, should be closely monitored.

Roles of specialized units in the medical side of care will be complex but necessary. The state-licensed pharmacies are required to maintain tight controls on their handling of controlled substances to avoid the high risk of diversion to abuse.[13] Thefts of drugs by nursing home employees have generated criminal investigations.[14]

Standing orders are utilized by the physician to give advance authorization for the use of certain medications by the nursing home staff. A prescription drug administered under standing orders is deemed to be a valid administration of the drug.[15]

Counsel for plaintiffs should recognize one's own limitations of knowledge before accepting a case from a potential plaintiff. The attorney will need to retain pharmacology and gerontology experts to understand the particular types of drugs and the adverse effects of their administration to elders. While the family may sincerely believe that the drugs were being used to harm their loved one, the lawyer

10. 42 C.F.R. § 483.60.
11. Hayward v. Jack's Pharmacy Inc., 115 P.3d 713 (Idaho 2005).
12. 42 C.F.R. § 483.450(e).
13. 21 C.F.R. pts. 1306, 1311.
14. *See, e.g.*, Hansen v. State, 928 N.E.2d 653 (Ind. Ct. App. 2010).
15. 42 C.F.R. § 483.60.

should reserve judgment at least until an experienced gerontologist or clinical pharmacology expert can advise about the merits of the potential case.

Chapter 13 discusses the adverse effects that can come from multiple drugs that have conflicting effects. This phenomenon, called "polypharmacy," should be detected in the clinical pharmacist's chart-review meetings and the physician's order could be questioned, so as to avoid side effects that could do harm to the patient.

The cost-control aspect of the prescription drug selection process involves the great economic pressure to substitute a generic version of a drug for the original manufacturer's pioneer drug. One of the significant aspects of nursing home use of generic drugs is the margin of therapeutic equivalence allowed by the Food and Drug Administration (FDA). In summary, the generic version of a drug is allowed onto the market, once the statutory exclusivity and patent periods of the pioneer expire, if the copy of that "pioneer" drug has effectiveness within a broad range around the expected dose that the pioneer product would deliver.[16] If the original "pioneer" version of the drug would dissolve in the bloodstream and deliver 20 milligrams of active ingredient to the brain, the generic drug can be accepted by the FDA if it delivers 16 to 24 milligrams to the brain, for example.[17]

If an injury such as a fall or dehydration can be traced in whole or in part to the effects of the drug, then counsel should use discovery to find records of the nursing home, the prescription entered by the physician for that patient, and the consulting pharmacist's chart review. A physician can always legally insist upon the patient receiving the original and more costly version by writing "no substitution" or checking a box on the face of the prescription. It is possible in some instances that negligence in the selection of a generic version of a very

---

16. *See* 1 James O'Reilly, Food & Drug Administration ch. 13 (West Thomson, 3d ed. 2008 Supp.).

17. *Id.* These are rough approximations; see bioequivalence approval criteria applied by FDA reviewers at 21 C.F.R. §§314.94(a)(7), 320.1, and 314.1279(a)(3)(iii)(A)(6) and see guidance at U.S. Food & Drug Admin., http://www.fda.gov/cder/guidance/4964dft.htm#P170_10281.

precise drug, chosen in order to reduce costs, had played a role in the negligent cause of the harm.

Counsel can work with medical and pharmaceutical experts to evaluate the particular drug that was chosen for the resident and then could obtain the FDA's publicly available file on the approval of this generic drug for this medical need,[18] as well as any adverse effect reports. Then counsel can determine from medical experts whether the adverse condition that was created in the patient may be linked to the chosen medication. If so, the expert can be asked, would the same negative effect of that generic drug have been manifested if the doctor had ordered the pioneer version of the drug? The Supreme Court's decisions about generic equivalence in the 2011 *Pliva* and 2013 *Mutual* cases[19] factor into the choices about suing a generic drug maker; it may be futile to argue about generic status in some circumstances.

Keep in mind that documentation of the health of the nursing home resident is in the hands of the medical and pharmacological providers. Records of the consultation and care planning meetings regarding patient medications may bring the consulting pharmacist under the microscope of "probable cause" evaluations if an avoidable patient harm incident occurs. Did the resident receive the careful attention that should be recorded in the nursing home records?

6:4 Laboratory Support

Clinical testing laboratories are an essential part of the chain of nursing home residents' health care. Labs receive samples from nursing homes and issue reports of their results. Elderly patients are prime customers for the Medicaid-reimbursed diagnostic tests of the patient's liver function, kidney function, and other medical needs.

---

18. *Id.* The bioequivalence section of the abbreviated new drug application will be of greatest interest where the pioneer drug had a narrow range of effectiveness or narrow range of avoidance of adverse effects.

19. PLIVA, Inc. v. Mensing, 564 U.S. 604 (2011); Mut. Pharm. Co. v. Bartlett, 570 U.S. 472 (2013).

The laboratory is an essential diagnostic partner of the resident's medical team. Did the nursing home file indicate that several bids were sought from competing lab service companies? Did the cheapest bid for lab service provide a questionable set of data points that has negligently weakened the medical care for that resident?

Now consider the actual drug dispensed to this patient. Was it the cheaper generic? Did it deliver all the potency of the pioneer drug? The generic drug maker's application that had been filed with the FDA is available under the Freedom of Information Act. The bioequivalence section of the abbreviated new drug application will be of greatest interest in situations where the pioneer drug had a narrow range of effectiveness or a narrow range of avoidance of adverse effects. These can be compared by a medical expert witness to provide useful data on bodily function and other indicators of disease problems.

Laboratory tests of a resident's blood are quite commonly reimbursed by Medicaid and Medicare when ordered by a physician and when the tests are reliably performed on samples taken from the nursing home residents. The clinical labs are overseen by the Centers for Disease Control and Prevention and by states, but generally not by the FDA. Did the nursing home document its need for services appropriately?

If there were abnormal results reported from the testing of specimens from that resident, the change of condition should be recorded by the nurses and then communicated to the medical director. The results may have signaled that the prescription should be changed—if the physician, the nurse, and the pharmacist had each acted on his or her obligations to the patient. If the laboratory is found to have made a significant error that concealed a disease state, then there may be a potential court action by the patient concerning inadequacies of the lab.

But such an action by a plaintiff is fraught with complications under the third-party-beneficiary issue in contract law: was the resident the beneficiary of a contract between the nursing home owner and the laboratory owner? The lab's defense will be that its duty was solely to the nursing home owner and to the medical director or other physician who ordered that test, and not to other parties. State case law will be the measure of accountability.

6:5 Rehabilitation

Some nursing homes or portions of nursing homes provide the service of short-term physical rehabilitation, not long-term care.[20] In the long-term care facility, licensed physical therapists should provide Medicaid-reimbursed specialized services, such as aiding the bed-limited patient to exercise sufficiently to avoid contractures of arm and leg muscles.[21]

Several types of therapists are likely to work with patients at the typical nursing home. Respiratory therapists are supportive of those patients with chronic difficulties in breathing. There may also be the need for a trained specialist in placement of the patient's nasogastric tube. Physical therapy professionals can work with individual patients on the training and equipment aided by staff to help patients with contractures, or to assist in the ability of mobile patients to continue to walk safely without falling. The occupational therapist will evaluate readiness of the patient to return home and handle routine household functions. Recreational therapists have a role in safe and steady ambulation, as well as in keeping patients healthy by assisting them to exercise; the more active patients without restraints can be active and thereby are more likely to avoid elopement and reduce their night-wandering situations.

6:6 Documentation

Record-keeping is the core of the defense in a nursing home tort action as well as in establishing regulatory compliance. The nursing home chart must be complete. "Charting by exception" is a policy that saves time for some nursing homes, as it assumes that actions had been normally taken, unless otherwise recorded. But this approach to documenting nurses' activities assumes that all is well, and this

20. 42 C.F.R. § 483.45.
21. 42 C.F.R. § 483.25(e).

type of assertion may be vulnerable to legal challenges in resident injury tort cases.[22]

Silence in the records is not helpful to the defense in litigation. It does not produce the specific record of timely action that the court would expect to encounter when causation of a patient's skin ulcer or other problem arose out of a pattern of staff neglect of the skin cleaning of this resident. The recording of patient care is an inherent tension—completeness versus delay/cost of data.

Records management is an area of nursing home administration that deserves more preventive scrutiny from the defense bar and insurance carriers. Evidence or deposition disclosures of document destruction of part or all of a recent patient's records signals a potential lapse of quality or a cover-up of a known violation. Sometimes the discovery of the documents will have a powerful impact on appeal for sustaining a judgment against the nursing home. The nursing home's own records of routinely passive or negligent care will be helpful for plaintiff; it will be a burden for the defense counsel to refute.[23]

6:7 The Role of Nursing Home Administration

The administrator of a nursing home has a major task. He or she is legally responsible in cases of what CMS or a state considers to be "substandard care."[24] The job of the administrator is to oversee operations in order to protect the residents and to carry out the operating policies of the corporation or other licensee.[25] Statutory reporting obligations for elder abuse or neglect cases typically fall upon the nursing home administrator. In an extreme case, the administrator could be criminally prosecuted and their conviction would be sustained along with that of the corporate owner.[26]

---

22. *See, e.g.*, Lama v. Borrs, 16 F.3d 473 (1st Cir. 1994).
23. Stogsdill v. Healthmark Partners, L.L.C., 377 F.3d 827 (8th Cir. 2004).
24. 42 C.F.R. § 483.75(d).
25. Cal. Health & Safety Code § 1416.2(a)(5).
26. State v. Serebin, 350 N.W.2d 65 (Wis. 1984).

The nursing home owner's conscious corporate budget decision to cut staff may have put some residents in danger, and their avoidable premature deaths would reflect badly upon the owners, managers, and administrator.[27] The individual accountability of the administrator arises because "the buck stops here," and liability follows from authority in some cases of conscious inattention.[28] Of course, each of the operating departments of the nursing home reports to the administrator: nursing, dietary, resident activities, social services, housekeeping, laundry, building maintenance, admissions, and business offices.[29]

Competent responses to resident or family complaints are an essential skill for the nursing home administrator. By the time a complaint gets to the stage of litigation, it is very likely that it has been aired with the administrator and not satisfactorily concluded. If these very direct interactions fail, litigation may follow.

The policy of the nursing home is typically set by the administrator working with a governing board, whose obligations include budgeting, staff selection, maintenance of elder care standards, and compliance with the rules of the state and of CMS. Their actual decisions can be communicated through the governing boards but are likely to have been made by distant management of a chain of nursing homes.[30] Plaintiff's counsel should chart the chain of responsibility.

6:8 Admissions

A facility should not admit a patient if the facility does not have the licensure, personnel, and capability to care for the patient's level of needs. For example, if a person must be fed by tubes, a skilled nursing

---

27. John Pray, State v. Serebin*: Causation and the Criminal Liability of Nursing Home Administrators*, 1986 Wis. L. Rev. 339.

28. State v. Boone Ret. Ctr., Inc., 26 S.W.3d 265 (Mo. Ct. App. W.D. 2000) (affirming conviction of nursing home administrator of two counts each of neglect of a nursing home resident); Mitchell v. State, 491 So. 2d 596 (Fla. Dist. Ct. App. 1986) (upheld conviction of nursing home operator for aggravated abuse).

29. Rebecca Perley & Kenneth Merchant, Nursing Home Administrator: Guide to an Amazing Career 4 (Cal. Dep't of Health Servs. 2006) http://www.cdph.ca.gov/certlic/occupations/Documents/NHA0906online.pdf.

30. 42 C.F.R. § 483.75.

facility with the right staffing is the only appropriate nonhospital setting, because of the risks of death involved in mistakes.

Discharge of a nursing home patient is required upon a change of condition that causes an inability for that home to continue providing care; only a qualified service provider should care for the needs of that person. Discharge for nonpayment of monthly bills is defensible, but plaintiff's attorney should question the nursing home owner's willingness to handle this resident until another placement is found.

6:9 Accounting

Litigation about nursing home problems rarely addresses billing errors and similar economic problems, except in the unusual cases of False Claims Act litigation concerning Medicare overbilling. Inept billing is potentially a matter of concern for business oversight, but tort cases like those addressed in this text will rarely involve financial issues other than understaffing. The financial data may involve proof at trial of the corporate owner's use of executive incentives to maximize profits by holding back service and personnel costs. The jury will be made aware that care of the resident was overlooked so that budget targets would be satisfied.

6:10 Staff Training and Selection

A nursing home that receives Medicaid or Medicare funding is required to have a staff sufficient to perform necessary services for its patients.[31] Training of staff in each of these service tasks, such as tube feeding, is essential. A nursing home is usually authorized by the state to conduct staff training using a state curriculum, but some nursing homes have been penalized for inadequate training conditions. They could be punished with restrictions, e.g., having state permission for training of certified nursing assistants (CNAs) withdrawn from that nursing home.

31. *Id.*

The tort litigator could find it interesting that the state had withdrawn the ability of this defendant nursing home to conduct its own training of its own people—a slap at the quality of the people who presently operate the facility, suggesting that they could not be relied upon to train the next generation of employees adequately. Jurors in a negligent harm case would find such state restrictions to be an indicator of serious problems inside the defendant nursing home.

6:11 Support Rules of Specialized Units

Proof of facilities' cleanliness truly matters in defense of a nursing home challenge regarding infections. The safety and security of the physical plant are overseen by the building maintenance staff. Chapter 7 addresses this topic. Examples of litigation issues are oxygen tank lapses, or nonfunctioning or absent alarms for patient wandering and security against intruders. Adequate maintenance of the home's patient service equipment and repairs to protective systems such as belt restraints are aspects of potential negligence. The adequacy of pest control may also be a source of negligence analysis.[32]

Maintenance failures that might have precipitated lawsuits will occasionally arise. Oxygen supplies and the functional connection of medical gases may become a source of fire risks or of mix-ups. Fall protection requires that the home install sufficient railings, fall guards, signage, exterior door locks, and so on.

Door-exit alarms should be maintained to diminish the prospect of an escaped "wanderer" who might die of exposure outdoors. Physical design of the facility to reduce exit risks is another potential method for avoiding liability lawsuits. What could go wrong? How would the resident be impacted? Why did the nursing home owner skimp on spending for safety functions?

---

32. 42 U.S.C. 483.70.

6:12 Illustrative Case

A contract dental provider performed what Executor described as "unnecessary" dental procedures on Decedent at her nursing home and extracted five of Decedent's teeth. Executor accused the nursing home of conspiring to profit from such dental procedures. Executor claims that the procedures were not medically necessary and were performed without Decedent's consent. He pleaded claims against the dental contractor for committing (1) fraud by misrepresenting the medical necessity of the dental procedures, (2) assault by performing the unnecessary tooth extractions, and (3) intentional infliction of emotional distress (IIED) for the same reason.[33]

33. Parker v. Symphony of Evanston Healthcare, LLC, No. 1-22-0391, 2023 WL 3806800 (Ill. App. June 5, 2023).

CHAPTER 7

Facility Safety Issues

7:1 Premises Safety Issues
7:2 Fire and Emergency Issues
7:3 Floods and Evacuations
7:4 Removal
7:5 Avoiding Preventable Errors
7:6 Facility Maintenance Issues
7:7 Stairway Accidents

7:1 Premises Safety Issues

Safety in the nursing home begins with planning for residents' communication to nursing home staff about risks.[1] The failure to plan is almost certainly a "plan to fail." The state or CMS program surveyors can penalize a nursing home that does not make it feasible for the patient to reach their call button from their bed.[2] The ability of the resident to obtain a safety-related response is essential.

1. Windsor Place Nursing & Rehab. Ctr. v. U.S. Dep't of Health & Hum. Servs., 649 F.3d 293 (5th Cir. 2011).

2. *Id.* (there was no need for a negative outcome to find that service offered was insufficient) (citing 42 C.F.R. § 483.25(a)(3)); *see* Ivy Woods Healthcare v. Thompson, 156 F. App'x 775 (6th Cir. 2005).

7:2 Fire and Emergency Issues

Litigation often follows the consequences of disastrous fires or floods, where injuries resulted from an alleged lack of adequate planning, preparation, or implementation of emergency plans. Nursing homes take a longer time to evacuate in fire, hurricane, and earthquake disasters, and their occupants are more sensitive to disruption and more challenging to evacuate than others might be. The plan to "shelter in place" makes sense where backup power and supportive services are available immediately after the storm passes. But the 2012 Hurricane Sandy's devastation of coastal New York City was a serious setback for hundreds of the area's nursing home residents. The tort liability risk of the nursing home management for disaster-related harm is a function of foreseeability of the event and the failure to have planned for responses to the contingent event.

Fire evacuation plans are included in the standard nursing home compliance evaluation, using the Life Safety Code as administered by each state. Federal investigators have found deficiencies that require much stronger regulatory oversight.[3] The plan should be exercised periodically to evaluate the feasibility of removing the immobile residents from the area of the fire.

7:3 Floods and Evacuations

New Orleans area nursing homes had grave problems with the flooding that followed Hurricane Katrina, and New York area homes were devastated by Hurricane Sandy in 2012, and some tragic deaths resulted. Planning obligations should be related to proximity of water and potential flooding.

7:4 Removal

State surveys of nursing homes include an evaluation of the nursing home's resident removal emergency plan, the feasibility of retaining

3. U.S. Gov't Accountability Office, GAO-04-660, Nursing Home Fire Safety (2004).

a bus or ambulance company to facilitate the removals, the safety of residents during and after the event, and the location of the emergency shelter to which patients will be removed. Rehearsals with staff and local emergency officials would be a prudent part of a nursing home's emergency plan, in coastal or other areas where severe weather might damage the facility's access to continuous power and water supplies.

7:5 Avoiding Preventable Errors

Breathing and enteral feeding apparatus that depends on continued electrical power is particularly at risk from the effects of natural disasters. Backup generator support is needed to sustain lives of patients, and the failure of the backup system can be alleged to have been a foreseeable failure of due care by the facility operator. Another preventable error is hooking up hoses and tubes to lines of oxygen and other medical gases. Improper connections can have fatal consequences. Jurors can readily understand the negligence claims.

7:6 Facility Maintenance Issues

Litigation arising out of injuries generally does not relate to the poor maintenance of the nursing home. The slips and falls that occur from floor spills and poor lighting are covered in Chapter 9. The bed rail collapses that could have been avoided by proper maintenance will result in settlements, so they will not be seen in appellate reports.[4]

But seven deaths and 15 injuries have been reported to the Food and Drug Administration (FDA) concerning mix-ups in medical gas lines.[5] In one case, criminal indictments were brought where a switch of gas lines occurred and four deaths resulted, when the wall-mounted outlet line for oxygen was inadvertently changed to distribute nitrogen instead into the breathing masks of patients.[6]

4. MeadowWood Nursing Home v. U.S. Dep't of HHS, 364 F.3d 786 (6th Cir. 2004).

5. FDA Public Health Advisory to Hospitals and Nursing Homes, re medical gas mix-ups (Mar. 2001) as FDA also did in 2005, see http://www.accessdata.fda.gov/scripts/cdrh/cfdocs/psn/printer-full.cfm?id=41.

6. *Indictments Issued in Nursing Home Deaths*, CINCINNATI ENQUIRER (Feb. 10, 2001).

The FDA warned users of inhalation gas lines for patients to use caution. Gas line error cases reveal striking similarities:

- The person connecting the vessel to the oxygen system (e.g., the delivery person or the facility employee) was not properly trained and did not understand that connection incompatibility is a built in safeguard.
- Prior to installing the cryogenic vessel to the oxygen supply system, the person making the connection did not examine the drug label applied to the cryogenic vessel to ensure that the product was medical oxygen.[7] Proper staff training could have avoided these fatal errors.

7:7 Stairway Accidents

One of the tragic flaws in some nursing homes has been the willingness of staff to override safety measures in order to enhance the employees' comfort or convenience. Leaving a secure door ajar to facilitate smokers' exits down to an outside door is one such flaw. The tragic cases of dead residents found in broken wheelchairs at the bottom of staircases can result in penalties by government[8] and will inevitably result in settlements of tort actions by survivors of the victims.

---

7. FDA Public Health Advisory to Hospitals and Nursing Homes, re medical gas mix-ups (Mar. 2001), as FDA also did in 2005, see http://www.accessdata.fda.gov/scripts/cdrh/cfdocs/psn/printer-full.cfm?id=41.

8. Asbury Ctr. v. U.S. Dep't of HHS, 77 F. App'x 853 (6th Cir. 2003).

CHAPTER 8

Liability for Neglect: Skin Ulcers and Infection Problems

8:1 Overview
8:2 Use of Clinical Practice Guidelines or CMS Guidelines as Evidence of the Standard of Care
8:3 Use of Regulatory Violations to Establish Negligence Per Se or as Evidence of the Standard of Care
8:4 Legal Issues
8:5 Dividing the Causes
8:6 Care Must Be Continuously Supervised
8:7 Record-Keeping Is Essential to Defense
8:8 Standard of Due Care
8:9 Short Staffing
8:10 Evidence
8:11 Defenses
8:12 Damages
8:13 Punitive Damages
8:14 Burns
8:15 Other Infection Concerns
8:16 Lessons from the Cases
8:17 Summary

8:1 Overview

A significant health problem for the elderly is the deterioration of normal skin as the layers of moist fresh skin begin to compress; the weight and pressure of the body rests upon one part of the body, as when a nursing resident is confined to his bed and his or her weight rests upon the right hip, right ankle, right foot, and so on.[1] These pressure points on the body may produce pressure sores, and, in the most severe condition, the pressure sores may eat through the skin into bone and produce a fatal infection.[2] A pressure sore is a "localized injury to the skin, muscle and/ or underlying tissue usually over a bony prominence as a result of pressure, or pressure in combination with shear and/or friction."[3] The potential for regulatory or tort liability for these conditions is a serious vulnerability for the nursing home operator.[4]

National experts have cited statistics that 10 to 20 percent of nursing home residents may develop ulcers and sores. These statistics may be severely underreported.[5] Once the sore develops, it must be dealt with properly. In the worst cases, ignored skin problems may degrade to the stage where amputation of a gangrenous limb is required in the worst cases.[6] These cases cost multiple millions of dollars to Medicare, Medicaid, and insurers every year. Federal studies have shown significant costs and losses attributable to pressure ulcers.[7]

Because of the seriousness of the risk and frequency of the sores, Center for Medicare and Medicaid Services (CMS) nursing home rules

---

1. Douglas Singh, Effective Management of Long-Term Care Facilities 290–91 (2005).

2. The most useful technical reference is Am. Med. Dirs. Ass'n, Clinical Practice Guideline: Pressure Ulcers in the Long-Term Care Setting (2008).

3. Nat'l Pressure Ulcer Advisory Panel, NPUAP Pressure Ulcer Stages/Categories, http://www.npuap.org/resorces/educational-and-clinical-resources/npuap-pressure-ulcer-stagescategories/.

4. Michael Stockham, *"This Might Sting a Bit": Policing Skin Care in Nursing Facilities by Litigating Fraud*, 87 Cornell L. Rev. 1041, 1062 (2002).

5. Zihan Chen, Lauren J. Gleason & Prachi Sanghavi, *Accuracy of Pressure Ulcer Events in US Nursing Home Ratings*, 60(10) Med. Care 775–83 (2022).

6. *See, e.g.*, Stogsdill v. Manor Convalescent Home, 343 N.E.2d 634 (Ill. App. Ct. 1976).

7. U.S. Gov't Accountability Office, GAO-05-78, Nursing Home Deaths: Arkansas Coroner Referrals Confirm Weaknesses in State And Federal Oversight of Quality of Care (Nov. 12, 2004), http://www.gao.gov/new.items/d0578.pdf.

require the nursing home to ensure that (1) new residents who enter without pressure sores do not develop them "unless the individual's clinical condition demonstrates that they were unavoidable," and (2) a resident who has a pressure sore "receives necessary treatment and services to promote healing, prevent infection and prevent new sores from developing."[8] These CMS norms serve as a standard of due care,[9] and can be enforced by federal civil penalty proceedings.[10] The reality in many understaffed nursing homes is that too few trained employees are available and willing to take the time to meet the ideal norms of skin care; the norms are recognized but not met in many instances.[11]

Pressure ulcers in nursing home residents are a common but serious condition and a crisis-level public health problem.[12] Unfortunately, the prevalence of pressure ulcers in nursing homes has not decreased since the implementation of the Omnibus Budget Reconciliation Act of 1987.[13] Approximately 11 percent of nursing home residents have a pressure ulcer of any stage in any one year, according to the National Center for Health Statistics.[14] In a nursing home population of approximately 2.3 million people,[15] that is a total of approximately 250,000 people in this country who suffer from pressure ulcers.

CMS has implemented several regulations relating to pressure ulcer reimbursement and public reporting.[16] These new regulations have affected how nursing homes are documenting pressure ulcer stages

---

8. 42 C.F.R. § 483.25(c).

9. Ctrs. for Medicare & Medicaid Servs., State Operations Manual, CMS Pub. No. 100-07, Appendix PP: Guidance to Surveyors for Long Term Care Facilities F314 [hereinafter CMS Survey Guidance].

10. *See, e.g.*, Harmony Court v. Leavitt, 188 F. App'x 438 (6th Cir. 2006).

11. Mildred Hogstel, Gerontology: Nursing Care of the Older Adult 402 (2006).

12. R.L. Abel et al., *Quality Improvement in Nursing Homes in Texas: Results from a Pressure Ulcer Prevention Project*, 6 J. Am. Med. Dirs. Ass'n 181–88 (2005); E. Park-Lee et al., *Pressure Ulcers among Nursing Home Residents: United States* (Nat'l Ctr. for Health Statistics 2009).

13. E.A. Coleman et al., *Pressure Ulcer Prevalence in Long-Term Nursing Home Residents since the Implementation of OBRA '87*, 50 J. Am. Geriatr. Soc. 728–32 (2002).

14. Park-Lee et al., *supra* note 12.

15. Nat'l Ctr. on Elder Abuse, Fact Sheet: Elder Abuse Prevalence and Incidence (2005), http://www.ncea.aoa.gov/Resources/Publication/docs/FinalStatistics050331.pdf

16. Since October 1, 2010, the resident assessment instrument (RAI) for long-term care, MDS 3.0 Section M, requires coding compliance to document if Stage II, III, IV (or pressure ulcers that cannot be staged) were present on admission. Ctrs. for Medicare & Medicaid Servs., Nursing Home Quality Initiative, MDS 3.0 for Nursing Homes and Swing

and other wound characteristics. This is because the documentation influences whether the nursing home (1) receives reimbursement for pressure ulcers present on admission; (2) is cited and fined if, for example, a pressure ulcer develops after a resident enters the facility; or (3) has its pressure ulcer rates listed on public websites. Not surprisingly, these new reporting measures have resulted in changes to nursing home polices and practices designed to reduce pressure ulcer incidence.

For example, CMS has implemented its revised guidance to health care surveyors for Tag F686, which deals with pressure ulcers. CMS found that pressure ulcers (both prevention and treatment) were the most cited condition in health quality checks performed by surveyors.[17] In addition, CMS made the troubling finding that there were great variances in the survey findings between state and federal teams. The revised guidance was intended to provide a more detailed guidance to surveyors in order to more consistently detect deficiencies in pressure ulcer assessment, prevention, and treatment. As more fully discussed below, CMS has included a section on pressure ulcer prevention and the definition of an *unavoidable* pressure ulcer. The term *unavoidable* means that the resident developed a pressure ulcer in spite of the facilities use of best practices to "(1) evaluate the resident's clinical condition and pressure ulcer risk factors; (2) define and implement interventions consistent with resident needs, goals and recognized standards of practice; (3) monitor and evaluate the impact of the interventions; and (4) revise the approaches as appropriate."[18]

According to a recent monograph by the National Pressure Ulcer Advisory Panel, new studies of specialized support surfaces used with individuals with impaired mobility have greatly added to the understanding of ulcer prevention. Support surfaces range from dynamic

---

Bed Providers (2012), http://www.cms.hhs.gov/Nursinghomequalityinits/25_NHQ-IMDS30.asp.

17. Julie Williamson, *Pressure's On*, McKnight's Long-Term Care News & Assisted Living (Mar. 1, 2008), http://www.mcknights.com/pressures-on/article/107737/.

18. Nat'l Pressure Ulcer Advisory Panel, Pressure Ulcers: Prevalence, Incidence, and Implications for the Future 228 (2012) (summarizing CMS Survey Guidance, *supra* note 9), http://www.hsag.com/App_Resources/Documents/PrU_LS1_F_314.pdf.

support surfaces including alternating-pressure mattresses, low-air-loss beds, and air-fluidized bed systems to static support surfaces (e.g., mattresses or mattress overlays placed on the top of the mattress and filled with water, gel, air, foam, or a combination). Of importance is that alternative foam mattresses (static support viscoelastic foam) can decrease the incidence of pressure ulcers in individuals at risk compared to standard hospital mattresses. Taking this one step further, alternating-pressure mattresses are more effective than standard foam mattresses in preventing pressure ulcers. Medical sheepskin overlays are superior in the reduction of the risk of pressure ulcers compared to standard care. And hydrocellular heel supports are superior to orthopedic wool padding. Notably, air-filled vinyl boots with foot cradles and low-air-loss hydrotherapy beds can actually increase the risk of ulcers compared with other pressure-relieving surfaces.[19]

There is limited evidence that other physical interventions can reduce the risk of pressure ulcers. These measures include seat cushions, alternating-pressure surfaces, electric profiling beds, low-tech constant-low-pressure supports, repositioning, or topical skin lotions and dressings. Repositioning and turning every two hours has been the mainstay in the majority of pressure ulcer prevention protocols.[20]

Robust clinical trials are still absent in the evaluation of nutritional interventions aimed at preventing pressure ulcers. One metaanalysis did reveal that, in comparison with standard care, oral nutritional supplements are associated with a significantly lower incidence of pressure ulcer development in at-risk residents. A similar conclusion was reached in a combined meta-analysis of oral nutritional supplements.[21]

Relevant to the discussion below of steps that should be taken to insulate the nursing home from liability is the substantial body of literature that reveals that there are common gaps in pressure ulcer prevention programs. These gaps include limitations in staff education and training, lack of physician involvement, limited involvement of

---

19. *Id.* at 228.
20. *Id.*
21. *Id.*

unlicensed caregivers, lack of a plan for communicating at-risk status, and limited quality improvement evaluations of bedside practices.[22]

These problems are becoming more present in the public eye as, within the last decade, the Internet has made pressure ulcer rates available to consumers, increasing public pressure for nursing homes to take measures focused on prevention. One example is the National Nursing Home Survey, which displays pressure ulcer prevalence in a specific care setting. The Agency for Healthcare Research and Quality (AHRQ) has developed a toolkit to assist in the creation of effective pressure ulcer prevention practices.[23]

8:2 Use of Clinical Practice Guidelines or CMS Guidelines as Evidence of the Standard of Care

The standard of care in a medical malpractice case is always the same, it is reasonable care. In order to provide reasonable care, a healthcare provider must "possess and use the care, skill and knowledge ordinarily possessed and used under like circumstances."[24] The majority of states limit the scope of the admissible evidence on the issue of what is reasonable care to what is called the "customary care rule." However, the use of customary care as a proxy for quality of care in medical malpractice cases is changing as the practice of medicine moves toward the provision of evidence-based care and the growing use of clinical practice guidelines ("CPGs").[25] For a complete discussion of this transformation and the serious issues surrounding the continued use of the customary care rule, see Chapter 26. Chapter 26

22. *Id.*

23. D. Berlowitz et al., Preventing Pressure Ulcers in Hospitals: A Toolkit for Improving Quality of Care (Agency for Healthcare Research & Quality, U.S. Dep't of Health & Human Servs. 2008), http://www.ahrq.gov/research/ltc/pressureulcertoolkit/putoolkit.pdf.

24. Burns v. Metz, 513 N.W.2d 505, 509 (Neb. 1994); Vergara v. Doan, 593 N.E.2d 185, 188 (Ind. 1992) (judging the physician's conduct by a "minimum standard of care for the particular practice"). For an excellent overview of medical malpractice law, see Dan B. Dobbs, The Law of Torts § 242, 631–34 (2000).

25. Katharine Van Tassel, Using Clinical Practice Guidelines and Knowledge Translation Theory to Cure the Negative Impact of the National Hospital Peer Review Hearing System on Healthcare Quality, Cost, and Access, 40 Pepperdine L. Rev. 911 (2013).

discusses these issues in the context of pressure ulcer case and the use of CMS guidelines to establish what is reasonable care.

Both nursing homes and plaintiffs can take advantage of the current state of the science on CPGs in states that have already adopted a broader rule for what evidence is relevant to establish the amount of care required under a particular circumstance. In these states, the amount of care required can be established using a risk-benefit analysis that relies upon empirical evidence. As described in Chapter 26, nursing homes can use this tort law to insulate themselves against liability.

Another way that CPGs can be used is as demonstrative exhibits to show the decision-making process that the nursing home used in caring for the resident-plaintiff.[26] Also, CPGs can be used to impeach an expert witness.[27]

The overall strategy discussed in Chapter 26 can also work well for the plaintiff. During the investigation phase, a plaintiff can review the records of the nursing home to determine if the CMS-suggested CPGs were adopted. If not, and an ulcer developed with all of its sequelae, this is likely to be a good case to continue to investigate. If the nursing home did adopt one of these CPGs, then the plaintiff can use the CPGs as a way to conduct a structured investigation into whether the CPGs were followed in the care of a resident who did develop a pressure ulcer. If it is clear that the nursing home followed the CPGs, then this likely will not be a case that a lawyer will want to pursue—at least under this theory. If any gaps or omissions are discovered, the case can be presented to a reviewing expert for analysis. As discussed in Chapter 26, there is a great deal of evidence that nursing homes in general have gaps in their adherence to ulcer prevention protocols. If, in the expert's opinion, these omissions were a substantial factor in bringing about the harm, they may be used to settle a case before trial even begins. At trial, the CPGs will provide the jury with a clear outline of the care that the nursing home should have provided. If the

26. Hinlicky v. Dreyfuss, 6 N.Y. 3d 636, 848 N.E.2d 1285 (2006).
27. Roper v. Blumenfeld, 309 N.J. Super. 219, 706 A.2d 1151 (1998).

home neglected to provide this clearly outlined care protocol without reasonable grounds, liability will likely follow.

8:3 Use of Regulatory Violations to Establish Negligence Per Se or as Evidence of the Standard of Care

In order to qualify to bring a cause of action for negligence per se, the plaintiff must meet two prerequisites: first, the plaintiff must be within the class of individuals the statute is designed to protect and, second, the risk of harm must be within the class of risks of harm that the statute is designed to protect against. The case of the injured nursing home resident fits squarely within this doctrine as the CMS regulations located in 42 C.F.R. part 483, subpart B are designed to protect this particular class of people, residents in nursing homes, against a long laundry list of risks of harm, one of which the plaintiff claims came to fruition.[28] More particularly, the residents of nursing homes are exactly the persons that CMS regulation § 483.25(c), regarding pressure ulcers, is designed to protect and the risk of developing a pressure ulcer is exactly the kind of risk the statute is designed to protect against.[29] For a full discussion of negligence per se, see Chapter 26.

In order to be able to make an argument for either negligence per se, or to introduce the violation of federal regulations as evidence of the standard of care, a lawyer new to nursing home litigation will be faced with trying to figure out the survey system, nomenclature and the use of Tags for the first time. Just a bit of background is likely to be of help.

To start off, all nursing facilities are subject to inspection or survey by virtue of two requirements. First, in order to receive payment under

---

28. Negligence Per Se-Federal Regulations, 57A AM. JUR. 2d Negligence § 755 (2013); McClain v. Mariner Health, Inc., 279 Ga. App. 410, 631 S.E. 2d 435 (2006). *Cf.* Satterwhite v. Reilly, 817 So. 2d 407 (La. Ct. App. 2d Cir. 2002), *writ denied*, 825 So. 2d 1193, 412 (La. 2002). (the court declined "to hold that 42 C.F.R. § 483.75(i) grant[ed] a private cause of action against a medical director of a nursing home or [establish] the standard of care or duty that a nursing home medical director owes to . . . patients of the nursing home he serves, or that a violation of the regulation[s] is negligence per se. The court concluded that "[t]he mere citation of federal regulations . . . [was] not suffice to meet this burden of proof.")

29. *See* CMS Survey Guidance, *supra* note 9, at 111–32.

Medicare or Medicaid, skilled nursing facilities and nursing facilities are required to be in compliance with the requirements located in 42 C.F.R. part 483, subpart B. To certify that they are in compliance, they must complete a Life Safety Code Survey and a Standard Survey.[30] There are two types of Standard Surveys, the Traditional Survey and the Quality Indicator Survey (QIS). CMS is in the process of a staged implementation of QIS as a replacement for the Traditional Survey. During this transition period, CMS deems the completion of either survey as meeting the qualification for certification under 42 C.F.R. parts 483.5–483.75. QIS is designed to generate more empirical data in a more cost effective and accessible way as well as to optimize the use of this data for quality and cost of care purposes.[31]

Second, nursing facilities must be licensed by the state in which they operate. As a general matter, state licensure standards follow federal certification standards. State personnel perform the vast majority of surveys—concurrently assessing compliance with both state licensure

---

30. Ctrs. for Medicare & Medicaid Servs., The Facility Guide to OBRA Regulations, and the Long Term Care Survey Process 1 (2013).

31. QIS is described as follows:

> The QIS is a two-staged, computer-assisted survey process with Stage 1 consisting of both computer analysis of offsite data as well as data collected by surveyors onsite from observations, interviews, and record reviews of large computer-selected resident samples. Stage 2 consists of systematic surveyor investigations of triggered issues and residents using the Guidance to Surveyors as well as a set of investigative tools known as critical elements protocols. In addition to the Stage 1 and Stage 2 sample-based investigations, the QIS also contains several facility-level tasks that are unstaged and are completed either on every survey or when triggered as areas of concern.

Reviews of large computer-selected resident samples. The information collected throughout Stage I is analyzed by computer to derive a set of approximately 160 Quality of Care Indicators (QCIs) that are used to compare the facility being surveyed to national norms. QCIs that score beyond a statistical threshold are computer-selected for Stage 2 review, and the relevant residents are also computer selected. Stage 2 consists of systematic surveyor investigations of triggered issues and residents using a set of detailed investigative tools known as critical elements protocols. In addition to the Stage 1 and Stage 2 sample-based investigations, the QIS also contains several facility-level tasks that are unstaged and are completed either on every survey or when triggered as areas of concern.

Ctrs. for Medicaid & Medicare Servs., CMS Manual System, Pub. 100-07 State Operations Provider Certification (January 4, 2008) (transmittal 31), http://www.cms.gov/Regulations-and-Guidance/Guidance/Transmittals/downloads/R31SOMA.pdf. For an excellent summary of the QIS, see Michael K. Lin, et al., *The Quality Indicator Survey: Background Implementation and Widespread Change*, 25 J. Aging & Soc. Pol'y 10–29 (2013).

and federal certification requirements. The federal government also provides training for state surveyors and periodically conducts inspections with federal surveyors as a check on the performance of state surveyors.[32]

What this means is that the primary regulatory focus for nursing facilities is compliance with the survey process and requirements established by CMS. These requirements are published in the SOM.[33] Compliance with these standards is evaluated both during the yearly survey but also during the investigation of a complaint. Any deficiency cited against the facility will result in regulatory and/or monetary penalties to the facility, will become a part of the public record about the facility, and may reflect poorly on the providers and facility. The SOM has multiple components and sections. Appendices P, PP, and R of the SOM are the three appendices related to the nursing home setting.

Each SOM Appendix has its own Tag designation (for example, F Tags are for long-term care facilities and G Tags are for home health agencies). When a survey identifies a deficient practice and noncompliance with the regulations and guidelines, the surveyor must name the specific Tag under which the deficient practice falls. This is how the citation is officially classified and documented. For some of the tags, CMS includes additional guidance to surveyors related to deficiencies for that particular tag, namely deficiency categorization and severity guidance.[34] The federal regulations governing the care provided to residents in nursing homes are increasingly supported by empirical research based on outcomes analysis.

---

32. These are called FOSS surveys (Federal Oversight and Support Surveys).

33. Ctrs. for Medicaid & Medicare Servs., State Operations Manual (2011), https://www.cms.gov/surveycertificationgeninfo/. Appendix P contains the survey protocol for long-term care facilities, Appendix PP contains the interpretive guidelines for long-term care facilities, and Appendix R describes the resident assessment instrument (which includes the minimum data set, MDS). Each appendix includes (1) the regulations, including the regulatory citation from the Code of Federal Regulations (C.F.R.); (2) the Tag numbers (the alpha-numeric indexing system used to denote specific sections in each SOM Appendix); and, (3) interpretive guidelines, also known as Guidance to Surveyors.

34. For example, Appendix PP contains 42 C.F.R. § 483.60, which deals with the standards for providing pharmacy services to a long-term care nursing facility. This section of the regulations is divided into three F Tags: F425, F428, and F431. The "F" indicates that the section pertains to long-term care facilities and can be found in Appendix PP.

8:4 Legal Issues

Claims for skin-related injury are usually brought in negligence and/or under state nursing home resident protection statutes. Only the very worst cases will get to litigation: the other enforcement channel, state surveys leading to civil penalties, is a more likely means of stimulating process improvement.[35] The primary challenge in liability litigation is usually establishing cause-in-fact. The plaintiff in the cases asserting nursing home negligence may use the pressure sore as a basis for arguing that the negligence of the nursing home produced a severe adverse health effect in the plaintiff's decedent. When the concern relates to the causation of a severe skin condition, however, the problem of proving cause-in-fact becomes a challenge.[36]

The primary challenge for proof relating to pressure sores is to separate the "unavoidable" sore from the sore that was caused by negligence such as lack of attention by the nursing home staff. There are multiple means of proving causation, and these can be tailored to specific situations.[37] The cases often show a series of related standard of care violations in wound care that, together with failings of the infection control system, result in imminent jeopardy to the health of the resident.[38]

The legal significance of the harm is different between the regulatory and the tort systems. Liability suits usually occur when serious harm was caused by the neglect of the resident by the nursing home. In the regulatory context, the fact that the pressure sore was eventually healed "does not negate the fact that the facility failed to provide

---

35. These surveys evaluate skin deterioration and wound healing. *See* 42 C.F.R. § 483.25(c)(2); Ctrs. for Medicaid & Medicare Servs., State Operations Manual (2011), https://www.cms.gov/surveycertificationgeninfo/.

36. Nursing Home Litigation: Investigation and Case Preparation 159–69 (Patricia Iyer ed., 1999).

37. *Id.*

38. *See, e.g.*, Barbourville Nursing Home v. U.S. Dep't of HHS, 174 F. App'x 932 (6th Cir. 2006).

the necessary treatment and services to promote healing and prevent new sores from developing."[39]

Careful pleading of the complaint is necessary in those states that divert medical services cases into pretrial evaluative and mediation alternatives. The nursing home case is not a medical malpractice claim and is not bound by malpractice case procedures if the claim made is related to duties of protection and support services and is not exclusively aimed at the medical and pharmacology issues.[40]

8:5 Dividing the Causes

When the lawyer examines a potential lawsuit against a nursing home for skin effect injuries and death, the key distinction that the advisory experts will draw is between "natural" and "negligent" causes. In the case of CMS penalties, if surveyors find that nursing home residents have skin ulcers and related problems, the defense has a difficult time overcoming judicial deference to the on-site view of the surveyors.[41] The burden is placed on the nursing home to show state and federal surveyors that "the individual's clinical condition demonstrates that [the skin ulcers] were unavoidable."[42] State courts have likewise held that the burden is on the nursing home to prove that a skin ulcer that developed while the person was a resident of the home had been "unavoidable."[43] The home "must show that it furnished the care necessary to prevent new sores unless they were unavoidable."[44] Several medical[45] and legal sources exist to aid the evaluative framework, but

39. Tri-County Extended Care Ctr. v. CMS, Dec. No. 2060 (HHS Departmental Appeals Bd., App. Div., Jan. 10, 2007), http://www.hhs.gov/dab/decisions/dab2060.pdf.

40. Integrated Health Care Servs. Inc. v. Lang-Redway, 840 So. 2d 974 (Fla. 2002).

41. *See, e.g.*, Livingston Care Ctr. v. U.S. Dep't of HHS, 108 F. App'x 350 (6th Cir. 2004).

42. 42 C.F.R. § 483.25(c)(1).

43. Emerald Oaks v. Agency for Health Care Admin., 774 So. 2d 737 (Fla. Dist. Ct. App. 2000). If the defendant places such expert testimony of unavoidability in the record, then the burden shifts back to plaintiff to bring forward its proof. Heritage Healthcare Ctr. v. Agency for Health Care Admin., 746 So. 2d 573 (Fla. Dist. Ct. App. 1999).

44. Pineview Manor v. Ohio Dep't of Health, 2003-Ohio-5762, 2003 WL 22434603 (Ohio Ct. App. Oct. 28, 2003).

45. Am. Med. Dirs. Ass'n, Clinical Practice Guideline: Pressure Ulcers in the Long-Term Care Setting (2008).

each case requires its own expert evaluation of the chart and of the potential plaintiff's witnesses.[46] CMS uses a definition that is focused on the quality of the ongoing care; if all the care steps are documented and the sore appears nevertheless, the sore is "unavoidable"; plaintiff will focus on how well the documentation matched the criteria of "implemented interventions."[47]

Plaintiff's counsel will focus on the documentation at the nursing home of when the skin ulcer was discovered and how it was treated, or not. The resident's entry examination may show that the resident did not have any ulcerations of the skin. If so, then the resident is to be protected from developing a sore.[48] When the resident is recorded to have a small sore, the care or cleaning may not be well documented, and the inference can be drawn that the care not recorded was not given.[49] The care plan for the resident, and the remedial plan the nursing home created and should have followed after it was cited by surveyors for allowing skin ulcers to form,[50] must be effective,[51] because a facility's failure to follow its own plan is useful to a future plaintiff.

The defense will focus on natural causes of the wound. As a matter of physiology, the skin of the elderly human is less likely to be able to withstand pressure before it deteriorates. Skin that is in constant contact with beds and chairs is compressed between the body weight and the hard surface, and the maintenance of skin quality is far more difficult. As a result of the greater rates of incontinence of the elderly person, skin condition breaks down. Urine, feces, and sweat, all concentrated on the skin under a diaper or cloth cover, may cause substantial degeneration of the epidermal layer of the skin. The staff may leave the resident soaked in urine, and this is recognized as a causal factor in the creation of skin ulcers.[52] And the resident may be uncooperative with

---

46. Nursing Home Litigation, *supra* note 36, at 402.
47. CMS Survey Guidance, *supra* note 9, at F330, F331.
48. 42 C.F.R. § 483.25 (c)(1).
49. Nursing Home Litigation, *supra* note 36, at 402.
50. *See, e.g.*, S. Valley Health Care Ctr. v. Health Care Fin. Admin., 223 F.3d 1221 (10th Cir. 2000).
51. Pineview Manor v. Ohio Dep't of Health, 2003-Ohio-5762, 2003 WL 22434603 (Ohio Ct. App. Oct. 28, 2003).
52. Lakeridge Villa Health Care Ctr. v. Leavitt, 202 F. App'x 903 (6th Cir. 2006).

the staff, but the CMS rules do not contain any exception for injury to residents who fail to fully cooperate.[53] Lack of cooperation occurs but is not an excuse for failing to follow a care plan.[54]

Proving the cause-in-fact of a sore by nursing home negligence is likely to require an expert's careful analysis, including review of charts and any available photographs, of the resident's skin condition, the probable sources of that skin deterioration, and the concern that the sore had gone untreated or undetected for a period of time longer than would have been acceptable with reasonable nursing care. The consequence of the skin ulcer problem may be amputation of the foot or other body part, or a fatal sepsis when the infection overcomes the body's weakened defenses.[55] But the consequences will certainly include infection, often to the extent of skin surgery to debride the area that is most wounded. The skin decomposes, bone may be exposed, infections arise, maggots may be found in the wound, and in some cases even death from septic infection may result.[56]

The breach of federal CMS standards of care can be used as a basis for tort actions arguing negligence, but doing so does not create a sufficient jurisdictional basis to remove the tort action to federal court.[57]

8:6 Care Must Be Continuously Supervised

From day to day, from hour to hour, the nursing staff in a nursing home is dealing with the skin consequences of resident immobility. Well-trained staff in adequate numbers are aware of the residents' skin problems early enough to intervene. Among immobilized elders, incontinence is a problem; the effect of pressure of bones on flesh during immobility is a problem; lack of staff for sufficiently frequent turning of bedridden persons is a problem; and each of these situations

53. Harmony Court v. Leavitt, 188 F. App'x 438 (6th Cir. 2006).
54. *Pineview Manor*, 2003-Ohio-5762, 2003 WL 22434603.
55. Sandoval v. Summit Care Corp., No. 633197-9 (Fresno Cnty. Cal. Super. Ct. 2003), *reported in* VERDICTS, SETTLEMENTS & TACTICS 20 (Jan. 2004).
56. NURSING HOME LITIGATION, *supra* note 36, at 402.
57. Pitts v. Davis Nursing Ass'n, 2005 WL 2244691, Case 5:05CV00234SWW (E.D. Ark. Sept. 13, 2005).

often leads to pressure sores. Dehydration while the resident also lacks adequate nutrition may also contribute as secondary factors in the skin deterioration.

8:7 Record-Keeping Is Essential to Defense

Tools for the assessment of the resident are well understood, but the need for adequate documentation of how the sore was avoided and the care that was actually given might be overlooked. Inadequacy of records is often disputed when these cases are litigated.[58]

Accuracy and timeliness of records really matters to both sides in these cases. It is said that what is chronicled gets done; what is done without any documentation is presumed not to have been done. In the case of skin ulcers, this record-keeping principle is essential to an understanding of the liability chain. The nursing home is far less likely to be able to defend a serious pressure ulcer if its staff has not chronicled the resident's turning, cleaning, showers, changes of underwear, and so on.[59] The rapid turnover of nurse aides, and the length of time before trial can be reached, means that the defense cannot rely on the eyewitness memory of employees, and must instill a culture of record-keeping accuracy. Fraudulent and back-dated resident records are seen in the worst cases with the largest payouts against the nursing home.[60] False charting when the resident was not there or otherwise could not be cared for results in serious liability.[61]

8:8 Standard of Due Care

The optimal actions in defense of the resident would be an overall commitment by the management of the nursing home to a policy of skin

---

58. Integrated Health Care Servs. Inc. v. Lang-Redway, 840 So. 2d 974 (Fla. 2012).

59. *See, e.g.*, Tri-County Extended Care Ctr. v. CMS, Dec. No. 2060 (HHS Departmental Appeals Bd., App. Div., Jan. 10, 2007), http://www.hhs.gov/dab/decisions/dab2060.pdf

60. *See, e.g.*, Boston v. 2510 Eagle Inc., No. 97-333 (Leon Cnty. Fla. Cir. Ct. 1999), *reported in* Verdicts, Settlements & Tactics 389 (Sept. 1999).

61. Dunson v. Blue Ridge Nursing Homes, No. 01A85157-1 (DeKalb Cnty. Ga. Cir. Ct. 2003), *reported in* Verdicts, Settlements & Tactics 63 (Feb. 2004).

protection. This commitment must begin on the first day of admission when skin care conditions are documented in the resident assessment files. It must continue through the training of nurses, certified nursing assistants (CNAs), and other staff, leading them to turn each of the immobilized residents on a two-hour cycle in order to reduce the risk of pressure sores. The commitment and policy must continue with prompt evaluation by a registered nurse of suspected areas of skin deterioration, with physician follow-up as needed. And it must continue to the physician's decision to surgically debride the worst deterioration, in those areas where potential infection can be reduced by removing layers of tissue or skin. Training is vital to assisting the execution of the strategy that will protect residents against pressure sores and subsequent infection; enforcing training by effective supervision is the best way to reduce liability and avoid state survey penalties.

The reality is that some sores will inevitably arise on the skin of elderly persons who are in fixed positions, such as bed-bound residents. Counsel for the plaintiff will be seeking to identify all the conditions under which this plaintiff's skin began to break down, and how the skin was subsequently demonstrated to be vulnerable to serious problems.

The standard of care can be determined by state regulations, by CMS rules, and by other standards applicable to the defendant's facility. Staffing must be sufficient to meet needs. Recently CMS established minimum staffing requirements for nursing homes.[62] However, the future of the minimum staffing requirements is unclear.[63]

In the summer of 2013, the Centers for Medicare and Medicaid Services expressed concern that double-digit Medicare profit margins for skilled nursing facilities and home health agencies are too high and are

62. 42 U.S.C. § 483.35(b); *see also* Medicare and Medicaid Programs; Minimum Staffing Standards for Long-Term Care Facilities and Medicaid Institutional Payment Transparency Reporting, 89 Fed. Reg. 40,876 (May 10, 2024), https://www.federalregister.gov/documents/2024/05/10/2024-08273/medicare-and-medicaid-programs-minimum-staffing-standards-for-long-term-care-facilities-and-medicaid.

63. Alejandra O'Connell-Domenech, *Trump, GOP Expected to Undo Biden's Divisive Nursing Home Rule*, The Hill (Dec. 11, 2024), https://thehill.com/policy/healthcare/5033563-nursing-home-staffing-rule-repeal-expected/.

not necessarily linked to the delivery of better care. Medicare Payment Advisory Commission Executive Director Mark E. Miller told a House Ways and Means Health Subcommittee that Medicare profit margins will be 12 percent for home health agencies in 2013 and up to 14 percent for nursing homes. In light of these profit margins, understaffing is likely to be seen by a jury as a way of placing profits over people.[64]

8:9 Short Staffing

Several of the court cases have cited nursing home staff shortages as a factor in the award of punitive damages. In the *Boston* case, ulcers were related to the conditions of severe neglect, under which the resident lost 43 pounds.[65] In the *Sandoval* case, a large jury award was imposed where lack of adequate staff was demonstrated, and the resultant sore was medically identified as the source of the sepsis that killed the decedent; $2.4 million was awarded for compensatory damages, and the nursing home settled for a confidential amount of punitive damages.[66] In the *Olson* case, there was ulcer-related sepsis as well as malnutrition affecting the resident, and the jury awarded $25 million.[67] In the *Morris* case in 2005, $12 million was awarded for skin ulcers with an indication of a reduction in staff to enhance the profitability of the nursing home. These cases and many others show that if the plaintiff can get to a jury with graphic photographs of the skin condition and the deterioration in that condition, the juries will be very generous in rewarding that victim of neglect. From the defense side, it is essential to demonstrate that the resident's skin condition arose so quickly that even with an immediate response, the resident would have incurred a similarly serious skin problem.

---

64. Steve Teske, *CMS Concerned over Nursing Home, Home Health Agency Profit Margins*, Health Care Pol'y Rep. (BNA) (June 21, 2013).

65. *2510 Eagle Inc.*, Verdicts, Settlements & Tactics 389.

66. Sandoval v. Summit Care Corp., No. 633197-9 (Fresno Cnty. Cal. Super. Ct. 2003), *reported in* Verdicts, Settlements & Tactics 20 (Jan. 2004).

67. Olson v. Chisholm Trail Living & Rehab. Ctr., No. 98-0-363 (Caldwell Cnty. Tex. Jud. Dist. Ct. 1999), *reported in* Verdicts, Settlements & Tactics 458 (Oct. 1999) (coma, malnourishment, dehydration, deep Stage IV pressure ulcer led to death of resident).

The expert testimony that will be received at the pretrial and trial stages of a skin case will involve medical testimony from dermatology experts and wound care nurses regarding the adequacy of the response given by the nursing home to the wound as it was developing. The documentation by the nursing home of the bathing of the resident, the shifting of an immobile resident to an alternate side, and the placing of clean underwear and sheets on the resident will all be used to demonstrate that the normal standard of care had in fact been satisfied. Conversely, the plaintiff will be seeking to get before the jury information relating to the handling of the initial discovery of the wound, and the delay in the treatment of that wound because of the short staffing inside the nursing home. The plaintiff will be seeking to get past summary judgment, so as to put the photographs in front of the jury. The defense will either settle the more egregious cases or assert that the plaintiff's expert lacks sufficient basis for reliable, relevant testimony about this resident's condition.

The plaintiff's efforts to determine whether the facility was, in fact, understaffed are aided by a requirement of the Patient Protection and Affordable Care Act that requires nursing homes to report a considerably expanded amount of information about the management and ownership of their facilities. CMS plans to collect this data in the Provider Enrollment and Chain Ownership System database. CMS displays some of this ownership information on the website Nursing Home Compare.[68]

8:10 Evidence

Pictures can "say it all": the jury will be shocked and disgusted by photos of maggots eating infected skin down to the bone, and plaintiffs will benefit from the jurors' revulsion. Some of these photos may be taken as part of emergency room care for the resident transferred to the hospital from the nursing home.

---

68. Ctrs. for Medicare & Medicaid Servs., Nursing Home Compare, http://www.medicare.gov/nursinghomecompare/.

A significant challenge for the defendant in these cases is that visually graphic photos and exhibits are put before the jury; the jury questions in these cases include what the standard of care should be, whether the nursing home's care fell below that limit, and whether the skin ulcers were made worse by treatment after the resident left the nursing home for a hospital.[69] As a leading trial lawyer has observed: "Cases involving decubitus ulcers are more notorious than the other categories [of harm] because they involve horrendous wounds usually depicted in unspeakable photographs."[70]

8:11 Defenses

Once the plaintiff has established a prima facie case the defense burden is to demonstrate that any one of a number of different causes could have produced the skin problem for the resident. Because multiple causes are possible, and experts can testify in favor of or against particular causes in causing the wound, establishing the cause-in-fact of neglect by the staff of the nursing home is essential.[71]

The rights of nursing home residents are protected by the CMS standards that very specifically focus on sores. The evaluation of skin condition is a part of the questions to be answered in the minimum data set, data that is gathered at the time the incoming resident is being evaluated.

The baseline of skin condition is recorded, and then the obligation falls on the nursing home to prevent "avoidable" skin problems. Presumably, the employees who will deal with nursing home residents as CNAs have been trained about skin care and skin cleaning during their preparation for the role of certified nursing assistant. The skin condition of a selection of nursing home residents is surveyed by state surveyors during their periodic evaluation, and the likelihood that

---

69. Mellies v. Nat'l Heritage Inc., 636 P.2d 215 (Kan. Ct. App. 1981).

70. Roger Rider & Ruben Krisztal, *Voir Dire, Opening Statement and Closing Argument*, in Nursing Home Litigation: Pretrial Practice and Trials 325 (Ruben Krisztal ed., 2d ed. 2003).

71. HCRA of Tex. Inc. v. Johnston, 178 S.W.3d 861 (Tex. App. 2005).

sores will appear can be predicted by the Breeden score, a method for ranking skin problems.

8:12 Damages

State common law and statutory norms of punitive damages are applied; the courts vary in their willingness to find extreme or egregious actions where the nursing home acted negligently toward the resident who developed the ulcers.[72] In the area of bedsore skin deterioration, after a certain point the risk and the probability of serious permanent harm becomes severe.[73]

8:13 Punitive Damages

Punitive damages can be awarded in these cases, as with the $850,000 in punitives in the *Schultz* decision, where the defendant nursing home had notice of the skin condition, falsified records, violated its own policies for resident care, and negligently dealt with the needs of the resident, showing "conscious disregard" for the resident and gross negligence.[74] Certain patterns of conscious reduction in available resident care staff have been documented in state ombudsmen reports and in surveys, and this has an effect on the ability to turn residents so as to avoid sores.[75]

8:14 Burns

In a small number of cases, courts have imposed liability based on an inference of negligence, where the burns sustained by the resident were not an allergic reaction but were physical results of the bathing

72. *Id.*
73. *Id.*
74. Convalescent Servs. Inc. v. Schultz, 921 S.W.2d 731 (Tex. App. 1996).
75. Statement of Sarah Slocum, Mich. State Long-Term Care Ombudsman and Sec'y of the Nat'l Ass'n of State Long-Term Care Ombudsman Programs, to the U.S. Senate Special Comm. on Aging (Nov. 15, 2007), http://www.aging.senate.gov/hearing.detail.cfm?id=300437.

of the defendant by a nursing home staff member.[76] Remedies are recognized for burns suffered by a nursing home resident.[77]

8:15 Other Infection Concerns

The problem of infection control is a constant headache for nursing home supervisors,[78] since nursing home residents are often incontinent, are prone to nausea, have open sores in some cases, and so on as they are being toileted, bathed, and handled by the staff of the nursing home.

In the case of urinary catheters, infections are predictable unless extensive time-consuming efforts are made in cleaning and maintaining the catheter.[79] If a case arose in which universal precautions for bloodborne pathogens had not been adequately followed, there might be a citation for OSHA violations.[80] Infection control cases generally rest on two separate theories: failure to prevent the infection and failure to respond properly to an infection. The former may occur, for example, when nursing home staff fail to utilize or are not provided with appropriate personal protective equipment (PPE) and spread infectious diseases or bacteria throughout a facility. The latter may occur when a resident begins exhibiting signs and symptoms of an infection that nursing staff fail to investigate by contacting a physician or transporting the resident to emergent care.

8:16 Lessons from the Cases

Skin ulcer cases attract punitive damages because of their very visible nature and because of the disgust that photos of the ulcers will generate among jurors. The temptation to falsely record care that had

---

76. Franklin v. Collins Chapel Conn. Hosp., 696 S.W.2d 16, 20 (Tenn. Ct. App. 1985).

77. *See, e.g.*, Ivy Manor Nursing Home v. Brown, 488 P.2d 246 (Colo. Ct. App. 1971); Ferguson v. Dr. McCarty's Rest Home, 142 N.E.2d 337 (Mass. 1957).

78. Douglas Singh, Effective Management of Long-Term Care Facilities 284–287 (2005).

79. *Id.* at 293.

80. 29 C.F.R. § 1910.1030.

not been given after the severity of the skin problem becomes evident leads the nursing home into greater jeopardy of punitive damages.

Large verdicts in ulcer and infection cases seem to be on the rise. This author posits that the rise may be due to the preventability of infections, which often have signs and symptoms appearing prior to serious injury occurring. When nursing homes ignore multiple opportunities to intercede on a resident's behalf, hefty verdicts can follow.

In 2005, in the *Morris* case, a $12 million punitive award and $830,000 in other damages for an amputation after a Stage IV pressure ulcer followed assertions of management cuts that had reduced resident care.[81]

Severe skin ulcers and sepsis brought on by poor care led to the award of $25 million, mostly punitive, in the 1999 *Olson* case.[82] A resident who died of a heart attack but had skin sores that manifested a lack of care and cleaning led to a $2.28 million verdict in the *Keaton* case in December 2007.[83] The apparently falsified records of the nursing home concerning skin ulcers and malnutrition brought a $2.3 million verdict in the 2002 *Rivera* case.[84] A resident with a severe sore was refused an air mattress and won a $2.2 million verdict, including $1 million in punitive damages, in the 2004 *Dunson* case.[85] The 2004 *Sandoval* case settled for an undisclosed amount after testimony of egregious conditions led to a $2.4 million compensatory award; the settlement came just before the jury could award punitive damages.[86]

81. Morris v. Longwood Mgmt. Co., No. BC-310030 (L.A. Cnty. Cal. Super. Ct. 2005), *reported in* VERDICTS, SETTLEMENTS & TACTICS 500 (Nov. 2005).

82. Olson v. Chisholm Trail Living & Rehab. Ctr., No. 98-0-363 (Caldwell Cnty. Tex. Jud. Dist. Ct. 1999), *reported in* VERDICTS, SETTLEMENTS & TACTICS 458 (Oct. 1999).

83. Keaton v. Beverly Enters. Inc., No. CV-2005-282-6 (Ouachita Cnty. Ark. Cir. Ct. 2007), *reported in* VERDICTS, SETTLEMENTS & TACTICS 550 (Dec. 2007).

84. Rivera v. Brentwood Place Three, No. 00-06777-E (Dallas Cnty. Tex. Jud. Dist. Ct. 2002), *reported in* VERDICTS, SETTLEMENTS & TACTICS 313 (July 2002) (successfully argued for "conscious indifference" by staff and alterations and incompleteness in records about resident care).

85. Dunson v. Blue Ridge Nursing Homes, No. 01A85157-1 (DeKalb Cnty. Ga. Cir. Ct. 2003), *reported in* VERDICTS, SETTLEMENTS & TACTICS 63 (Feb. 2004) (physician ordered air mattress but nursing home considered it too expensive; allegations of false charting of care when resident was not there to receive care).

86. Sandoval v. Summit Care Corp., No. 633197-9 (Fresno Cnty. Cal. Super. Ct. 2003), *reported in* VERDICTS, SETTLEMENTS & TACTICS 19 (Jan. 2004) (extensive evidence of neglect leading from clean skin to Stage IV ulcers and sepsis; medical testimony connected patient's death to the infection from the poorly treated sores).

Amputation followed poor care of a skin ulcer in the 2004 *Rodriguez* case, with a punitive damage award of $5 million and $300,000 in compensatory damages.[87] In the 1999 *Boston* case, doubts about accuracy of resident charts were expressed for a resident with skin ulcers who had also lost 43 pounds, and $1.5 million was awarded.[88]

Maggots found in an infected sore led to amputation in the 2006 *Stewart* case, leading to an award of $1.2 million.[89] The judge in the 2001 *Boatwright* case refused to allow award of punitive damages, but the compensatory damages were $1.2 million.[90] Other skin wound cases included $800,000 against Nexion[91] and $600,000 in the *Hall* case.[92]

More recently, an Ohio jury awarded $5 million in wrongful death damages to the family of an 84-year-old man who died from sepsis caused by an undiagnosed *C. difficile* infection.[93] A Florida jury awarded $12.3 million to a woman who suffered from a Stage IV pressure injury; she became totally wheelchair-bound.[94] A 69-year-old woman suffered multiple injuries at a nursing home that changed hands four times during her year-and-a-half-long residency. Most notably, she developed a Stage IV pressure ulcer that became septic, causing her death. The Pennsylvania jury awarded her estate $19 million, including $15 million in punitive damages.[95]

---

87. Rodriguez v. Marion Mem'l (Buena Vista Cnty. Ga. Dist. Ct. 2004), *reported in* Verdicts, Settlements & Tactics 313 (July 2004).

88. Boston v. 2510 Eagle Inc., No. 98-333 (Leon Cnty. Fla. Jud. Cir. Ct. 1999), *reported in* Verdicts, Settlements & Tactics 389 (Sept. 1999).

89. Stewart v. Renova Health Ctr., No. 05-2005-CA-006508 (Palm Beach Cnty. Fla. Cir. Ct. 2006), *reported in* Verdicts, Settlements & Tactics 13 (July 2006).

90. Boatwright v. Healthcare Ctr., No. CV-00-1193 (Pulaski Cnty. Ark. Cir. Ct. 2001), *reported in* Verdicts, Settlements & Tactics 347 (Aug. 2001) (court refused to send punitive damage issue to jury; gangrene from Stage III pressure ulcers; demand for $3 million, offer of $100,000).

91. Washington v. Nexion Health, No. 63836-A (Webster Parish, La. Dist. Ct. 2006), *reported in* Verdicts, Settlements & Tactics 313 (June 2006) (Stage IV pressure sore took 18 months to heal).

92. Hall v. Alden Wentworth Rehab. Ctr. (Cook Cnty. Ill. Cir. Ct. 2007), *reported in* Verdicts, Settlements & Tactics (Oct. 2007).

93. Huls v. Laurel Health Care Co., Case No. 18OT08-0187 (Knox Cnty. Ohio Ct. Com. Pl. June 24, 2022).

94. Reed v. Life Care Ctrs., Case No. 2018-CA-013297-O, 2022 WL 2229485 (Fla. Cir. Ct. Mar. 11, 2022).

95. Newlin v. Vita Healthcare Grp., Case No. CV-2020-008216 (Delaware Cnty. Pa. Ct. Com. Pl. Dec. 20, 2023).

8:17 Summary

Who can sue? The resident or his or her personal representative.

What is the duty of care? A skilled nursing facility must comply with federal and state norms for adequate care of residents' medical conditions, including "avoidable" deterioration of skin condition.

What is the injury? Physical ulceration of skin and resulting infections, including amputation, removal of diseased skin, and death.

How do you prove that substandard care was the cause of the injury? Expert nursing witness testimony establishes the standard of care in the skilled nursing home environment.

Whom should you sue? The institution that admitted the resident, as well as subentities or affiliated companies that contractually were responsible for the care.

How do you go about proving your case? Obtain the medical records, nursing charts, daily care records, hospital admission data, photographs of skin condition, and so on, and deliver them to the expert nursing witness and/or dermatology physician. Examine the admission forms for the baseline skin condition upon the resident's entering the facility, and upon later treatment at a hospital or by a dermatologist. Establish a chronology of observation, recognition, measurement, and treatment that can form the basis for the expert witness opinion.

CHAPTER 9

Fall-Related Injuries

9:1 Introduction
9:2 Resident Assessments by Nursing Homes
9:3 Measures to Avoid Fall Injuries
9:4 Resident Evaluation
9:5 Procedures and Documentation
9:6 Response to the Fall Event
9:7 Transportation Concerns
9:8 Fall Cases Are Not Simple
9:9 Legal Implications of Fall Injuries
9:10 Proving Nursing Home Negligence in the Fall Case
9:11 Assembling the Proof of Causation
9:12 Few Fall Cases Reach Appellate Levels
9:13 Evaluating Potential Litigation
9:14 Plaintiff's Theory of the Case
9:15 Policies and Noncompliance
9:16 Examples of Fall Injury Cases

9:1 Introduction

As a general matter, for people over 65, falls are the most common cause of nonfatal injuries[1] and accidental death.[2] The costs associated

1. Ctrs. for Disease Control & Prevention, WISQARS Leading Causes of Nonfatal Injury Reports, http://www.cdc.gov/injury/wisqars/index.html.
2. *Id.*

with falls are considerable.[3] The annual estimated costs associated with nonfatal, fall-related injuries were roughly $50 billion in 2015. Costs associated with fall-related deaths were approximately $754 million in that same year.[4] Fall-related injuries were the third most common readmitting diagnosis in the first month after discharge from the hospital behind septicemia and heart failure.[5]

These statistics make some sense as, with age, the body loses some of its agility and stability during activities of daily living. The aged person tends to have a less steady gait and less stability upon rising to a standing position, and will face other issues with lessened vision, diminished muscle tone, potentially severe pain, and other sources of physical instability. The result is that an aged person is more likely to fall more frequently, and the concentration of elderly persons inside the nursing home is, in part, a reflection of the fact that families and friends can no longer accommodate them with the risks of falling during everyday activities. The parent, relative, or friend will presumably expect the resident to be safer inside the nursing home, according to the conventional wisdom.[6]

Unfortunately, an average of 43 percent of the residents in long-term care facilities have one fall every year,[7] and 29 percent to 55 percent of residents are reported to fall during their stay.[8] In context, these

3. Leanne Currie, *Fall and Injury Prevention*, *in* Agency for Health Care Research & Quality, Resident Safety and Quality: An Evidence-based Handbook for Nurses 1 (2008).

4. Curtis S. Florence, Gwen Bergen, Adam Atherly, Elizabeth Burns, Judy Stevens & Cynthia Drake, *Medical Costs of Fatal and Nonfatal Falls in Older Adults*, 66(4) J. Am. Geriatrics Soc'y 693–98 (2018).

5. Geoffrey J. Hoffman, Haiyin Liu, Neil B. Alexander, Mary Tinetti, Thomas M. Braun & Lillian C. Min, *Posthospital Fall Injuries and 30-Day Readmissions in Adults 65 Years and Older*, 2(5) JAMA Network Open e194276 (2019).

6. Marshall Kapp, *At Least Mom Will Be Safe There: The Role of Resident Safety in Nursing Home Quality*, 12 Quality & Safety in Health Care 201 (Dec. 2003).

7. L.Z. Rubenstein et al., *The Epidemiology of Falls and Syncope*, 18 Clinics in Geriatric Med. 141–58 (2002) (the range of the percentage of residents reported to fall each year is 16 to 75 percent, with a mean of 43 percent).

8. D.K. Kiely et al. *Identifying Nursing Home Residents at Risk for Falling*, 46 J. Am. Geriatr. Soc. 551–55 (1998); P.B. Thapa et al., *Injurious Falls in Nonambulatory Nursing Home Residents: A Comparative Study of Circumstances, Incidence, and Risk Factors*, 44 J. Am. Geriatr. Soc. 273–78 (1996).

numbers are more startling as many residents have no opportunity to fall as they are bedridden or otherwise immobilized.[9]

Approximately half of all nursing home residents fall annually. About one in three of those that fall will fall two or more times in a year.[10] Thus, families may have a perception that their loved one is less safe, and are dismayed when a fall occurs and a search for litigation counsel may follow. However, it is important for all to keep in mind that the overall increase in injury rates is likely because long-term care residents are more vulnerable than those who can function in the community.[11] In addition, fall reporting is likely to be more accurate by nursing homes than self-reporting of individuals living in the community.[12]

Because such a large percentage of nursing home residents fall annually, the challenge for the nursing home operator is to protect the interests of the elderly resident without appearing to be overly controlling of the resident's sense of freedom for safe movement within the nursing home. The challenge for a potential plaintiff's attorney is to be selective, and to avoid taking cases where the explanation for this injury is so plausible that no jury would be likely to return a substantial verdict.

Falls and related injuries have had varying definitions.[13] Falls may be caused by intrinsic or extrinsic factors. "Intrinsic factors are those that have a physiologic origin, and extrinsic factors are those precipitating from environmental or other hazards. Identifying whether a fall was caused by an intrinsic or extrinsic risk factor is critical to the choice of an appropriate fall prevention intervention."[14] One definition of a

---

9. Medical-Legal Aspects of Long-Term Care 222 (Jeffrey Levine ed., 2003).

10. *The Falls Management Program: A Quality Improvement Initiative for Nursing Facilities, Chapter 1. Introduction and Program Overview*, Agency for Healthcare Rsch. & Quality (Dec. 2017), https://www.ahrq.gov/patient-safety/settings/long-term-care/resource/injuries/fallspx/man1.html.

11. M.Q. Vu et al., *Falls in the Nursing Home: Are They Preventable?*, 5 J. Am. Med. Dir. Ass'n 401–06 (2004).

12. Medical-Legal Aspects of Long-Term Care, *supra* note 9, at 222.

13. J. Close et al., *Prevention of Falls in the Elderly*, 353 Lancet 93–97 (1999); T. Masud et al., *Epidemiology of Falls*, 30 Age & Ageing 3–7 (Nov. 2001) (4 Supp).

14. Currie, *supra* note 3, at 1.

fall in a person living in the community is "an event which results in a person coming to rest unintentionally on the ground or lower level, not as a result of a major intrinsic event (such as a stroke) or overwhelming hazard."[15] Researchers modified this definition for nursing home residents to define a fall as "unintentionally coming to rest on the ground, floor, or other lower level, but not as a result of syncope or overwhelming external force."[16]

9:2 Resident Assessments by Nursing Homes

A complete assessment is done of all residents when they enter a nursing home and annually thereafter. This assessment provides a comprehensive review of each resident's functional capabilities and helps nursing facility staff identify health problems. This analysis is conducted pursuant to a resident assessment instrument (RAI). The RAI has three parts: the minimum data set (MDS), the resident assessment protocols (RAPs), and the utilization guidelines. The MDS is a multifactored screening and assessment tool that measures a resident's functional capacities. The MDS data is then evaluated using the RAP in order to identify health problems that need to be addressed. The utilization guidelines are then used to evaluate the problem and create a care plan with the interventions necessary to deal with the problem. For each identified problem, the care plan must explain the interventions that will be used to address the problem and must describe the desired goal and the methods that will be used to measure progress toward that goal.[17]

In the nursing home setting, the long-term care MDS[18] is used for reporting all aspects of care. The current version, MDS 3.0, was

---

15. M.E. Tinetti et al., *Risk Factors for Falls among Elderly Persons Living in the Community*, 319 N. Eng. J. Med. 1701–07 (1988).

16. J.V. Agostini et al., *Prevention of Falls in Hospitalized and Institutionalized Older People* (Agency for Healthcare Research & Quality 2001).

17. Medical-Legal Aspects of Long-Term Care, *supra* note 9, at 43–64.

18. Ctrs. for Medicaid & Medicare Servs., Long Term Care Minimum Data Set (MDS), http://www.cms.gov/Research-Statistics-Data-and-Systems/Files-for-Order/IdentifiableDataFiles/LongTermCareMinimumDataSetMDS.html.

implemented in 2010 and has received regular updates since its implementation. The MDS captures fall and injury histories through the initial complete assessment that is then performed yearly thereafter, as well as the quarterly updates that occur in between. During these assessments, residents are evaluated for balance and for the ability to perform activities of daily living with the goal being to apply fall-prevention measures should the resident be deficient in these areas. A more recent development in the long-term care setting, the Nursing Home Quality Initiative, promotes the collection of a list of enhanced quality indicators, including those that track declines in functional and cognitive status.[19]

MDS information from the state databases is sent to the national MDS database at the Centers for Medicaid & Medicare Services (CMS). This collected MDS data is used to place the nursing home into a particular Resource Utilization Group (RUG) category. The RUG category determines the per diem rate paid to the nursing home for a resident whose stay is covered under Medicare Part A. The MDS data also is used to create the nursing home's quality indicator and quality measure reports, some of which are publicly reported and some of which are used by surveyors during the survey process.

9:3 Measures to Avoid Fall Injuries

CMS regulations require that "[t]he services provided or arranged by the facility must . . . meet professional standards of care." The Interpretive Guidelines explain that "'[p]rofessional standards of quality' means services that are provided according to accepted standards of clinical practice." What will be considered to be "accepted standards of clinical practice"? The Interpretive Guidelines only permit the use of standards that are published by a limited list of sources, including licensing boards, professional organizations, current professional

---

19. Ctrs. for Medicare & Medicaid Servs., Nursing Home Quality Initiative, http://www.cms.gov/Medicare/Quality-Initiatives-Patient-Assessment-Instruments/NursingHomeQualityInits/index.html?redirect=/nursinghomequalityinits/ (last modified May 28, 2013).

journals, clinical literature, or the clinical practice guidelines published by the Agency of Health Care Policy and Research.

One of the most oft-cited set of guidelines in the area of fall prevention of older adults are those of the American Geriatrics Society and British Geriatric Society's clinical guidelines for the prevention of falls. These guidelines were first published in 2001 and were updated for the first time in 2010.[20] In addition to the past recommendations of a multifactorial fall risk assessment for all older adults who present with a fall or who have gait and balance problems, the 2010 guidelines call for a multifactorial fall risk assessment for individuals who simply report difficulties with gait or balance. "The history of fall circumstances is more specific in the 2010 guidelines, including questions about frequency of falling, symptoms at time of fall, and injuries from fall. New specific recommendations for assessment include examination of the feet and footwear, functional assessment (assessment of activity of daily living skills, including use of adaptive equipment and mobility aids, as appropriate); assessment of the individual's perceived functional ability and fear related to falling; and environmental assessment, including home safety."[21]

Based on this multifactorial fall risk assessment, individualized, targeted interventions to address the risks and deficiencies identified in the assessment must be strategized.[22] Interventions could consist of a mixture of a variety of types of exercises, such as those that focus on balance, strength, endurance, and physical therapy, as well as vitamin D supplementation and environmental safety precautions.[23] For example, a Cochrane Review of 111 trials (55,303 participants) concluded that multiple-component group exercise,

20. Am. Geriatrics Soc'y, British Geriatrics Soc'y, *Summary of Updated American Geriatrics Society/British Geriatrics Society Clinical Practice Guidelines for Prevention of Falls in Older Persons*, 59 J. AM. GERIATR. SOC. 148–57 (2011).

21. *Id.* at 149.

22. Y.L. Michael et al., *Interventions to Prevent Falls in Older Adults: An Updated Systematic Review* (2010) (Evidence Synthesis No. 80, AHRQ Publ'n No. 11-05150-EF1, Agency for Healthcare Research & Quality).

23. Resident-Centered Outcomes Research Inst., Preventing Injuries from Falls in the Elderly, http://www.pcori.org/funding-opportunities/funding-announcements/preventing-injuries-from-falls-in-the-elderly/.

individually prescribed multiple-component exercise, and tai chi resulted in reduced rates of falls.[24]

The optimal means for reducing the risk of falls in the nursing home environment is the individualized multifactorial intervention by a team consisting of medical, nursing, physical therapy, and other staff members. The risk factors for each elder resident should be considered as the group targets the means of intervention to avoid the continued occurrence of serious harmful falls. The planning phase is well understood in the technical literature,[25] and gaps and omissions by a particular nursing home may be a root cause of the negligence that precipitated a particular resident's fall.

The assessment of the resident's risk factors will allow the nursing home to target interventions to solve his or her particular problems. Education of the staff, of the family, and of others who come into contact with the resident may be helpful; consultation with the resident's "support system" who care for that individual resident, and ideally with the resident if he or she is competent, is probably the best strategy to combat nursing home falls. In practice, many nursing homes lack sufficient staff to monitor even those who are most prone to falls. Staff have the benefit of specific federal guidance on safe lifting and moving of the residents,[26] but this standard of care is not mandatory. The question of negligent omission or failure to adequately supervise the resident is a jury question.[27]

9:4 Resident Evaluation

Because the CMS and state nursing home standards of care include the creation of a plan for the handling of each resident's needs, the

---

24. L.D. Gillespie et al., *Interventions for Preventing Falls in Older People Living in the Community*, 9 Cochrane Database Sys. Rev. (2012).

25. Douglas Singh, Effective Management of Long-Term Care Facilities 288–89 (2005) (charts of optimal fall prevention decisions).

26. NIOSH, NIOSH Publ'n 2006-117, Safe Lifting and Movement of Nursing Home Residents (2006), http://www.cdc.gov/niosh/docs/2006-117.

27. *See, e.g.*, Dusine v. Golden Shores Convalescent Ctr., 249 So. 2d 40 (Fla. Dist. Ct. App. 1971) (leaving a resident unobserved for 20 minutes while the restraint vest is untied).

plan will be examined as step one in the evaluation of potential liability. Risks of falls should be reflected in the document known as the resident assessment protocol, including the minimum data set, which give information to the nurses and aides regarding the potential vulnerability of the resident.

In evaluating the risk of a fall for a particular resident, the professional staff of the nursing home should evaluate the potential complications that would result if a fall occurred, based on the unique condition of the resident. It may be that the fall or other injury triggers an adverse effect in the elder, such as internal bleeding after a fall which bruises the rib cage, or a concussion that impairs brain function. The protocol for most nursing homes will be to send the resident to a hospital emergency room for tests to determine the extent of injuries.

Ideally, the health professionals at the nursing home will develop a plan for managing the risks of falls after the chart gives an indication of vulnerability. Once the plan is in place, these professionals can manage the many different causes of falling, including ways to treat dizziness, leg or foot problems, and the like.

An expert advisor has suggested that the prudent nursing home will provide relevant measures to address the risk of falling.[28] The resident movement of high risk should be monitored closely, and some nursing homes prefer to use bedside alarms when the resident leaves the bed, so that an aide can promptly investigate. In the worst cases, a restraint produces accidental strangulation, or a staff nurse or aide disconnects the resident call button to limit the demands that a resident places on their needs for service.

It is important, of course, for the managers of the nursing home to direct staff to particularly monitor the movements of an individual resident whose assessment forms show a history of vulnerability to falls, or show other factors that trigger a high risk of falls. Such an individual deserves special attention.

---

28. Doe v. Roe Skilled Nursing Facility, Confidential Docket No. (Orange County Super. Cal. July 6, 2012), *addressed in Improper Transfer of Patient from Wheelchair*, 49 TRIAL 14 (2012).

An 89-year old nursing home patient who had undergone hip surgery on his left side was being transferred from a wheelchair to his bed. A certified nursing assistant allegedly lifted his left leg over his right, causing a left femur fracture that necessitated revision surgery and a lengthy recovery. He sued the nursing home, alleging that the nurse transferred him improperly and should have enlisted another employee's help. The case was settled for $150,000.[29]

An expert witness in a Louisiana case noted that a nursing home "gave little attention to implementing/revising clinical interventions to address the decedent's safety needs in light of her obvious 'high risk' for falls." The records failed to demonstrate that the facility investigated the cause of her falls, revised her care plan, instituted appropriate restraint monitoring and release, or utilized fall-prevention techniques or services to protect the decedent from injury. So the expert stated that these violations resulted in the fall and subsequent hip fracture as well as her continued physical decline and death due to complications from her immobility. A second expert testified that a fall and hip fracture suffered at the nursing home significantly contributed to the decedent's death. The patient had been ambulatory prior to the hip fracture and was unable to return to her baseline functional status after her fall and surgery, and she became bedridden and immobile. She died as a result of complications of Alzheimer's-type dementia, hypertensive and atherosclerotic cardiovascular disease, and the left hip fracture, which contributed significantly to her death because it caused a marked decline in her status. But the court found that the evidence presented was not sufficient to establish that plaintiff would be able to satisfy her evidentiary burden of proof at trial.[30]

---

29. Doe v. Roe Skilled Nursing Facility, Confidential Docket No. (Orange Cnty. Super. Ct. Cal. July 6, 2012), *addressed in Improper Transfer of Patient from Wheelchair*, 49 Trial 14 (2012).

30. Ballard v. Plantation Mgmt. Co., LLC, 2012 WL 992097 (La. Ct. App. 1st Cir. March 23, 2012).

9:5 Procedures and Documentation

The procedures in place to avoid fall risks should satisfy CMS and state regulatory requirements. In an appropriate case, the legal advisor should prepare for possible litigation by auditing the nursing home's documentation of its performance. This tracking of injury results can be performed on a retrospective basis, examining the home's experience with falls and their consequences. The records of the nursing home should be complete on these issues; the criminal conviction of nursing home administrators for falsities in record-keeping serves as a warning of the need for accuracy.[31]

The fall-prevention-program evaluation can be performed by a nursing home consultant reporting to the legal counsel (for reasons of legal privilege protection) while conducting quality improvement activities. The audit may lead to changes relating to the handling of resident transfers, improvements in staffing, changes in the delivery of medication that causes instability, and other changes. Templates on a program to intervene with high-risk residents are available.[32]

9:6 Response to the Fall Event

The defense of a fall case begins when the nursing home administrator learns of the injury from the fall and acts to have physicians evaluate the harm. Delays in medical treatment after the fall can result in punitive damages.[33] The home's protocol for medical follow-up after a fall is important evidence for the plaintiff; it is intended to protect the injured person from further problems with an unrecognized injury. There is a duty on the nursing home to promptly evaluate the effect of the fall and to obtain medical follow-up promptly.[34]

---

31. United States v. Bell, 2006 WL 952214 (W.D. Pa. April 12, 2006).

32. Mildred Hogstel, Gerontology: Nursing Care of the Older Adult 401 (2001).

33. Bremenkamp v. Beverly Enters.-Kan., 762 F. Supp. 884, 894 (D. Kan. 1991); Watts v. Golden Age Nursing Home, 127 Ariz. 255, 619 P.2d 1032 (1980); Thibodeaux v. Stonebridge, L.L.C. , 873 So. 2d 755 (La. Ct. App. 5 Cir. 2004).

34. *Bremenkamp*, 762 F. Supp. at 887.

Once the injury is evident and the resident has been transported or given care on the scene, the nursing home has passed the responsibility on to the hospital, unless the resident is returned to the home. Negligence that occurs in transport of a resident by nursing home staff can sometimes result in liability, for example, if the event results in a fatal wheelchair fall for the resident.[35]

Often the effects of the fall are acute—pain, obvious swelling, unconsciousness, and so on. But for some individual residents, the head trauma consequences of falling may be delayed a few weeks, depending upon the impact and the preexisting condition of the resident. Sometimes a person who cannot speak suffers an effect that is masked by an existing condition, such as a stroke, causing difficulty of communication, and sometimes the seriousness of the fall is not immediately evident. Proper procedure is to have an immediate evaluation by the registered nurse on duty, and an emergency room transfer of the resident if any lasting or severe harm appears to have occurred. The nursing home may terminate the employee who dropped the resident and will be liable for a CMS penalty for inadequate employee training.[36]

9:7 Transportation Concerns

In addition to the nursing home facility itself, the operator has responsibility for safety in the transportation of its residents to hospitals and physician appointments. So the failure to safely secure residents when they are passengers in the home's transport vehicles can be a subset of CMS surveyor complaints and can lead to a civil penalty.[37]

9:8 Fall Cases Are Not Simple

The injuries to nursing home residents from falls can be trivial, or seriously harmful, and in some cases fatal. Many seemingly innocuous

---

35. Penny v. Sunbridge Healthcare, No. 02-C-378 (Cass Cnty. Tex. 2003), *reported in* Verdicts, Settlements & Tactics 422 (Oct. 2003).

36. *In re* Epsom Healthcare Ctr., Dec. No. CR1749 (HHS Departmental Appeals Bd. 2008).

37. *In re* SunBridge Care, Dec. No. 2170 (HHS Departmental Appeals Bd. 2008).

environments become troublesome for elderly residents: some fall from beds,[38] some in bathrooms,[39] some in interior hallways,[40] some in outdoor areas, and some from wheelchairs or walkers. The falls that precipitate litigation tend to be the most avoidable falls with the most severe effects, such as hip fractures and head trauma.[41]

The issue of negligence in protecting the resident from falls is usually one for the jury in these nursing home cases.[42] The reader is cautioned not to expect an easy surrender by the nursing home or its insurer after the resident's fall occurs. The mere fact of a fall does not create an inference of negligence.[43] The nursing home need not have a staff member following each ambulatory resident.[44] As an expert plaintiff's litigator has written, "[A] case involving a fall is better if it was the tenth fall that resulted in serious injury, rather than the first," because the pattern of negligent conduct makes the finding of nursing home liability easier to achieve.[45]

The legal liability of the nursing home, in the instance of an injury to a resident caused by a fall, is potentially serious. But these cases are not open-and-shut plaintiff cases. Winning a contested case will require the plaintiff to demonstrate that the fall was avoidable, based upon norms of similar accidents in similar situations, and that if the nursing home staff had been more attentive to the victim, the fall would not have occurred.[46] Res ipsa loquitur arguments are usually

---

38. *See, e.g.*, Smith v. Gravois Rest Haven Inc., 662 S.W.2d 880, 883 (Mo. Ct. App. 1983).

39. *See, e.g.*, Laidlaw v. Andrew Freedman Home, 32 A.D.2d 754, 300 N.Y.S.2d 979 (1969).

40. Parker v. Ill. Masonic Warren Barr Pavilion, 299 Ill. App. 3d 495, 701 N.E.2d 190 (1998).

41. Because "it is common knowledge that an elderly person often suffers a broken hip in a fall," no expert testimony is needed to show causation between a fall and a broken hip. Smith v. Gravois Rest Haven Inc., 662 S.W.2d 880, 883 (Mo. Ct. App. 1983).

42. Thus the plaintiff carries the burden to show duty, breach of duty, proximate cause, and damages, and can use direct or circumstantial evidence. Parker v. Ill. Masonic Warren Barr Pavilion, 299 Ill. App. 3d 495, 701 N.E.2d 190 (1998).

43. Booty v. Kentwood Manor Nursing Home, 483 So. 2d 634, 639 (La. Ct. App. 1986) (citing Tait v. W. World Ins. Co., 220 So. 2d 226 (La. Ct. App. 1969)).

44. *Booty*, 483 So. 2d at 639.

45. Allen Fuller, *Settlement Strategies*, *in* NURSING HOME LITIGATION: PRETRIAL PRACTICE AND TRIALS 581, 584 (Ruben Krisztal ed., 2d ed. 2003).

46. Kildron v. Shady Oaks Nursing Home, 549 So. 2d 395 (La. Ct. App. 1989).

not welcomed because of the existence of multiple possible alternative causes for a fall.[47]

Expert testimony may be needed for the plaintiff to indicate the failings of the nursing home staff, in dealing with all the signs of instability, weakness, or other disturbances that signaled the likelihood of a serious fall.[48] In some cases, however, expert testimony is not always necessary.[49]

To make things more complicated, in many states, a fall may be considered medical malpractice requiring submission to a medical review panel prior to filing a claim with the court. Other states differentiate between "professional" negligence and ordinary negligence. The Court of Appeals of Tennessee has stated, "Not all injuries in a hospital, nursing home or other health care facility are the result of professional negligence; they may be solely attributable to ordinary or simple negligence."[50] An appeals court in Georgia stated, "In cases involving a person's fall while in the care of medical professionals, it can be difficult to distinguish professional negligence from ordinary negligence."[51] In order to determine if a negligent act is "professional" or "ordinary," courts have either created a test[52] or tried to define the difference between a professional and a nonprofessional.[53]

9:9 Legal Implications of Fall Injuries

The fall injury case most likely to be pursued by a plaintiff's attorney is one in which death or serious harm followed a fall event, which event had been typical of the systemic problems of this nursing home's poor care for residents. Evidence of the fall, beyond the clinical records and

---

47. *See, e.g., id.*; *Booty*, 483 So. 2d 634; Cannon v. McKendree Vill., Inc., 295 S.W.3d 278 (Tenn. Ct. App. 2008).

48. Tudor v. Wheatland Nursing L.L.C., 42 Kan. App. 2d 624, 214 P.3d 1217 (Kan. Ct. App. 2009).

49. Brown v. Tift Cnty. Hosp. Auth., 635 S.E.2d 184 (Ga. Ct. App. 2006).

50. Padgett v. Baxley & Appling Cnty. Hosp. Auth., 741 S.E.2d 193 (Ga. Ct. App. 2013).

51. Brown v. Tift Cnty. Hosp. Auth., 635 S.E.2d 184 (Ga. Ct. App. 2006).

52. Munson v. Lakewood Quarters Ltd. P'ship, 965 So. 2d 448 (La. Ct. App. 2007).

53. Myers v. Heritage Enters., Inc., 354 Ill. App. 3d 241, 820 N.E.2d 604 (Ill. App. Ct. 4th Dist. 2004).

hospital admission reports, may be weak, since the incompetent or confused elder may have no recollection, the nursing home records may be incomplete,[54] and the home's current employees may be the only witnesses. The cause of the particular injury from this fall may be hard to isolate as a legal matter of proof. Depositions, family testimony, photographs, and clinical records are the sources for information about the harmful event.

The mere occurrence of a fall inside the nursing home does not mean that negligence occurred or that the CMS rules on accident avoidance have been violated.[55] Some falls are the result of an aged person's spontaneous bone fracture or other physiological reason for collapse. Others have a cause that is not internal to the condition of the individual. On some occasions, the cause may be external, resulting from a slippery floor, the height of the bed, the lack of grip bars, or other physical and protective measures. These events prompt specific attention to how this injury occurred as an event; the prudent plaintiff's counsel also examines the systemic failings within the nursing home that allowed such an event to occur.

A survey of the case law suggests that the defendant nursing home is found not to be liable in more cases than those in which the home is found to have been negligent.[56] Defense counsel tend to have represented numerous homes in similar cases, and their experience with the jury defense of such cases makes a difference for their rate of success, compared to the one-time tort litigator whose nursing home case may be his or her only such claim in years.

The nursing home more often can be found to be negligent where the resident was dropped or had previously fallen, or where the nursing home is on notice of the resident's predisposition to fall but took

54. Falsification of nursing home records to conceal violations is a criminal offense. United States v. Bell, 2006 WL 952214 (W.D. Pa. April 12, 2006).

55. *See, e.g.*, Czehowski v. Avery Manor, 2004 WL 5294390 (Mass. Super. Sept 17, 2004).

56. This results from a necessarily unscientific survey of 1996–2008 cases in the West-Thomson newsletter *Verdicts, Settlements & Tactics*, which records several dozen nursing home tort action outcomes that were voluntarily reported by defense and plaintiffs' counsel.

few or no steps to prevent the fall.[57] This notice of the individual's preexisting fall risk would be the basis for a negligence case, in which the nursing home failed to take appropriate steps under its policies to protect this vulnerable resident from falling again, and the nursing home is found to have been negligent.[58]

Getting to punitive damages for the fall injury requires a special effort for the plaintiff's counsel. Contingent fee plaintiff representation usually involves a younger, more active person who has lost substantial income potential as a result of the injuries. As one experienced plaintiff's counsel has cautioned: "Few [residents of nursing homes], if any, can be expected to survive long enough to appear before a jury and, even if they did, their dementia and poor health would prevent them from testifying in any coherent manner."[59] In seeking damages for serious misconduct, the home's failure to obtain rapid medical attention after the fall injury occurs can be a basis for damages.[60]

9:10 Proving Nursing Home Negligence in the Fall Case

Negligence in whatever context is a broad concept, one that requires proof of a breach of duty that proximately caused the injury.[61] Plaintiff must connect the negligence to the injury, and will fail if the evidence to show the connection is absent or inadequate.[62]

Nursing homes are not hospitals, so the case law of hospital accidents is not usually a good guide to outcomes.[63] The safety culture of nursing homes is significantly less than in hospitals, with smaller staffs, high use of temporary agency workers, and "action . . . not being taken

57. Forum Group at Moran Lake Nursing & Rehab. Ctr., LLC v. Terhune, 733 S.E.2d 808, 811 (Ga. Ct. App. 2012).

58. Giandana v. Providence Rest Nursing Home, 815 N.Y.S. 2d 526 (App. Div. 2006).

59. Patrick Ford, *Punitive Damages in Nursing Home Cases, in* Nursing Home Litigation: Pretrial Practice and Trials 429 (Ruben Krisztal ed., 2d ed. 2003).

60. Powell v. Parkview Estate Nursing Home, 240 So. 2d 53 (La. Ct. App. 1970); Domoroski v. Smithtown Ctr. for Rehab. & Nursing Care, 95 A.D.3d 1165, 945 N.Y.S.2d 345, (N.Y. App. Div. 2d Dep't 2012).

61. *See, e.g.*, Bremenkamp v. Beverly Enters.-Kan., 762 F. Supp. 884, 887 (D. Kan. 1991).

62. Palmer v. Intermed Inc., 270 Ark. 538, 606 S.W.2d 87 (1980).

63. Stogsdill v. Manor Convalescent Home, 35 Ill. App. 3d 634, 343 N.E.2d 589 (1976).

to improve resident safety."[64] The case law of compensation for nursing home falls is relatively constant from state to state, and will impose a sufficient duty of supervision for the staff of a nursing home, with the fall proven to be a breach of that duty of care.[65] A nursing home is not an insurer of "no falls," but must act reasonably within its role as protector of the residents. The general standard of care required of a nursing home is that degree of care, skill, and diligence usually exhibited by such homes generally in the community.[66] Res ipsa loquitur assertions will not succeed in the typical nursing home case.[67] The case law of fall injuries indicates that the courts are willing to impose liability when the courts perceive that the nursing home staff did not do enough to attend to the safety needs of the injured resident.[68]

These cases involve a matrix of reasons for their various resident falls, and it is difficult to generalize what juries may do with any particular pattern of facts. But to the extent that one can speculate, it appears likely that the jurors will be very sympathetic to the fallen resident's injuries or death, once the nursing home is shown to have knowledge of the risk of falls.[69] This sympathy arises because jurors are concerned about their own family, or even themselves, being subjected to a future lapse in judgment by the staff of a similar nursing home.

The defense counsel, aware of this pattern of jury empathy, will seek to win summary judgment by pointing out the gaps in the plaintiff's case, or by presenting evidence in a manner that cuts off the plaintiff's assertions, or by barring expert testimony through a motion to exclude the plaintiff's designated nursing home expert. When all else fails the nursing home might admit liability, and go before the jury on the matter of damages alone.

---

64. N.G. Castle & K.E. Senon, *A Culture of Resident Safety in Nursing Homes*, 15 QUALITY & SAFETY IN HEALTH CARE 405 (2006).

65. For example, leaving an unstable person standing alone, after notice of the propensity of this person to fall, is a negligent act. Lathan v. Murrah Inc., 174 S.E.2d 269 (Ga. Ct. App. 1970).

66. Padgett v. Baxley & Appling Cnty. Hosp. Auth., 741 S.E.2d 193, 199 (Ga. Ct. App. 2013).

67. Palmer v. Intermed Inc., 270 Ark. 538, 606 S.W.2d 87, 88 (1980); MacAlpine v. Martin, 205 So. 2d 347 (Fla. Dist. Ct. App. 1967).

68. Brown v. Tift Cnty. Hosp. Auth., 635 S.E.2d 184 (Ga. Ct. App. 2006).

69. *See, e.g.*, Lathan v. Murrah Inc., 174 S.E.2d 269 (Ga. Ct. App. 1970).

Circumstantial evidence can be used by the plaintiff to establish negligence, where the unattended resident's fall is linked to the nursing home's negligence by a reasonable showing of facts.[70] Or there may be equal interpretations to be drawn from the same set of facts, and the injured resident may be unable to testify about their view of what had occurred.[71]

The CMS survey of nursing home conditions after a resident's death from a fall led to a $365,000 civil penalty, which was sustained by the appellate court; the lack of adequate staffing led to inadequate supervision of a resident who was known to wander, and who fell down a stairwell and died.[72]

9:11 Assembling the Proof of Causation

One major problem for plaintiffs tends to be the lack of adequate proof of causation. The elder may be dead or incompetent to testify; the staff members are silenced, forgetful, or have departed for other jobs; the records are incomplete or perhaps have been cleansed of incriminating statements.

Plaintiff has the burden of proving that negligent acts breached the duty of care in a manner that proximately caused the harm. The court must have before it some evidence that the fall was proximately caused by the nursing home's agents, employees, or facilities. In the absence of proof of such a proximate cause, the plaintiffs would be denied compensation.[73]

To establish that the cause-in-fact of the fall was within the legal responsibility of the nursing home, the plaintiff must show with reasonable certainty that the nursing home's specific negligent acts or omissions caused this particular fall to occur. Under the case law, the plaintiff has the burden to demonstrate (1) that the fall had occurred;

---

70. Bremenkamp v. Beverly Enters.-Kan., 762 F. Supp. 884, 887 (D. Kan. 1991) (citing Gunn v. Hi-C-Home, 260 Or. 404, 490 P.2d 999, 1001 (1971)).

71. Drucker v. Goscar Inc., 184 Neb. 475, 168 N.W.2d 534 (1969).

72. Asbury Ctr. v. U.S. Dep't of HHS, 77 F. App'x 853 (6th Cir. 2003).

73. MacAlpine v. Martin, 205 So. 2d 347 (Fla. Dist. Ct. App. 1967).

(2) that the fall caused injury; (3) that the nursing home was on notice of the potential risk; and (4) that the nursing home had actual notice of the potential for a fall—all of which are typically documented in the resident records. Where the proof of causation lies outside the knowledge of the lay juror, many states require that the causal link between the defendant's negligence and the plaintiff's harm be established by expert testimony.[74]

Eyewitness testimony about the events of the actual fall will be very important, but it is not the sole key to success. Defining the reason for the fall, months or years afterwards, is probably going to be speculative. There will be many factual disputes among qualified experts, augmented by the eyewitness testimony of those staff members who were present at the time of the fall. Perhaps a former employee who has quit the nursing home will be more forthright about what really happened; current employees may be more fearful of retribution. The jury in each one of these cases must determine whether the nursing home breached the standard of care, and whether the negligent omission or action by the nursing home would be deemed the proximate cause of the injury.[75]

9:12 Few Fall Cases Reach Appellate Levels

The tort law cases alleging negligence involving harm from a fall tend to present the extreme situations, or situations with the more extreme consequences, for which settlement was not deemed acceptable by one side. Most complaints do not lead to lawsuits. In the case law, negligence by the employees of the nursing home is usually found when the resident's representative can demonstrate that the nursing home had been on notice, but had not taken sufficient action to deal with the potential risk of a fall. In the appellate cases, reviewing trial court decisions regarding falls, the nursing homes try to win these cases by asserting that the nursing home had provided a reasonable amount of

74. Pitts v. Wingate at Brighton, Inc., 82 Mass. App. Ct. 285, 972 N.E.2d 74 (Mass. App. Ct. 2012).

75. Thibodeaux v. Stonebridge, L.L.C., 873 So. 2d 755 (La. Ct. App. 2004).

due care, and that the resident's mental and physical condition made the act of falling unavoidable, if not unforeseeable.

In an Iowa case, an obese resident was dropped by two workers who attempted to lift her; the nursing home's care plan for her was that "2–3" workers were to be used. On appeal of a penalty, the court found that the facts showed the accident would have occurred even with a third employee present. The court declined to give deference to state surveyor findings and a state penalty against the nursing home was reversed.[76]

Plaintiffs lost a Massachusetts case claiming negligent failure by a nursing home to supervise a resident who fell from a chair and died. Counsel failed to lay a sufficient foundation for admission of documents; failed to authenticate the CMS regulation on accidents; failed to bring in experts to show a violation occurred; and then failed on appeal to show prejudice, that is, that exclusion of the regulation injuriously affected the resident's rights.[77]

9:13 Evaluating Potential Litigation

A very effective tool in the evaluation of the potential lawsuit concerning a fall is a look back at the assessment of the incoming resident's condition when he or she entered the nursing home. The document forms a base line of notice regarding the vulnerabilities. Attorneys working on either side of these cases often use the survey instrument, on a format prepared by the federal Centers for Medicaid and Medicare Services, for the guidance of the inspection/survey teams which examine nursing homes every 15–18 months. (This is described elsewhere in this text as the CMS Guidance for Surveyors, colloquially known as the "watermelon book" because of the colors of its pages).

---

76. Parkview Nursing & Rehab. Ctr. v. Iowa Dep't of Inspections, 2001 WL 726397 (Iowa Ct. App. June 29, 2001).

77. Higgins v. Lifecare Ctrs. of Am., 808 N.E.2d 1257 (Mass. App. Ct. 2004).

Another useful tool is the "Falls and Fall Risk" clinical practice guideline of the American Medical Directors Association (AMDA).[78]

The simplest way to evaluate a claim of negligence in a potential lawsuit concerning a nursing home resident fall is to first ask about the resident's preadmission history of falling; then ask whether the resident's chart indicated to the staff that he or she is at risk of falling; then asking whether the resident has recently fallen under similar circumstances; then inquiring about witnesses before, during, and after the fall; and then determining the causes and the frequency of that person's falls since the event in question. Counsel representing the injured person should obtain and use the clinical practice guideline of AMDA, as it provides a useful professional standard of care.[79]

Case evaluation includes a prediction of juries' receptivity to damage awards. Higher-rise nursing homes recognize that patient falls from a fifth-floor window are fatal. A special interrogatory asking a jury to determine whether it was reasonably foreseeable to a nursing home that its resident would commit suicide or act in self-destructive manner encompassed not only the deliberate act of suicide but also accidental death. The jury answered no, but generally found negligence. On appeal, the jury's negative answer was found to be inconsistent with the general verdict of negligence, so the verdict was reversed.[80]

After a nursing home resident was dropped on the floor while being transferred from chair to bed, the lawsuit specifically alleged that the nursing home failed to provide the resident with the appropriate degree of care when transferring him from his chair to his bed, allowing only one aide to transfer him, failing to properly train its employees in the appropriate methods of transferring a resident from chair to bed, allowing the resident's head to strike the wall, and other acts or omissions to be learned through discovery. They also alleged that the

---

78. Am. Med. Dirs. Ass'n, Clinical Practice Guideline, Falls and Fall Risk (2011), https://paltmed.org/sites/default/files/2024-10/FALLS_CPG_08092024.pdf.

79. *Id.*

80. Garcia v. Seneca Nursing Home, 2011 Ill. App. (1st) 103085, 956 N.E.2d 1005, 353 Ill. Dec. 877 (2011).

nursing home was vicariously liable under respondeat superior. Then a state law was invoked by the defense that required the claim first be reviewed by a medical advisory panel.

The physical action of handling this resident to transfer him from his geri-chair to his bed is covered by the Medical Malpractice Act. The resident's claims must be submitted to a medical review panel.

9:14 Plaintiff's Theory of the Case

As with any negligence cause of action, the plaintiff needs to have a clear theory of the case regarding the facts as they occurred and of the safer alternatives, that is, what should have been done differently in order to satisfy the standard of care. There are several ways to approach this. One approach is to show a breach of the nursing home's own standards, and when this is possible, settlement is likely and the facts may be the hardest for the defense. Another is to demonstrate the patterns of past similar falls within the same nursing home, articulated by evidence from discovery and depositions of current and (especially for plaintiff) former employees. Another option is to have an expert gerontology physician determine this injured individual's patterns of weakness, and then testify that the resident's clinical chart demonstrated knowledge on the part of the nursing home about his or her vulnerability toward falling.

The most likely scenario for the award of negligence-related damages is that a resident who was unable to walk safely alone was allowed to roam "loose" despite a clinical chart indicating instability or inability to walk. The chart should show an awareness of that vulnerability on the part of the nursing home administration; a pattern of small or minor bruises from previous falls; probably witness testimony of a pattern of unanswered requests for assistance by the means of a call button used by the victim; and then the showing of an attempt to walk alone, in the absence of a prompt response to the resident's call by the nurses or aides.

Sometimes the nursing home conceals the circumstances of a fall, and it may also obstruct access to or lose key records, and there may be additional charges of spoliation of evidence.[81] Former employees who quit because the home had inadequate staffing at the time of the resident's fall are helpful witnesses.[82] These are useful in establishing a claim for punitive damages for recurring falls, inadequate safeguards, and tampered records.[83]

Bringing an action for negligence does not preclude a parallel claim of violation of rights under state elder protection statutes. The terms of these statutes vary, but a nursing home that deprives a resident of a "right or benefit" under New York law can be held liable for the same acts or omissions that give rise to a negligence cause of action.[84]

9:15 Policies and Noncompliance

Plaintiff's counsel need not look very far to find standards that apply to the fall-prevention, postfall reporting, and resident care issues. CMS and state long-term care agencies have regulations and guidance documents that set the underlying "floor" of nursing home care for virtually all nursing homes. (The Department of Veterans Affairs facilities have their own rules and norms,[85] which are uniquely federal in their restricted set of remedies.[86]) The decision of the nursing home as an institution may be deemed adequate as a policy of handling residents, but more likely, the lawsuit will be brought when the individual demonstrates that he or she was harmed by individual employees' failure to follow that policy of the employer. "Owners and

---

81. Rinaldi v. City View Nursing & Rehab. Ctr., 2005 WL 3215146 (Ohio Ct. App. December 1, 2005); *accord*, Smith v. Manor Care of Canton, 2006 WL 636975 (Ohio Ct. App. March 13, 2006).

82. Bremenkamp v. Beverly Enters.-Kan., 762 F. Supp. 884, 887 (D. Kan. 1991).

83. Patrick Ford, *Punitive Damages in Nursing Home Cases, in* NURSING HOME LITIGATION: PRETRIAL PRACTICE AND TRIALS 429, 431 (Ruben Krisztal ed., 2d ed. 2003).

84. Pasqua v. Bon Secours N.Y. Health Sys. Inc., 13 Misc. 3d 1036, 827 N.Y.S.2d 548 (N.Y. Sup. Ct. 2006) (tort law had not provided sufficient remedies, so separate nursing home law was adopted, and each can be applied.).

85. Joe Murphy, *Making Falls Reduction a Full Time Job*, 8 TOPICS IN PATIENT SAFETY 1 (VA Nat'l Ctr. for Patient Safety, May/June 2008), http://www.patientsafety.va.gov/TIPS/Docs/TIPS_MayJune08.pdf.

86. 28 U.S.C. § 2680, 38 C.F.R. § 14.605.

operators of nursing home facilities are liable to residents for injuries caused by the negligent acts of their employees."[87]

9:16 Examples of Fall Injury Cases

In the *Smartt* case, a jury awarded a massive $33 million verdict after extensive evidence of nursing home negligence, including falls, leg contractures, sores, and neglect.[88] The *Palmer* case produced a $7 million award of which $5 million was punitive; the bed rails were incorrectly handled and there was no mattress to cushion the fall.[89] In the *Terhune* case, nearly $38 million was awarded due to systemic problems at the nursing home.[90]

In the *Smith* case, the cover-up allegation and claims of inadequate supervision led to a $4.5 verdict.[91] In the *Matteo* case, the doctor's order for the use of safety restraints was not followed, and the jury awarded $943,000.[92] In the *Wilks* case, a high-risk resident was not restrained as the doctor had ordered; the fall led to a $216,000 jury award.[93]

Staff errors in dropping residents are usually settled without full reported case outcomes. The *Hoel* case resulted in a $4.5 million verdict, where the drop was part of a pattern of neglect, sepsis, and malnutrition. The *Johe* case settled for $185,000 after a drop that occurred with a staff mistake in using the Hoyer sling to lift the resident. The *Penny* case brought a $2 million jury verdict for wheelchair rollaway and

---

87. Myers v. Heritage Enters., Inc., 354 Ill. App. 3d 241, 820 N.E.2d 604 (Ill. App. Ct. 4th Dist. 2004).

88. Smartt v. NHC Healthcare, No. 2182 (Warren Cnty. Tenn. 2007), *reported in* Verdicts, Settlements & Tactics 149 (Apr. 2007) (eight falls; last one produced untreated hip fracture, no medical care for seven days; doctor's orders ignored and hip reinjured; Stage IV pressure ulcer; urosepsis infection led to heart attack).

89. Palmer v. S. Ala. Nursing Home, Civ. No. CV-00-2775 (Mobile Cnty. Ala. 2001), *reported in* Verdicts, Settlements & Tactics 49 (Feb. 2002).

90. Forum Group at Moran Lake Nursing & Rehab. Ctr., LLC v. Terhune, 733 S.E.2d 808 (Ga. Ct. App. 2012).

91. Smith v. Parks Methodist Ret. Vill., No. A-114050 (Ector Cnty. Tex. 2004), *reported in* Verdicts, Settlements & Tactics 462 (Oct. 2004).

92. Matteo v. Geisinger Wyo. Valley Med. Ctr., No 7248-C (Luzerne Cnty. Pa. 1998) *reported in* Verdicts, Settlements & Tactics 547 (Dec. 1998).

93. Wilks v. Ave. Care Ctr., No. 95-L-5369 (Cook Cnty. Ill. 1999), *reported in* Verdicts, Settlements & Tactics 302 (July 1999).

fall;[94] an employee released the resident's wheelchair, which rolled into a parking lot where she fell out; the resident had had 15 prior falls. A San Diego nursing home concealed the reason for the injury from a fall, after an elderly resident was left alone in a wheelchair inside the nursing home and the individual movement alarm was shut off; she fell and hit her head; a $475,000 settlement was reached in 2002.[95]

94. Penny v. Sunbridge Healthcare, No. 02-C-378 (Cass Cnty. Tex. 2003) *reported in* VERDICTS, SETTLEMENTS & TACTICS 422 (Oct. 2003).

95. Anonymous case (San Diego Super. Ct. Cal. May 16, 2002), *reported in* VERDICTS, SETTLEMENTS & TACTICS 251 (June 2002).

CHAPTER 10

Liability for Neglect: Wandering, Elopement, and Escape

10:1 Overview
10:2 Response When Residents Escape
10:3 Why Residents Wander
10:4 Safety versus Secure Buildings
10:5 Staff Responsibilities
10:6 Framing the Complaint
10:7 Lessons from the Cases
10:8 Summary

10:1 Overview

Nursing homes are paid to assume the duty of care for persons whose dementia or other mental difficulties make them more vulnerable when they "wander" on public streets or into areas of natural hazards. "Wandering" is an umbrella term for behaviors along a spectrum of conduct that have been observed among persons with mental impairments; for example, disorientation and aimless movement to an undefined end point, and getting "lost" along the way. One professional society defined it as "meandering, aimless or repetitive locomotion that exposes a person to harm and is incongruent with boundaries, limits or obstacles."[1] Experts estimate that there will be 500,000 wandering

1. American Nursing Diagnosis Association definition, *quoted in* Evidence-Based Protocols for Managing Wandering Behaviors 5 (Audrey Nelson & Donna Algase eds., 2007) [hereinafter Nelson].

persons among the 15 million Alzheimer's residents by 2040.[2] In 1994, it was estimated that 3 percent of residents wander out of their facilities each year.[3]

Mortality of nursing home residents with dementia almost doubled when wandering was present.[4] Falls and fractures are likely to result; drowning sometimes occurs;[5] vehicle-pedestrian accidents are inevitable among this group of wanderers.[6] Inside the home, the errant wanderer may not be able to find his or her way back to the facility.[7] In one tragic case, an elder was locked into a freezer and suffered frostbite and death.[8] "Wandering poses a significant safety challenge for care providers."[9]

The aimless wandering around the facility that marks one type of dementia can be contrasted to the type that manifests as an escape attempt as the resident with dementia seeks to leave for what is perceived as an urgent mission; for example, picking up children or meeting with a friend outside. Both types have the potential to seriously injure the resident, by falling on stairs,[10] precipitating confrontations, pedestrian traffic deaths[11] or getting lost or even drowning.[12] The resident with a mission comes with special concerns such as a possible confrontation when attempting to return the resident to the facility.

Escape by an elderly resident from a nursing home is called "elopement," and it is a substantial concern with dementia residents. Elopement is a form of wandering behavior that is usually associated with dementia. Approximately half of nursing home residents suffer

---

2. NINA SILVERSTEIN ET AL., DEMENTIA AND WANDERING BEHAVIOR 35 (2006).
3. NELSON, *supra* note 1, at 58.
4. *Id.* at 60.
5. First Healthcare Corp. v. Hamilton, 740 So. 2d 1189, 1200 (Fla. Dist. Ct. App. 1999).
6. *See, e.g.*, Murphy v. Allstate Ins. Co., 295 So. 2d 29 (La. Ct. App. 1974).
7. Wandering is also profoundly difficult to manage. *See, e.g.*, Ellen Scott, *Punitive Damages: Lawsuits against Nursing Homes*, 23 J. LEGAL MED. 115 (2002).
8. Bebe Med. Ctr. v. Bailey, 913 A.2d 543 (Del. 2006).
9. NELSON, *supra* note 1, at 61.
10. *See, e.g.*, Booty v. Kentwood Manor Nursing Home, 483 So. 2d 634 (La. Ct. App. 1986).
11. Lorraine Mion, *Physical Restraints*, *in* MEDICAL-LEGAL ASPECTS OF LONG-TERM CARE 257 (Jeffrey Levine ed., 2003).
12. Daniels v. Twin Oaks Nursing Home, 692 F.2d 1321 (11th Cir. 1983).

from some form of dementia. Some research has found that about 20 percent of residents with dementia are reported to have wandered.[13]

To establish nursing home liability, the plaintiff must show that the facility failed to meet the standard of care by using reasonable care to prevent the elopement, and that the facility responded inappropriately after the elopement occurred. Wandering should be discussed in the periodic assessments of "each resident's functional capacity." These assessments must be conducted within 14 days after the resident's admission to the facility, or "within 14 calendar days after the facility determines, or should have determined, that there has been a significant change in the resident's condition," quarterly, and annually.[14]

Counsel should carefully examine the Centers for Medicaid & Medicare Services (CMS) rules[15] and study some of the excellent secondary resources concerning responses to the problems caused by elopement.[16]

The resident's unauthorized departure from the building or from its protective area can produce a very adverse or fatal consequence. The pattern of departures may have been known upon initial admission,[17] once known to the staff,[18] it should be included in the chart, posted on signs on the door of the resident's room, and included as part of new staff training. A resident who is not adequately supervised might wander and fall off a roof or out of a window, for example.[19]

Sometimes the survivors of the deceased resident may sue the nursing home for the inadequate protection given by the negligent custodians.[20] The law of negligence applies; the claim of res ipsa

---

13. Staci Yandle, *Protect the Innocent: Establish Elopement Liability*, 49 Trial 36 (Mar. 2013).
14. Yandle, *supra* note 13.
15. 42 C.F.R. § 483.25.
16. Yandle, *supra* note 13; Nina M. Silverstein, *Why Long-Term Care Facilities Should Be Concerned about Wandering Behavior*, 19 Advice & Advs. 17 (2002); *see also* Jeannette Wick & Guido Zanni, *Aimless Excursions: Wandering in the Elderly*, 21 Consultant Pharmacist 608 (Aug. 2006).
17. McGillivray v. Rapides Iberia Mgmt. Enters., 493 So. 2d 819 (La. Ct. App. 1986).
18. *Booty*, 483 So. 2d 634.
19. Richards v. Broadview Heights Harborside Healthcare, 782 N.E.2d 609 (Ohio Ct. App. 2002); Eichenbaum v. First United Lemberger Ladies Chair, 186 N.Y.S.2d 498 (N.Y. Sup. Ct. 1959).
20. *Daniels*, 692 F.2d 1321.

loquitur might be asserted in a proper case,[21] but that may not supply proof of proximate causation.[22] The lack of adequate staffing and the conscious reduction in protective resources can result in serious repercussions for the responsible managers, even possibly a successful criminal prosecution.[23]

A nursing home is under a duty to "exercise such reasonable care for a resident's safety as his known mental and physical condition may require."[24] This is not an assurance of absolute safety; the circumstances of the cases will vary.[25] For example, in a case where a resident diagnosed with cancer jumped off the roof of the nursing home, the court held that a jury could consider whether the nursing home violated CMS and state rules. The court went on to find that the nursing home had "the duty to exercise reasonable care to prevent decedent from harming herself" if it had knowledge of the risk,[26] even if exercising such reasonable care meant only that defendant took measures to keep decedent safe until decedent's responsible person could move her to a more secure facility.[27]

The cognitively impaired resident who escapes is not deemed to be contributorily negligent or partially responsible, because the mental state of such persons is not such that they can be deemed at fault for their unauthorized travels.[28]

The implementation of an effective system of protection against wandering is a normal task in operating a facility for persons with

---

21. The claim of res ipsa loquitur ("the event speaks for itself") is sometimes of value when there is only one cause. Franklin v. Collins Chapel Connectional Hosp., 696 S.W.2d 16 (Tenn. Ct. App. 1985); Virginia S. v. Salt Lake Care Ctr., 741 P.2d 969 (Utah Ct. App. 1987). But it cannot be applied where multiple causes could have been present. Guffey v. Integrated Health Servs., 1 S.W.3d 509 (Mo. Ct. App. 1999); Tait v. W. World Ins. Co., 220 So. 2d 226 (La. Ct. App. 1969); Ivy Manor Nursing Home v. Brown, 488 P.2d 246 (Colo. Ct. App. 1971).

22. Daniels v. Twin Oaks Nursing Home, 692 F.2d 1321 (11th Cir. 1983).

23. State v. Serebin, 350 N.W.2d 65 (Wis. 1984); John Pray, *State v. Serebin*, 1986 Wis. L. Rev. 339.

24. Golden Villa Nursing Home v. Smith, 674 S.W.2d 343 (Tex. App. 1984).

25. Though it is not an insurer, the nursing home must meet the duty to give a reasonable standard of care to the resident. Powell v. Parkview Estate Nursing Home, 240 So. 2d 53 (La. Ct. App. 1970).

26. McCoy v. Alvista Care Home Inc., 391 S.E.2d 419 (Ga. Ct. App. 1999).

27. Klein v. BIA Hotel Corp., 49 Cal. Rptr. 60 (Cal. Ct. App. 1996).

28. Fields v. Senior Citizens Ctr., 528 S.E.2d 573 (La. Ct. App. 1988); *Powell*, 240 So. 2d 53.

dementia. Planned interventions are well understood in the professional literature[29] and designs could actually work against wandering,[30] but, as with other issues, short staffing may foil the best-intended plans. One expert says that a 1:5 staff-to-resident ratio is optimal and a 1:6 ratio is adequate.[31]

CMS and its state agencies prohibit the routine use of drugs to control the wandering behaviors; there must be valid medical reasons for the use of drugs and adequate reviews of the medication plan.[32]

Alarms and security measures to prevent departures are expected, and their absence or their conscious disablement by staff can be a source of escapes.[33] Hindsight is applied in tort cases; the custom of leaving doors open[34] for staff members who smoke, or disabling alarms because they might malfunction, builds a case for a future plaintiff's claim of negligent supervision. Architecture and planning are great opportunities to confine a wanderer, but the actual operators in those facilities may be so negligent that the plaintiff easily convinces a jury to award damages.

These are sad cases with great appeal to a jury in a civil tort case.[35] Drowning, freezing, disappearing in a swamp, and other exposure deaths are some of the results of the departure of a disoriented resident who cannot find the way back to the home; the person also can be injured or killed by traffic, trains, and other foreseeable collisions. Death that is avoidable may be hard to defend; that may be the reason why so few of these cases reach appellate court decision stages.

---

29. *See, e.g.*, Mildred Hogstel, Gerontology: Nursing Care of the Older Adult 404 (2006).

30. Silverstein et al., *supra* note 2, at 120–25 (recommending environmental audit of the facility to change those factors that would facilitate escape).

31. *Id.* at 149.

32. 42 C.F.R. § 483.12; Ctrs. for Medicare & Medicaid Servs., State Operations Manual, CMS Pub. No. 100-07, Appendix PP: Guidance to Surveyors for Long Term Care Facilities F600, F605 [hereinafter CMS Survey Guidance].

33. Booty v. Kentwood Manor Nursing Home, 483 So. 2d 634 (La. Ct. App. 1986).

34. *Id.*

35. Silverstein et al., *supra* note 2, at 115.

10:2 Response When Residents Escape

The prudent nursing home has a good working relationship with local police, fire, and emergency medical services. The standard of care upon an external unauthorized departure is a call to the police to assist in locating and returning the wandering person before he or she is injured. Liability for damages may be enhanced if the resident dies outside and the home had taken few efforts to find him or her. The immediate follow-up search may help to find and return the resident, though some die while wandering prior to their discovery by the staff.[36]

10:3 Why Residents Wander

Mental impairments usually accompany the urge to escape. The wandering resident may be restless from loneliness, disorientation, a desire to "return home," and so on. Risks of elopement increase as cognitive function decreases.[37] The literature of neurophysiology and cognitive psychology has expanded greatly as more and more Alzheimer's disease research is being published worldwide.[38] As a psychology text cautions: "The added medical problems of older people with Alzheimer's disease who wander from home or a facility and become lost only magnify their physical vulnerability."[39]

The care plan for each resident should be altered when there is a significant change in mental condition; this care plan should include measures to allow staff to watch out for potential wandering.

36. McGillivray v. Rapides Iberia Mgmt. Enters., 493 So. 2d 819 (La. Ct. App. 1986).

37. Nursing Home Litigation: Investigation and Case Preparation 170 (Patricia Iyer ed., 1999).

38. *See, e.g.*, Silverstein et al., *supra* note 2 (as of 1990, estimates were that 4 million Americans had Alzheimer's or related brain disorders); Nat'l Ctr. on Elder Abuse, Research Brief: How at Risk Are People with Dementia? (2012), http://www.ncea.aoa.gov/Resources/Publication/docs/Dementia_ResearchBrief_web508.pdf (Currently, approximately 5.3 million Americans have Alzheimer's disease. In 2030, approximately 7.7 million people will have Alzheimer's disease, and the number will increase to 16 million by 2050).

39. *Id.* at 21.

10:4 Safety versus Secure Buildings

The requirement for ease of egress during fires or emergency evacuations needs to be balanced against the risks of wandering residents dying or harming themselves.

Physical security measures are well understood. Fixing the doors so they close automatically and open with coded keypads is one approach. Designing the nurses' station so that all exit doors and corridors can be viewed is an ideal architectural approach. Alarms can be used for exit doors and for fall-prone residents when the resident gets out of bed.

Negligence comes when staff leaves doors open for their convenience as smokers. Some alarms are tampered with by staff to reduce their noisy distractions, and these situations result in facilitating the unfortunate resident departures and establishing a basis for a negligence claim. One lawsuit involved a freeway pedestrian's death after she escaped from a nursing home; the alarm was turned off while a group of visitors was leaving, and a similar escape by another resident under similar circumstances had put the nursing home on notice of the risk.[40]

10:5 Staff Responsibilities

Staff alerts about particular "likely wanderers" are important. Nursing homes should train, plan, and respond urgently to wandering and elopement when residents leave without authorization. This problem can be contained, and failure to do so can cause avoidable deaths and injuries.[41]

Receptionists and door greeters should be prepared to gently restrain a departing resident whose demented state cannot comprehend the dangers outdoors. Nursing homes should not use drugs as "chemical restraints" that slow down a person enough to prevent wandering, but

---

40. Love v. CF&H Corp., 89 S.W.2d 68, 73 (Tex. App. 2002).
41. CMS Survey Guidance, *supra* note 32 (interpreting 42 C.F.R. § 483.25(h)).

some still do so.[42] The ultimate protection may be the assignment of a designated "Mr. Jones-watcher" from among the aide staff, but this is a higher cost than most for-profit homes can easily sustain.

The next best option is an alarm device for the resident, such as a bracelet that sets off an alarm when the resident passes the exit door. A room alarm or other means to track the location of the wanderer could be a significant benefit.

In rare cases, the wandering person commits a violent act against another person; the nursing home employee who observes the wanderer with any potential weapon should take immediate action before the violent act occurs.[43] To not act under these circumstances would be negligence in the protection of the vulnerable residents.

10:6 Framing the Complaint

A key aspect of success will be the plaintiff attorney's story to the jury about pain and suffering and other noneconomic damages. These would include damages for mental anguish and distress by the escaped wanderer, and loss of dignity established through having friends and members of the clergy testify. Expert testimony should also be used to establish noneconomic damages. An expert on elder liability has suggested: "Typically, the defense will argue or insinuate that due to dementia, the resident did not experience any pain or distress. This is not true. A geriatric psychiatrist, forensic psychiatrist, or other mental health professional familiar with dementia and Alzheimer's can convey effectively to the jury the elopement's impact on the resident."[44]

Negligent failure to appropriately assess a nursing home resident's elopement risk would be the basis for the claim. An assessment should consider "whether the resident exhibits cognitive impairment with respect to memory, communication, or decision-making; is independently mobile; suffers from depression, agitation, or anxiety; wanders

---

42. Charlotte Digregorio, Everything You Need to Know about Nursing Homes 116 (2005).
43. Riley v. Maison Orleans II Inc., 829 So. 2d 479 (La. Ct. App. 2002).
44. Yandle, *supra* note 13.

or has a past history of wandering; verbalizes a desire or intent to leave the facility; exhibits "exit seeking" behavior; accepts residency in the nursing home; and recognizes and responds appropriately to danger."[45] When the risk is identified, an individual care plan for that resident should be established with meaningful interventions and strategies to prevent elopement. The care plan should have been reviewed and revised "to accommodate changes in the resident's physical or mental condition that would increase the risk for elopement, such as prior wandering incidents or elopement attempts."[46]

The individual plan should be tied in to "facility-wide technological interventions to prevent resident wandering and elopement. Electronic devices such as door alarms, elopement warning systems, and video surveillance cameras can significantly reduce the risk of elopements. To be effective, door alarms should be designed to trigger only when certain individuals attempt to exit. This will reduce false alarms. Elopement warning systems, such as Wander Guard, use transmitting wristbands that alert the facility staff when a chair, bed, or door alarm is activated by a resident's movement."[47]

The negligence of the staff in the nursing home is the basis for the complaint in most cases. Unreasonable failure to protect is a negligent act, but the nursing home is not an insurer and does not have a duty to place an attendant to watch each resident at all times.[48] Sometimes state laws allow a private cause of action. But the plaintiff must pay close attention; not all states have an elder protection statute that covers the circumstances of escapes.[49]

10:7 Lessons from the Cases

To reduce liability, the prudent nursing home should have a plan to identify the potential of cognitively impaired residents to escape or

---

45. *Id.*
46. *Id.*
47. *Id.*
48. *Id.;* Tait v. W. World Ins. Co., 220 So. 2d 226 (La. Ct. App. 1969).
49. No private cause of action was found in a New York escape case, Begandy v. Richardson, 134 Misc. 2d 357, 510 N.Y.S.2d 984 (N.Y. Super. 1987).

wander. Those who are identified can be fitted with bed alarms and bracelets that set off alarms when they pass an exit, or can be otherwise marked so that staff is alerted.

A review of the cases can show lessons to be applied in other cases.[50] Punitive damages were allowed where a nursing home had ample notice of several past escapes but left a door ajar despite warnings, and the resident escaped and drowned.[51] A nursing home escaped punitive damages by showing that its efforts to transfer the wandering resident to a more secure facility had been unsuccessful as of the date of the last escape.[52] Expert testimony will be needed to explain the "degree of care, skill, and diligence" that comparable nursing homes in the community would use in rendering treatment to a wandering-prone resident; this evidence is needed to create the standard against which the nursing home's performance is to be measured.[53]

On the other hand, whether the failure to lock a door allowing a resident to elope and suffer a fatal fall amounts to negligence is a matter within the common knowledge of the jury.[54] "[E]ven though limited medical testimony may be required on the issue of (1) a plaintiff's capacity for 'self-control' to demonstrate a defendant's negligence in its 'supervision or custodial care' or (2) failure to protect a plaintiff from a known danger, the need for this limited testimony is insufficient to translate an ordinary negligence claim into medical malpractice."[55] Similarly, it was within the common knowledge of the jury to decide whether it was negligence to allow a resident suffering from dementia who had a history of attempted elopement to leave the nursing home by passing both nurse's stations and the reception desk in a wheelchair, culminating in a fatal fall down the front steps. A complaint alleging

50. James Rigelhaupt, Annotation, *Hospital's Liability for Resident's Injury or Death Resulting from Escape or Attempted Escape*, 37 A.L.R.4th 200 (1985).

51. First Healthcare Corp. v. Hamilton, 740 So. 2d 1189 (Fla. Dist. Ct. App. 1999).

52. Love v. CF&H Corp., 89 S.W.2d 68, 73 (Tex. App. 2002).

53. Rosemont Inc. v. Marshall, 481 So. 2d 1126 (Ala. 1985).

54. Ostrum v. Manorcare Health Serv., 2007 WL 188132 (E.D. Mich. January 22, 2007).

55. *Id.; see also* Reiss v. Stamford Hosp., 205 WL 2009560 (Conn. Super. Ct. August 2, 2005); George Beauvais v. Conn. Subaccute Corp. of Waterbury, 2000 WL 1657845 (Conn. Super. Ct. September 19, 2000).

that a medical judgment for supervision had been made, but negligently followed, does not sound in malpractice.[56]

These cases can have sad endings. After a wandering resident has not been found for more than a year, state probate proceedings can be initiated and a wrongful death case can be brought on the assumption that the resident died.[57]

The deficiencies uncovered in many nursing homes during post-escape litigation tends to be a lack of staff to monitor the alarms and signals, and a lack of staff to follow up with the search for the escapee; the plaintiff should put on evidence of what the proper staffing should have been to be equivalent to better-run facilities.[58] Sometimes the alarms are turned off, and that brings a finding of negligence.[59] The staff's lack of adequate supervision that allows an escape while alarms are not operational can be a jury question on negligent care.[60] A standard of "ordinary care" was applied where a resident wandered out of a facility into freezing weather and died.[61]

Three federal appeals of nursing home penalties illustrate some of the complex issues that escapes can cause. In one case, a demented resident was able to flip a switch to open an outside door; the staff put a piece of paper over the switch; the paper did not fool the resident, who opened the door anyway and escaped six times.[62] The federal appeal decision upheld the $3,050-per-day penalty because the home had a duty to install a more secure alarm system once this wander risk was evident, or to assign a single worker to supervise this one resident to prevent his wandering.

In another case, the argument on appeal by the nursing home was that resident escape was a volitional choice by the resident that should

---

56. Kelly v. Bridgeport Health Care Ctr., Inc., 2178 LEXIS (Conn. Super. Ct. September 2, 2010).

57. Daniels v. Twin Oaks Nursing Home, 692 F.2d 1321 (11th Cir. 1982).

58. *Rosemont*, 481 So. 2d at 1130–31.

59. *Love*, 89 S.W.2d at 73.

60. Bailey v. Rose Care Ctr., 817 S.W.2d 412 (Ark. 1991).

61. McGillivray v. Rapides Iberia Mgmt. Enters., 493 So. 2d 819 (La. Ct. App. 1986).

62. Liberty Commons Nursing & Rehab.-Alamance v. CMS, Dec. No. 2070 (HHS Departmental Appeals Bd., App. Div., Mar. 9, 2007), http://www.hhs.gov/dab/decisions/dab2070.pdf.

not be penalized. The receptionist at the front door of the nursing home knew of the wandering behavior, and while distracted by a call failed to stop the resident from his escape. The penalty was upheld because the receptionist's negligent conduct breached the nursing home's own policies.[63]

Death of a wandering resident drew a civil penalty in another case, where the use of an alarm device could have detected the fact that the resident was opening a window and departing the ground-floor room through that window.[64] In the federal appeals, nursing home duties under the CMS regulation[65] have been clarified, and it appears likely that judges in tort trials would, if asked, admit the federal investigative results and give great deference to the expertise of the hearing and appeals officers when evaluating the seriousness of the nursing home's misconduct.

An expert in elopement litigation suggested: "Litigants should also demand production of the entire resident chart, which should include fall risk, cognitive decline, and wandering assessments; minimum data sets (MDS), which are comprehensive assessment tools; behavior tracking logs; psychiatric assessments, evaluations, and progress notes; incident and accident reports; activity assessments and progress notes; resident care plans; activities of daily living flow sheets; narrative nursing notes; nursing monthly summaries; and physician progress notes and orders."[66]

10:8 Summary

Who can sue? The resident or his or her personal representative.

What is the duty of care? A skilled nursing facility with knowledge of an incompetent resident's risks from unsupervised movement either inside or outside the facility, or both, has a duty to protect and

63. Brightview Ctr. v. CMS, Dec. No. 2132 (HHS Departmental Appeals Bd., App. Div., Nov. 21, 2007), http://www.hhs.gov/dab/decisions/DAB2132.pdf.

64. Briarwood Nursing Ctr. v. CMS, Dec. No. 2115 (HHS Departmental Appeals Bd., App. Div., Sept. 17, 2007), http://www.hhs.gov/dab/decisions/dab2115.pdf.

65. 42 C.F.R. § 483.20; CMS SURVEY GUIDANCE, *supra* note 32, at F272.

66. Yandle, *supra* note 13.

supervise that resident's movements by reasonable methods and practices.

What is the injury? Death or substantial trauma from accidental injuries.

How do you prove that substandard care was the cause of the injury? Expert witness testimony establishes the standard of care in this community, and the expert will evaluate the failed "safeguards" in the facility that failed to contain the wandering resident.

Whom should you sue? The facility operator and relevant affiliated companies, as well as drivers who actually collided with the wandering resident after departure.

How do you go about proving your case? Use expert witness testimony based on credible reconstruction of the escape and the eventual end point of the resident's journey; resident charts demonstrating awareness of the potential for wandering; admission records and subsequent records indicating prior departures; police reports of the search and of the accident that caused trauma.

CHAPTER 11

Use of Resident Restraints

11:1 Overview
11:2 Restraints and Uses
11:3 Restraint-Injury Litigation
11:4 CMS and State Norms
11:5 FDA Hazard Alerts
11:6 Summary

11:1 Overview

Controlling the movement of residents within the nursing home is sometimes necessary to reduce the risk of harmful conflicts, aggressive behaviors, wandering, falls, and so on.[1] Pharmaceutical means of restraining residents with psychotropic drugs are covered in Chapter 13, Liability for Prescription Drugs. This chapter covers physical devices used to restrain the nursing home resident, including straps, vests, or jackets.[2] Restraints also include seat belts, bedside rails, hand mitts, and chair tray tables.[3] In some instances, restraint is beneficial—a mitt covering the hands may prevent removal of a feeding tube from the stomach,[4] and a secure portion of a facility may prevent a violent

1. *See generally* Jeffrey Levine, *Medical and Legal Aspects of Chemical and Physical Restraint in the Nursing Home*, 75 Am. Jur. Trials 1 (2007).

2. Douglas Singh, Effective Management of Long-Term Care Facilities 292 (2005).

3. Ctrs. for Medicare & Medicaid Servs., State Operations Manual, CMS Pub. No. 100-07, Appendix PP: Guidance to Surveyors for Long Term Care Facilities PP-60 [hereinafter CMS Survey Guidance].

4. Mildred Hogstel, Gerontology: Nursing Care of the Older Adult 397 (2001).

resident from assaulting others.[5] Physical restraints should be ordered by a physician, not simply used for the convenience of the nursing staff.[6] Misuse, regardless of actual harm caused, violates the CMS rules[7] and could lead to a serious injury.[8]

Subcategories of the torts related to falls include inappropriate use of restraints, which sometimes cause injuries in and of themselves, and inadequate medical response to the fall by delaying treatment or neglecting appropriate treatment.

11:2 Restraints and Uses

Restraint devices may entrap the resident as he or she moves; side rails may collapse[9] or cause other problems for the resident who should remain in bed. The physical injuries caused by straps and vests include arm injury, strangulation, and the effect of falls from wheelchairs.[10] That is why physician orders are usually required for resident restraints, and excessive use is subject to penalties during surveys of nursing home compliance.[11]

Unexpected but foreseeable outcomes may befall the user of the restraint. In one case, $220,000 was awarded where a restraint choked the resident between the mattress and the footboard of his bed.[12] In another case, workers physically restrained the resident, and she died of suffocation.[13] Bedside rails must be kept in good condition to avoid accidents.[14] CMS norms applied by nursing home surveyors

---

5. Associated Health Sys. Inc. v. Jones, 366 S.E.2d 147 (Ga. Ct. App. 1988).

6. 42 C.F.R. § 483.13; Saunders v. Beverly Enters. (unreported), *discussed in* Ellen Scott, *Punitive Damages in Lawsuits against Nursing Homes*, 23 J. Leg. Med. 115, 126 (2002).

7. Lakeridge Villa Health Care Ctr. v. Leavitt, 202 F. App'x 903 (6th Cir. 2006).

8. *Id.*; *see also* Clermont Nursing & Convalescent Ctr. v. Leavitt, 142 F. App'x 900 (6th Cir. 2005) (wrist restraint tied to bed, wrapped around chest, could injure the resident).

9. *See, e.g.*, MeadowWood Nursing Home v. U.S. Dep't of HHS, 364 F.3d 786 (6th Cir. 2004).

10. Kujaswki v. Arbor View Health Care Ctr., 407 N.W.2d 249 (Wis. 1987).

11. 42 C.F.R. § 483.13(a); *Lakeridge Villa*, 202 F. App'x 903.

12. Adams v. Ashtabula Cnty. Nursing Home, No. 99-CV-193 (Ashtabula Cnty. Ohio Com. Pl. June 15, 1999), *reported in* Verdicts, Settlements & Tactics 340 (Aug. 1999).

13. Colwell v. Baker, CV697-1103C (Cape Girardeau Cnty. Mo. Cir. Ct. 1998), *reported in* Verdicts, Settlements & Tactics 442 (Oct. 1998).

14. *MeadowWood*, 364 F.3d 786.

expressly prohibit the use of side rails "unless they are necessary to treat a resident's medical symptoms."[15] CMS requires an individualized determination of how the restraint fits with the individual care plan for this resident.[16] Surveyors will ask and the nursing home staff must respond to a series of questions about the decision to place a restraint on a resident.[17]

11:3 Restraint-Injury Litigation

Before very recent times, restraint use was practically normal and accepted, and tort liability arose only if there had been negligence in the use of the restraint.[18] Those cases looked to normal practices and attributed liability only in the extreme cases. The proof used standard negligence approaches.[19]

CMS regulations,[20] guidance to surveyors,[21] and enlightened opinions among specialists in the field recommend against the use of restraints because of their risks and because they signal to the resident the message of captivity and suggest that immobility would be preferred by the staff. Exceptions are made for the orders of a physician that the resident be restrained and for use of restraints as a short-term emergency response.[22] The subset of fall cases dealing with restraints is a category in which the nursing home is likely to be penalized by public enforcers[23] and is particularly vulnerable to tort claims for damages.[24] Studies show that prolonged use of restraints increases the likelihood of a resident's serious harm from falling. Restraint use is also associated with harmful side effects, including decreased mobility

---

15. CMS SURVEY GUIDANCE, *supra* note 3, at P-61.
16. *Id.*
17. *Id.*
18. Annotation, *Hospital's Liability for Injuries Sustained by Resident as a Result of Restraints Imposed on Movement*, 25 A.L.R.3d 1450 (1969).
19. *See, e.g.*, 24 AM. JUR. PROOF OF FACTS 3d *Nursing Home Liability* § 73.
20. 42 C.F.R. § 483.13.
21. CMS SURVEY GUIDANCE, *supra* note 3, at PP-59.
22. Dusine v. Golden Shores Convalescent Ctr., 249 So. 2d 40 (Fla. Dist. Ct. App. 1971).
23. MeadowWood Nursing Home v. U.S. Dep't of HHS, 364 F.3d 786 (6th Cir. 2004).
24. *See, e.g.*, Powell v. Parkview Estate Nursing Home, 240 So. 2d 53 (La. Ct. App. 1970).

and increased anger, anxiety, fear, depression, and humiliation of the individual wearing the restraint.

Bed fall cases often involve the use of side rails as restraints. In some cases, the side rails of the institution's beds are raised to prevent movement by the resident, and these side rails have the effect of preventing mobility unless the resident tries to climb over that rail. In theory, the individual should ring the call button and an aide should respond promptly to assist the resident in using the toilet. Because the CMS standards on restraints are not being followed carefully in some nursing homes, and restraints are sometimes excessively used to make up for staff shortages, the failure to reasonably control restraints will result in a potential injury situation.[25]

An Oregon jury awarded $1 million in punitive damages to the survivors of a person who was restrained for 24 hours a day without a physician's order, contrary to the CMS rules. To free himself, the resident set himself on fire, and subsequently died of burns.[26]

In cases alleging negligent failure to apply restraints, the courts have sometimes enforced the home's policy and held it to be negligence not to restrain especially vulnerable residents.[27] One court dismissed the negligence complaint alleging improper nonuse of a restraint, where the nursing home had a policy against using restraints, the resident was not under a doctor's order for the use of restraints, and there was no other requirement for the use of a restraint.[28]

11:4 CMS and State Norms

The restraints used on residents are limited by federal rules to emergencies and in certain nonemergency situations as directed by a

---

25. Evan Meyers, *Physical Restraints in Nursing Homes*, 10 ELDER L.J. 217 (2002).

26. Saunders v. Beverly Enters, No. 89C-10930 (Marion Cty. Or. filed March 18, 1999), *discussed in* Julie Braun & Elizabeth Capezuti, *The Legal and Medical Aspects of Physical Restraints and Bed Siderails and Their Relationship to Falls and Fall-Related Injuries in Nursing Homes*, 4 DEPAUL J. HEALTH CARE LAW 1, 38 (2000).

27. Marotta v. Whitehall of St. Petersburg, 195 So. 2d 225 (Fla. Dist. Ct. App. 1967).

28. Abrahams v. King St. Nursing Home, Inc., 245 A.D.2d 251 (App. Civ. 2d Dep't 1997).

physician.[29] The excessive use of restraints is a violation punishable by civil penalties[30] because it affects the dignity of residents and can be "emotionally and physically devastating."[31] The federal agency regulating nursing homes found that "despite their problematic history which included risks of misuse and potential for severe and even fatal consequences, such restraints also provide benefits in some situations, when their use is carefully controlled."[32]

State laws may also forbid the use of "bodily or chemical restraints on a mentally ill person which is not in compliance with Federal and State laws and regulations."[33] But the inability to use a set of restraints on a particular resident does not prevent the nursing home from safeguarding vulnerable residents by restricting the access of an assaultive or aggressive resident to the areas where vulnerable residents reside.[34]

In CMS penalty cases against nursing homes for excessive use of restraints, CMS attorneys must make a prima facie showing that there was a "potential for even minimal harm to the resident from the few instances in which the [restraint] was not released per the physician's orders, assuming that the record of routine care is accurate."[35]

11:5 FDA Hazard Alerts

Counsel for plaintiff in a physical restraint device injury case should become familiar with the Food and Drug Administration's (FDA) safety alerts on resident restraint devices.[36] The misuse of the restraint may

29. 42 C.F.R. § 483.13, 42 U.S.C. § 1819(c)(I)(A)(ii).

30. Lakeridge Villa Health Care Ctr. v. Leavitt, 202 F. App'x 903 (6th Cir. 2006).

31. Proposed Rules, Protective Restraints, 57 Fed. Reg. 27,397 (June 19, 1992); Cross Creek Health Care Ctr. v. Health Care Fin. Admin., Dec. No. 1665 (HHS Departmental Appeals Bd., App. Div., July 14, 1998), http://www.hhs.gov/dab/decisions/dabl665.html.

32. Proposed Rules, Protective Restraints, 57 Fed. Reg. 27,397 (June 19, 1992).

33. People v. Johnson, 595 N.E.2d 1381 (Ill. App. Ct. 1992).

34. Associated Health Sys. v. Jones, 366 S.E.2d 147 (Ga. Ct. App. 1988).

35. Evergreene Nursing Care Ctr. v. CMS, Dec. No. C-05-386 (HHS Departmental Appeals Bd., Civ. Remedies Div., Aug. 18, 2005), http://www.hhs.gov/dab/decisions/CR1337.htm.

36. *See* U.S. Food & Drug Admin., Medical Device Safety Communications, http://www.fda.gov/MedicalDevices/Safety/AlertsandNotices/; U.S. Food & Drug Admin., Medical Device Safety Archive, http://www.fda.gov/MedicalDevices/Safety/AlertsandNotices/ucm312901.htm; U.S. Food & Drug Admin., Medical & Radiation Emitting Device Recalls, http://www.accessdata.fda.gov/scripts/cdrh/cfdocs/cfres/res.cfm.

have violated a warning or contraindication placed on the restraint or in its FDA-reviewed labeling instructions.

11:6 Summary

Who can sue? The resident or his or her personal representative; in wrongful death cases, a person described in the state wrongful death legislation.

What is the duty of care? The use of resident restraints should follow the directions given by the manufacturer and in any labeling required by the FDA for these types of restraints. Use of restraints may be limited for this type of resident by state nursing home standards.

What is the injury? Death by strangulation, fall-related trauma, and other injuries from use or misuse of the restraints.

How do you prove that substandard care was the cause of the injury? Use expert witness testimony concerning proper use of restraints and concerning the contraindications for restraint use on certain residents.

Whom should you sue? The facility and affiliated relevant corporations; in rare situations, the prescriber and perhaps the restraint manufacturer or supplier may have been negligent, or be liable under product liability laws, along with the facility staff.

How do you go about proving your case? Gather the physical evidence including the actual restraint; photograph the scene; depose the employee(s) who found the resident who was harmed by the restraint; obtain the restraint manufacturer's labeling and warnings; obtain the resident chart; depose the physician who gave express permission for the restraint to be utilized.

CHAPTER 12

Assault and Abuse

12:1 Overview
12:2 Long-Term Care Ombudsmen Programs
12:3 Incidence of Abuse
12:4 Overview of Intentional Harm: Abuse by Caregivers
12:5 Overview of Neglect by Caregivers
12:6 Overview of Abuse by Other Residents and Nonemployee Third Parties
12:7 Criminal Aspects
12:8 Definitions
12:9 Sources of Assaults
12:10 Regulatory Duty of Care for Protection of Residents
12:11 Nursing Home Response to Assaults
12:12 Framing the Complaint for Civil Tort Liability
12:13 State Alternative Malpractice Remedies
12:14 Defending the Nursing Home's Supervision
12:15 Rape and Sexual Assault
12:16 Effects of Shock and Public Outrage
12:17 Allegations of Concealment of the Assault
12:18 Allegations of Employee Hiring and Supervision Errors
12:19 CMS and State Penalties
12:20 Punitive Damages
12:21 Liability Insurance
12:22 Evidentiary Issues
12:23 Governmental Immunity
12:24 Effect of Resident Assault on Liability to Employees

12:1 Overview

In 1986, the Institute of Medicine issued its now-famous report, *Improving the Quality of Care in Nursing Homes,*[1] detailing the shocking degree of abuse in nursing homes. This report triggered the passage of the Nursing Home Reform Act of 1987, part of the Omnibus Budget Reconciliation Act of 1987 (OBRA). OBRA provided nursing home residents protections from abuse and neglect, commonly referred to as "elder abuse," over and above common law tort and criminal law provisions.

"Elder abuse" is a general term that includes a range of harmful actions and inactions that affect older adults. This conduct includes, among others, seven overall categories: physical, sexual, emotional, verbal, and psychological abuse; financial exploitation; neglect; and in some cases, self-neglect.[2] The terms "elder mistreatment" or "elder maltreatment" have been used by researchers to indicate the same concepts. Some definitions exclude self-neglect as a form of elder abuse by limiting the definition to encompass only abuse, neglect, or exploitation from third parties such as a caregiver or other person in a position of trust.[3]

The 2006 amendments to the Older Americans Act provide clear definitions for the terms "elder justice,"[4] "exploitation,"[5] "neglect,"[6] and "self-neglect."[7] Unfortunately, these definitions and others have not been uniformly adopted across federal agencies, states, or state agencies which hampers the uniformity and reliability of the data collection on this serious problem.

---

1. Inst. of Med., Improving the Quality of Care in Nursing Homes (1986), http://www.iom.edu/Reports/1986/Improving-the-Quality-of-Care-in-Nursing-Homes.aspx.
2. U.S. Dep't of Health & Human Servs., Congressional Report on the Feasibility of Establishing a Uniform National Database on Elder Abuse (Mar. 2010), http://aspe.hhs.gov/daltcp/reports/2010/elderCR.htm.
3. T. Tatara et al., Types of Elder Abuse in Domestic Settings (Elder Abuse Info. Series No. 1, Nat'l Ctr. on Elder Abuse, 1999), http://www.ncea.aoa.gov/Resources/Publication/docs/fact1.pdf.
4. Older Americans Act Amendments of 2006, Pub. L. No. 109-365, 109th Congress § 102(17).
5. *Id.* at § 102(18)(A).
6. *Id.* at § 102(38).
7. *Id.* at § 102(47).

The pervasiveness of nursing home abuse, based on what data there is, is a serious, and likely growing, public health issue. In 2020, there were more than 15,000 nursing homes[8] housing approximately 1.3 million residents.[9] Research indicates that more than 40 percent of people over the age of 65 will enter a nursing home before they die.[10] Unfortunately, "[o]ver 50% of nursing home staff admitted to mistreating . . . older residents" (this mistreatment included physical violence, mental abuse and neglect).[11] One survey of certified nursing assistants found that 17 percent had pushed, grabbed, or shoved a nursing home resident. Fifty-one percent reported they had yelled at a resident and 23 percent had insulted or sworn at a resident.[12] Seven percent of all complaints regarding institutional facilities reported to long-term care ombudsmen were complaints of abuse, neglect, or exploitation.[13]

Of special concern are the high rates of abuse of those with dementia. As described below, one of the root causes of abuse and neglect is the frustration of caregivers dealing with those with behavioral disorders common to people with dementia. In one U.S. study, 20 percent of caregivers expressed fears that they would become violent with the people for whom they cared for.[14] Three international studies found

---

8. Nat'l Acads. of Scis., Eng'g & Med., The National Imperative to Improve Nursing Home Quality: Honoring Our Commitment to Residents, Families, and Staff (The National Academies Press 2022), https://nap.nationalacademies.org/catalog/26526/the-national-imperative-to-improve-nursing-home-quality-honoring-our; Nat'l Ctr. on Elder Abuse, Fact Sheet: Elder Abuse Prevalence and Incidence (2005), https://www.vdh.virginia.gov/content/uploads/sites/18/2016/04/finalstatistics050331.pdf [hereinafter NCEA Fact Sheet]. Roughly two out of three residents are women, and six of seven are 65 years or older. Nat'l Ctr. on Elder Abuse, *Research Brief: Elder Mistreatment in Long-Term Care* (Aug. 2022), https://pfs2.acl.gov/strapib/assets/RB_LTC_ec96f4dd2e.pdf [hereinafter NCEA Research Brief].

9. *Id.*

10. C. Murtaugh, et al., *The Amount, Distribution, and Timing of Lifetime Nursing Home Use*, 35 Med. Care 204–18 (1997), http://www.ncbi.nlm.nih.gov/pubmed/9071254.

11. M. Ben Natan, et al., *A Study of Factors That Affect Abuse of Older People in Nursing Homes*, 17 Nursing Mgmt. 20–24 (2010), http://www.ncbi.nlm.nih.gov/pubmed/21229867.

12. K. Pillemer, et al., *A Model Abuse Prevention Program for Nursing Assistants*, 33 Gerontologist 128–31 (1993), http://gerontologist.oxfordjournals.org/content/33/1/128.abstract.

13. Nat'l Ctr. on Elder Abuse, Research Brief: Abuse of Residents of Long Term Care Facilities (2012), http://www.ncea.aoa.gov/Resources/Publication/docs/LTCF_ResearchBrief_web508.pdf.

14. K. Pillemer, et al., *Violence and Violent Feelings: What Causes Them among Family Caregivers?*, 47 J. Gerontology S165-S172 (1992).

overall rates of abuse of people with dementia by their caregivers ranging from 34 to 62 percent.[15] In a U.S. study, caregiver abuse and neglect of people with dementia was detected in 47.3 percent of the surveyed caregivers.[16] This problem is likely to grow worse. Currently, approximately 6.7 million Americans of all ages have Alzheimer's disease. In 2030 approximately 7.7 million people will have Alzheimer's disease, and the number will increase to 16 million in 2050.[17]

The actual number and severity of intentional harm and sexual assaults on nursing home residents, whether by strangers, staff, or other residents, is difficult to determine.[18] This population is highly vulnerable and is composed of people who may be immobilized, incoherent, or otherwise incapacitated. This means that many abused or neglected elders are incapable, or are unwilling, to self-report.[19]

This tracks a general tendency among victims of intentional harm to underreport, fearing retribution by a known assailant[20] or the hassles of the law enforcement system; and even those nursing home residents

---

15. C. Cooney, et al., *Abuse of Vulnerable People with Dementia by Their Carers: Can We Identify Those Most at Risk?*, 21 INT'L J. GERIATRIC PSYCHIATRY 564–71 (2006); C. Cooper et al., *Abuse of People with Dementia by Family Carers: Representative Cross Sectional Survey*, 339 BRITISH MED. J. 339 1–5 (2009); E. Yan, et al., *Abuse of Older Chinese with Dementia by Family Caregivers: An Inquiry into the Role of Caregiver Burden*, 10 INT'L J. GERIATRIC PSYCHIATRY 2561 (2010).

16. *Alzheimer's Disease Facts and Figures*, ALZHEIMER'S ASS'N, https://www.alz.org/alzheimers-dementia/facts-figures#:~:text=in%20the%20U.S.-,Prevalence,living%20with%20Alzheimer's%20in%202023 (last visited Dec. 16, 2024).

17. NAT'L CTR. ON ELDER ABUSE, RESEARCH BRIEF: HOW AT RISK FOR ABUSE ARE PEOPLE WITH DEMENTIA? (2012), http://www.ncea.aoa.gov/Resources/Publication/docs/Dementia_ResearchBrief_web508.pdf.

18. Data regarding elder abuse, whether in long-term care facilities or in private homes, is both incomplete and unreliable. According to Karl Pillemer and David Finkelhor, "[d]ata on elder abuse in domestic settings suggest that 1 in 14 incidents, excluding incidents of self-neglect, come to the attention of authorities." NCEA Research Brief, *supra* note 8. Abuse is also inflicted on younger, incapacitated residents. *See, e.g.*, Vandalia Park v. Leavitt, 157 F. App'x 858 (6th Cir. 2005).

19. *See, e.g.*, Bezark v. Kostner Manor, Inc., 172 N.E.2d 424, 426 (Ill. App. Ct. 1961).

20. In general, confidentiality laws are not thought to hinder the collection of data on elder abuse by ombudsman representatives, but they do interfere with sharing that information across enforcement and service systems. Ombudsmen are prohibited from sharing information about cases with law enforcement unless they have the specific consent of the resident or his or her guardian. Residents may be reluctant to allow the ombudsman to report to law enforcement or the state's licensing agency for fear of retaliation by the perpetrator(s). Some ombudsman representatives reportedly find this to be a significant and frustrating barrier.

who are coherent and willing to report may not be believed by police or prosecutors. This problem is likely to be somewhat ameliorated if ombudsmen programs adopt a new proposed requirement that reports of abuse remain anonymous if requested.[21]

12:2 Long-Term Care Ombudsmen Programs

To give a bit of background, state long-term care ombudsmen are charged with protecting the rights of residents of long-term care facilities. Ombudsmen advocate for residents' rights and quality care, educate consumers and providers, and resolve residents' complaints. Under the federal Older Americans Act, every state is required to have an ombudsman program that addresses complaints and advocates for improvements in the long-term care system.[22]

The ombudsman program was established in 1972 as a demonstration program under the Older Americans Act, but no final regulations implementing the program have been issued. "'In the absence of regulatory guidance, there has been significant variation in the interpretation and implementation of [the law] among states,' [the Administration on Aging, "AoA"] said. In addition, the Institute of Medicine recently identified the lack of federal guidance as a challenge for state implementation that contributed to an absence of fully implemented state ombudsman programs, AoA said."[23] In response, the AoA issued a rule intended to clarify responsibilities of ombudsmen assisting the elderly

---

U.S. Dep't of Health & Human Servs., Congressional Report on the Feasibility of Establishing a Uniform National Database on Elder Abuse (Mar. 2010), http://aspe.hhs.gov/daltcp/reports/2010/elderCR.htm.

21. *Id.*

22. The quality and uniformity of data collected and reported by ombudsmen may be limited by low staffing levels and different levels of training about reporting for staff and volunteers across states. In 1995, the Institute of Medicine published an evaluation of long-term care ombudsman programs that recommended one full-time ombudsman for every 2,000 nursing facility beds in the state. Most states rely heavily on volunteers to operate their ombudsman programs in addition to paid staff. Ombudsman representatives are trained to be advocates, not protective services caseworkers or forensic investigators, and may not report all complaints to the National Ombudsman Reporting System or to a state's survey agency or nurse aide registry. *Id.*

23. 45 C.F.R. pt. 1324.

in long-term care facilities nationwide. The amendment addressed responsibilities of state agencies housing long-term care ombudsman offices not to disclose the identity of any person sending a complaint to the ombudsman or the identity of any resident of a long-term care facility.

In particular, under the rule, the ombudsman must maximize resident participation in resolving the complaint by ensuring resident confidentiality, discussing the complaint with the resident and/or his or her representative, determine the resident's wishes for the resolution of the complaint, advise the resident of his or her rights, develop a plan of action with the resident, investigate the complaint, and determine whether the complaint is resolved to the resident's satisfaction.[24]

Nursing home ombudsman complaints fell during the COVID-19 pandemic.[25] The decline is likely linked to pandemic lockdowns. Complaint numbers have continued to rise steadily in the post-pandemic era.[26] As of July 2023, nursing homes nationwide averaged 8.5 deficiencies per facility.[27] Approximately 26 percent of facilities were cited for serious deficiencies, reflecting either "actual harm" or "immediate jeopardy" to residents.[28] Of the citations nationwide as of July 2023, 70 percent were for quality of care, 55 percent were for resident rights violations, 53 percent were for pharmacy services, 50 percent were for food and nutrition services, 47 percent were for the comprehensive resident-centered care plan, 46 percent were for infection control, and 31 percent were related to abuse, neglect, and exploitation.[29]

24. *Id.* pt. 1324.19(b).

25. National Long-Term Care Ombudsman Resource Center, 2023 NORS Multi-Year Complaint Trend Report (May 15, 2024), https://ltcombudsman.org/uploads/files/support/NORS_MultiYrTrendFFY_2019_2020_2021_2022_2023.xlsx.

26. *Id.*

27. *Average Number of Deficiencies per Certified Nursing Facility: 2024*, KFF, https://www.kff.org/other/state-indicator/avg-of-nursing-facility-deficiencies/?currentTimeframe=0&sortModel=%7B%22colId%22:%22Location%22,%22sort%22:%22asc%22%7D (last visited Dec. 17, 2024).

28. *Percent of Certified Nursing Facilities Receiving a Deficiency for Actual Harm or Jeopardy: 2024*, KFF, https://www.kff.org/other/state-indicator/of-facilities-w-serious-deficiencies/?currentTimeframe=0&sortModel=%7B%22colId%22:%22Location%22,%22sort%22:%22asc%22%7D (last visited Dec. 17, 2024).

29. *Percent of Certified Nursing Facilities with Top Ten Deficiencies: 2024*, KFF, https://www.kff.org/other/state-indicator/percent-of-certified-nursing-facilities-with

12:3 Incidence of Abuse

A 2002 study by congressional investigators found that one-third of the nursing homes surveyed had been cited for abuse, and that imminent jeopardy or actual harm had been found in 1,600 homes.[30] Physical abuse accounted for approximately 4,500 reported incidents per year.[31] Sexual abuse was the least reported of several categories of abuse.[32] Of the complaints involving institutional facilities made to long-term care ombudsmen, seven percent were complaints of abuse, neglect, or exploitation.[33] A study conducted in 2000 that involved the interviews of 2,000 nursing home residents revealed that 44 percent of those interviewed stated that they had been abused and 95 percent stated that they had been neglected or seen another resident neglected.[34] A study conducted by the U.S. General Accountability Office in 2008 showed that that state surveys commonly miss neglect and abuse problems in licensed facilities. According to this study, 70 percent of state surveys miss at least one deficiency and 15 percent fail to identify actual harm and immediate jeopardy of nursing home residents.[35]

Of note is that this problem with abuse and neglect is likely to grow as the population ages and more adults enter the nursing home population. People 65 and older numbered 55.8 million in the 2020 census,

---

-top-ten-deficiencies-2014/?currentTimeframe=0&sortModel=%7B%22colId%22:%22Location%22,%22sort%22:%22asc%22%7D (last visited Dec. 17, 2024).

30. House Report, addressed in John Parisi, *Fighting Fraud in Long Term Care, in* Nursing Home Litigation: Pretrial Practice and Trials 275 (Ruben Krisztal ed., 2d ed. 2003).

31. Office of Inspector Gen., Dep't of Health & Human Servs., No. OEI-09-02-00160, State Ombudsman Data: Nursing Home Complaints 11 (July 2003), http://oig.hhs.gov/oei/reports/oei-09-02-00160.pdf.

32. *Id.* at 14. OIG did not provide more information about sexual abuse incidents in this report. Federal regulations also prohibit mental or verbal abuse. *See* Salmon v. Dep't of Pub. Health & Addiction Servs., 788 A.2d 1199, 1203 (Conn. 2002) (citing 42 U.S.C. § 1395i-3(c)(1)(a)(ii) (2008)).

33. U.S. Dep't of Health & Human Servs., Admin. on Aging, 2010 National Ombudsman Reporting System Data Tables (2010), http://www.aoa.gov/aoa_programs/elder_rights/Ombudsman/National_State_Data/2010/Index.aspx.

34. K. Broyles, *The Silenced Voice Speaks Out: A Study of Abuse and Neglect of Nursing Home Residents* (2000) (report from the Atlanta Long Term Care Ombudsman Program and Atlanta Legal Aid Society to the National Citizens Coalition for Nursing Home Reform).

35. U.S. Gov't Accounting Office, GAO-08-517, Nursing Homes: Federal Monitoring Surveys Demonstrate Continued Understatement of Serious Care Problems and CMS Oversight Weaknesses (2008).

representing 16.8 percent of the U.S. population. This is about one in every six Americans.[36] Looking ahead, by 2030, there will be 72.1 million people over 65 years old in the United States, comprising about 19 percent of the population.[37] The U.S. Census Bureau projects that, until around 2034, the majority of the older population will be relatively young—age 65–74. However, by 2034, all of the baby boomers will be over 70. To put this aging of the older population in perspective, in 2010, only 14 percent of older Americans were over 85. By 2050, more than 21 percent of the older population will be 85 and older. This growth is notable as this oldest segment of our elders requires the greatest amount of support and care.[38]

Educating judges about the extent of this problem and the public policy impact of judicial decisions regarding abuse and neglect on overall public health policy will act to help a plaintiff's case. Importantly, it will also help judges to better understand how the law can influence how nursing homes operate and care for their residents

12:4 Overview of Intentional Harm: Abuse by Caregivers

For purposes of tort law, it is important to distinguish *abuse* from *neglect*. Abuse is an affirmative act that is intended to cause harm.[39] In contrast, neglect is generally the failure to act to provide care that is necessary to avoid injury.[40] Just a quick pointer on terminology that is likely to be of help in avoiding confusion in reading case law in this area. In common law tort cases, assault and battery are two different causes of action. Assault is the intent to put another in imminent apprehension of a touching that is harmful. In contrast, a cause of action for battery arises when actual physical harm has occurred. In

---

36. Zoe Caplan & Megan Rabe, *The Older Population: 2020*, U.S. CENSUS BUREAU (May 2023), https://www2.census.gov/library/publications/decennial/2020/census-briefs/c2020br-07.pdf.

37. U.S. Dep't of Health & Human Servs., Admin. on Aging, Aging Statistics, http://www.aoa.gov/AoARoot/Aging_Statistics/index.aspx (last visited June 21, 2013).

38. U.S. CENSUS BUREAU, THE NEXT FOUR DECADES—THE OLDER POPULATION IN THE UNITED STATES: 2010 TO 2050 (May 10, 2010).

39. MEDICAL-LEGAL ASPECTS OF LONG-TERM CARE 279 (Jeffrey Levine ed., 2003).

40. *Id.*

both criminal law and in many state civil statutes that create a private cause of action for elder abuse, the term "assault" is used to refer to conduct that, in tort common law, is referred to as battery. The reader will see that the term "assault" is, at times, incorrectly used in civil tort cases when, in fact, the correct term that should be used is battery.

The dated "bad apples" approach to preventing abuse by caregivers in nursing homes is grounded in the idea that abuse is caused by evil-minded perpetrators motivated by outright malice, gratuitous infliction of harm, or reckless disregard for the safety of residents. Thus, the answer to the problem of abuse was single-mindedly driven by the goal of identification and then removal of these bad apples. To this end, the Centers for Medicaid & Medicare Services (CMS) requires nursing homes to have processes in place to "[s]creen potential employees for a history of abuse, neglect or mistreating residents . . . which includes attempting to obtain information from previous employers and/or current employers, and checking with the appropriate licensing boards and registries."[41] One such registry is the National Practitioners Data Bank (NPDB) set up by the Health Care Quality Improvement Act (HCQIA).[42] Under HCQIA and its regulations, multiple different organizations are required to report information that allegedly reflects poor quality resident care by physicians.[43] NPDB reports include not only physicians and dentists but also nurses and nurse's aides.[44] In addition, the list of entities that can query the NPDB has expanded to include "private sector hospitals, nursing homes, and other organizations so that they may be used when making employment, affiliation, certification, or licensure decisions."[45]

---

41. Ctrs. for Medicare & Medicaid Servs., State Operations Manual, CMS Pub. No. 100-07, Appendix PP: Guidance to Surveyors for Long Term Care Facilities 47 (2006) (referring to Guidelines for 42 U.S.C. § 483.13(c)(1)(ii)(A) & (B) for F226) [hereinafter CMS Survey Guidance].

42. *See* 42 U.S.C. § 11101 (2006).

43. U.S. Gov't Accountability Office, GAO-01-130, National Practitioner Data Bank: Major Improvements Are Needed to Enhance Data Bank's Reliability 7 (2000), http://www.gao.gov/assets/240/230998.pdf.

44. HHS National Practitioner Data Bank for Adverse Information on Physicians and Other Health Care Practitioners, 45 C.F.R. pt. 60, §§ 60.1–60.16 (2012).

45. U.S. Dep't of Health & Human Servs., Data Bank: Legislations & Regulations, http://www.npdb-hipdb.hrsa.gov/resources/section1921.jsp. Thus: "Hospitals and their human

The reality is that while some abuse is caused by bad apples, the root causes of most abuse are more complicated and call for multifactored interventions. The most prevalent trigger of an act of physical abuse is a resident's own behavior. For example, when a resident refuses to cooperate with a caregiver who is trying to complete an assigned task quickly in order to move on to the next task on a long laundry list of other tasks that must be finished by the end of the work period, the caregiver may become frustrated. This frustration can lead to an impulsive physical response that does not come close to the stereotype of the unprovoked malicious attack.[46] Another common problem is the use of physical punishment by caregivers for perceived wrongdoing on the part of the resident that is in keeping with the norms of the caregivers' cultural background.[47] Important to the creation of both preventive measures and liability avoidance is that impulsive physical abuse is more prevalent than malicious abuse.

One of the most common root causes for impulsive physical abuse is unrelieved stress and burnout from understaffing. Another common root cause is the failure of nursing homes to train staff members in appropriate strategies to deal with both stress and uncooperative and disruptive resident behaviors. As the resident safety movement points out, these are systems failures, not individual failures.[48] Thus, the solutions for the most common causes of abuse include systematic changes in order to ensure adequate staffing and training. These systematic changes must be continuously evaluated and improved upon in a cycle referred to in quality improvement circles as "continuous quality improvement." CMS recognizes this continuous quality improvement

---

resource departments and nurse recruitment offices now have access to licensure actions on all types of health care professionals. They may query the Data Bank on all types of health care professionals including nurses, nurse aides, and other allied health care professionals when making their hiring decisions. The ability to perform preemployment screenings of potential health care employees is an invaluable resource that can enhance the hiring process and increase an organization's efforts toward patient safety." *Id.*

46. C.K. Beck, *Interventions for Treating Disruptive Behavior in Demented Elderly People*, 29 Nursing Clinics of N. Am. 143–55 (1994).

47. Medical-Legal Aspects of Long-Term Care, *supra* note 39, at 293.

48. Inst. of Med., To Err Is Human: Building a Safer Health System (Linda T. Kohn et al. eds., 2000).

approach by requiring that nursing home administrations adopt and implement seven anti-abuse policies.[49] These prevention policies, and the procedures to implement them, should stress zero tolerance for abuse. Minimum staffing levels should be set along with optimum staffing goals. Employees should be trained in stress management, behavior management, and the care of dementia residents on an ongoing basis.[50] Policies and practices should be instituted to identify and investigate possible abuse as well as protect residents during these investigations. If neglect or abuse is found, an appropriate system of interventions should be created, implemented, and assessed on an ongoing basis. Policies and practices for reporting acts of abuse must also be established.[51]

What does all of this mean for litigating the nursing home case?

Under the "bad apples" approach to abuse, it follows that a nursing home can be found directly liable for negligent hiring by failing to use reasonable care in doing background checks before hiring the abusive worker when a reasonable investigation would have disclosed a propensity to commit abuse. The nursing home may also be found directly liable for the failure to protect the resident if there was reasonable notice that the resident was at risk of abuse by an employee. However, it is unlikely that a cause of action for the respondeat superior liability of the nursing home will be successful. An employer can be found liable under respondeat superior for the acts of its employees that cause harm when those acts are committed within the scope of their employment. However, the intentional torts of employees, though committed while on the job, are not considered to be committed within the scope of employment.

Adding to the foregoing causes of action, under the continuous quality improvement approach to the prevention of abuse, the nursing home can be found directly liable for the failure to use reasonable care in training the employees in the appropriate interventions to deal with uncooperative or aggressive residents as well as what measures

49. CMS Survey Guidance, *supra* note 41, at F226 (2006).
50. *Id.*
51. *Id.*

to avoid as they rise to the level of abuse. The nursing home can also be held directly liable for failure to use reasonable care to provide a proper level of staffing that contributes to abuse. Under this theory, the use of the substantial factor test for causation will assist a lawyer in establishing liability. One resource that is of help during the preliminary investigation, before discovery of the actual nursing home records, is the information that CMS currently provides on the staffing levels of nursing homes on its Nursing Home Compare webpage.[52]

Nursing homes do well in defending against these claims if they have clear written policies and practices in place that are reasonable under the circumstances unique to the particular nursing home and that clearly comply with CMS regulations. To help in their defense, nursing homes must regularly document their adherence to these policies and practices and regularly assess whether these policies and practices are having their desired effect or if reasonable new interventions should be implemented. As discussed in Chapter 8, compliance with CMS regulations and nationally recognized clinical practice guidelines with auspice authenticity is good evidence that the nursing home complied with the standard of care.

12:5 Overview of Neglect by Caregivers

In contrast to abuse, which generally is a single act of impulsive physical harm or a malicious act by a caregiver, neglect is a pattern of failure to provide care necessary to avoid harm. This pattern generally occurs over a period of time and results in an injury or injuries. This pattern of failures can be on the part of one member of a caregiving team or it can be a failure on the part of the entire team. The root causes of neglect can be the same resident behavior problems that give rise to impulsive acts of abuse—obstructive or belligerent behavior that interferes with the delivery of care. Commonly, neglect occurs when a nursing home is understaffed. It can also arise out of a lack of understanding

52. Ctrs. for Medicare & Medicaid Servs., Nursing Home Compare, http://www.medicare.gov/nursinghomecompare/.

of the special needs of the elderly in the areas of nutrition, skin care, strength and mobility, polypharmacy, and the special issues associated with dementia, among many other areas. Finally, as discussed in earlier chapters, it can result from a continued reliance upon customary care practices and the failure to adopt best practices based upon clinical practice guidelines. For a full discussion of the negative effect of these customary care practices, see Chapter 26.

In this situation, the employees will be liable in negligence or medical malpractice for the failure to exercise reasonable care for the safety of the resident. The nursing home will be liable under the doctrine of respondeat superior for the acts of their employees committed within the scope of their employment. The nursing home will also likely be held directly liable for the failure to use reasonable care to adequately train and supervise these employees. This neglect will likely also violate CMS's standard of care as reflected in its regulations. As discussed in prior chapters, the violations of these regulations may give rise to a cause of action for negligence per se in some states, and in others, can be good evidence of the standard of care. For a full discussion of negligence per se, see Chapter 26.

To better understand nursing home neglect, the statutory definition is helpful. "Neglect is the failure of the facility, its employees or service providers to provide goods and services to a resident that are necessary to avoid physical harm, pain, mental anguish, or emotional distress."[53] Notice, first, that a nursing home can neglect a resident both by the actions of its employees and by the actions of "service providers," potentially opening nursing homes to liability for independent contractors, contrary to typical norms for vicarious/respondeat superior liability. Likewise, a nursing home's "failure . . . to provide goods and services that are necessary to avoid physical harm, pain, mental anguish, or emotional distress"[54] can be broadly interpreted. Such failures can include failing to provide consistent toileting practices, allowing residents to develop pressure injuries through a lack

53. 42 C.F.R. pt. 483.5.
54. *Id.*

of turning and repositioning, and allowing residents to become malnourished because staff cannot feed them their meals as needed. The list of causes is equally as long as the list of effects.

12:6 Overview of Abuse by Other Residents and Nonemployee Third Parties

The harm committed by nonemployee third parties and other residents should be evaluated differently from that of nursing home employees. Tort liability on the part of the nursing home in this situation is likely to be grounded solely in its failure to protect the residents under its care. Thus, the issues will be whether the nursing home (1) had notice of the risk of harm from the third party or other resident and (2) failed to take reasonable steps to avoid that risk. There will not be any issue of respondeat superior liability.

The sexual or physical assault of a nursing home resident is not an easy topic to think about, talk about, or debate in public. By virtue of their physical and mental issues, the residents of nursing homes are the persons least capable of protecting themselves from harm from third parties. Therefore, the amount of care that must reasonably be exercised to protect the safety of these residents is much greater than that which would be owed to an average person. The amount of care should be seen to be proportional to the degree of vulnerability of each resident and the risk of harm from the failure to protect.[55] Jury pools drawn from elders and those who have had relatives or friends in nursing homes are particularly sensitive to plaintiffs whose injuries occurred while they were captive victims of those who intentionally inflict harm.

Tied to the failure to prevent avoidable risks is the potential for liability on the back end: namely, failing to appropriately respond once an incident has occurred. Nursing homes, especially those that are generally poorly performing, do not wish to advertise their failures, even when state and federal laws and regulations require it. For

55. *See, e.g.*, Shepard v. Mielke, 877 P.2d 220 (Wash. Ct. App. 1994).

example, many states have laws for mandatory reporting of any allegations of abuse or neglect.[56] The same can be said for allegations of sexual assault. However, given the number of lawsuits filed against nursing homes based upon allegations that have never been reported to any governmental agency, there can be little doubt that nursing home employees do little to police activities within their own walls. Residents themselves fear retaliation if they report abuse.[57]

In the context of resident-on-resident assaults, a nursing home's liability is multifaceted. As a threshold matter, all residents must be assessed to determine their individual care needs. Nursing homes also have the responsibility to provide a safe environment for their residents. Often, in a resident-on-resident assault, both parties are victims. The aggressor typically suffers from a mental condition like dementia. The assaulted resident is the target of the aggressor's efforts to fulfill an unsatisfied need.

By way of example, imagine two residents sharing a room. The aggressor resident, John, suffers from dementia with a known history of aggression. A careful discussion with John's family during the intake process would have disclosed that his aggression is triggered by loud noises. However, due to a speedy and inadequate intake process, this fact is never disclosed. John is placed in a shared room with a fellow resident who suffers from significant hearing loss, requiring the television in their shared room to be very loud. Due to diminished capacity, John is unable to verbalize his needs. John assaults his roommate due to his needs being unmet upon admission.

As a second example, imagine a memory care ward where Jane and Joan are both residents. Jane is known to walk the halls of the unit, entering other residents' rooms. Jane frequently becomes confused due to her dementia. Without proper redirection and assurance from staff, Jane can become aggressive. One night, Jane is once again walking the halls. Staff are aware of this. But, because they are understaffed, even

56. *See* 42 C.F.R. pt. 483.12(c).

57. Nada Hassanein, *Why Aren't Nursing Home Residents Reporting Abuse? Fear of Retaliation, Study Finds*, USA Today (June 16, 2023), https://www.usatoday.com/story/news/health/2023/06/16/nursing-home-residents-fear-retaliation/70317690007/.

more so than usual on the night shift, they make no effort to stop Jane. Jane enters Joan's room. Jane sees Joan sleeping in bed. Confused by her condition and the fact that every room is outfitted in an identical fashion, Jane believes Joan is trespassing and sleeping in Jane's bed. Jane drags Joan from the bed, causing Joan to fall to the floor and suffer significant injuries.

12:7 Criminal Aspects

We begin with a nontort reality: assault is a crime.[58] Crimes should be prosecuted wherever possible. Assault on elders tends to be treated as an aggravated level of crime under state statutes.[59] The crime of assault can occur in different levels of violence; slapping residents could be prosecuted as an aggravated battery.[60] More frequent use of criminal law remedies is needed.[61] Unlike most interpersonal interactions that may occur in the nursing home setting, assaults are subject to mandatory reporting under most state rules.[62]

The revulsion and shame evoked by the crime of assault on an immobile sick person poses a problem for the institutional defendant in civil cases, making settlements more likely to be substantial.[63] When an individual sexually assaults or physically attacks a nursing home resident, civil liability usually follows, and this liability falls on the home because the actual assailant is usually unknown, unavailable, or unable to pay.

Nursing home operators have responsibility for protection of their residents from intentional harm by employees, strangers, or other

---

58. Robert Polisky, *Criminalizing Physical and Emotional Elder Abuse*, 3 ELDER L.J. 377 (1995).

59. Ana Ramares, Annotation, *Criminal Assault or Battery Statutes Making Attack on Elderly Person a Special or Aggravated Offense*, 73 A.L.R.4th 1123 (1989).

60. People v. Johnson, 595 N.E.2d 1381 (Ill. App. Ct. 1992).

61. Michael Davidson, *Governmental Responses to Elder Abuse and Neglect in Nursing Homes*, 12 ELDER L.J. 327 (2004).

62. James Buchwalter, Annotation, *Validity, Construction, and Application of State Civil and Criminal Elder Abuse Laws*, 113 A.L.R.5th 431 (2003).

63. NURSING HOME LITIGATION: INVESTIGATION AND CASE PREPARATION 170 (Patricia Iyer ed., 1999).

residents. While they are not insurers of complete safety,[64] they owe a duty of ordinary care to protect the vulnerable residents, and this protective duty is a great responsibility.[65] Courts readily find that the nursing home has responsibility for "every aspect of [the resident's] wellbeing."[66] The duty of care relates directly to the vulnerable condition of the residents.[67] That is why liability for assault cases poses a high risk for damage awards against the owner of the nursing home, as well as to nursing home administrators.[68]

The nursing home assault event may be subject to criminal prosecution, if the assailant is found and is competent to stand trial. It is estimated that over one-half of the sexual abuse cases from nursing homes result in a criminal conviction, but only a quarter of those convicted go to prison.[69] In a 2007 rape case, a nursing home aide was convicted and sent to prison, while the nursing home was penalized for violating federal CMS standards.[70] There will be a carryover from the criminal conviction to the nursing home's potential liability in tort for the assault.[71] In some cases, the nursing home itself might be a source of problems to its community by admitting or hiring criminals, probationers, and registered sex offenders.[72] And it can be argued that planned, for-profit understaffing of the caregiving role in nursing homes is itself a form of corporate criminal negligence.[73]

---

64. Francis v. Lafon Nursing Home, 840 So. 2d 1281 (La. Ct. App. 2003).

65. *See, e.g.*, Bezark v. Kostner Manor, 172 N.E.2d 424 (Ill. App. Ct. 1961).

66. Guernsey v. Country Living Pers. Care Homes, No. crY.A.3:CV-04-0423, 2006 U.S. Dist. LEXIS 31450 (M.D. Pa. May 19, 2006).

67. *Bezark*, 172 N.E.2d at 426–27.

68. Hill v. Beverly Enters.-Miss., Inc., 305 F. Supp. 2d 644, 648 (S.D. Miss. 2003).

69. Robert Hawks, *Grandparent Molesting: Sexual Abuse of Elderly Nursing Home Residents & Its Prevention*, 8 MARQ. ELDER'S ADVISOR 159, 179 (2006).

70. Rolling Hills Rehab Ctr. v. CMS, Dec. No. 2119 (HHS Departmental Appeals Bd., App. Div., Oct. 5, 2007), http://www.hhs.gov/dab/decisions/dab2119.pdf.

71. Jennifer Phan, *The Graying of America: Protecting Nursing Home Residents by Allowing Regulatory and Criminal Statutes to Establish Standards of Care in Private Negligence Actions*, 2 HOUS. J. HEALTH L. & POL'Y 297 (2003).

72. Emerald Park Health Care Ctr. v. CMS, Dec. No. CR-1462 (HHS Departmental Appeals Bd., Civ. Remedies Div., June 20, 2006), http://www.hhs.gov/dab/decisions/CR1462.htm.

73. Victoria Vron, *Using RICO to Fight Understaffing in Nursing Homes*, 71 GEO. WASH. L. REV. 1025 (2003).

The downside of using criminal penalties is that proof to a jury of each element of the statutory offense—proof beyond a reasonable doubt—is constitutionally required but hard to achieve. Most prosecutors are quite busy with dockets crammed with more readily proven violations. Here, the complaining witness may be dead by the time of trial,[74] so the local prosecutor may permit plea bargains that are unlikely to deter nursing home abuse. And appellate courts cannot be counted on to be sympathetic to the trial court findings, based on the specific terms of state elder abuse legislation.[75] So criminal prosecutors have numerous incentives to accept the predator's pleas to lesser offenses.

12:8 Definitions

State criminal laws specify what "abuse" will be[76] and what is required to establish an "assault." For example, Wisconsin appellate courts affirmed convictions on 12 counts of elder abuse, defined as "any act or failure to act which causes suffering, misery or physical harm to a person confined."[77] Between 2004 and 2005, Wisconsin had 4,234 allegations of abuse, of which 23 were fatal and 353 were deemed life-threatening.[78] The elder abuse standard in Louisiana punishes intentional or criminally negligent acts or omissions causing "unjustifiable" pain and suffering.[79]

Sexual assault includes the standard definition used in each state's criminal statutes, words usually covering any unconsented-to touching of a person for sexual reasons, including oral or vaginal intercourse.

---

74. Hawks, *supra* note 69, at 174 (more than one-half of sexual assault victims die within one year).

75. People v. Johnson, 595 N.E.2d 1381 (Ill. App. Ct. 1992).

76. Klein v. Mo. Dep't of Health & Senior Servs., 226 S.W.3d 162 (Mo. 2007) (construing Mo. Rev. Stat. § 198.006 by its plain meaning: striking a nursing home resident "necessarily involves physical injury or harm. . . . The statute does not require a physical manifestation of injury or harm.").

77. State v. Serebin, 350 N.W.2d 65 (Wis. 1984).

78. John Pray, *State v. Serebin*, 1986 Wis. L. Rev. 339; *see also Listening Session: Abuse of Our Elders: How We Can Stop It: Hearing Before the U.S. Senate Special Comm. on Aging* (July 18, 2007) (testimony of Robert Blancato, Elder Justice Coal.), http://www.aging.senate.gov/hearing_detail.cfm?id=279115&.

79. State v. Brenner, 486 So. 2d 101 (La. 1986).

Physical assault includes the unconsented touching of another person, typically with an adverse result for the victim of the assault who is bruised, beaten, or knocked down. State criminal statutes can form the basis for defining the civil tort offense, except where a state supreme court has permitted common law tort recovery for "assault" (assault and battery as described above) in a broader range of factual settings.

The state statutory term "elder abuse" includes striking the resident, even in the absence of long-term harm, since striking a person inflicts pain and the state abuse laws do not require "a physical manifestation of injury or harm."[80] The CMS use of "abuse" refers to intentional actions by the nursing home or its staff.[81] The term "abuse" can include slapping the resident.[82] And physical abuse claims require the plaintiff to show that "inappropriate physical contact" occurred.[83]

Some states define "abuse and neglect" to include infliction of pain, injury, or "mental anguish," or depriving the resident of services "necessary to maintain the health and welfare of an adult, or a situation in which an adult is unable to provide or obtain the services that are necessary to maintain that person's health or welfare."[84] The term "neglect" relates to the duty that the caregiver owes to the incompetent elder.[85] For example, a home that allows a resident to engage in risky behaviors is "neglecting" the safety of the elder and there must be adequate written procedures to prevent harm.[86]

The "duty of care" of the nursing home facility is a jury issue. The nursing home is not the guarantor, per se, of its residents' safety.[87] Nevertheless, it has both a moral and a legal obligation to provide

---

80. Klein v. Mo. Dep't of Health & Senior Servs., 226 S.W.3d 162 (Mo. 2007).

81. Woodstock Care Ctr. v. HCFA, Dec. No. 1726, at 21 (HHS Departmental Appeals Bd., App. Div., May 30, 2000), http://www.hhs.gov/dab/decisions/dab1726.pdf.

82. People v. Johnson, 595 N.E.2d 1381 (Ill. App. Ct. 1992).

83. Stevens v. Axelrod, 162 A.D.2d 1025 (N.Y. App. Div. 1990).

84. TENN. CODE ANN. § 71-6-120(1) (2000), *quoted in* Conley v. Life Care Ctrs. of Am., 236 S.W.3d 713 (Tenn. Ct. App. 2007).

85. *In re* Conservatorship of Gregory, 95 Cal. Rptr. 336 (Cal. Ct. App. 2000).

86. Centerclair Inc. v. CMS, Dec. No. CR-1747 (HHS Departmental Appeals Bd., Civ. Remedies Div., Mar. 10, 2008), http://www.hhs.gov/dab/decisions/civildecisions/2008/CR1747.pdf.

87. Bezark v. Kostner Manor, Inc., 172 N.E.2d 424, 426–27 (Ill. App. Ct. 1961) (citing Sylvester v. Nw. Hosp. of Minneapolis, 53 N.W.2d 17 (Minn. 1952); Tabor v. State, 62 N.Y.S.2d 380 (Ct. Cl. 1946); RESTATEMENT OF TORTS § 320).

adequate care to its residents in maintaining safe facilities and preventing assaults on its residents wherever possible. This duty is assessed under the ambiguous standard of "reasonable care." What conduct will amount to reasonable care will vary in accordance with residents' mental and physical capacities, and the standard of homes generally in the community if the state either follows the locality rule or if a statute so designates the standard.[88] One element that will generally be considered is whether a nursing home had notice of potential dangers, and upon other factors pertaining to the legal elements of negligence and liability.[89] CMS does not demand that nursing homes be "unconditional guarantors of favorable outcomes," but CMS rules "impose an affirmative duty to provide services [to avoid harm] . . . to the highest practicable degree."

12:9 Sources of Assaults

Protection of nursing home residents from harm includes protection from intentional physical violence, including assaults by nursing home staff,[90] visitors,[91] other residents,[92] or intruders. The law views each assault as criminal;[93] the legal consequences vary according to

88. 83 A.L.R.3d 871 (Supp. 2013).

89. Basic elements of negligence and liability include duty, breach of duty, causation, and harm. "A person acts negligently if the person does not exercise reasonable care under all the circumstances. Primary factors to consider in ascertaining whether the person's conduct lacks reasonable care are the foreseeable likelihood that the person's conduct will result in harm, the foreseeable severity of any harm that may ensue, and the burden of precautions to eliminate or reduce the risk of harm." RESTATEMENT (THIRD) OF TORTS § 3. "Where there is greater danger and hazard, there must be a corresponding exercise of attention for the purpose of preventing injury to another, to exercise what the law terms 'ordinary care.'" *Bezark*, 172 N.E.2d at 426–27 (citing Commonwealth Elec. Co. v. Melville, 70 N.E. 1052 (Ill. 1904)). *See id.* at 427 (regarding "notice"). Medicare/Medicaid-certified long-term care facilities are required by federal statute to keep residents free from abuse and from restraints unrelated to medical symptoms, and "facility[ies] must develop and implement written policies and procedures that prohibit mistreatment, neglect, and abuse of residents and misappropriation of resident property." 42 C.F.R. § 483.13 (2008). Additionally, all allegations must be investigated and reported to authorities immediately. *Id.*

90. Niece v. Elmview Group Home, 929 P.2d 420 (Wash. 1997).

91. *See, e.g.*, Shepard v. Mielke, 877 P.2d 220 (Wash. Ct. App. 1994).

92. *See, e.g.*, Associated Health Sys. v. Jones, 366 S.E.2d 147 (Ga. Ct. App. 1988).

93. Tort cases often follow the conviction of the assaultive employee. Doe v. Westfall Health Care Ctr., 755 N.Y.S. 2d 769 (N.Y. App. Div. 2002); *Niece*, 929 P.2d 420.

categories of assailant, with the fewest remedies in the case of an incompetent mentally deficient resident as the attacker, and the greatest likelihood of punitive damages where the attack is perpetrated by a staff member. Nursing home administrators, nurses, and staff are often the target of prosecutions.[94]

The civil liability for intentional harm by employees is most significant; action against nursing homes for negligent hiring is a risk, imposing a duty of care in the selection of workers at a time when turnover is very high and the pool of available workers is less skilled, less loyal, and less experienced than the employers and residents would desire. Intruder or visitor assault is the most difficult case, as plaintiffs have difficulty showing that the nursing home and its staff should have known of the risk of harm and failed to use reasonable measures to protect against it.[95] A rape should be reported to police immediately; whether such an assault is a foreseeable event for which the nursing home is civilly liable will be a matter for the jury to decide.[96]

12:10 Regulatory Duty of Care for Protection of Residents

Federal and state requirements for nursing homes receiving Medicare and Medicaid funds are enforced by surveys[97] and money penalties.[98] Under federal law, the nursing home has a legal duty to provide care necessary "to attain or maintain the highest practicable physical, mental, and psychosocial wellbeing" of its residents.[99] The operator must ensure that "[e]ach resident receives adequate supervision and assistance devices to prevent accidents."[100]

State laws can expand and augment these responsibilities, and some of these laws allow private enforcement lawsuits.[101] The plaintiff in a

---

94. 83 A.L.R.3d 871 (Supp. 2013).
95. K.L. v. Riverside Med. Ctr., 524 N.W.2d 300 (Minn. Ct. App. 1995).
96. *Shepard*, 877 P.2d 220.
97. CMS Survey Guidance, *supra* note 41.
98. *See, e.g.*, Harmony Court v. Leavitt, 188 F. App'x 438 (6th Cir. 2006).
99. 42 C.F.R. § 483.25 (2008).
100. *Id.* at § 483.25(h)(2).
101. Robin Miller, Annotation, *Construction and Application of State Resident Bill of Rights Statutes*, 87 A.L.R.5th 277 (2001).

tort action for nursing home assault may want to use the state statutes that are specific to protection of nursing home residents, but a careful drafting of the pleadings will be necessary; a statute dealing with "care and services" is not necessarily violated by failure to protect the resident's bodily integrity.[102] Be careful and conservative in the drafting of a complaint to cover what the statute covers. Very few victims of assault attempt a suit against the nursing home, and those that do so are not assured of success.[103] It is significant that the nursing home may be a well-situated defendant in a situation where the aggressor was an incompetent resident.

The reader should note that while CMS and state findings of regulatory violations can, in many cases, provide the grounds for negligence per se, some courts have found that the existence of a regulatory norm does not determine civil tort outcomes. These courts have criticized the CMS rules as too vague and general a standard for the courts to apply a negligence per se finding for their violation.[104] For example, one federal appellate panel ruled in a nursing home abuse case that "the duty of care owed to residents by a nursing home under common or state law is unrelated to the duty of care owed by a long term care facility to a severely disabled resident under federal regulations."[105] (For a full discussion of negligence per se and a critique of this approach, see Chapter 26.) This situation is likely to change fairly quickly as the nation transitions from customary care to evidence-based care based on uniform national standards grounded in clinical practice guidelines.[106]

The CMS rules are enforced by civil penalties, and the rules do not contain an exception where the resident was "difficult to work with."[107]

---

102. Doe v. Advisors Healthcare, No. XOI-CV-020170300S, 2005 Conn. Super. LEXIS 1036 (Conn. Super. Ct. Mar. 24, 2005).

103. Hawks, *supra* note 69, at 187.

104. Conley v. Life Care Ctrs. of Am., 236 S.W.3d 713 (2007); Frantz v. HCR Manor Care, No. 5-2374-2002, 2003 WL 23473921 (Pa. Com. Pl. Dec. 12, 2003).

105. Woodstock Care Ctr. v. HCFA, Dec. No. 1726, at 12 (HHS Departmental Appeals Bd., App. Div., May 30, 2000), http://www.hhs.gov/dab/decisions/dab1726.pdf.

106. See Chapter 8:2, Use of Clinical Practice Guidelines as Evidence of the Standard of Care, and 8:3, Use of Regulatory Violations to Establish Negligence Per Se or as Evidence of the Standard of Care.

107. Harmony Court v. Leavitt, 188 F. App'x 438 (6th Cir. 2006).

One Ohio nursing home was assessed a civil penalty of $33,650, upheld on appeal,[108] for failing to prevent assaults on its residents to a degree that residents were in "imminent jeopardy" of physical harm.[109] The appeals board upheld an administrative judge's finding that the home was liable for failing to protect residents from "accidents," as the rules required,[110] because "repeated unprovoked assaults were tolerated" by the home.[111] The attackers lacked the mental ability to plan or execute "volitional acts," so as to the resident victims, what had occurred was an "accident" that the home failed to prevent by failing to adequately supervise the assailants.[112]

Awareness of the aggressive behaviors of nursing home residents put the home on notice that altercations could be "uncontrolled behaviors rather than willed acts," and so would be within the CMS requirement to prevent "accidents."[113] The home's defense asserted that state officials misled the home when it transferred the assailant into the home despite knowing of that person's past mistreatment and overmedication at a Veterans Affairs nursing facility; the combative resident had been recorded as "agitated 141 times and aggressive 134 times" and interventions had been ineffective.[114] This sets up the case for a negligent failure to protect the victim from another resident's uncontrolled and violent behavior. In these cases the nursing homes themselves will likely be found liable, as well as the nursing home administrators.[115]

---

108. Woodstock Care Ctr. v. Thompson, 80 F. App'x 962 (6th Cir. 2003).
109. *Woodstock Care Ctr. v. HCFA*, Dec. No. 1726.
110. 42 C.F.R. § 483.25(h)(2) (2008).
111. *Woodstock Care Ctr. v. HCFA*, Dec. No. 1726, at 6.
112. *Id.* at 6–8.
113. *Id.* at 20.
114. *Id.* at 12.
115. Casas v. Paradez, 267 S.W.3d 170, 176 (Tex. App.—San Antonio 2008).

12:11 Nursing Home Response to Assaults

When an assault occurs, time is of the essence and action must be taken, even if the facts are not yet fully confirmed.[116] If the intentional harm is the result of the act of one of the nursing home residents, documentation of the interventions that have been taken to deal with the violent resident is essential to the future defense.[117] A cover-up invites serious damages if the facts go to a jury.[118] The prudent nursing home will send the injured resident to the emergency room as soon as possible for treatment and, where appropriate, a rape kit evaluation. Delay in medical treatment, without adequate justification,[119] is grounds for a negligence case.[120] Criminal law enforcement authorities should be advised at the same time,[121] and a report must be made to the state long-term care monitoring agency.[122] That agency probably has a regulation that requires the immediate submission of a report to state officials. Delay by the nursing home supervisors can count against the nursing home in a subsequent enforcement case.[123]

Lack of a long-term injury from the assault does not excuse the nursing home from liability. The plain meaning of a state elder abuse law punishing assault is interpreted from its literal terms.[124] In the negligence context, the defense benefits from the proximate cause requirement that the attack must have been "foreseeable" because of past patterns of violence or other indications of harmful conduct.[125]

---

116. Rolling Hills Rehab. Ctr. v. CMS, Dec. No. 2119 (HHS Departmental Appeals Bd., App. Div., Oct. 5, 2007), http://www.hhs.gov/dab/decisions/dab2119.pdf.

117. NURSING HOME LITIGATION: INVESTIGATION AND CASE PREPARATION 177 (Patricia Iyer ed., 1999).

118. Hawks, *supra* note 69, at 176–77.

119. Collier v. AMI Inc., 254 So. 2d 170 (La. Ct. App. 1971).

120. Blum v. Sunrise Cmty. Inc., No. 02-10806 CA23 (Miami-Dade Cnty. Fla. Jud. Cir. Ct. 2003) (significant delay in transfer to hospital after assault by employee caused injury, led to $9 million settlement), *reported in* VERDICTS, SETTLEMENTS & TACTICS 422 (Oct. 2003).

121. Delay in reporting a possible crime "could have prejudiced effective investigation and enforcement." *Rolling Hills Rehab. Ctr.*, Dec. No. 2119, at 12.

122. Delay in filing the report of the assault may be punished. Vandalia Park v. Leavitt, 157 F. App'x 858, 863 (6th Cir. 2005).

123. *Rolling Hills Rehab. Ctr.*, Dec. No. 2119.

124. Klein v. Mo. Dep't of Health & Senior Servs., 226 S.W.3d 162 (Mo. 2007).

125. K.L. v. Riverside Med. Ctr., 524 N.W.2d 300 (Minn. Ct. App. 1994).

Professional license revocation is another possible remedy against the nursing home supervisors who fail to act to prevent assault. A nurse who observed an impaired male resident in the act of sexually assaulting an immobile and incapacitated resident, and then told two aides to "let him finish," had her license revoked; the courts upheld the sanction.[126] The errant employee may be placed on a list of employees who are not eligible to work in nursing homes in the state.[127] These listings act as bans on future employment, and appeals of the ban may lead to a remand for the development of further information.[128] A defendant nursing home is likely to respond to a claim that it had knowledge of the resident-assailant's behavior with a claim that it tried, but was unable, to have this resident transferred; one case was won by a defense claim that only the family or a physician could order the transfer of the assailant to another home.[129]

12:12 Framing the Complaint for Civil Tort Liability

The torts of assault and battery are well recognized in common law. While the duty to protect residents applies "whether the assault was committed by an employee, a visitor, or by someone coming in off the street,"[130] it is a serious obligation to be enforced in tort damages. Proof of the cause of injury in fact by a rape is straightforward.[131] In those states that have created specific statutory remedies "to redress the abuse of nursing home residents," the terms of the statute should also be examined prior to drafting the elements of the claims.[132]

In the nursing home setting, the physical contact of staff with residents is usually helpful, benign, and not tortious. But where the assault occurs in the course of resident care—for example, hitting to restrain

---

126. Yaw v. Dep't of Health Servs., No. 703447, 1993 Conn. Super. LEXIS 1263 (Conn. Super. Ct. May 12, 1993).

127. These will be found via the website of the state long-term care agency.

128. Salmon v. Dep't of Pub. Health, 788 A.2d 1199 (Conn. 2002).

129. Dupree v. Plantation Pointe L.P., 892 So. 2d 228 (Miss. 2004).

130. Niece v. Elmview Group Home, 929 P.2d 420 (Wash. 1997); *accord*, Regions Bank v. Stone Cnty. Skilled Nursing Facility, 49 S.W.3d 107 (Ark. Ct. App. 2001).

131. Healthcare Ctrs. of Tex. v. Rigby, 97 S.W.3d 610 (Tex. App. 2002).

132. Doe v. Westfall Health Care Ctr., 755 N.Y.S.2d 769 (App. Div. 2002).

an uncooperative resident—it is unacceptable and tortious.[133] The nursing home itself is likely to be sued for negligence after the assault becomes known to the family of the resident.[134] Likewise, knowledge by the staff of the violent or overtly sexual aggression by a resident toward other residents gives rise to a duty to protect the victim. In one case, failure to remove or restrict access after the first assault, and then waiting 18 hours after a rape to call police, was "wanton conduct and reckless indifference" that was indefensible and reprehensible and warranted $800,000 in punitive damages.[135] The victim of the assault or his or her conservator can be awarded damages for both the physical pain and the emotional trauma.[136] The harsh emotional effects of becoming a victim can be severe, and can be compensated.[137] In some instances, a wrongful death action by the court-appointed personal representative may be appropriate.[138] Where an injury was caused by another resident and the nursing home had knowledge of the potential harm that could be caused by that person, the injured resident's estate can bring actions for negligent omissions in protecting the resident.[139]

Laws and rules may be helpful, but classic tort actions will be a primary means of inducing the nursing home to avoid actions that rise to the level of assault and battery. The federal CMS standards for nursing homes provide the government-recognized standard of care, but they do not create a private cause of action for enforcement of the federal norms.[140] Recall, though, that they might provide good evidence of what conduct meets the standard of care. On the other hand, state-specific laws may give a right of action to the injured elder."[141]

---

133. Rodebush v. Okla. Nursing Homes Ltd., 867 P.2d 1241 (Okla. 1993).

134. Hawks, *supra* note 69, at 185–86.

135. Guernsey v. Country Living Pers. Care Home, No. 3:CV-04-0423, 2006 U.S. Dist. LEXIS 31450 (M.D. Pa. May 19, 2006).

136. *Id.*

137. Beth Rom-Rymer, *Demonstrating Trauma: Effects of Sexual Abuse on the Elderly*, *in* NURSING HOME LITIGATION: PRETRIAL PRACTICE AND TRIALS 547 (Ruben Krisztal ed., 2d ed. 2003).

138. *See, e.g.*, OHIO REV. CODE § 2125.02 (2008).

139. Mast v. Magpusao, 225 Cal. Rptr. 689 (Cal. Ct. App. 1986).

140. Brown v. Sun Healthcare Group, 476 F. Supp. 2d 848 (E.D. Tenn. 2007); Conley v. Life Care Ctrs. of Am., 236 S.W.3d 713 (2007); Brogdon v. Nat'l Healthcare Corp., 103 F. Supp. 2d 1322 (N.D. Ga. 2000).

141. Deerings W. Nursing Ctr. v. Scott, 787 S.W.2d 494 (Tex. App. 1990).

Assault and battery tort cases can be brought in civil courts under the specific state protection laws for nursing home residents, medical liability laws,[142] or common law negligence for foreseeable harm, or under general laws like the wrongful death statute; an action under contractual obligations is sometimes available but may be less desirable procedurally.[143] If the state statutory cause of action is successful, attorney fee awards are also possible against the nursing home.[144]

Unlike many neglect cases, the nursing home abuse case is not a medical malpractice cause of action, and courts are reluctant to accept defense claims that it must be handled as a malpractice claim would be handled.[145] The negligence of the nursing home is established by showing that its management had notice of the possibility of violent behavior by the assailant.[146]

In addition to bringing causes of action for assault and battery, an injured plaintiff may also plead in the alternative by filing a claim for negligent infliction of emotional distress.[147] However, other residents who witnessed the abusive conduct may have trouble establishing the contemporaneous observation element, though some states have a more relaxed standard.[148] For a discussion of the cause of action for intentional or negligent infliction of emotional distress, see Chapter 26. In one case, an employee who was fired for violent behavior and taking residents' medications for unauthorized illegal sale was enjoined by the court from further contact with that nursing home, at the employer's request. The temporary restraining order, obtained without prior notice in fear of the violent reaction of the ex-employee, was upheld on appeal.[149]

---

142. Diversicare Gen. Partner, Inc. v. Rubio, 185 S.W.3d 842, 853 (Tex. 2005).

143. Stiffelman v. Abrams, 655 S.W.2d 522 (Mo. 1983) (death of resident by staff member assault).

144. Morgan v. Galilean Health Enters. Inc., 977 P.2d 357 (Okla. 1998).

145. Alcoy v. Valley Nursing Homes, 630 S.E.2d 301 (Va. 2006).

146. Coastal Health Servs. Inc. v. Rozier, 335 S.E.2d 712 (Ga. Ct. App. 1985).

147. Doe v. Advisors Healthcare, No. X01CV020170300S, 2005 Conn. Super. LEXIS 1036 (Conn. Super. Ct. Mar. 24, 2005).

148. Hope v. Royal Healthgate Nursing & Rehab. Ctr., A-5072-07T2, 2008 WL 5273084 (N.J. Super. App. Div. December 22, 2008).

149. Jennings Guest House v. Gibson, 971 So. 2d 506 (La. Ct. App. 2007).

Negligence per se claims for violating the CMS or state rules are arguable, but are not sure winners.[150] The tort law concept of negligence per se will not be sufficient to establish a case where there is no witness testimony about the facts of the claim.[151] If there are alternative causes possible, then negligence per se does not apply. Courts are reluctant to supply the cause; it is not enough just to show that there had been injuries.[152] The local standard of care in the state rules applies; these are more specific than the federal norms. In Kansas, disputes over proof without expert testimony led an appellate court to hold that the duty of reasonable care within the community can be determined by jurors without expert testimony.[153] In Wisconsin, the court held that the jury could decide the reasonableness of not using a restraint on a wheelchair; no expert testimony was needed, because restraints are a matter of routine care.[154]

12:13 State Alternative Malpractice Remedies

Nursing homes in which sexual assault and elder abuse have allegedly occurred may try to dismiss the tort action by forcing the cause of action into the alternative channels of state "malpractice" statutory processes. Because the failure to prevent an assault is not a delivery of medical service, most courts reject this argument as a lack of security at a nursing home was not within the category of professional negligence of a health care provider.[155] The California Supreme Court agreed that limits on exemplary damages that apply to hospitals did not apply in suits against nursing homes,[156] and that special provisions

150. Conley v. Life Care Ctrs. of Am., 236 S.W.3d 713 (Tenn. Ct. App. 2007).

151. Makas v. Hillhaven Inc., 589 F. Supp. 736 (M.D.N.C. 1984).

152. "It is necessary that the manner and circumstances of the damage or injury be of a kind that do not ordinarily happen in the absence of someone's negligence." May v. Triple C Convalescent Ctrs., 578 P.2d 541 (Wash. Ct. App. 1978).

153. Juhnke v. Evangelical Lutheran Good Samaritan Soc'y, 634 P.2d 1132 (Kan. Ct. App. 1981) (nursing home's conduct was "so obviously lacking in reasonable care and had such serious consequences" that it was within normal experience of the general public).

154. Kujawski v. Arbor View, 470 N.W.2d 249 (Wis. 1987).

155. Alcoy v. Valley Nursing Homes, 630 S.E.2d 301 (Va. 2006).

156. Covenant Care v. Super. Ct., 86 P.3d 290 (Cal. 2004).

for professional negligence did not apply to nursing home instances of elder abuse.[157]

The logical conclusion that intentional acts of assault (sexual or otherwise) are not within the realm of medical malpractice is becoming more and more embraced.[158] However, some courts remain reluctant to abandon medical malpractice in the context of an assault due to the distinction between the patient-caregiver relationship in a nursing home and that of a host-invitee in a general premises case.[159]

Unfortunately, of greater concern to the practicing attorney in pursuing a nonmedical claim for assault against a nursing home is whether or not any judgment will be collectible. Failure to assign liability for the assault to the nursing home could result in a judgment that is only worth the paper it is printed on. For example, in the context of an employee assault upon a resident, a nursing home (and its insurer) will contend that the employee's act was outside the scope of employment and is not, therefore, covered by insurance. Such an approach, therefore, should be made with caution and particular attention to theories of liability such as negligent hiring, retention, and supervision.

In terms of a resident-upon-resident assault, litigators should anticipate efforts to place blame upon the resident aggressor as the solely responsible party—a person who is almost certainly judgment proof. Thus, care should be taken to determine the nursing home's role in failing to prevent or respond to the assault and make that the focus of liability.

12:14 Defending the Nursing Home's Supervision

The nursing home as an entity does not consent to or participate in the assault, of course. But it has an obligation to use reasonable care

157. *Id.*

158. Reaux v. Our Lady of Lourdes Hosp., 492 So. 2d 233 (La. Ct. App. 1986) (claims of assault, rape, and battery do not make a case of medical malpractice); Afamefune v. Suburban Hosp., Inc., 385 Md. 677 (2005) (sexual assault did not occur while rendering medical care and did not constitute a medical malpractice claim).

159. Diversicare Gen. Partner, Inc. v. Rubio, 185 S.W.3d 842.

for the protection of the security of its vulnerable residents.[160] The more immobilized or helpless the victim, the greater the amount of care imposed by law that must be used for the physical safety of that person. Whether supervision was "adequate" depends in part on the resident's inability to protect himself or herself from harm.[161] Shortages of staff are linked statistically, in a general way, to a higher volume of liability suits against nursing homes.[162] Defense efforts to deny a duty of protection or even to assert consent by the elder to the sexual assault are unlikely to be persuasive in the nursing home context. However, if it can be established that the nursing home staff had no prior notice of a particular staff member's potential for harming residents, the nursing home is likely to be able to avoid liability.[163]

The outcome of a tort case for negligent failure to protect a resident from intentional harm will often turn upon the foreseeability of the risk of assault. This is a fact issue that should be determined by the jury, not on summary judgment. The jurors are likely to find that administrators or owners of the home could have prevented the assault through greater supervision or more robust security measures.

A successful defense by a nursing home asserted that assault had been a random unpredictable act, they had no notice of prior violence or violent tendencies,[164] and that the payments needed for guards to be posted "would be grossly out of proportion to the security gained," or would have been an unreasonable burden on the nursing home.[165] The court examined the cost-benefit equation and noted: "The question is whether the foreseeable likelihood of harm warrants the burden imposed to prevent that harm."[166]

160. Niece v. Elmview Group Home, 929 P.2d 420 (Wash. 1997).

161. Franklin Care Ctr. v. CMS, Dec. No. CR1694 (HHS Departmental Appeals Bd., Civ. Remedies Div., Nov. 20, 2007), http://www.hhs.gov/dab/decisions/CR1694.pdf.

162. Christopher Johnson et al., *Predicting Lawsuits against Nursing Homes in the United States 1997–2001*, 39(6) HEALTH SERVS. RES. 1713, 1724 (2004).

163. *Niece*, 929 P.2d 420.

164. Rodriguez v. Terence Cardinal Cooke Health Care Ctr., 771 N.Y.S.2d 516, 517 (N.Y. App. Div. 1st Dep't 2004).

165. Piazza v. Regeis Care Ctr., L.L.C., 852 N.Y.S.2d 53, 55 (N.Y. App. Div. 1st Dep't 2008).

166. K.L. v. Riverside Med. Ctr., 524 N.W.2d 300 (Minn. Ct. App. 1995).

Respondeat superior liability imposed on the custodial home for the actions of the employee has been hotly debated; Indiana applies vicarious liability[167] while Washington has declined to recognize this common law doctrine.[168] The claimed defense that a nursing home could not lawfully use physical restraints on a violent resident will not insulate the nursing home from liability when the home could have used alternative measures, such as supervising the movements of the violent resident or denying him access to vulnerable residents.[169] Depositions can be used to show notice, ability to segregate the violent resident from other residents, and prior knowledge of the past record of the resident's assailant.[170]

12:15 Rape and Sexual Assault

Within the category of assault cases, sexual assault is the most troublesome case for the defendant nursing home to defend.[171] The facts can be especially horrible.[172] The fact patterns are profoundly disturbing, even haunting, and have extreme effects on jurors that defendant nursing homes should fear.[173] Though no firm figures are available, as this is the "least detected, least reported, and least acknowledged form of elder abuse," sexual assault is a serious abuse concern for elderly residents.[174] Jury members can understand the shock and shame of the victim and are more likely to punish the home's lack of adequate protections.[175] Perhaps 53,000 such assaults occur each year but very

167. Stropes v. Heritage House Children's Ctr., 547 N.E.2d 244 (Ind. 1989).

168. Niece v. Elmview Group Home, 929 P.2d 420 (Wash. 1997).

169. Christian Care Ctrs., Inc. v. Golenko, 328 S.W.3d 637, 648 (Tex. App.–Dallas 2010); Associated Health Sys. v. Jones, 366 S.E.2d 147 (Ga. Ct. App. 1988).

170. Fink v. Commonwealth (Roanoke Cnty., Va. Cir. Ct., 2005), *reported in* Verdicts, Settlements & Tactics 207 (May 2005).

171. Hawks, *supra* note 69.

172. Guernsey v. Country Living Pers. Care Homes No. 3:CV-04-0423, 2006 U.S. Dist. LEXIS 31450 (M.D. Pa. May 19, 2006).

173. Rom-Rymer, *supra* note 137.

174. Hawks, *supra* note 69, at 159.

175. A jury award of $350,000 was settled for $322,000; the mental care facility was on notice after the first sexual assault that another could occur; it inadequately protected the victim. Peay v. Panorama Res-Care, No. 87-CI-701 (Warren Cnty. Ky. Cir. Ct. 1991), *reported in* Verdicts, Settlements & Tactics 312 (Sept. 1992).

few reach the stage of reported court decisions.[176] A verdict of $800,000 in punitive damages on top of $300,000 actual damages was awarded in 2006, where the assailant was a convicted sexual predator, admitted into a nursing home in shackles and handcuffs upon completion of his prison term, and no protective measures were taken in the nursing home during the few months before the rape occurred.[177] Within the categories of assault that have been reported, the fewest such reports are of sexual assault. Studies suggest that the perpetrators are overwhelmingly lower-paid male aides working at the nursing home where the rape occurs.[178] A few cases have drawn extensive coverage,[179] as when the Senate heard from the family of a 90-year-old rape victim that her survivors felt "disbelief, fear, numbness, pain, anger, bitterness, shock, outrage, and our hearts broken."[180] Utah appellate courts allowed use of res ipsa loquitur negligence actions against a nursing home, where an incompetent resident was found to be pregnant, and no explanation of the rape was ever found.[181] We can speculate that revulsion about the crime is so great that there are cases that go unreported, out of apprehension that the criminal system would broadcast the nursing home rape case as a headline story, driving potential residents/customers away. Posttraumatic stress disorder is a possible mental consequence of the assault, if the victim is conscious and understands what had occurred.[182] Mandatory reporting laws were intended to counterbalance this incentive to suppress the news of the event.[183]

Even if it reports the rape allegation, the nursing home will be deeply criticized; the management has minimal benefit from the postrape outcomes. The home will have to pay lawyers during the

---

176. Hawks, *supra* note 69, at 173.

177. *Guernsey*, 2006 U.S. Dist. LEXIS 31450.

178. Hawks, *supra* note 69, at 171.

179. Examples of headline elder abuse stories are in testimony of Blancato, *supra* note 78.

180. *Listening Session: Abuse of Our Elders: How We Can Stop It: Hearing Before the U.S. Senate Special Comm. on Aging* (July 18, 2007) (testimony of Jennifer Coldren, Rome, N.Y.) (rapist had worked in several facilities before this incident; was convicted and sentenced to 30 years in prison), http://www.aging.senate.gov/hearing_detail.cfm?id=279115&.

181. Virginia S. v. Salt Lake Care Ctr., 741 P.2d 969 (Utah Ct. App. 1987).

182. Rom-Rymer, *supra* note 137.

183. *Id.* at 551 (42 states mandate reporting of the sexual assault).

inevitable investigation, can be expected to pay large damages if the case is proven, and may face insurance premium increases. In addition, the home may be unable to pay for (1) exterior door security, if the rapist came from outside, or (2) interior assault prevention, finding a way to restrict movement of the incompetent assailant, because forcing a transfer of a nursing home resident who is incompetent but violent is a complicated process.[184] In spite of this, a nursing home in Kentucky was held liable for a rape that was committed by an individual who had never entered the facility or had any prior contact with the resident even though the home argued that these criminal acts were unforeseeable.[185] From the nursing home's position, the sexually aggressive resident who is mentally incompetent but "acting out" is hard to deal with; only a doctor can order restraints, and the family must cooperate to move the resident to another home.[186] The defense will assert a lack of foreseeability of the violent assault.[187] Accepting a criminal with a sexual predator designation, right out of prison, is a recipe for disaster (and punitive damages),[188] and can be in violation of statutory duties.[189]

Pregnancy of the rape victim is reported on rare occasions from the institution in which a mentally disabled person is confined.[190] The burden on the plaintiff is to prove cause-in-fact; for example, "but for" the nursing home's silence, the family could have arranged for an abortion had they been told of the assault that caused pregnancy early enough.[191] This would not be an issue for most of the immobilized nursing home population, who are postmenopausal.

---

184. Dupree v. Plantation Pointe L.P., 892 So. 2d 228, 233 (Miss. 2004) (home not negligent where assailant was a resident with dementia who could not readily be transferred elsewhere).

185. Murphy *ex rel.* Reliford v. EPI Corp., 2002-CA-002173-MR, 2004 WL 405754 (Ky. Ct. App. March 5, 2004).

186. *Dupree*, 892 So. 2d at 233.

187. *See, e.g.*, K.L. v. Riverside Med. Ctr., 524 N.W.2d 300 (Minn. Ct. App. 1994).

188. Guernsey v. Country Living Pers. Care Homes, No. 3:CV-04-0423, 2006 U.S. Dist. LEXIS 31450 (M.D. Pa. May 19, 2006).

189. Maplewood Care, Inc. v. Arnold, 2013 Ill. App. (1st) 120602.

190. McDaniel v. Ong, 724 N.E.2d 38 (Ill. App. Ct. 1999).

191. *Id.*

The split in the Texas Supreme Court in the *Rubio* case shows the significance of a court's distinction between premises liability and inadequate nursing home supervision.[192] The majority in a closely split decision rejected a lawsuit brought after the two-year statute of limitations for medical suits; dissenters argued for the status of premises liability instead.

The future prevention of sexual abuse will be affected by cost and personnel considerations.[193] As a scholar has speculated, jury awards will be so significant that costs will drain the funds of the affected home, so conditions of staffing will become worse. "The ideal answer to this problem must be outside of civil litigation, especially considering that very few victims of sexual abuse will even attempt a civil suit against the nursing home."[194]

While judgments can be significant, they may not necessarily be worth much. The potentially overlooked pitfall in litigating a nursing home sexual assault case is the issue of linking the rapist's conduct to that of the nursing home and, ideally, its parent company. A common defense in these cases is foreseeability. Could the nursing home foresee that the resident would potentially sexually assault someone else? Could the nursing home foresee that its employee would potentially sexually assault someone else? Absent foreseeable conduct, the unwary litigant may end up in the unfortunate position of the nursing home escaping liability on summary judgment or via another procedural mode. Thus, if trial proceeded against the tortfeasor, a sizeable (but unobtainable) judgment might be rendered against a judgment-proof defendant.

Likewise, the same risk arises for sexual assaults by employees. In order to access deep pockets to satisfy judgments, litigants must contend that the conduct either was foreseeable or occurred in the course and scope of employment.[195] Defendant nursing homes will certainly

192. Diversicare v. Rubio, 185 S.W.3d 842 (Tex. 2005).

193. Pamela Teaster & Karen Roberto, *Sexual Abuse of Older Adults*, 44 Gerontologist 788 (2004).

194. Hawks, *supra* note 69, at 187.

195. Our Lady of Peace, Inc. v. Morgan, 297 Va. 832, 832 S.E.2d 15 (2019).

contend that it was neither. Litigants further face the possibility of protracted litigation due to reluctant insurers who do not care to pay settlements or judgments for nursing home employees' bad acts.

12:16 Effects of Shock and Public Outrage

Posttraumatic stress disorder for the rape or assault victim has long-term adverse effects on the resident's mental health.[196] Potential shock value of a rape or serious injury from assault makes these cases newsworthy; this kind of news can lead to withdrawal of residents by their families, and could deter new applications for care. The privacy of the resident should be protected by law enforcement, medical, and social service agencies because of the sensitivity of these allegations. The cases are also potentially attractive for a plaintiff's attorney; the attorney should be retained early enough to assure that the necessary evidence will be preserved.

The reality is that situations in these cases are ugly and cases are very likely to be settled by the nursing home or its insurer, as there can be dramatic, even horrific, sets of testimony and exhibits in open court that will reach the news media and will inevitably place the nursing home in a very bad light even if a defense verdict is rendered.

12:17 Allegations of Concealment of the Assault

The jury propensity to punish the nursing home would increase if there were indications that a cover-up of the crime had been attempted by the nursing home staff.[197] This is especially true if the assault had been by an employee who was fired for the gross misconduct. Fraud in nursing home record-keeping that conceals substandard care can be criminally prosecuted.[198]

---

196. Rom-Rymer, *supra* note 137, at 548.

197. The cover-up of a sexual assault in the records of the defendant nursing home led to a $12 million verdict in 2000 in the *Collins* case. Collins v. Beverly Enters.-Fla., No. 98-433-CA (Taylor Cnty. Fla. Cir. Ct. 2000), *reported in* Verdicts, Settlements & Tactics (Nov. 2000).

198. U.S. v. Bell, No. 02:04CR0212, 2006 WL 952214 (W.D. Pa. Apr. 12, 2006).

Mandates for reporting of assault and abuse must be met and penalties can be imposed by CMS or the state for violations.[199] In some cases, a separate count of violation of state protective laws might be included in the litigator's complaint. Evidence that the nursing home administrator told the supervisor not to follow policy and not to telephone relatives of the assaulted resident was admitted into evidence in a tort trial, and formed part of the basis for a $1.2 million punitive damages award.[200]

12:18 Allegations of Employee Hiring and Supervision Errors

Where the intentional harm was committed by a nursing home employee, a claim of "negligent hiring" is likely to be brought.[201] The nursing home has a duty to guard against a foreseeable source of harm from bad conduct of its employees.[202] For example, an Ohio nursing home employee sexually abused at least 24 residents and was believed to have abused about 100 during his 20-year career.[203] Assaults by a violent employee whose background had not been checked would trigger "negligence in hiring" liability against the nursing home.[204] In Indiana, nursing homes may escape liability for negligent hiring if misrepresentations were made about the employee by former employers. If this occurs, plaintiffs can bring suit against the former employer.[205] Federal auditors found many weaknesses in the background checks that are actually run on prospective employees by nursing homes.[206]

---

199. Vandalia Park v. Leavitt, 157 F. App'x 858, 863 (6th Cir. 2005).
200. Rodebush v. Okla. Nursing Homes Ltd., 867 P.2d 1241 (Okla. 1993).
201. Jennifer Marciano, *Mandatory Criminal Background Checks of Those Caring for Elders*, 9 ELDER L.J. 203 (2001).
202. Niece v. Elmview Grp. Home, 929 P.2d 420 (Wash. 1997).
203. *Ohio Nurse Accused of Raping Elderly*, ASSOCIATED PRESS (Jan. 23, 2008).
204. Deerings W. Nursing Ctr. v. Scott, 787 S.W.2d 494 (Tex. App. 1990).
205. Passmore v. Multi-Mgt. Servs., Inc., 810 N.E.2d 1022, 1026 (Ind. 2004).
206. *Listening Session: Abuse of Our Elders: How We Can Stop It: Hearing Before the U.S. Senate Special Comm. on Aging* (July 18, 2007) (testimony of Gregory Demske, Assistant Inspector for Legal Affairs, Office of Inspector Gen., U.S. Dep't of Health & Human Servs.), http://www.aging.senate.gov/hearing_detail.cfm?id=279115&.

And retaining employees with known problems can be a source of many further difficulties for residents.[207]

The action of the employee is the cause-in-fact of the harm; it is not sufficient that the employee have mental problems, if the identical action would have been taken by any other responsible employee.[208] The intentional harm claim is unlike the typical nursing home case, where the nursing home acts in a respondeat superior role and the claim against the negligence of the individual employee is easily dismissed.[209] Because the turnover of certified nursing assistants exceeds 70 percent a year, the nursing home may argue that it is unable to be very selective of its new employees.[210]

In a case that awarded $200,000 in punitive damages, a Texas court stated that upon hiring "an unlicensed and potentially mentally and morally unfit nurse, it is reasonable to anticipate that an injury would result as a natural and probable consequence of that negligent hiring."[211] Prior criminal convictions for felony assault and battery, escape, and weapons charges were not checked in another case of resident assault that resulted in a $1.2 million verdict.[212] The criminal trial information will almost always be available on the record before the civil cause of action is heard. Evidentiary battles over employee hiring records may delay the trial.[213]

In some cases, the civil suit brings out information that leads to discipline such as probation or discharge of the employee who committed the assault.[214] Some percentage of the staff assaultive behaviors might have been predicted and avoided by more rigorous screening;

---

207. Charlotte Digregorio, Everything You Need to Know about Nursing Homes 106 (2005).

208. Smith v. Silver Spring-Wheaton Nursing Home, 220 A.2d 574 (Md. 1996).

209. *See, e.g.*, Slobin v. Boasiako, 19 Misc. 3d 1110 (N.Y. Super. Ct. Mar. 18, 2008).

210. American Health Care Ass'n, Results of the 2002 AHCA Survey of Nursing Staff Vacancy and Turnover in Nursing Homes (2003), http://www.ahcancal.org/research_data/staffing/Documents/Vacancy_Turnover_Survey2002.pdf.

211. Deerings W. Nursing Ctr. v. Scott, 787 S.W.2d 494 (Tex. App. 1990).

212. Rodebush v. Okla. Nursing Homes Ltd., 867 P.2d 1241 (Okla. 1993).

213. *In re* Lavernia Nursing Facility, 12 S.W.3d 566 (Tex. App. 1999).

214. Limbaugh v. Coffee Med. Ctr., 59 S.W.2d 73 (Tex. 2001).

available state lists of persons who were dismissed for misconduct at a prior nursing home[215] are a source that the hiring team should check before hiring a staff member. In those cases in which the tort liability of the nursing home turned upon the failure to check with prior employers, the plaintiff's suit might fail if there is not sufficient evidence that the other employers would have truthfully expressed the risk of hiring this employee.[216] Punitive damages can be awarded for "conscious indifference" where the nursing home did not ask for a copy of the state license for a new employee and that employee assaulted a person; the court held that the nursing home "consciously jeopardized the health, welfare and safety of its residents and visitors" by allowing the unlicensed aide to "create a dangerous situation."[217]

12:19 CMS and State Penalties

Adequate supervision to protect against "accidents" is the regulatory basis for the duty to avoid assaults.[218] The CMS rules do not make the nursing home strictly liable for whatever assault occurs, but the nursing home must take all reasonable steps to mitigate foreseeable risks of harm from accidents.[219] Where the state or federal survey team finds unreported acts of intentional harm, it will penalize the nursing home if the home fails to follow the required procedures for reporting of these attacks, and these can be sizeable penalties.[220]

A federal appeals court held that the nursing home does *not* have the freedom to "exercise some judgment when determining whether an investigation [of abuse allegations is] warranted."[221] The court upheld a penalty against the nursing home where intentional harm had occurred. And in a tort suit the state findings about conditions

215. *See, e.g.*, Mo. Rev. Stat. § 198.070 (2000) (abuse by nursing home employee), *upheld in* Klein v. Mo. Dep't of Health & Senior Servs., 226 S.W.3d 162 (Mo. 2007).
216. Long v. Brookside Manor, 885 S.W.2d 70 (Tenn. 2001).
217. Deerings W. Nursing Ctr. v. Scott, 787 S.W.2d 494 (Tex. App. 1990).
218. 42 C.F.R. § 483.25(h)(2) (2008).
219. Franklin Care Ctr. v. CMS, Dec. No. CR1694 (HHS Departmental Appeals Bd., Civ. Remedies Div., Nov. 20, 2007), http://www.hhs.gov/dab/decisions/CR1694.pdf.
220. 42 U.S.C. § 1395i-3(h)(2)(B)(ii) (2000).
221. Vandalia Park v. Leavitt, 157 F. App'x 858, 863 (6th Cir. 2005).

in the nursing home and for other residents will be admissible and relevant.[222]

In cases where abuse but not assault is claimed because there was no physical conduct, a court dismissed administrative agency findings of abuse where the accused employee had ordered the resident to stand in the hallway of the nursing home.[223]

Although the federal standards are applied, the state courts that enforce the standards in enforcement cases will apply the state law that implements the federal norms, so it will apply state interpretations in the case law.[224]

12:20 Punitive Damages

Punitive damages are intended to punish misconduct and to deter future misconduct, above and beyond the compensation for economic and noneconomic damages.[225] These damages may be allowed under state statutes that protect the nursing home resident, as well as under state tort law for egregious conduct in the failure to protect the resident.[226] Punitive damages in the nursing home context have been called "the functional equivalent of deputizing nursing home residents and their attorneys to prosecute misdeeds when government enforcement is lax."[227] The Ohio legislation allows punitive damages without proof of malice for the failure to provide adequate and appropriate care.[228]

12:21 Liability Insurance

The nursing home liability carrier is likely to deny coverage for intentional harm, as the "events" defined into the policy tend to be limited to

222. Sprosty v. Pearlview Inc., 666 N.E.2d 1180 (Ohio Ct. App. 1995).
223. Stevens v. Axelrod, 557 N.Y.S.2d 809 (App. Div. 4th Dep't 1990).
224. Salmon v. Dep't of Pub. Health, 788 A.2d 1199 (Conn. 2002).
225. BMW v. Gore, 517 U.S. 559 (1996).
226. *See, e.g.*, Guernsey v. Country Living Pers. Care Homes Inc., No. 3:CV-04-0423, 2006 U.S. Dist. LEXIS 31450 (M.D. Pa. May 19, 2006); Covenant Care Inc. v. Super. Ct., 86 P.3d 290, 297 (Cal. 2004).
227. Michael Rustad, *Heart of Stone*, 35 N. Mex. L. Rev. 337, 358 (2005).
228. Ohio Rev. Code § 3721.17(I).

accidental occurrences. If the policy excludes "abuse," then intentional harm inflicted by an employee on a resident might be abuse, but the same type of harm by a fellow resident or a nonemployee third party is not excluded as "abuse"[229] as the conduct of the nursing home will be covered as a negligent act, that is, the failure to use reasonable care to protect the injured resident from harm.

Contract exclusions are a matter for the court, not for the jury, to decide.[230] The lower-paid staff members who may commit an attack may be held to be outside of the "professional service" coverage definitions of a nursing home liability policy.[231] Some courts believe that "professional services" liability cannot include the attack on a resident, and allow denials of insurance coverage.[232] Other courts regard protection of the resident as being within the scope of professional services, therefore requiring coverage by the reluctant insurance carrier.[233] When the insurance policy excludes physical abuse, an assault by a demented resident is not excluded.[234]

12:22 Evidentiary Issues

Proving the case often requires testimony from those, other than the accused wrong doer, who had knowledge of the events. Sometimes the injured resident will be unavailable to testify. The injured resident is likely to be frightened and agitated when the intentional harm occurs, and the immediate statements he or she makes at the time are likely to be admitted into evidence under an exception to the hearsay rule as an excited utterance or a present sense impression.[235] Later statements that discount the harm may be admitted but do not eliminate the basis for criminal charges.[236]

---

229. Riley v. Maison Orleans II Inc., 829 So. 2d 479 (La. Ct. App. 2002).
230. *Id.*
231. Lexington Ins. Co. v. Educare Cmty. Living Corp., 149 F. App'x 326 (5th Cir. 2005).
232. *Id.*
233. Regions Bank & Trust Co. v. Stone Cnty. Skilled Nursing Facility, 49 S.W.3d 107, 113 (Ark. 2001).
234. *Riley*, 829 So. 2d 479.
235. State v. Oismaiye, 740 A.2d 338 (R.I. 1999).
236. *Id.*

Nursing home records showing the threat of violence by a resident toward another can be used as part of the evidence that the nursing home failed to take adequate actions.[237] The Government Accountability Office studied the rate at which convicts were being sent to nursing homes after prison.[238] The home has a duty to its residents under federal law to provide appropriate care to prevent any reasonably foreseeable harm that might occur as a result of admitting a former felon if convicted of a violent crime .[239] And expert witness testimony is not necessary to establish this duty.[240]

Privacy protections for medical records under Health Insurance Portability and Accountability Act (HIPAA) regulations will not shield a resident's records from civil discovery when that resident is accused of intentionally harming another nursing home resident.[241]

12:23 Governmental Immunity

Prior to 2023, a plaintiff's ability to hold a county- or state-owned nursing home accountable for abuse or neglect was limited. State immunity laws and tort caps could make pursuing such cases strategically and financially challenging. However, the Supreme Court changed the game significantly in June 2023.

In *Health & Hospital Corp. v. Talevski*,[242] the Supreme Court determined that the rights conveyed by the Federal Nursing Home Reform Act could be enforced against a county-owned nursing home through a civil rights suit under 42 U.S.C. § 1983. Notably, "[t]he unnecessary-restraint and predischarge-notice provisions . . . both reside in 42 U. S. C. §1396r(c), which expressly concerns '[r]equirements *relating to residents' rights*.' This framing is indicative of an individual 'rights-creating'

---

237. Coastal Health Servs. Inc. v. Rozier, 335 S.E.2d 712 (Ga. Ct. App. 1985).

238. U.S. Gov't Accountability Office, GAO-06-326, Long-Term Care Facilities: Information on Residents Who Are Registered Sex Offenders, or Are Paroled For Other Crimes (Mar. 31, 2006), http://www.gao.gov/new.items/d06326.pdf.

239. Woodstock Care Ctr. v. HCFA, Dec. No. 1726, at 12 (HHS Departmental Appeals Bd., App. Div., May 30, 2000), http://www.hhs.gov/dab/decisions/dab1726.pdf.

240. Mast v. Magpusao, 225 Cal. Rptr. 689, 691 (Cal. Ct. App. 1986).

241. Crawford v. Care Concepts Inc., 625 N.W.2d 876 (Wis. 2001).

242. 143 S. Ct. 1444 (2023).

focus. Examined further, the text of the unnecessary restraint and pre-discharge-notice provisions unambiguously confers rights upon the residents of nursing-home facilities."[243]

Claims under 42 U.S.C. § 1983 are not capped by statute. Suit must be filed against a "person" within the meaning of the statute.[244] There are many other intricacies involved in pursuing such claims. However, the complexities of pursuing section 1983 claims are beyond the scope of this text. Attorneys seeking to pursue such claims would be wise to consult a civil rights attorney with experience in these claims.

12:24 Effect of Resident Assault on Liability to Employees

Normally, workers' compensation applies to injuries caused by resident contact, whether the contact was accidental or deliberate. The litigation often turns upon the state law definition of the exception to workers compensation exclusivity known as "intentional torts," that is, the employer had knowledge that injury would be likely to occur to its employee.

A nursing home knew of a resident's dementia and propensity for combative behavior when it admitted him as a resident.[245] However, the resident had been released from a hospital to return to nursing home care; and the nursing home, which had residents with similar problems, believed that the resident could be provided appropriate care in a nursing home setting. After a staff member was attacked and died, the appeals court found that the plaintiff's "intentional tort" evidence fell short of establishing that the nursing home either consciously desired to bring about the nursing home employee's injury or death, or believed that such was substantially certain to follow from that resident's admission as a resident. There was no evidence indicating that the assaultive resident had ever attacked anyone before the attack on this employee. The heart of the plaintiffs' claim was that after knowing of the resident's condition, the nursing home failed to take precautions

243. *Id.* at 1457.
244. 42 U.S.C. § 1983.
245. Lloyd v. Shady Lake Nursing Home, Inc., 92 So. 3d 560 (La. Ct. App. 2d Cir. 2012).

to protect the staff member from injury. This was held to be a claim of failure to provide a safe workplace and was deemed to be exclusively recoverable under workers' compensation. The appellate court concluded that it was the stress from the attack by a demented resident that overwhelmed the nursing home employee's already burdened cardiovascular system and led to her death. The nursing home proved by clear and convincing evidence that the nursing home employee's death was a compensable personal injury by accident arising out of and in the course of her employment, so tort remedies were not available.

CHAPTER 13

Pharmaceuticals

13:1 Overview
13:2 Medication Management
13:3 Inappropriate Use of Antipsychotic Medications
13:4 Adverse Drug Interactions
13:5 Polypharmacy
13:6 Overview of Relevant Litigation
13:7 What Drug-Related Problems Are Likely to Arise in Nursing Homes?
13:8 Shared Liability: Malpractice or Drug Problems?
13:9 Malpractice by Misprescribing
13:10 Risks of Negligent Polypharmacy
13:11 Overdosing of Pharmaceuticals
13:12 Negligent Misdelivery
13:13 Drugs as a Resident Restraint Option
13:14 Inattentive Medical Oversight
13:15 Medical Device Problems

13:1 Overview

Medications are invented, developed, and marketed with strict federal oversight or may be so familiar and well known that no close supervision by means of "prescription" is needed. In the general population, the volume of prescription medications used in the United States is remarkably large. Studies show that in 2008, there were more than 2.3 billion "drug mentions" at office visits in the United States in which there was medical documentation in a physician's record of a drug provided, prescribed, or continued. Also, more than 711 million visits in the United States in 2008 were "drug visits," meaning drugs were either provided or prescribed. In a 2011 study, the Centers for Disease Control and Prevention stated that prescription drug sales by retail outlets exceeded $234 billion.[1]

Mirroring the stunning levels of use of medications in the larger population, medications are also an integral part of the care provided to residents of nursing facilities. The drugs are used to attempt to realize various outcomes, such as "curing an illness, diagnosing a disease or condition, arresting or slowing a disease process, reducing or eliminating symptoms, or preventing a disease or symptom."[2]

A study of 33,301 nursing facility residents revealed that an average of 6.7 medications was prescribed per resident, with 27 percent of residents taking nine or more medications.[3] This pattern of multiple prescriptions issued by multiple caregivers is referred to by many as "polypharmacy." Analysis of antipsychotic drug use by 693,000 Medicare nursing home residents found that 28.5 percent of the doses received were excessive and 32.2 percent lacked appropriate indications for use.[4]

Why is this elderly resident receiving a prescription for this particular drug? Was the drug cleared by the Food and Drug Administration (FDA) for use in the elders for this medical need? If not, there may be a significant liability issue.[5] Promotional efforts to expand use of medications in the elderly, before the drug has its required approval

1. Ryanne Dent, *No Duty to Warn of Drug Interactions: A Dangerous Prescription*, 46 J. Marshall L. Rev. 533 (2013).

2. Ctrs. for Medicare & Medicaid Servs., State Operations Manual, CMS Pub. No. 100-07, Appendix PP: Guidance to Surveyors for Long Term Care Facilities 190 (2006) ("Overview" for Tag 329).

3. D.E. Tobias et al. *General and Psychotherapeutic Medication Use in 328 Nursing Facilities: A Year 2000 National Survey*, 15 Consultant Pharmacist 34–42 (2001).

4. B.A. Briesacher et al., *The Quality of Antipsychotic Drug Prescribing in Nursing Homes*, 165 Arch. Intern. Med. 1280–85 (2005).

5. 1 James O'Reilly, Food & Drug Administration 15:47 (3d ed. 2013 Supp.).

for medical use in elders, generated billions of dollars of penalties against certain pharmaceutical companies.[6]

13:2 Medication Management

The Centers for Medicaid and Medicare Services (CMS) requires that the nursing home have a proper medication management plan for every resident. The goal of this plan is to ensure appropriate medication selection and prescribing (including dose, duration, and type of medication(s)). An appropriate medication management plan may help to stabilize or improve a resident's outcome, quality of life, and functional capacity. Without the constant vigilance that this plan requires, a broad range of adverse consequences such as medication interactions, depression, confusion, immobility, falls, and related hip fractures can result from any medication or combination of medications, or the use of a medication without adequate indications, in excessive dose, for an excessive duration, or without adequate monitoring.[7]

Elders are more at risk for the side effects that can be associated with medications simply because of the physiologic changes that come as part of the aging process. Elders commonly have multiple different medical conditions and many of these conditions may affect the absorption, distribution, metabolism, or elimination of medications from the body.[8]

Appropriate medical management includes continuous evaluations by the interdisciplinary team of whether there are means other than medications to accomplish the same goals. Education and training of both staff and providers concerning which alternative approaches are feasible may minimize the need for medications or reduce the dose

6. Press Release, Dep't of Justice, Eli Lilly and Company Agrees to Pay $1.415 Billion to Resolve Allegations of Off-label Promotion of Zyprexa (Jan. 15, 2009); John B. Reiss, *Your Business in Court and at Federal Agencies*, 68 Food & Drug L.J. 1 (2012).

7. Medical-Legal Aspects of Long-Term Care 179–219 (Jeffrey Levine ed., 2003).

8. Ctrs. for Medicare & Medicaid Servs., State Operations Manual, CMS Pub. No. 100-07, Appendix PP: Guidance to Surveyors for Long Term Care Facilities 190 (2006) ("Overview" for Tag 329).

and duration of those medications.[9] Litigants in nursing home pharmaceutical overuse cases should carefully study the FDA files about proper use of this drug.

13:3 Inappropriate Use of Antipsychotic Medications

According to a CMS report, off-label prescriptions of antipsychotic medications are frequently given to residents with dementia to try to deal with related behavioral and psychological symptoms (BPSD).[10]

This potentially inappropriate use of antipsychotics in this population raises serious questions regarding the proper behavioral health management of nursing home residents.[11] There is strong empirical evidence that antipsychotics have limited benefits for nursing home residents.

On the other hand, the evidence is strong that these antipsychotic drugs are likely to result in adverse consequences such as the risk of movement disorders, falls, hip fractures, cerebrovascular accidents, and death. Adding just one additional drug on top of already heavily medicated elders may be the last straw that triggers a cascade of adverse effects and drug interactions.

The CMS has taken notice of the risk for adverse events due to polypharmacy and overuse of many different types of medications to nursing home residents. As a first step in dealing with these problems, CMS has focused surveys on the overuse of antipsychotics, in an effort to reduce the overall use of these agents in nursing homes.

---

9. W.A. Ray et al., *Reducing Antipsychotic Drug Use in Nursing Homes: A Controlled Trial of Provider Education*, 1 Arch. Intern. Med. 713–21 (1993).

10. Dep't of Health & Human Servs., CMS 2012 Nursing Home Action Plan 28 (2012), http://www.cms.gov/Medicare/Provider-Enrollment-and-Certification/CertificationandComplianc/Downloads/2012-Nursing-Home-Action-Plan.pdf.

11. Ctrs. for Medicare & Medicaid Servs., Advanced Copy: Dementia Care in Nursing Homes: Clarification to Appendix P State Operations Manual (SOM) and Appendix PP in the SOM for F309-Quality of Care and F329-Unnecessary Drugs (May 24, 2013), http://www.cms.gov/Medicare/Provider-Enrollment-and-Certification/SurveyCertificationGenInfo/Policy-and-Memos-to-States-and-Regions-Items/Survey-and-Cert-Letter-13-35.html.

Both nursing homes and plaintiff's lawyers can expect to see an increase in surveyor citations for deficiencies for failure to properly manage medications. If a resident is injured, for example by fall or wandering, as a result of polypharmacy and/or the inappropriate use of antipsychotics, these deficiencies may become either evidence of a violation of the survey standard of care or of negligence per se.

CMS expects surveyors to evaluate other important classes of medications for unnecessary use, such as antibiotics, anticoagulants, proton pump inhibitors and others (Survey Tag F329 focuses on the importance of looking at all medications as well as implementation of nonpharmacological approaches to optimize the care of residents in nursing homes). The CMS is taking a multidimensional approach to the problem of inappropriate use of antipsychotic medications in nursing homes.

CMS has pointed out that "the potential overuse of antipsychotic agents is a symptom of a much larger problem—namely that many nursing facilities may not have a systematic plan to provide comprehensive behavioral health management to residents with diagnoses such as dementia and BPSD."[12] For example, a list of 45 recommendations for stopping certain customary care practices was made in "an educational initiative called Choosing Wisely, directed at both residents and physicians, under the auspices of the American Board of Internal Medicine Foundation and in partnership with Consumer Reports"[13]

---

12. *Id.*

13. Roni Caryn Rabin, *Doctor Panels Urge Fewer Routine Tests*, N.Y. Times (Apr. 4, 2012), http://www.nytimes.com/2012/04/04/health/doctor-panels-urge-fewer-routine-tests.html.

> U.S. specialty societies representing more than 500,000 physicians developed lists of Five Things Physicians and Patients Should Question in recognition of the importance of physician and patient conversations to improve care and eliminate unnecessary tests and procedures. These lists represent specific, evidence-based recommendations physicians and patients should discuss to help make wise decisions about the most appropriate care based on their individual situation. Each list provides information on when tests and procedures may be appropriate, as well as the methodology used in its creation. In collaboration with the societies, Consumer Reports has created resources for consumers and physicians to engage in these important conversations about the overuse of medical tests and procedures that provide little benefit and in some cases harm.

One of the items on this list of "don'ts" is an American Geriatrics Society recommendation against the prescription of benzodiazepines or other sedative hypnotics in older adults as a first choice for insomnia, agitation, or delirium because the use of these medications doubles the risk of car accidents, falls and hip fractures in elderly patients.[14]

13:4 Adverse Drug Interactions

Current medication references and pertinent clinical protocols should be used by both staff and practitioners to ensure the safe administration and monitoring of medications. One readily available source of information about the risks associated with a particular medication is the package insert that the FDA requires that manufacturers include inside the medication packaging. This package insert lists the adverse reactions and potential safety hazards associated with the medication, and what to do if these risks occur.[15]

Another source of medication information is the facility's pharmacist. A pharmacist has ready access to listings or descriptions of most significant risks, recommended doses, medication interactions, cautions, and so on that can be found in widely available standard references and computer software and systems that provide up-to-date information. She or he should have been paid for active participation for the resident's needs.

Because clinical testing of medications is not frequently done on older adults, much of the medication information found in many of these references is not specific to older adults or nursing home residents. In some states, the pharmacist does not have a general duty to warn residents, particularly of drug interactions.

ABIM Found., Lists, http://www.choosingwisely.org/doctor-patient-lists/ (last visited on Mar. 16, 2013).

14. Am. Geriatrics Soc'y, *Five Things Physicians and Patients Should Question*, Choosing Wisely, http://www.choosingwisely.org/doctor-patient-lists/american-geriatrics-society/ (last visited on Mar. 16, 2013).

15. Joseph P. Nathan & Etty Vider, *The Package Insert*, U.S. Pharmacist (May 15, 2015), https://www.uspharmacist.com/article/the-package-insert.

The Medicare State Operations Manual, Appendix PP, Guidance to Surveyors provides an excellent list of recognized clinical resources available for understanding the overall treatment and management of medical problems, symptoms, and medication consequences and precautions for use by nursing homes and by plaintiffs' lawyers.[16]

13:5 Polypharmacy

What would seem to be an obvious problem occurs when a resident is taking prescription medications ordered by multiple prescribers. The U.S. medical specialty societies representing more than 500,000 physicians developed lists of "Five Things Physicians and Patients Should Question" in recognition of the importance of physician and patient conversations to improve care and eliminate unnecessary tests and procedures. These lists represent specific, evidence-based recommendations that physicians and patients should discuss to help make wise decisions about the most appropriate care based on their individual situation. Each list provides information on when tests and procedures may be appropriate, as well as the methodology used in its creation. In collaboration with the societies, *Consumer Reports* has created resources for consumers and physicians to engage in these important conversations about the overuse of medical tests and procedures that provide little benefit and in some cases cause harm.

Sadly, polypharmacy is likely very common as many residents receive orders for medications from several practitioners, for example, attending and on-call physicians, consultants, and nurse practitioners. A proper medication management plan will clearly identify for each resident which medical professional has the overall responsibility for prescribing and identifying the indications for use of medications, for providing and administering the medications, and for monitoring the resident for the effects and potential adverse consequences of the

16. Ctrs. for Medicare & Medicaid Servs., State Operations Manual, CMS Pub. No. 100-07, Appendix PP: Guidance to Surveyors for Long Term Care Facilities (2011) http://cms.gov/Regulations-and-Guidance/Guidance/Manuals/downloads/som107ap_pp_guidelines_ltcf.pdf.

medication regimen. This is especially important when care is being delivered or ordered by diverse sources such as consultants, providers, or suppliers (e.g., hospice or dialysis programs). In this day of electronic medical records, there is no excuse for a failure on the part of the nursing home to appropriately manage this important aspect of the resident's care.[17]

13:6 Overview of Relevant Litigation

Pharmaceutical drug issues represent a large proportion of the claims that families and survivors have brought against nursing homes for injuries to an elderly relative. The nursing home that is subject to CMS and state standards has a clear obligation to handle pharmaceuticals safely under the supervision of the medical director and the consulting pharmacist.[18] Nursing home residents are among the most frequent and substantial users of pharmaceuticals and medical devices,[19] making them more prone to errors in misdelivery, overuse, or inappropriate mixed use of conflicting drugs.

Elders present special problems for the prescribing physician.[20] Because the elderly person will generally have decreased liver and kidney function, the medication will stay in the body longer and its side effects will have more negative consequences.[21] The pharmaceuticals used inside nursing homes include those that are prescribed for the individual residents and those that are included in the home's "standing orders" for administration by nurses from the stock of available medications as needed.[22]

---

17. Ctrs. for Medicare & Medicaid Servs., Advanced Copy: Dementia Care in Nursing Homes, *supra* note 11.

18. 42 C.F.R. §§ 483.60(a), 483.65(c).

19. Carlos Rojas-Fernandez, *Adverse Drug Events*, *in* Medical-Legal Aspects of Long-Term Care, at 179–180.

20. A useful source is Mildred Hogstel, Gerontology: Nursing Care of the Older Adult 353 (2006).

21. Michelle Meadows, *Medication Use and Older Adults*, FDA Consumer, July–Aug. 2006), http://www.athealth.com/consumer/disorders/olderadultsmeds.html.

22. The role of standing orders is explained in lay terms in Charlotte Digregorio, Everything You Need to Know about Nursing Homes 97 (2005).

Defenders of the nursing home in a pharmaceutical injury case will be focused on adequacy of the consulting pharmacist's monthly reviews,[23] the nurse's records about the resident's condition, and the physician's orders. Have they been properly recorded and coordinated?

The role of the consulting pharmacist in the periodic review of medications should not be overlooked if the resident was affected by the drugs, directly (overdosing) or indirectly (affecting gait and stability).[24] The prudent counsel will investigate the statutory provisions relating to the pharmacist's duties to determine potential liability.[25]

13:7 What Drug-Related Problems Are Likely to Arise in Nursing Homes?

The problems discussed in this chapter include four types of errors:

- misprescribing
- polypharmacy
- misdosing
- misdelivery

The rate of adverse effects from drugs in the nursing home setting appears to be substantial. CMS regulations require special care by the nursing home operator to ensure that "residents are free of any significant medication errors."[26] This is one of the requirements on which the nursing home must achieve "substantial compliance," defined as "a level of compliance with the requirements of participation such that any identified deficiencies pose no greater risk to resident health or safety than the potential for causing minimal harm."[27]

---

23. 42 C.F.R. § 483.65(c)(1).

24. Hogstel, *supra* note 20, at 392 ("The pharmacist is responsible for monitoring or reviewing the system of drug administration for each resident.").

25. Johnson *ex rel.* Johnson v. Badger Acq. of Tampa LLC, 983 So. 2d 1175, 1181 (Fla. 2d Dist. App. 2008).

26. 42 C.F.R. § 483.25(m)(2) (2008).

27. 42 C.F.R. § 488.301 (2008).

Drug errors or excessive doses are closely linked to the appearance of other problems in the resident's health, as CMS has told its surveyors of nursing homes, since overdosing, excessive duration of use, or prescribing without adequate monitoring "may increase the risk of a broad range of adverse consequences such as medication interactions, depression, confusion, immobility, falls, and related hip fractures."[28] These are avoidable injuries with enormous costs to the insurance and Medicaid systems.[29] The best defense that can avoid these problems is an active pharmacist review of the prescribed medications, with attention to interactions and contraindications that can pose safety risks for the resident.[30] Some of the larger nursing home pharmaceutical suppliers provide consulting pharmacy services as well as unit-dose packaging labeled for each resident.[31]

13:8 Shared Liability: Malpractice or Drug Problems?

Litigation over nursing home negligence may also include claims concerning medical malpractice, but the two systems do not necessarily intersect in all cases. The role of the medical director is broad and powerful, at least on paper.[32] The consulting pharmacist has defined duties to perform and must sign off regularly on the medication orders for each resident.[33] The registered nurses' implementation of the care plan on a daily basis may not always follow the physician's directives and instructions, and that omission may be a source of tort liability for the nursing home.[34]

Nursing home residents are among the highest-volume consumers of pharmaceuticals and individual medical devices, about twice the

28. Ctrs. for Medicare & Medicaid Servs., State Operations Manual, CMS Pub. No. 100-07, Appendix PP: Guidance to Surveyors for Long Term Care Facilities F329, PP-356 [hereinafter CMS Survey Guidance].

29. Rojas-Fernandez, *supra* note 19, at 180.

30. Steven Zlotnick, *Pharmacology and the Elderly, in* Nursing Home Litigation: Investigation and Case Preparation 254 (Patricia Iyer ed., 1999).

31. Omnicare Inc., 2007 Annual Report (2008).

32. Douglas Singh, Effective Management of Long-Term Care Facilities 271 (2005).

33. CMS Survey Guidance, *supra* note 28, at F426.

34. Negligence claims would use the physician's directives as the standard of due care.

rate of use by elders not in nursing homes.[35] Blood thinners, cardiac medications, blood pressure drugs, and other medications are commonplace in the nursing home population. The average 75-year-old has three chronic conditions and takes five prescription drugs.[36] The injuries associated with these drugs are estimated to be 80 percent avoidable.[37]

The drug-related side effects that occur in the nursing home are sometimes easily avoidable with more attention to detail by the professionals involved. Adverse drug events among nursing home residents "are associated with significant morbidity, mortality, and increased healthcare costs."[38] There may be complexity to allocating the liability among the prescribing physician, the nurse who administers the drug, the manufacturer who prepared warnings for the drug, and the pharmacist who delivered the dosage. If a tort action is brought after a severe adverse reaction, counsel may wish to include as defendants the drug maker, any intermediate packager of the drug, the physician prescriber, and the nursing home that employed the nurses and aides who dispensed the drug.

13:9 Malpractice by Misprescribing

CMS standards for the use of medications in nursing homes[39] are linked closely to those of its sister agency, the FDA. The FDA approves drugs for specific disease conditions or "indications for use." Use of prescriptions outside of the indication of use that has been approved by the FDA is considered "off-label" usage. Some assert that doctors generally have no duty to inform residents that the drug being prescribed was not intended for the prescribed use.[40] This, of course, is subject to the doctrine of informed consent.

35. Rojas-Fernandez, *supra* note 19, at 180.
36. Meadows, *supra* note 21.
37. Rojas-Fernandez, *supra* note 19, at 180.
38. *Id.* at 179.
39. 42 C.F. R. § 483.25(1), (m) (2008).
40. Steven R. Salbu, *Off-Label Use, Prescription, and Marketing of FDA-Approved Drugs: An Assessment of Legislative and Regulatory Policy*, 51 Fla. L. Rev. 181, 190 (1999).

Elders need special consideration because of their physiological changes that are a normal part of aging but that place them at a higher risk of adverse effects.[41] The indications for use of the drug may be taken from the labeling approved by the FDA or from relevant clinical practice guidelines.[42]

The prescribing of a drug that is "contraindicated" for a person who has certain medical problems may be a basis for the physician's tort liability after an adverse consequence to the resident. This malpractice liability would fall upon the medical director or the resident's own "attending" physician.[43] The pharmacist should catch this contraindication as well, even more so as there are computer programs specifically designed to aid pharmacists in this screening process. Moreover, one of the goals of the movement to adopt electronic medical records is to provide everyone on the resident's care team with notice of the medications that the resident is currently taking in order to avoid these types of medical errors.

A failure to consult the electronic medical record, or to note the new prescription therein, will qualify as a medical error.

The FDA approves certain prescription drugs for certain indications, shown on their labeling, but physicians are legally permitted to prescribe for off-label uses. This act of prescribing is subject to individual liability in malpractice tort cases, and to state medical board discipline, should a serious drug-related problem arise for the resident. Prescribing a particular drug, notwithstanding the label warnings of the risks of severe adverse effects on that type of resident, can be a form of medical malpractice if the adverse event occurs, unless the adverse side effect occurs in a very small percentage of users or if the physician obtains the resident's informed consent.[44]

Malpractice is judged by a range of measures from the locality rule, the same or similar community rule or the national rule, as more fully

---

41. Tina Champion, *The Elderly Suing Doctors: Reasons and Recovery*, 12 ALB. L.J. SCI. & TECH. 895, 899 (2002).

42. CMS SURVEY GUIDANCE, *supra* note 28, at F329, PP-354.

43. Champion, *supra* note 41, at 901.

44. Robicheaux v. Adly, 827 So. 2d 429, 437 (La. Ct. App. 3d Cir. 2002), *writ denied*, 836 So. 2d 100 (La. 2003).

discussed in Chapter 8, but in nursing home cases, according to some courts, norms of medical practice that are lower than the federal CMS norms cannot be accepted.[45]

The physician's decision to prescribe the inappropriate, unsafe, or just "wrong" drug can seriously harm or kill the resident. A prescribing error can have very serious negative consequences in the nursing home setting.[46] If it does, the resident should be able to sue and receive compensation from the prescribing physician for injuries sustained as a result of the misprescribing decision.[47] The standard of care for medical professionals applies: was this treatment of the resident consistent with the amount of care that a physician of similar education, training, and experience would provide under similar circumstances? Some statutes require a plaintiff to proffer evidence of what care should have been given in place of the care that was given, that is, what drug alternative regimen should have been prescribed.[48]

Experts in gerontology and pharmacology recognize the special problems that nursing home residents will encounter.[49] A lack of formal training in the interactions between these two specialties has contributed to the deficiencies in implementation of some resident care plans. A controversial list of "potentially inappropriate medications for persons over age 65," the Beers List, may be relevant to the prescribing decision.[50] It does not automatically support a claim for malpractice by misprescribing, as these consensus lists of inappropriate drugs carry no regulatory status. Plaintiff's counsel should seek early expert evaluation.

The problem of drug-drug interactions is one that requires close scrutiny by the prescribing physician,[51] and not merely the pharma-

45. Hayward v. Jack's Pharmacy Inc., 115 P.3d 713 (Idaho 2005).
46. DiGregorio, *supra* note 22, at 96,114–20.
47. *See, e.g.*, Formella v. Ciba-Geigy Corp., 300 N.W.2d 356, 358 (Mich. Ct. App. 1980); Fleming v. Prince Georges Cnty., 358 A.2d 892 (1976).
48. Shaw v. BMW Healthcare, Inc., 100 S.W.3d 8, 14 (Tex. App.—Tyler 2002).
49. Rojas-Fernandez, *supra* note 19, at 179.
50. *Id.* at 191; *see also* Kimberley Rask et al., *Çan an Algorithm for Appropriate Prescribing Predict Adverse Events?*, 11 Am. J. Managed Care 145 (2005).
51. Rojas-Fernandez, *supra* note 19, at 186.

cist that fills the prescriptions.[52] Warfarin, a commonly used blood thinner, interacts badly with certain other drugs, with serious negative consequences.[53]

The attending physician does not come to the nursing home as often as the resident's family may expect; and so it is the obligation of the nurses and the medical director to be sensitive to allergies, adverse effects, and complications that require interventions and changes in medications.[54] The warning signs of potential serious adverse effects from a new or changed medication should alert the nurse to the possible need for prompt corrective action. A change of medications may need to be considered along with concerns about withdrawal; sometimes the body rebels against the elder's decision to cease intake of a continuing dose of a particular pharmaceutical chemical.[55]

13:10 Risks of Negligent Polypharmacy

One category of problems is the polypharmacy of multiple physicians administering multiple medications for the same resident: drugs may conflict, neutralize the effect of other drugs, or have contraindications.[56]

Experts have warned that close monitoring is necessary "since the elderly are more sensitive to the effects of these drugs, both beneficial and untoward."[57] These can produce severe adverse effects leading to serious injury.[58] Special attention is needed to avoid drug interactions.[59]

The negligent omission that causes harm is the failure of the prescribing physician to check for other medications that may have a conflicting effect. Some drugs clash in the digestive tract or may cause

---

52. Est. of Sharp v. Omnicare, Inc., 879 So. 2d 34, 36 (Fla. 5th Dist. App. 2004).
53. Meadows, *supra* note 21.
54. Rojas-Fernandez, *supra* note 19, at 182.
55. *Id.* at 184.
56. *Id.* at 186.
57. These increase the risks of "receiving unnecessary medications"; so the facility should "clearly identify who is responsible for prescribing and identifying the indications for use of medications." CMS Survey Guidance, *supra* note 28, at F329, PP-358.
58. Zlotnick, *supra* note 30, at 271.
59. Hogstel, *supra* note 20, at 346, 350.

harmful reactions when combined in the elderly resident who has a compromised immune system, weakness in muscle tone, and so on.

This area of pharmaceutical prescribing and delivery is a significant liability concern when errors occur. The bodies of elderly residents may be more dramatically affected by a mistake in medications; the cumulative effect of chronic medications delivered several times a day to the resident may make the initial error more severe as the body receives multiple doses of the harmful drug. Expert advice is essential to the plaintiff's case.

For example, a list of 45 recommendations for stopping certain customary care practices was made in "an educational initiative called Choosing Wisely, directed at both residents and physicians, under the auspices of the American Board of Internal Medicine Foundation and in partnership with Consumer Reports."[60]

One of the items on this list of "don'ts" is an American Geriatrics Society recommendation against the prescription of benzodiazepines or other sedative hypnotics in older adults as a first choice for insomnia, agitation, or delirium, because the use of these medications doubles the risk of car accidents, falls, and hip fractures in older adults.[61]

13:11 *Overdosing of Pharmaceuticals*

Another category of resident harm allegations is that of drug overdosing, caused by a miscommunication of the physician or pharmacist (or, in some cases, by the nurse providing the tube feeding or intravenous injection). The FDA cautions elders that these errors in dosing—for example, a weekly dose taken as a daily dose—can have serious adverse effects.[62] Mistakes in dosing caused 41 percent of the fatalities in an FDA study of drug adverse effects during the 1990s.[63]

---

60. Roni Caryn Rabin, *Doctor Panels Recommend Fewer Tests for Patients*, N.Y. Times, Apr. 4, 2012.

61. AGS Choosing Wisely Workgroup, *American Geriatrics Society Identifies Five Things That Healthcare Providers and Patients Should Question*, 61(4) J. Am. Geriatrics Soc'y 622–31 (2013).

62. Michelle Meadows, *Strategies to Reduce Medication Errors*, FDA Consumer (May-June 2003), http://www.mamashealth.com/doc/mederrors.asp.

63. Meadows, *Medication Use and Older Adults*, *supra* note 21.

The CMS standards look at the dose and duration that the drug maker has recommended; if either is exceeded, the chart should contain "a documented clinical rationale" for the benefit of this use or dose.[64] The plaintiff's lawyer will probe the records, often without finding this clinical rationale until the expert witness is engaged. Some overdose cases arise out of failure to check necessary blood or fluid levels and adjust doses accordingly.[65] A New York statute imposes a duty on the nursing home to monitor dosages and effectiveness of drugs.[66] Failure to monitor can be categorized as medical malpractice.[67]

A nursing home medical director owes a duty of care regarding how long a drug is to be used for a resident.[68] For example, the jury in the *Lutz* case awarded $2.25 million for a deceased resident who had been given an overdose for 12 days and went unmonitored for two and a half months. The chain owner of the nursing home had relaxed its policy; the state imposed a substantial penalty against the nursing home and this came into evidence in the tort case.[69]

In the *Barn Hill* case, CMS imposed penalties after a temporary unlicensed nurse was assigned without supervision to care for 29 residents. She used the wrong-sized needle for insulin and gave four residents serious overdoses of insulin; one became "critical, near death" before being sent to the hospital. Standards of practice require that medications be delivered within one hour of the time designated by the prescriber, but dosing at this home lagged by several hours and inadequately responded to the severe reaction by an overdose victim. On appeal of the CMS penalty, the appeals panel held that there is no "human error" exception since institutions should have systems

64. CMS Survey Guidance, *supra* note 28, at F329, PP-353.

65. D'Esposito *ex rel.* D'Esposito v. Haym Salomon Home for the Aged, 886 N.Y.S.2d 66 (N.Y. Sup. Ct. 2009); *see also* Greenbriar Nursing & Rehab. Ctr. v. U.S. HHS, 686 F.2d 521 (8th Cir. 2012).

66. 10 N.Y. Comp. Codes R. & Regs. § 415.12.

67. D'Esposito *ex rel.* D'Esposito v. Haym Salomon Home for the Aged, 886 N.Y.S.2d 66 (N.Y. Sup. Ct. 2009).

68. Hayward v. Jack's Pharmacy, 115 P.3d 713 (Idaho 2005).

69. Lutz v. Brian Ctr. Nursing Care, No. 95-CV-1290 (Catawba Cnty. N.C. Super. Ct. May 27,1997), *reported in* Verdicts, Settlements & Tactics 351 (Aug. 1997).

in place to control against foreseeable human errors. Penalties were upheld against the nursing home operator.[70]

13:12 Negligent Misdelivery

A third category is the delivery of the wrong medication to the resident, as a result of misidentification or mistake[71] by an aide or nurse who is handing out medications to the residents.[72] This is a "significant medication error" and it includes cases of not delivering the drugs that have been prescribed for a resident.[73] Few are as dramatic as the nursing home error that connected nitrogen tanks to the home's oxygen distribution system and killed several residents,[74] but errors do occur. Training and in-service sessions with a pharmacist have been often recommended.

13:13 Drugs as a Resident Restraint Option

Medicare rules and CMS survey instructions are clear that drugs should not be used as a restraint or discipline for nursing home residents, except where recommended by experts as a means to avoid the problem.[75] Former employees of the nursing home may be the optimal witnesses to describe lapses in the pharmaceutical delivery system.[76]

One setting for this event is the delivery by the nursing home aide of a set of daily medications to a room with three residents; the wrong resident gets the drugs intended for another person in the group room.

---

70. Barn Hill Care Ctr. v. CMS, Dec. No. 1848 (HHS Departmental Appeals Bd., App. Div., Sept. 24, 2002), http://www.hhs.gov/dab/decisions/dab1848.html.

71. *See, e.g.*, Kunz v. Little Co. of Mary Hosp. & Health Care Ctrs., 373 Ill. App. 3d 615, 869 N.E.2d 328((2006).

72. Fatigue and stress can lead to misdelivery by the overworked aides, *see* DIGREGORIO, *supra* note 22, at 114.

73. 42 C.F.R. § 483.25(m) (2008); *see also* Hazel Hawkins Mem'l Hosp. v. CMS, Dec. No. CR1753 (HHS Departmental Appeals Bd., Civ. Remedies Div., Mar. 18, 2008), http://www.hhs.gov/dab/decisions/civildecisions/2008/CR1753.pdf.

74. Meadows, *Medication Use and Older Adults*, *supra* note 21.

75. Zlotnick, *supra* note 30, at 253.

76. Patrick Ford, *Punitive Damages in Nursing Home Cases*, *in* NURSING HOME LITIGATION: PRETRIAL PRACTICE AND TRIALS 429, 448 (Ruben Krisztal ed., 2d ed. 2003).

Or the specific drugs may be delivered properly, but the pharmacist may have erroneously assigned the drugs to a person for whom they were not intended by the prescribing doctor. The pharmacist sending unit doses to the nursing home has the same obligation of care as the neighborhood pharmacist filling a regular customer's prescription.[77] The larger pharmaceutical suppliers are dealing with many unit-dose obligations; for example, the 1.4 million nursing home residents served by Omnicare will have prescriptions filled at a rate of 600 per hour by using unit-dose cards with resident-specific labels.[78]

13:14 Inattentive Medical Oversight

Some state laws protecting the rights of nursing home residents include a right to sue for deprivation of "adequate and appropriate medical care."[79] The physician who attends the nursing home resident, or the home's designated medical director, is accountable for proper medical supervision, and litigants will focus on the acts or omissions of that doctor.[80] Both common law negligence and statutory nursing home resident rights can be asserted.[81]

The nursing home may be liable under these state laws for significant medication errors and failure to adequately plan for and provide relief.[82] If the nursing home plan includes directions that include treatment by staff before physician or pharmacist consultation, the adherence to these directions can provide the basis for liability.[83] The nurse who fails to deliver a resident's medication without adequate explanation can be prosecuted, in an appropriate case.[84]

---

77. *See* Hayward v. Jack's Pharmacy, 115 P.3d 713 (Idaho 2005).

78. OMNICARE INC., 2007 ANNUAL REPORT 5 (2008).

79. N.Y. PUB. HEALTH LAW § 2801-d (2008), *interpreted in* Slobin v. Boasiako, 2008 WL 818940 (N.Y. Sup. Ct. Mar. 18, 2008).

80. Gerald Taylor, *Handling Witnesses: Deposing the Medical Director, in* NURSING HOME LITIGATION: PRETRIAL PRACTICE AND TRIALS 99 (Ruben Krisztal ed., 2d ed. 2003).

81. Zeides v. Hebrew Home, 753 N.Y.S.2d 450 (App. Div. 2002).

82. Morisett v. Terence Cardinal Cooke Health Care Ctr., 797 N.Y.S.2d 856 (N.Y. Super. 2005).

83. Life Care Ctr. Tullahoma v. Sec. of U.S. Dep't of Health & Human Servs., 453 F. App'x 610, 612 (6th Cir. 2011) (unpublished).

84. People v. Spence, 648 N.Y.S.2d 636 (App. Div. 1996).

Several nursing home cases have brought big verdicts for inadequate medical supervision of the resident's condition. The *Parish* case settled for $1.3 million and the *Lutz* case awarded $2 million; deterrence of future inadequacies in resident care and oversight were the likely basis for these large sums. The *Lutz* decision was a useful example: charting of the resident's condition stopped when Medicare payments ran out.[85]

In emergency circumstances, medication injections may suppress an agitated resident,[86] and some states require physician certification of the use of chemical restraints.[87] These regulations often show up in the form of references to the resident's rights and responsibilities.[88] Some homes have improperly used psychotropic medicines and chemical restraints to punish residents and prevent them from seeking help.[89]

A state survey team will review medication use among Medicaid-funded residents[90] and may impose a civil penalty against a nursing home that uses sedatives and other drugs as a means of discipline or to assure compliance by the residents. This limitation on drug use was a congressional decision in the 1987 legislation,[91] so it is well known as a constraint, even if not always followed in practice.

Experts in nursing home pharmacy have cautioned that the side effects of medications used for this constraint purpose may be adverse and may lead to litigation against the prescriber and the nursing home.[92] Some plaintiffs have had trouble establishing a causal connection between use of drugs and alleged side effects such as death or

---

85. Lutz v. Brian Ctr. Nursing Care, No. 95-CV-1290 (Catawba Cnty. N.C. Super. Ct.), *reported in* VERDICTS, SETTLEMENTS & TACTICS 351 (Aug. 1997); *see also* Greenbriar Nursing & Rehab. Ctr. v. U.S. HHS, 686 F.2d 521 (8th Cir. 2012).

86. 42 C.F.R. § 483.13(a) (2008); CMS SURVEY GUIDANCE, *supra* note 28, at F222.

87. Fine v. Woodside Manor Nursing & Convalescent Home, 830469, 1984 WL 6860 (Ohio Ct. App. 1st Dist. April 18, 1984); Adam v. Sisters of Bon Secours Nursing Care Ctr., No. 292144, 2011 WL 3903146 (Mich. Ct. App. September 6, 2011), *appeal denied*, 810 N.W.2d 572 (Mich. 2012).

88. *Adam*, 2011 WL 3903146.

89. Benun v. Super. Ct., 20 Cal. Rptr. 3d 26, 28 (Cal. Ct. App. 2d Dist. 2004).

90. 42 C.F.R. § 483.13(a) (2008); CMS SURVEY GUIDANCE, *supra* note 28, at PP-59.

91. SINGH, *supra* note 32, at 294.

92. Zlotnick, *supra* note 30, at 267 ("When a chemical restraint results in decline of a resident's functional status, physical harm or death, a malpractice investigation might ensue.").

heart attacks.[93] The psychiatric tort liability cases suggest that sedation would be an appropriate part of a restraint program under psychiatric institution policies;[94] these may or may not be permissible tactics in the nursing home context.

The real-world practice seems to be that nursing homes routinely, but perhaps less frequently,[95] sedate those "problem residents" who are aggressive or likely to wander, with the sedation euphemistically called "behavior modification."[96]

Harm through medication errors has been observed. In the *Daughters of Miriam*[97] case, a temporary nurse working at a nursing home gave the wrong medicine to several residents; injected drugs into a resident who was prescribed pills; and attempted to administer insulin to a nondiabetic resident who refused to accept the medication. Harm was shown where the erroneous injection occurred; the manufacturer's precautions for administration of the medication state that injection of the medication will cause pain, tenderness, and muscle necrosis. These symptoms and the pain felt by the resident were sufficient "harm" to trigger the protections of federal CMS rules.

The temporary nurse in the *Miriam* case was immediately terminated, and the nursing home successfully resisted some of the penalties sought against it by state surveyors under the CMS regulations.[98]

13:15 Medical Device Problems

A separate category of federal regulation relates to medical devices such as catheters, heart monitors, bed restraints, feeding tubes, and so on. These devices come with their own specific sets of risks, most of

93. Braud v. Woodland Vill. L.L.C., 54 So. 3d 745, 751 (La. Ct. App. 4th Cir. 2010) *writ denied*, 60 So. 3d 1254 (La. 2011).

94. Williams v. Wasserman, 164 F. Supp. 2d 591 (D. Md. 2001).

95. 75 Am. Jur. Trials 1 (originally published in 2000).

96. DiGregorio, *supra* note 22, at 116.

97. Daughters of Miriam Ctr. v. CMS, Dec. No. CR1357 (HHS Departmental Appeals Bd., Civ. Remedies Div., Sept. 29, 2005), https://www.hhs.gov/sites/default/files/static/dab/decisions/alj-decisions/2005/CR1357.htm.

98. *Id.*

which are anticipated by label warnings and limitations. In practice, restrictions or limitations on use are sometimes ignored or downplayed.

CMS rules and guidance require that the resident be given "assistance devices" that meet the needs of the resident.[99] These devices may include indwelling catheters, the longtime use of which increases the risk of bacterial infections to 40 times that of noncatheter residents.[100] Because of the known safety risks, CMS has set a high amount of care for staff members to regularly check and clean the residents who use catheters.[101]

The FDA requires reports of adverse events in which the device was utilized and harm resulted. The FDA tracks the safety issues that may arise with certain devices.[102] The failure of nursing home employees to use a medical device in accordance with its instructions is admissible as some evidence of the negligent provision of medical care,[103] and the use of the device in direct conflict with the product warnings may be evidence of negligent conduct by the nursing home.

---

99. 42 C.F.R. § 483.25(h)(2) (2008); *see also* CMS SURVEY GUIDANCE, *supra* note 28, at F324; Ivy Woods Healthcare & Rehab. Ctr. v. Thompson, 156 F. App'x 775 (6th Cir. 2005).

100. CMS SURVEY GUIDANCE, *supra* note 28, at F315, PP-254.

101. *Id.* at PP-256.

102. FDA, Form FD-3500. *See* U.S. Food & Drug Admin., MedWatch: The FDA Safety Information and Adverse Event Reporting Program, http://www.fda.gov/medwatch; U.S. Food & Drug Admin., MAUDE—Manufacturer and User Facility Device Experience, http://www.accessdata.fda.gov/scripts/cdrh/cfdocs/cfmaude/search.cfm.

103. Dove v. Ty Cobb Healthcare Sys., Inc., 699 S.E.2d 355, 356 (Ga. Ct. App. 2010).

CHAPTER 14

Food-Related Harms

14:1 Food-Related Litigation
14:2 Why Litigation Occurs
14:3 Types of Harm from Food
14:4 Chronic Risk: Weight Loss and Wasting
14:5 Lessons from the Cases
14:6 Acute Risk: Choking and Aspiration
14:7 Expert Testimony
14:8 Tube and Pump Feeding
14:9 Responsibility for Care and Feeding
14:10 Dehydration
14:11 Setting the Standard of Care
14:12 Evaluations of Resident Nutritional Needs
14:13 Assembling the Case
14:14 Baseline Evaluations

14:1 Food-Related Litigation

The content and quality of the food served at the nursing home will vary, of course, and it is required that there be a dietetic needs evaluation as part of the resident assessment at the time of entry, which flags for the staff this resident's vulnerabilities and needs.[1]

A special nutritional caution or need, such as a warning that the resident is diabetic, should be flagged on the chart for that resident. The feeding to a resident of a food not indicated for him or her because

1. 42 C.F.R. § 483.35(b) (2008).

of allergenic concerns or diabetic concerns would be negligent and should be avoided by staff training and by careful marking of the dietetic chart.

Nursing home food is not perfect, and its delivery is rarely perfect. These cases may seem easy to win because of jury empathy, but the path to plaintiff success is strewn with barriers.[2]

The relatively small number of reported appellate cases that have dealt with food and liquid issues can be subdivided into several categories. The first category is malnutrition, poor care, and inadequate monitoring of resident meals and liquids that cause serious physical harm or death.[3] Malnutrition becomes a source of medical problems as skin does not have the nutrients to heal and skin ulcers worsen.[4] This line of cases asserts that the negligence or intentional acts of the facility harmed residents as a result of management's efforts to cut costs. The food inadequacies are often driven by budget pressures on the nursing home that induce the home to save money. So the management buys the lowest-quality food and reduces the hours it pays for the contract services of the dietician/nutritionist who must formulate the plan for feeding residents.[5]

The second category of risk is choking on food by a resident who is unable to fully swallow, or who lacks the mental capacity to navigate a dining experience with normal care to avoid choking or aspirating the food.[6] Each nursing home is required to perform (initially and periodically thereafter) a "comprehensive, accurate assessment of the

---

2. A useful synopsis is Janet McKee, *The Role of Nutrition in Evaluating Nursing Home Care, in* Nursing Home Litigation: Pretrial Practice and Trials 429, 456 (Ruben Krisztal ed., 2d ed. 2003).

3. Muccianti v. Willow Creek Care Ctr., No. 625122-7 (Fresno Cnty. Cal. Super. Ct. 2001), *reported in* Verdicts, Settlements & Tactics 209 (May 2001) ($5.2 million award for death from malnutrition, dehydration, and quick dismissal from home after Medicare ran out).

4. Rodriguez v. Marion Mem'l Home, No. SVOICV-1082 (Muscogee Cnty. Ga. Super. Ct. 2004), *reported in* Verdicts, Settlements & Tactics 313 (July 2004) ($5.2 million award).

5. Roy Turner, *An Overview of the Use of NG and PEG Feeding Tubes in a Nursing Home Environment*, Am. Ass'n for Justice Nursing Home Litigation Group Seminar, Fall 2007, at 1–3.

6. Golden v. Sunrise Assisted Living Mgmt., No. 01-L-012539 (Cook Cnty. Ill. Cir. Ct. July 21, 2005), *reported in* Verdicts, Settlements & Tactics 405 (Oct. 2005) (decedent choked on ham, aspiration pneumonia followed, died in 13 days; jury verdict for $990,026 for plaintiff).

resident's ability to eat and drink without assistance."[7] This should identify those who need special interventions because they cannot safely eat solid foods by themselves.[8]

The third category encompasses injuries related to tube feeding. Tube feeding is regulated by CMS standards and will be closely examined during surveyor visits.[9] When properly performed and maintained, tube feeding can benefit the resident who has lost the ability to swallow.[10] The risk events are those in which obstructions in the tube, misplacement of the tube, tearing of an internal organ during tube implantation, tube feeding without raising the resident's head, or other tube-related injury results in a serious adverse effect on the resident, including infection, bowel problems, or aspiration into the lungs of the resident from the tube-fed liquid food material.

14:2 Why Litigation Occurs

An unknown number of deaths occur in elderly or infirm persons as a result of problems related to feeding. Some aspirate liquid food into the lungs during a badly managed tube feeding and die of pneumonia. Some starve or die of thirst, harm that could have been prevented by better care.

Some choke on solid food that should not have been served to them, if the speech therapist had properly diagnosed their swallowing problem and if the designated feeding aide had properly fed the resident. The few reported appellate cases in this field are only the small tip of the iceberg, in this as in many other fields, since deteriorated health conditions may appear natural rather than caused by malnutrition. An unknown tiny fraction of cases where problems such as malnourishment could be asserted will be litigated; the majority will be dropped

7. 42 C.F.R. § 483.30(a) (2008); CTRS. FOR MEDICARE & MEDICAID SERVS., STATE OPERATIONS MANUAL, CMS PUB. NO. 100-07, APPENDIX PP: GUIDANCE TO SURVEYORS FOR LONG TERM CARE FACILITIES F353, PP-529 [hereinafter CMS SURVEY GUIDANCE].

8. McKee, *supra* note 2, at 525.

9. CMS SURVEY GUIDANCE, *supra* note 7, at F369.

10. Nancy Collins & Victoria Castellanos, *Nutrition and Hydration*, *in* MEDICAL-LEGAL ASPECTS OF LONG-TERM CARE 125, 144 (Jeffrey Levine ed., 2003).

or settled, so the case law is an imperfect guide to the reality of this aspect of elder care.

Standards of due care related to nursing home food can be established from federal[11] and state rules, from CMS survey guidance,[12] from the nursing home's policy manual, and from expert testimony about standard practices for evaluation of swallowing capacity of residents, and evaluation of their needs for tube feeding. There are both standards for feeding and requirements for records of what food and drink have been offered. These combine with the required assessment of nutritional needs to aid the lawyer who is evaluating a potential liability claim. When an elderly resident of a nursing home is brought to a hospital suffering from the effects of severe malnutrition or dehydration, suspicion of "elder abuse" may be raised. When family members observe the elder, with his or her body wasting away as a result of undernourishment or dehydration, the family or responsible persons are likely to be surprised, and may remove that resident to another facility before considering a lawsuit.

There may be litigation about the ill treatment of that elderly person, intended to provide a deterrent to neglect by that nursing home operator in the future. So the prudent plaintiff's counsel will not overlook the liquid and nutritive needs of the resident as a possible source for recovery of compensation.

In practice, the poor outcomes from deficient resident feeding patterns are closely tied to labor costs, with high turnover of staff and inadequate numbers of paid staff to feed each resident who requires such aid.[13]

The CMS rules require adequate feeding staff, with paid feeders for the most functional residents, but with a CNA or nurse handling the

11. 42 C.F.R. § 483.35 (2008).

12. CMS Survey Guidance, *supra* note 7, at F373.

13. For an exceptionally thorough review, see Sarah Greene Burger, Jeanie Kayser-Jones & Julie Prince Bell, Malnutrition and Dehydration in Nursing Homes: Key Issues in Prevention and Treatment (Nat'l Citizens' Coal. for Nursing Home Reform, July 1, 2000), http://www.commonwealthfund.org/Publications/Fund-Reports/2000/Jul/Malnutrition-and-Dehydration-in-Nursing-Homes--Key-Issues-in-Prevention-and-Treatment.aspx.

feeding of those who have swallowing difficulties or more complex needs.[14] Money is the root of all evil, and in the specific issue of lawsuits related to feeding, the deterrent effect of a lawsuit alleging inadequacy or misconduct will be minimal, if it is covered by the home's liability insurance.

When the injury is a choking incident or aspiration of food into the lungs, the death or serious injury is scrutinized to determine whether it would have been preventable with adequate supervision of the feeding employees. These paid feeding employees should each have completed a state-approved course on feeding of such types of impaired residents.[15]

Policies of the nursing home will be scrutinized to determine the standard of negligence in administering food programs. For example, one nursing home allowed residents to take food from the dining area to their individual rooms; then a person slipped on a grape dropped in the hall, and the policy of allowing food to be removed was used as a basis for negligence claims.[16]

14:3 Types of Harm from Food

Two types of feeding situations bear close scrutiny in the nursing home context, where food or drink is related to the actual injury condition. The first is the chronic long-term loss of weight and/or severe symptoms of dehydration, which should alert the nursing home to the need for an intervention relating to diet or other medical remedial measures. CMS requirements[17] and state rules mandate that a nutrition assessment be performed on each entering resident within 14 days of admission, so this will provide litigants with a baseline, which is then augmented by study of the resident records kept on the amount

14. 42 C.F.R. § 483.35(b) (2008); CMS SURVEY GUIDANCE, *supra* note 7, at F373, PP-519 ("Paid feeding assistants are not permitted to assist residents who have complicated eating problems. . . . Nurses or nurse aides must continue to assist residents to eat or drink who require the assistance of staff with more specialized training.").

15. 42 C.F.R. § 483.30(a) (2008); CMS SURVEY GUIDANCE, *supra* note 7, at F353, PP-529.

16. Markowitz v. Helen Homes, 826 So. 2d 256 (Fla. 2002).

17. 42 C.F.R. § 483.35 (2008).

of food offered and eaten on a daily basis. Often, in cases of poor documentation, the only evidence of a resident's decline will be their apparent weight loss. In some residents, wasting is a symptom of their disease. In others, it is a natural process before dying. Nevertheless, in some instances, wasting is due to an egregious lack of reasonable care leading to starvation.

Dehydration and malnutrition will make the resident's skin ulcers and sores more severe and slower to heal. Malnutrition was one cause of death in a case that produced a $65 million award.[18] Charts indicating the resident's needs may be challenged as negligence. The second subcategory of harm is the acute problem of choking on solid food that was mistakenly given to a person who had been known to the nursing home to have an impaired ability to swallow food. Acute problems with food and drink may include failure to monitor the patient's feeding tube for obstructions or misconnections.

In some cases, failure to adequately maintain and monitor the feeding tube is the source of the problem. The resident's head must be elevated in bed and the pump must be monitored before the tube feeding can be safely administered. For those residents who receive special liquid nutrition, a feeding tube blockage may be fatal, and the aspiration into the lungs of tube-delivered liquids can be a source of life-threatening pneumonia.

14:4 Chronic Risk: Weight Loss and Wasting

The long-term loss of weight or symptoms of dehydration should alert the nursing home to the need for dietetic and perhaps medical intervention. Weight loss during the last period of life is a common phenomenon, but a loss such as 17 pounds in 75 days indicates a need for medical intervention.[19] The resident should be screened for the loss

---

18. Estate of West v. Vari-Care Inc., No. CV 91-0617, 1993 WL 631314 (Baldwin Cnty., Ala. Cir. Ct. Nov. 1993).

19. Lutz v. Brian Ctr. Nursing Care, No. 95-CV-1290 (Catawba Cnty. N.C., Super. Ct. 1997), *reported in* VERDICTS, SETTLEMENTS & TACTICS 351 (Aug. 1997).

of weight that seriously impairs his or her ability to function or ability to recover from other medical conditions.[20]

Loss of weight alone proves nothing. By the CMS rules, severe weight loss that is clinically avoidable violates the regulations for due care of residents.[21] But the plaintiff's lawyer is cautioned that weight loss during the final months of life in an elderly person is a common phenomenon of the cycle leading to natural death. The person who is alleged to have suffered a severe loss of weight that impairs his or her ability to function and to recover from medical conditions should be screened for distinctions between the expected, natural deterioration and deterioration that is attributable to negligent maintenance.[22]

A severe-weight-loss chart is in CMS Survey Guidance, regarding negligent care.[23] In some instances the drastic weight loss is the fault of negligent work by the nursing home staff.[24] Distant family members who sporadically come to visit the nursing home resident may wrongly conclude that the staff is "starving" their loved one. The key to assessing the case may be in the statements of others whose similar experiences in that home were comparably bad, or in records of state investigations of the nursing home for food-related resident neglect.[25]

14:5 Lessons from the Cases

These situations have been litigated over many decades.[26] An unscientific survey of jury verdicts in this field showed several results since

---

20. 42 C.F.R. § 483.25(i) (2008).

21. 42 C.F.R. § 483.25(i) (2008). A severe-weight-loss chart is in CMS SURVEY GUIDANCE, *supra* note 7, at F326, PP-338.

22. An instructive case of malpractice asserting the resident's declining weight is *Slobin v. Boasiako*, 19 Misc. 3d 1110 (Nassau Cnty. N.Y. Super. Ct. Mar. 18, 2008).

23. *See* CMS SURVEY GUIDANCE, *supra* note 7, at F326, PP-338.

24. *See, e.g.*, Marsh v. Bay Convalescent Ctr., No. 93-3758B (Bay Count). Cir. Ct. 1995), *reported in* VERDICTS, SETTLEMENTS & TACTICS 106 (Mar. 1996) (very severe dehydration and malnutrition after 35 days in a nursing home led to death; $400,000 settlement).

25. Diabetic care was alleged to be inadequate but the nursing home won a defense verdict with the argument that CMS and state rules were too complex to fully comply, Truehill v. W. Med. Ctr., No. 722908 (Orange Cnty. Cal. Super. Ct. 1996), *reported in* VERDICTS, SETTLEMENTS & TACTICS 496 (Nov. 1996).

26. Robert Brazener, Annotation, *Hospital's Liability for Injury Allegedly Caused by Improper Diet or Feeding of Resident*, 42 A.L.R. 736 (1972).

1996. Punitive damages of $92 million, later lowered to $11,855,000, were imposed where malnutrition and dehydration were proven against a nursing home.[27] A pattern of neglect of a partially paralyzed resident allowed him to deteriorate until he was too ill to recover; $250 million in damages were awarded.[28]

The dietary manager for a nursing home told state surveyors that a resident who had lost 17 pounds in 75 days showed that her nursing home had "dropped the ball" on that resident's nutrition needs; a $1,385,000 settlement was reached.[29] And malnutrition with a loss of 27 percent of body weight in 15 months was another serious concern, which led to a $380,000 settlement just before trial.[30]

A defendant claiming that CMS and state requirements were too complex to be absolutely and completely satisfied showed that natural causes were the source of the plaintiff's problems and won a defense verdict in the *Truehill* case.[31] A claim of malnutrition was tied in to one of inadequate care for a skin lesion and wrongful discharge of the resident in the *Muccianti* case,[32] and plaintiff won $5.2 million. Dehydration led to verdicts in two other cases awarding $100,000[33] and $400,000.[34]

In some cases, the nutrition sufficiency question becomes entangled with "right to die" issues of suspending the delivery of nutrition to a sick person who is unable to communicate his or her wishes and

---

27. Estate of Hary v. Horizon/CMS Healthcare Corp., No. JVR-212802, 1997 WL 831687 (Tarrant Cnty. Tex. Dist. Ct. Nov. 1997).

28. Rhodes v. HEB Nursing Home, *cited in* Julie Braun & Elizabeth Capezuti, *A Medico-Legal Evaluation of Dehydration and Malnutrition among Nursing Home Residents*, 8 ELDER L.J. 239, 277 (2000).

29. Parish v. Beverly Enters., CV-1-99-7216CC (Clay Cnty. Ct. Mo. July 2003), *reported in* VERDICTS, SETTLEMENTS & TACTICS 277 (July 2003).

30. Case name withheld (Franklin Cnty. Va. Cir. Ct. 2003), *reported in* VERDICTS, SETTLEMENTS & TACTICS 379 (Sept. 2003).

31. Truehill v. W. Med. Ctr., No. 722908 (Orange Cnty. Cal. Super. Ct. 1996), *reported in* VERDICTS, SETTLEMENTS & TACTICS 496 (Nov. 1996).

32. Muccianti v. Willow Creek Care Ctr., No. 625122-7 (Fresno Cnty. Cal. Super. Ct. 2001), *reported in* VERDICTS, SETTLEMENTS & TACTICS 209 (May 2001).

33. Anonymous v. Anonymous (L.A. Super. Ct. June 30, 1997), *reported in* VERDICTS, SETTLEMENTS & TACTICS 426 (Oct. 1997) (renal failure due to profound dehydration).

34. Marsh v. Bay Convalescent Ctr., No. 93-3758B (Bay Cnty. Fla. Cir. Ct. 1995), *reported in* VERDICTS, SETTLEMENTS & TACTICS 106 (Mar. 1996).

who has not given a directive regarding sustaining life.[35] A surviving spouse cannot simply direct the cessation of food and water through the resident's feeding tube; most courts will require the intervention of a judicial officer in a "right to die" proceeding before deeming the termination of life-sustaining services to be proper.[36]

14:6 Acute Risk: Choking and Aspiration

Experts believe that difficulty in swallowing food affects one-half to three-quarters of elderly nursing home residents, and some have substantial difficulty with eating and take considerable time to eat.[37] Malnutrition and dehydration could result. But if the wrong food is negligently given to an impaired eater, choking will follow,[38] with aspiration of food into the lungs being possible, and the catastrophe is a direct result of the negligent action of the supervisor and aide. Death can result and liability is likely to be imposed.

The standard of care for a resident whose swallowing is impaired is to have a trained staff member feed the individual resident with sufficient time and liquids to aid digestion and avoid choking or aspiration of the food. Understaffed homes may have as many as 14 residents to be fed by one aide.[39]

The nursing home staff must be ready to respond immediately if choking occurs, so that the tools and techniques are readily available; to do less would risk a fatal consequence.[40]

Choking to death on food seems to be a remote and rare event, but where the nursing home selected the menu, provided the feeding tray, and could have supervised the eating period for the resident, a negligence suit following a choking incident can be difficult to defend.

---

35. Alan Meisel, *Barriers to Forgoing Nutrition and Hydration in Nursing Homes*, 21 Am. J. Law & Med. 335 (1995).

36. Grace Plaza of Great Neck Inc. v. Elbaum, 588 N.Y.S.2d 853 (App. Div. 1992), *aff'd*, 623 N.E.2d 513 (N.Y. 1993).

37. Braun & Capezuti, *supra* note 28, at 239, 277.

38. Mildred Hogstel, Gerontology: Nursing Care of the Older Adult 172 (2001).

39. Charlotte Digregorio, Everything You Need to Know about Nursing Homes 100 (2005).

40. *Id.*

An Alabama case brought a $750,000 verdict when a nursing home allowed the wife of a resident to feed him; he choked to death, and the family sued the nursing home for negligence.[41]

Training the staff employees who feed these residents requires attention to safeguards such as remedial measures like the Heimlich maneuver, and attention to placing the right food for that resident at the right spoon or fork size into the mouth. "Liability may result if certain foods are served to dysphagic residents through error or lack of knowledge."[42] Sticky foods like peanut butter are unlikely to be well handled by a stroke victim, and peanut-flavored cookies served to a resident with allergies could result in sudden adverse reactions. Tube-fed residents are susceptible to a similar pattern of mistakes in the foods chosen, with similarly serious outcomes.[43]

14:7 Expert Testimony

These few litigated nutrition cases will perhaps involve intense disagreements among expert witnesses about the cause and effect of the individual's harm and the connection between the individual's lack of food or water and the subsequent serious injury, for example, renal failure or instability leading to collapse. In the cases involving choking, an expert with nursing home experience will assess the policy, the statements of witnesses recorded by police or state surveyors, and other documents, and then will determine whether the standard of care was met.

Cases involving a steady decline in the resident's weight while under a physician's care may present conflicting expert affidavits.[44] The minimal standard of care will be correlated with state regulations and with the federal CMS standards. In the CMS Guidance for Surveyors of nursing homes, for example, the survey team must determine

---

41. Crowne Invs. Inc. v. Reid, 740 So. 2d 400, 402 (Ala. 1999).
42. Braun & Capezuti, *supra* note 28, at 278.
43. *Id.*
44. DiGregorio, *supra* note 39, at 98.

if the nursing home has[45] qualified staff in sufficient numbers to provide assistance to eat or drink to those residents who require such assistance.[46]

14:8 Tube and Pump Feeding

Residents who cannot safely eat normal food can be fed by one of several types of tubes, some entering the nose and some surgically implanted to feed through the stomach or the intestine.[47] This service is delivered to residents in the skilled nursing home or hospital setting, since tube feeding is a high-risk skilled service that ordinary care homes cannot provide.[48] Misplaced tubes can be fatal if their erroneous installation into the stomach or intestine punctures an internal organ, fills the abdominal cavity and causes peritonitis, causes reflux resulting in aspiration pneumonia, or clogs and thereby blocks the flow of liquids that the body needs to sustain itself. These tube cases carry substantial liabilities for the nursing home supervisors and nurses, especially a nurse who tries to reinstall a surgically placed tube into the stomach but misses the mark.

Feeding tube usage is disfavored for most residents by CMS norms, yet it saves time for the staff and allows the billing of Medicaid for the additional "medically necessary" services including tube placement and maintenance.[49] Risks of tube feeding include aspiration of food into the lungs, infection, diarrhea, nausea, dislodgement of the tube, and increased use of restraints to prevent the person from pulling out the tube.[50]

The proper location of a tube must be ascertained by a doctor or nurse.[51] Death could result from staff member or nurse errors in

45. Slobin v. Boasiako, 19 Misc. 3d 1110 (Nassau Cnty. N.Y. Super. Ct. Mar. 18, 2008).
46. 42 C.F.R. § 483.30(a) (2008); CMS Survey Guidance, *supra* note 7, at F353, PP-530.
47. Douglas Singh, Effective Management of Long-Term Care Facilities 350 (2005).
48. Hogstel, *supra* note 38, at 388.
49. 42 C.F.R. § 483.25(g) (2008); CMS Survey Guidance, *supra* note 7, at F322.
50. Jackie Nasso & Lisa Celia, Dementia Training: Inservice Training Modules for Long-Term Care 150.
51. Cockerham v. Lassalle Nursing Home Inc., 930 So. 2d 239 (La. Ct. App. 2006).

dealing with the misplaced or clogged feeding tube.[52] Tube feeding is subject to specific federal rules and guidance.[53] Informed consent is required, and failure to adequately inform and obtain consent may be a basis for a negligence per se claim.[54] Critics of nursing home management assert that the tube system is both a cost-saving and money-making aspect of the care given at a facility.[55] Fatal consequences can result from mishandling of the tube feeding system.[56] Major tort damage cases have involved these tubes.[57]

These cases have involved postdeath claims that tube feeding should have been performed on a resident who was losing weight.[58] Federal standards fix the norm as "unavoidable"; the tubes are not used for feeding "unless the resident's clinical condition demonstrates that use of a naso-gastric tube was unavoidable."[59] There are potential liability problems with several aspects of this procedure, though it may be absolutely necessary for sustaining the life of a resident who is paralyzed or who for other reasons cannot eat normally. Tube feeding is one of the most likely reasons for injury litigation in the nursing home setting.[60] Often this is the result of poor handling of feeding tubes by the aides in the nursing home; better care requires following specific protective steps.[61] Courts do impose liability where feeding tubes were not properly used or where the expected nutritional materials were not supplied to the injured person.[62]

Some plaintiffs' counsel who have studied this field believe that the rate of use of tube feeding is excessive and that the reason for its use

---

52. Liguori v. Beverly Enters., 762 So. 2d 1069 (Fla. Dist. Ct. App. 2000).

53. 42 C.F.R. § 483.25(g) (2008) (duty to prevent aspiration pneumonia in nasogastric tube feeding); CMS Survey Guidance, *supra* note 7, at F322.

54. Diggs v. Susquehanna Ctr., No. 944S1996, 1996 WL 1044797 (Pa. Com. Pl. Dec. 9, 1996).

55. DiGregorio, *supra* note 39, at 209.

56. *Cockerham*, 930 So. 2d 239.

57. $63 million in punitive damages and $15 million in compensatory damages were awarded in *Sauer v. Advocat Inc.*, No. crv 2000-5 (Ark. Cir. Ct. 2001).

58. Slobin v. Boasiako, 19 Misc. 3d 1110 (Nassau Cnty. N.Y. Super. Ct. Mar. 18, 2008).

59. 42 C.F.R. § 483.25(g)(1) (2008).

60. Marshall Kapp, *At Least Mom Will Be Safe There: The Role of Resident Safety in Nursing Home Quality*, 12 Quality & Safety in Health Care 201 (Dec. 2003).

61. DiGregorio, *supra* note 39, at 135.

62. *See, e.g.*, HCRA of Tex. Inc. v. Johnston, 178 S.W.3d 861 (Tex. App. 2005).

goes beyond medical necessity and instead reflects a desire to save labor cost on the part of the nursing home administration. If the resident is not mobile, and not fully capable of self-care, the expensive alternative is to assign an aide to hand-feed that person, three times a day. The less expensive option for the facility's administration is to obtain a physician's order for feeding, along with a pump and surgically placed tube, which allows the staff member to enter the resident's room, start the pump for delivery of the liquid through the tube, and then go on to other residents. This labor cost savings, when multiplied by dozens of residents, is significant, and it also transfers the cost item from general labor expense to Medicare-reimbursed surgical and postsurgical services. The medical procedure of implanting the tube for feeding and then supervising its use will be important cost items for Medicare.

14:9 Responsibility for Care and Feeding

Counsel should be aware of how difficult this particular dietary responsibility can be for the nursing home. Feeding is literally life-sustaining, but it is a challenging assignment to maintain the fluid and food intake in a resident who rejects both because he or she is in pain, is mentally challenged and uncooperative, or has difficulty in swallowing.

The optimal demonstrated means by which to carry through this obligation is the use of trained CNAs or feeding assistants[63] who rely upon a coaxing and coaching approach. The nursing home may also need to use a one-to-one feeding arrangement by assigning a particular aide to feeding or supervising the eating of dietician-planned meals. Paid feeding assistants must be trained before being assigned to feed residents; it is likely to be cited as a violation if paid assistants for feeding had not been adequately trained.[64]

Enteral feeding in particular is generally limited to residents in the skilled nursing home or hospital setting, since tube feeding is

---

63. CMS Survey Guidance, *supra* note 7, at F353, PP-530.
64. *Id.* at PP-530.

a high-risk skilled service that ordinary care homes lack. This ideal standard of care is not what really happens, according to an expert report done for the Commonwealth Fund: the ideal is one staffer to two or three residents; the reality as of the 2000 study was seven to nine residents to be fed at daytime meals and 12 to 15 residents in the evening, with the result that "[r]esidents are fed quickly or forcefully and sometimes not fed at all."[65]

Lack of appropriate feeding assistants is a problem where staff members have been lost at a 93 percent turnover rate.[66] Also of concern to CMS surveyors is "coughing and/or choking episodes related to the paid feeding assistant using poor techniques indicating lack of appropriate supervision."[67] Tort liability flows if the nursing home was on notice of the prior choking history of a vulnerable resident, and then failed to offer assistance, and the resident choked to death on the food.[68]

This individual feeding process is of course expensive and labor intensive, and therefore may be resisted by the financial side of the nursing home management team. Discovery of internal e-mails and corporate documents will demonstrate the risk/cost balance done by some nursing home chains. Plaintiffs' lawyers have expressed significant alarm that the costs paid by Medicare for tube feeding is high, and the nursing home thereby saves the personnel cost for a person to perform the hand-feeding tasks.[69]

Responsibility for inadequate or improper tube feeding occasionally becomes a question for a jury. Several tort cases have addressed tube feeding. One was a throat aspiration, in which the resident choked; recklessness was alleged, and a defense verdict was given.[70] In the other, the tube was not cleaned and it malfunctioned; the defendant admitted liability, and the jury awarded $2.9 million.[71] In another case

---

65. *See* BURGER ET AL., *supra* note 13.

66. *See id.* at viii.

67. CMS SURVEY GUIDANCE, *supra* note 7, at PP-530.

68. Beverly Enters.-Va. v. Nichols, 441 S.E.2d 1 (Va. 1994).

69. Turner, *supra* note 5.

70. Platt v. Palmer, No. 06-CC-04201 (Orange Cnty. Super. Ct. Mar. 27, 2007), *reported in* VERDICTS, SETTLEMENTS & TACTICS (Apr. 2007) (defense verdict).

71. Carrasco v. Healthcare & Ret. Corp., No. 02-L-7024 (Cook Cnty. Ill. Cir. Ct. Aug. 11, 2006), *reported in* VERDICTS, SETTLEMENTS & TACTICS (Sept. 2006).

involving an assisted living home, the home admitted the negligence of its staff; the award was $990,000.[72]

14:10 Dehydration

Providing adequate water is essential to sustaining life, and will be among the aspects of performance examined by the survey teams.[73] The CMS survey norms[74] are violated by a nursing home's failure to insist that the resident drink sufficient liquids and some courts will allow a negligence per se claim for dehydration.[75] That is because, as CMS emphasizes to its surveyors of nursing home compliance, inadequate hydration results in weight loss, urinary tract infections, and fecal bowel impaction.[76]

In the chronic injury cases, the subtle signs of dehydration should not be overlooked. Dehydration results in problems with wound healing, in the urinary tract, in stability, and gait problems as the resident walks, and so on.[77]

Lack of adequate liquid intake is remediable by having staff members constantly prompt the residents to drink their liquids, so that they have an adequate supply on a continuing basis. This, however, may involve more staff time and personal attention to residents than the budget for that particular nursing home has allowed. The consequence may be that the slow and quiet deterioration of the resident's condition goes too far before the dehydration becomes visible. Medical staff must perform the hand-feeding tasks.

---

72. Golden v. Sunrise Assisted Living Mgmt., No. 01-L-012539 (Cook Cnty. Ill. Cir. Ct. July 21, 2005), *reported in* VERDICTS, SETTLEMENTS & TACTICS (Oct. 2005) ($990,000 award).

73. *Id.*

74. 42 C.F.R. § 483.25(j) (2008).

75. Goda v. White Cliff Leasing P'ship, No. 2002-917, 2003 WL 22841695 (Pa. Com. Pl. May 21, 2003).

76. CMS SURVEY GUIDANCE, *supra* note 7, at P-46.

77. *See, e.g.*, Caruso v. Pine Manor Nursing Ctr., 538 N.E.2d 722, 725 (Ill. App. Ct. 1989).

14:11 Setting the Standard of Care

The best means of winning these cases is to establish the amount and type of care that is reasonable under the circumstances and to demonstrate in the acute cases that this care was not provided, for example, by delivering the wrong food tray to a resident—which resulted in an acute injury such as choking or aspiration.

The amount and type of care that is reasonable under the circumstances for safe and adequate feeding can be drawn from the CMS guidelines, state guidelines, the AMDA guidelines, and other means of articulating best practices or a required mandatory practice in dealing with resident feeding habits and practices. The witness testimony comparing the condition of the plaintiff when he or she was hospitalized to the condition of a comparable person under normal nursing home care will be very instructive.

The Woodland Hills case involved a resident who consumed less liquid than the facility's registered dietician had recommended, but the fact that a resident consumed less fluid than recommended is not determinative. The question under the CMS regulation is "whether or not a resident was properly hydrated and proper hydration is primarily determined by looking for signs and symptoms of dehydration."[78] The appeals panel found evidence of a diagnosis of dehydration for this nursing home resident, when made by treating physicians in a hospital setting, to be highly credible and probative.[79]

14:12 Evaluations of Resident Nutritional Needs

The content and quality of the food served at the nursing home will vary, of course, and it is required that there be a dietetic needs evaluation as part of the resident assessment at the time of entry, which flags for the staff this resident's vulnerabilities and needs.[80]

78. Woodland Vill. Nursing Ctr. v. CMS, Dec. No. CR1367 (HHS Departmental Appeals Bd., Civ. Remedies Div., Nov. 16, 2005), http://www.hhs.gov/dab/decisions/CR1367.htm.

79. *Id.*

80. 42 C.F.R. § 483.35(b) (2008).

A special nutritional caution or need should be flagged on the chart for that resident, such as a warning that the resident is diabetic. The feeding to a resident of a food not indicated for him or her because of allergenic concerns or diabetic concerns would be negligent, and should be avoided by staff training and by careful marking of the dietetic chart.

14:13 Assembling the Case

An expert on the defense of nursing home liability claims told a trade journal interviewer in 2007 that settlements are most common; dismissals are second;[81] and a very small percentage of these cases actually go to trial, verdict, and final disposition.[82]

Resident malnutrition, falls, and skin ulcers are the top three claim types for the defenders of nursing homes.[83] Malnutrition leading to death or serious illness is attractive to an experienced plaintiff's counsel; these cases "almost always have the basis for punitive damages because they involve conscious neglect by almost all of the staff of the nursing home for extended periods of time."

If the injury directly resulted from an acute "misfeeding" form of negligence, the claim of allergic reaction harm or choking injury is likely to be settled. If it proceeds to litigation, the most useful witnesses may be former employees who left the nursing home and who have a perspective on the lack of adequate attention given to dietetic restrictions.[84]

In the case of chronic malnutrition issues, the discovery of poor conditions at the nursing home by a state surveyor or the discovery of a resident's physical crisis at the emergency room by a physician treating that nursing home resident may suggest a pattern of malnutrition

---

81. Paul Hamlin, *Claims Management: From Report to Resolution*, LONG-TERM LIVING, June 30, 2007, http://www.ltlmagazine.com/article/claims-management-report-resolution.

82. Patrick Ford, *Punitive Damages in Nursing Home Cases*, *in* NURSING HOME LITIGATION: PRETRIAL PRACTICE AND TRIALS, *supra* note 2, at 429.

83. *Id.* at 448.

84. CMS SURVEY GUIDANCE, *supra* note 7, at PP-519.

that is beyond what would be expected in that person, given his or her age and circumstances.

Proving a negligent feeding pattern will probably require one or two experts with registered dietitian credentials and sufficient experience to be able to determine the nursing home's variations from normal standards of dietetic care.

In some cases, the court has permitted the nursing home to withhold supportive measures. The guardian of a 92-year-old nursing home resident was granted a court order authorizing it, as guardian of person and property of the incapacitated person, to act on his behalf in withholding consent to his intubation with a percutaneous endoscopic gastronomy (PEG) feeding tube, to diagnostic testing, and to medical treatment of metastasized cancer, and further authorizing it to act on his behalf in granting consent to palliative and/or hospice care and in executing orders of "do not resuscitate" (DNR) and "do not intubate" (DNI). New York's Family Health Care Decision Act allowed such an order.[85]

14:14 Baseline Evaluations

Baseline evaluations of weight, caloric intake, restrictions, allergies, and so on should be in the chart, as a result of the incoming resident assessment that must be performed by a registered dietician within 30 days of admission. In this aspect of preparing for possible tort cases, it will be essential to study the dietitian's initial and annual assessment of the incoming resident. The CMS guidance requires such a dietary assessment to be performed by the dietitian within 30 days after the new resident enters the nursing home.[86] If this is not done, the nursing home may be vulnerable to a penalty from the state surveyors of long-term care.[87]

---

85. *In re* N. Manhattan Nursing Home, 32 Misc. 3d 754, 928 N.Y.S.2d 810 (Sup. Ct. 2011).
86. 42 C.F.R. § 483.35 (2008).
87. CMS Survey Guidance, *supra* note 7, at PP-519.

CHAPTER 15

Liability for Infections and Other Injuries

15:1 Overview of Nursing Home Infection Challenges
15:2 CMS Targets HAIs in New Initiatives
15:3 Importance of Metrics for Measurement of Infection Rates
15:4 Ongoing Survey and Certification Work Related to HAIs
15:5 Infection Issues
15:6 Bathing, Scalding, and Drowning
15:7 Insects

15:1 Overview of Nursing Home Infection Challenges

Plaintiffs in the nursing home case that involves communicable diseases should be able to discern evidence that the plaintiff resident had developed an infection that is attributable to the nursing home.[1] Nursing home patients often develop infections and skin problems (e.g., pressure ulcers).[2] Conjunctivitis, gastroenteritis, and influenza are also common.[3]

1. CTRS. FOR MEDICARE & MEDICAID SERVS., STATE OPERATIONS MANUAL, CMS PUB. NO. 100-07, APPENDIX PP: GUIDANCE TO SURVEYORS FOR LONG TERM CARE FACILITIES 337 (2011) ("Overview").

2. L.E. Nicolle et al., *Infections and Antibiotic Resistance in Nursing Homes*, 9 CLINICAL MICROBIOLOGY REVS. 1–17 (1996).

3. C. Richards, *Infections in Residents of Long-Term Facilities*, 50 J. AM. GERIATR. SOC. 676 (2002).

While confirming and ameliorating an infectious outbreak can be costly in both time and money, planning ahead by creating an effective facility-wide infection prevention and control program can help to contain costs and reduce adverse consequences. An effective program relies upon the active support and knowledge of the facility's administration, the entire interdisciplinary team, residents, and visitors. The CMS State Operations Manual includes a list of excellent clinical practice guidelines to help in these efforts.[4]

Recognizing and managing infections from the time of a resident's admission to the facility and throughout his or her stay are critical aspects of the infection prevention and control program. Of great importance is that the staff consistently follow recognized infection control practices while providing care (e.g., hand hygiene, handling and processing of linens, use of standard precautions, and appropriate use of transmission-based precautions). Finally, great care must be used to cohort or separate infectious residents.[5]

Once a resident is found to have an infectious condition, that resident must be fully reassessed because older adults may have coexisting diseases that complicate the diagnosis of an infection (e.g., joint degeneration versus infectious arthritis, COPD versus pneumonia), and they may also have atypical or nonspecific signs and symptoms related to infections, such as altered mental status, function or behavior, and impaired fever response.[6]

An additional challenge for the nursing home is to balance the promotion of the resident's rights while trying to prevent the spread of infection. This calls for a systematic approach that learns from the experience of others.

---

4. Ctrs. for Medicare & Medicaid Servs., State Operations Manual, CMS Pub. No. 100-07, Appendix PP: Guidance to Surveyors for Long Term Care Facilities 395–97 (2011).

5. *Id.* at 337.

6. *Id.*

15:2 CMS Targets HAIs in New Initiatives

Hospital- or healthcare-acquired infections (HAIs) are a major problem. According to a 2012 report from CMS, HAIs are mostly preventable, but they occur far too often in nursing homes. CMS identifies multiple factors that contribute to this problem, "including but not limited to understaffed facilities, staff without the appropriate training or time to identify infections early, overtreatment with antibiotics, the increasing clinical complexity of the average nursing home resident, and frequent transitions between care settings that lead to person-person transmission of HAIs. Additionally, nursing homes frequently lack a systematic approach to prevent and identify HAIs."[7]

The impact on all the stakeholders is great, because HAIs reduce nursing home residents' quality of life and increase the risk of an acute hospitalization (with all of its associated negative sequelae), morbidity, and mortality. HAIs also further strain the limited resources of the provider community.

For these reasons, the CMS Division of Nursing Homes (DNH) has set the reduction of HAIs as a priority. Steps that have been, or are being, taken include the creation of a new chapter on reducing HAIs in the long-term care environment to provide to the HHS Secretary. This chapter will add to the National Action Plan to Prevent Healthcare Associated Infections: Roadmap to Elimination (the National Action Plan).

15:3 Importance of Metrics for Measurement of Infection Rates

The first step in this plan is to create metrics that can be used to quantify the current rate of high frequency and high cost HAIs, such as *C. difficile* infection, urinary tract infections (both noncatheter- and catheter-associated), catheter care processes, and the vaccination rates

---

7. Dep't of Health & Human Servs., CMS 2012 Nursing Home Action Plan 27 (2012), http://www.cms.gov/Medicare/Provider-Enrollment-and-Certification/Certificationand Complianc/Downloads/2012-Nursing-Home-Action-Plan.pdf.

of both residents and staff for influenza and pneumonia. This will help to establish robust baseline estimates of the burden of HAIs in nursing homes (mostly by utilizing the nursing home module of the National Health Safety Network surveillance tool), and to track the progress of HAI reduction initiatives.

At the same time, the CMS Division of Nursing Homes (DNH) developed a study with the Centers for Disease Control and Prevention (CDC) to evaluate state action plans to address HAIs in nursing homes. This study had three phases. The first phase consists of a data collection effort in order to determine what the state survey agencies or departments of health are already doing to reduce HAIs in nursing homes. Second, an in-depth analysis of a few states that appear to be more aggressive in their efforts to eradicate HAIs was performed. Finally, DNH and the CDC took the lessons learned from individual state's experiences to better train nursing home surveyors to identify potential risk for HAIs. For the nursing home plaintiff's case preparation efforts, this background research can set up the claim support and facilitate settlement.

15:4 Ongoing Survey and Certification Work Related to HAIs

In 2009, CMS combined several of its enforcement and penalty tags into one infection control Tag at F441 and expanded the interpretive guidance from eight to 38 pages.[8]

This expansion of federal guidance is rich in information that will both help the nursing home in its risk management, regulatory compliance, and litigation defense efforts, as well as assist the plaintiff's lawyer in identifying deficiencies that resulted in harm to the resident. CMS's focus on this issue is likely to bring far more cited deficiencies because, in addition to the policy change, train-the-trainer sessions were held jointly by CMS and the CDC to heighten awareness of infection control issues and to increase surveyor confidence in citing these deficiencies.[9]

---

8. *Id.*
9. *Id.*

CMS posts on the Nursing Home Compare website the new set of quality measures based on the MDS 3.0 instrument. Some of these measures address HAI-related domains such as resident vaccinations, urinary tract infections, and catheterization. Additionally, CMS will be able to analyze data from the MDS related to multidrug resistant organisms. Finally, CMS will explore analyses that link the nursing home residents with acute care hospitalizations for infections as either the primary or secondary diagnoses. This data will be of great use for prospective residents choosing a nursing home as well as for plaintiffs pursuing an HAI claim against a nursing home.

15:5 Infection Issues

Relatively few nursing home liability appellate cases relate to infection; this is not because there are few infections, but because the proof of infectious disease causation can be particularly difficult. Indeed, health care facilities generate infections in previously uninfected persons. The hospital-acquired infection is one of the top ten causes of death tracked by CDC.[10] The linkage of infection with nursing home quality issues is understood among infection control professionals.[11]

CDC's Guidelines for Environmental Infection Control in Health-Care Facilities[12] offer a useful standard against which to measure nursing home performance, perhaps aided by former employees who actually witnessed the conditions as of the time of the passage of the infection to the plaintiff.

If the cause can be identified with a particular source within the nursing home, it may be possible to find expert witness testimony that the

---

10. *See* Health-Care-Associated Infections in Hospitals: Leadership Needed from HHS to Prioritize Prevention Practices and Improve Data on These Infections, U.S. GOV'T ACCOUNTABILITY OFFICE, GAO-08-283, (Mar. 2008) http://www.gao.gov/products/GAO-08-283.

11. *See, e.g.*, Ctrs. for Disease Control & Prevention, Get Smart for Health Care, http://www.cdc.gov/getsmart/healthcare/; M. Yates, *A Study of Infection in Elderly Nursing Home, Residential Home and Community Based Residents*, 43 J. Hosp. Infection 123 (1999); R.A. Garibaldi, *Infections among Residents in Nursing Homes*, 305 New. Eng. J. Med. 731 (1981).

12. Ctrs. for Disease Control & Prevention, Guidelines for Environmental Infection Control in Health-Care Facilities, http://www.cdc.gov/mmwr/preview/mmwrhtml/rr5210a1.htm (issued 2003).

standard of care for infection control had been breached by the defendants. Proving cause in fact in a negligence case is a daunting task if other sources of viral or bacterial exposure might have caused the harm.

Transmission of disease by workers inside the nursing home appears to be cited often among critics, using anecdotal information, but there is a shortage of specific detailed data on which a plaintiff can build a case. The exception could be a federal or state OSHA workplace inspection.

Liability for Infections and Other Injuries can become many times greater than injury rates for the average employment setting, so this may be a fruitful avenue for plaintiff's counsel to pursue.[13]

Periodic inspections will evaluate and may impose penalties for noncompliance relating to disease transmission under the OSHA Bloodborne Pathogens (BBP) standard. The BBP standard requires the worker who comes into contact with feces, blood, urine, and other bodily fluids to be protected by universal precautions, typically gloves and necessary protective gear.[14] A pattern of violations around protecting workers' health may aid the plaintiff's assertion that the disease transmission that harmed the plaintiff had come from negligent actions of the nursing home employees. The expert witness needed to support this assertion will be an epidemiologist or infectious disease physician.

Bladder infections and catheter use appear to be correlated among nursing home residents, but some of these assertions are anecdotal rather than epidemiological,[15] so the claims might not survive pretrial scrutiny that would be needed to sustain a tort case.

15:6 Bathing, Scalding, and Drowning

Bathing of residents in scalding water can produce serious burns. But it is especially difficult to prove liability when the resident cannot express a feeling of pain or has lost feeling in a part of his or her

---

13. *See* Occupational Safety & Health Admin., Nursing Homes and Personal Care Facilities, http://www.osha.gov/SLTC/nursinghome/index.html.

14. 29 C.F.R. § 1910.1030.

15. Charlotte DiGregorio, Everything You Need to Know about Nursing Homes 84 (2005).

body that is in contact with the extreme heat. These cases come to light when serious burns are treated at a hospital and thereafter state reporting requirements for "elder abuse" result in the notification to a state long-term care hotline.

Residents should be assisted in bathing, consistent with personal privacy and dignity. The occasional cases of bathtub drowning are likely to be a result of negligent supervision of the impaired elder.

15:7 Insects

CMS requires that an appropriate pest control program be in place.[16] Ordinarily, pest control would be a minor part of the nursing home maintenance budget. But in some tropical climates, ants are aggressive and can bite humans, especially those unable to protect themselves from harm. Insect attacks are preventable and horrid events, so plaintiffs would be likely to obtain a settlement before a jury decision.

Two CMS penalty appeals are instructive on this issue. The state survey results for a Florida nursing home revealed that a nursing home's pest control had been defective. The resident was hospitalized after being found covered with fire ants and their bites.[17]

In a comparable case, the nursing home argued on appeal that it had done all that it could do to prevent ant bites on its residents.[18] These cases are typically settled with minimal publicity, so the case law is relatively infrequent.[19]

16. 42 C.F.R. § 483.70(h)(4).

17. Lake Mary Health Care v. CMS, Dec. No. 1031 (HHS Departmental Appeals Bd., App. Div., May 14, 2007), http://www.hhs.gov/dab/decisions/dab2081.pdf.

18. *In re* Emerald Shores Health & Rehab. Ctr. v. CMS, Dec. No. CR1385 (HHS Departmental Appeals Bd., Civ. Remedies Div., Dec. 22, 2005, http://www.hhs.gov/dab/decisions/CR1385.htm.

19. Two ant-bite injury cases drew million-dollar verdicts: Tewcyzynski v. Hoffman, No. 1999-29188 (Harris Cnty. Tex. Jud. Dist. Ct. May 12, 2003), *reported in* 23 Verdicts, Settlements & Tactics 22 (Aug. 2003); Devers v. Huntsville Health Servs., 2300 Jud. Cir. Ct. (Huntsville, Ala., June 28, 2002), *reported in* 22 Verdicts, Settlements & Tactics 388 (Sept. 2002).

CHAPTER 16

Admission and Discharge

16:1 Overview
16:2 Rationale for Placing Resident in the Home
16:3 Economics of Admission Balancing
16:4 Admission Agreements and Brochures
16:5 Involuntary Discharge
16:6 Appeal of Involuntary Discharge
16:7 Patient Movement within Nursing Homes

16:1 Overview

Medicaid-accepting facilities are subject to specific CMS rules regarding discharge rights of patients.[1] This subcategory of litigation deals with the nursing home that discharges the resident without the consent of the resident or his or her guardian. Such litigation occurs infrequently but it may be the source of an exceptional verdict if foreseeable harm to the resident results.

16:2 Rationale for Placing Resident in the Home

The family's rationale for seeking nursing home care may be fear of the family's inability to prevent further harm to a frail elderly relative. There may be a concern that an acute injury may occur at home, and an expectation that the nursing home would be a safer residential

1. 42 C.F.R. § 483.12.

setting. A statement from the primary care physician, past hospital reports, and memos regarding the patient's mental condition can all be included when the nursing home is asked to make a bed available for the prospective resident. Mutual decisions about the resident's appropriate "fit" with this facility are made by the facility administrator, the hospital discharge planner (where appropriate), and the family members of the resident.

The relevance of this decision to litigation is that the defense may in some instances question the family members' motives in the lawsuit. Defense counsel may impeach their claims of concern for the institutionalized person. The defense would argue that the family that projects its sorrow to the jurors, appearing as a group of saddened survivors, actually had rarely visited and had done little to protect the patient during his or her life. Jurors may be receptive to the defense assertions; if the nursing home conditions had been so terrible, the defense counsel will argue, why was the patient not moved elsewhere?

16:3 Economics of Admission Balancing

Nursing homes exist either to make money or to carry through on a charitable purpose. As a practical and economic matter, the better quality for-profit nursing homes must manage their admissions so that they have a mix of "private pay" and "public pay" (Medicare/Medicaid) patients. The mixing of payors and rates per bed makes sense; the Medicaid population is large, so by charging private paying patients more, it will offset the lower rates of state Medicaid. A few residents among the private-pay group will have long-term care insurance (a trend that will likely rise in future years). Others have affluent families or independent means; and some are not aged but are temporarily disabled persons of working age who have employer-paid insurance and whose short-term rehabilitation need can be met during a brief stay at that nursing home.

The majority of the "public pay" cases are patients in nursing home beds that are contractually dedicated to be available for eligible beneficiaries of government programs like Medicaid, Medicare, and Veterans programs. The majority are Medicaid beds administered by states and governed by the rules of the state and of the Centers for Medicaid and Medicare Services (CMS). The Medicare and Medicaid residents typically arrive as posthospital referrals who have been discharged from a nearby acute care hospital.[2]

The patient's eligibility is verified, and the home's licensed level of service under state Medicaid rules will be compared to the patient's set of needs. Key decisions about appropriate nursing home placement are made by the hospital management's discharge planner, with advice from the social worker and the concurrence of the family. The discharge planner has an essential role in feeding the nursing home with new enrollees while keeping the quality of the nursing home's results high, so that the hospital is not penalized by Medicare for excessive numbers of readmitted, relapsed ill patients.

Older and more frail residents of nursing homes may begin their journey in the hospital and are likely to be readmitted as hospital inpatients if and when their move to that nursing home results in inadequate care or falls, injuries, or assaults occur. Readmission to the nursing home with a "bed hold" after a hospitalization is completed is not automatic, but it tends to be presumptive based on state Medicaid policy.[3]

Special attention is given to avoiding the risk that the patient will return with hospital-acquired infections or illnesses that could spread rapidly among the nursing home population.[4]

16:4 Admission Agreements and Brochures

Lawsuits that may be brought alleging poor care of residents will often claim a breach of an implicit contractual duty of care, which contract is construed to exist from the admission booklet or other

---

2. O. Intrator et al., *Maintaining Continuity of Care for Nursing Home Residents: Effect of States' Medicaid Bed-Hold Policies and Reimbursement Rates*, 44 HEALTH SERVS. RESEARCH 33 (2009).

3. *Id.*

4. CDC studies of disease transmission merit close examination with the assistance of a skilled epidemiological expert witness.

written agreements. Careful drafting of these agreements is difficult but essential for a future defense.[5]

Counsel to the nursing home will typically oversee the drafting of its admission paperwork, to exclude or disclaim statements that later could be called a basis for breach of warranty claims, or as breach of disclaimer or promise. Typically, admission contracts for the nursing home will be written to expressly disclaim any other expressions or promises that were not included in the written agreement.

The use of a contract requiring arbitration of claims is especially controversial, as discussed in a later chapter of this text.[6]

16:5 Involuntary Discharge

Litigation may arise following an involuntary discharge of the client from the nursing home. For federal and state-funded Medicaid/Medicare patients, there is a specific statutory[7] requirement for adequate advance notice of the reasons and date of the transfer.[8]

Dismissal from a nursing home poses the quandary for the family or support network: where can we safely place this patient? An aggressive, violent resident can be moved out with virtually no notice; this is done to protect the safety of other residents. Most other transfers take time to arrange and must be done with advance notice.[9] The contractual provisions of the admissions agreement should spell out the conditions under which the nursing home may opt for the eviction or dismissal of the resident. The nursing home that no longer wants a particularly difficult resident may assert that the patient's condition had changed and the level of care needed was in excess of the nursing home's abilities.

---

5. Amy DeLaney, *Maneuvering the Labyrinth of Long Term Care Admissions Contracts*, 4 Nat'l Acad. Elder Law Att'ys J. 35, 57 (2008).

6. See Chapter 29.

7. 42 U.S.C. § 1305.

8. 42 C.F.R. § 482.12(a)(4); *see* Ctrs. for Medicare & Medicaid Servs., State Operations Manual, CMS Pub. No. 100-07, Appendix PP: Guidance to Surveyors for Long Term Care Facilities F-203, PP-47.

9. 42 C.F.R. § 483.12(a)(5)(ii)(B).

The resident who receives notice of discharge may file for an administrative appeal as provided by the CMS rules.[10] Or the nursing home may discover a medical need for this patient to have hospital care, and upon the patient's return from the hospital, the facility may be "unable to find an available bed" for this patient. The litigation may arise when the person or their guardian sues for damages for wrongful dismissal. Winning such a case in the face of the preadmission contract language would be a long shot at best, and these cases are rare for a reason: relatively few of those nursing home residents who are wealthy enough to afford to pay lawyers by the hour would wish to litigate in order to reside in a home where they are no longer welcome.

If the patient is sent to the emergency room from the nursing home, the federal Emergency Medical Treatment and Active Labor Act requires the hospital to screen the patient and stabilize the patient's condition.[11] The nursing home usually has a contract with one or more hospitals under which its residents will receive hospital inpatient treatment when needed. Reentry rights for transfers back into the nursing home usually expire if the person does not return from the hospital within 30 days, indicating a serious illness or condition.

An intriguing book authored by the daughter of a long-term nursing home resident made the somewhat cynical observation: "Usually they try to keep patients for as long as they can do the absolute minimum for them, as long as the patients can be controlled through medication, and as long as the family members don't complain much."[12]

---

10. 42 C.F.R. §§ 483.200 *et seq.*

11. Emergency Medical Treatment and Active Labor Act, 42 U.S.C. § 1395dd; Galen v. Roberts, 525 U.S. 249 (1999); Burditt v. U.S. Dep't of HHS, 934 F.2d 1362 (5th Cir. 1991); George Smith, *Patient Dumping: Implications for the Elderly*, 6 Elder L.J. 165 (1998); Andrew McClurg, *Your Money or Your Life*, 24 Wake Forest L. Rev. 173 (1989).

12. Charlotte Digregorio, Everything You Need to Know about Nursing Homes 69 (2005).

16:6 Appeal of Involuntary Discharge

Once the nursing home has certified a certain number of beds for Medicaid patients, the Nursing Home Resident Protection Amendments[13] apply and restrict the eviction of current Medicaid residents even if the home drops its Medicaid contract.[14] States may go further and restrict the ability to discharge categories of patients who had spent down their personal wealth but were not yet eligible for Medicaid. Appeal rights are found in the CMS regulations.[15]

16:7 Patient Movement within Nursing Homes

Litigation about involuntary discharge does not include transfers within the nursing home itself. The person who remains in the home but in what they perceive to be a less desirable location or group may complain to the home, to the CMS surveyor,[16] or to the ombudsman, but rarely if ever would anyone who wished to remain as a resident take the steps to appeal[17] or, worse yet, sue for an intra–nursing home retransfer.

---

13. 42 U.S.C. § 1305, 113 Stat. 7 (1999).
14. 42 C.F.R. § 483.12(o).
15. 42 C.F.R. § 483.200.
16. 42 C.F.R. § 483.10(o).
17. 42 C.F.R. § 483.206.

CHAPTER 17

Assembling the Complaint

17:1 Overview
17:2 Elements of Knowledge
17:3 Elements of Due Care
17:4 Elements of Corporate Responsibility
17:5 Public Defendants
17:6 Statute of Limitations Defenses
17:7 False Claims Act Whistleblower Claims
17:8 Damages
17:9 Attorney Fee Requests

17:1 Overview

This chapter briefly addresses the drafting of the plaintiff's complaint in the nursing home action.[1] The state procedural aspects of tort complaint elements and drafting are best known to each state's practitioners, so this chapter is simply an overview of lessons from other nursing home cases. Other chapters address the selection of plaintiffs, defendants, and causes of action to be encountered in this litigation.

As discussed in an earlier chapter, the causes of action for injury to the elder will include both negligence and a claim for violation of a state nursing home protective statute, if one is available. Class actions

1. Other reference works on point are the multivolume sets ATLA, LITIGATING A TORT CASE, ch. 63, and DAVID COUCH, LIBBY EDWARDS & DAVID HOEY, LITIGATING NURSING HOME ABUSE CASES (compiling forms and state rules).

are possible but tend to be rare and complex.[2] Complaint drafting should emphasize that ordinary care activities were negligently managed; the more one focuses on the medical aspects of care, the more likely one will be to run afoul of state medical malpractice laws and their prodefendant prerequisites.[3]

17:2 Elements of Knowledge

The complaint should aver that each defendant had knowledge of the patient's condition or vulnerability before the incident that precipitated the suit. In an assault case, the presence of substantial cautionary information in the clinical file of an aggressive patient may put the nursing home on notice that he or she might attack a defenseless resident, like the injured plaintiff. Several days of chart entries about the pressure ulcer in the plaintiff's hip should contain information about skin treatment that was used before a Stage III ulcer developed that required hospital treatment. The resident assessment report[4] performed at the time of admission may show that the patient could not swallow, so the staff was on notice that leaving the demented patient alone in the dining room with a sandwich may result in her choking.[5]

Knowledge of the risk, prior to the event, is likely to be found in the records of the nursing home, e.g., "Watch out for Ms. Jones's wandering," and this knowledge sets up the foreseeability needed for a negligence claim for not having safeguarded the patient. Knowledge of the risk also may be shown in order to set up a case under the state nursing home statutory causes of action. The intersection of negligence case law and the duties created by a state protective statute for nursing home residents will be the right place for the complaint drafter to begin.[6] Some common law duties were breached; some statutory duties

---

2. *See, e.g.*, Flemming v. Barnwell Nursing Home & Health Facilities, Inc., 15 N.Y.3d 375, 938 N.E.2d 937 (2010).

3. *See, e.g.*, Estate of French v. Stratford House, 333 S.W.3d 546 (Tenn. 2011).

4. 42 C.F.R. § 483.20.

5. *See, e.g.*, Sharp v. Parkview Care Ctr., Inc., 940 So. 2d 724, (La. Ct. App. 2d Cir. 2006) (choked on sandwich).

6. MARGARET JASPER, NURSING HOME NEGLIGENCE (Oxford Oceana 2002).

may have been violated; and perhaps some contractual elements may need to be raised in the initial complaint (or may be waived if the statute of limitations has passed on an extra cause of action). In some cases, the abuse of nursing home residents may amount to criminal activity.[7]

Vicarious liability is frequently claimed where employees have been arrested for perpetrating harm on nursing home residents.[8]

17:3 Elements of Due Care

The complaint drafter should look for each of the elements of due care expressed in state case precedents. The drafter should ask, What are the norms of reasonable patient care that my plaintiff will assert should have been followed in her case, but that were allegedly overlooked or done poorly by the nursing home staff?

External and objective sources of quality standards are very helpful. A Centers for Medicare and Medicaid Services (CMS) regulation that was violated is a great help in those states that allow negligence per se arguments.[9] A CMS Manual or Guidance document[10] is likely to be helpful on point; the more clearly applicable, the easier it will be to show that its violation harmed the plaintiff. If the nursing home is voluntarily accredited by a group like the Joint Commission, or claims to be an adherent to norms of an elite standardized body, then counsel should find the accreditation agency's standard on this issue, and reference should be made by the plaintiff to that failure of compliance by the nursing home. The American Medical Directors Association guidelines[11] and the American Health Care Association guidance documents and periodicals on nursing home liability may be useful.[12] The

---

7. Diana Harris & Michael Benson, Maltreatment of Patients in Nursing Homes (2005).

8. Sande Buhai & James Gillman, *Honor Thy Mother & Father: Preventing Elder Abuse through Education & Litigation*, 36 Loyola L.A. L. Rev. 565 (2003).

9. See 42 C.F.R. § 483 for specific regulatory imposition of duties.

10. Ctrs. for Medicaid & Medicare Servs., http://www.cms.gov/Medicare/Medicare-Fee-for-Service-Payment/SNFPPS/BestPractices.html.

11. Am. Med. Dirs. Ass'n, http://www.amda.com/tools/guidelines.cfm.

12. Am. Health Care Ass'n, Liability, http://www.ahcancal.org/research_data/liability/Pages/default.aspx.

admissions brochure may brag about the groups that endorse the quality of this nursing home; if so, breach of that set of standards may be an additional complaint element since an implied warranty may have been formed in the claims of quality.

In the absence of a direct external command, the norm of duty can be drawn by the plaintiff from the nursing home's own procedure manual or policy statement set—because it is especially negligent for the nurses or staff to fail to follow the home's own program directives.[13] This showing of a clear violation of defendant's own written policies by an employee will later produce a revision of policies that have failed in practice. This may lead to an earlier settlement offer, to avoid the fallout of a public trial litigating such a violation by the nursing home.

Was the employee guilty of a crime? Vicarious liability and failure to comply with state laws on screening of health care service workers should be considered. Plaintiff should strive to show that a more careful inquiry by the nursing home into the employment history of a violent employee would have prevented the assault on the plaintiff. Counsel wants jurors to be asking, "Why did this criminal get hired for access to such a vulnerable group of new victims?" This history of the worker may be essential to lay a foundation for the plaintiff's arguments of employer accountability and proximate causation.[14]

17:4 Elements of Corporate Responsibility

Because of the recent trend of nursing home corporations to disperse their potential liabilities among a ring of weak corporations, the complaint should name the entity that is the official state license holder first, then name the parent corporation, as well as each of the companies that may have been responsible.[15] The corporation whose name appears on the license and the patient admission forms and on letters

13. These would be found in discovery of the defendant's procedure manuals.
14. Long v. Brookside Manor, 855 S.W.2d 70 (Tenn. Ct. App. 1994).
15. Sara Jurand, *Lack of Insurance Hinders Recovery in Nursing Home Cases*, 42 TRIAL 14 (Feb. 2006).

to the patient's representative should also be a named defendant, and "John Doe Corporation" and "John Doe Partnership" may be named to preserve the cause of action against other entities that may have been internally connected to the decisions that affected the plaintiff. An amended complaint may later insert the corporate identities found after discovery.

Understaffing is at the root of many negligent failures in the nursing home, especially regarding falls and medication errors.[16] Budget questions concerning numbers of staff and budgeting for staff member pay will be part of the discovery process. Use of a forensic accounting expert may be advisable to track the financial assets that may have been shuffled to avoid liability.[17] To set up these depositions, the counsel for plaintiff should ask the designated corporate witness under Rule 30(b)(6) of the Federal Rules of Civil Procedure or an analogous state rule to detail each corporation that provided any of the services related to this patient in this nursing home during these periods.[18] Eventually the jury may draw a skeptical view of the defense if the owner manipulated each role to avoid "owning" the problem.

17:5 Public Defendants

If the nursing home enjoys state sovereign immunity, be certain that you understand the case law of the state exemptions, and plead accordingly. Your case may or may not involve a "discretionary function" under state immunity law or the Federal Tort Claims Act, and the state entity may have been negligent in allowing this event to occur.[19]

Additionally, liability may exist under 42 U.S.C. § 1983. Refer to section 12:23 for a more detailed discussion of potential tort liability under federal civil rights legislation.

---

16. An excellent review is Jeffrey Levine, *Understaffing in Nursing Homes*, *in* MEDICAL-LEGAL ASPECTS OF LONG-TERM CARE 65 (Jeffrey Levine ed., 2003).
17. Jurand, *supra* note 15.
18. FED. R. CIV. P. 15.
19. Limbaugh v. Coffee Med. Ctr., 59 S.W.2d 73 (Tenn. 2001).

17:6 Statute of Limitations Defenses

The statute of limitations is another constraint on the complaint drafting team. The two years (typically) allowed by the state's tort statute, for filing of the action, begins to run upon occurrence of the assault, fall or other event.[20] In some cases, the wrongful death statute requires an action be filed within two years after the date of death, even though the nursing home may have discharged the person before she or he died. The three or four years for the tort statute of limitations (depending on the state law) usually begins with the event, such as a fall or assault, that created the injury.[21] Plaintiffs' attorneys should proceed with caution in determining the relevant statute of limitations. In the wake of tort reform, many nursing home claims have been lumped into the medical malpractice statute of limitations. These statutes are often as little as one year.

17:7 False Claims Act Whistleblower Claims

A qui tam (False Claims Act) suit can be brought where the employee of the nursing home notified state officials that the home had insufficient staff and supplies to meet patient needs. Management told two nurses that there was not enough money to hire more staff or purchase additional supplies. As a result, residents developed excessive pressure sores, were subject to a scabies epidemic, and received inadequate attention to their personal hygiene, among other abuses. The nurses were fired and sued using a state whistleblower action. The facility's owner was allegedly siphoning off money received from Medicare and Medicaid and using it for his own purposes instead of patient care. The plaintiffs charged that the defendants' actions caused patients to suffer infections, skin disorders, and deprivation of required medication. The jury awarded about $28.11 million.[22]

20. Diversicare Gen. Partner Inc. v. Rubio, 185 S.W.3d 842 (Tex. 2005).

21. Crockett v. Medicalodges Inc., 799 P.2d 1022 (Kan. 1990).

22. United States v. Momence Meadows Nursing Ctr., Inc., No. 2 04 C 2289 (CD. Ill. Feb. 8, 2012); *see* 49 TRIAL 8 (May 2012).

17:8 Damages

The complaint must plead damages according to state procedures for civil litigation. Wrongful death and other injury claims are addressed in other chapters. For purposes of drafting the complaint, counsel should include the costs and traumatic consequences for the elder, as well as the pain. One must beware of nursing home lobbyists' success in capping or avoiding punitive damage remedies through state legislation.[23]

17:9 Attorney Fee Requests

The complaint in a statutory nursing home abuse case should seek an award of attorney fees in addition to damages, where the state nursing home protective statute or state case precedents allow the fee awards.[24] Common law negligence actions generally do not allow recovery of the winner's attorney fees.

---

23. J. Shanahan, *Statutory Limits on Punitive Damages in Nursing Home Negligence Tort Actions*, 4 J. HEALTH CARE L. & POL'Y 373 (2001); PETER WINBURN & REBECCA ADELMAN, FRENCH REVOLUTION: REDEFINING THE BATTLE LINES.

24. Sprosty v. Pearlview Inc., 106 Ohio App. 3d 679, 666 N.E.2d 1180 (1995).

CHAPTER 18

Defendants

18:1 Overview
18:2 Interconnected Corporations
18:3 Deposing Corporate Representatives
18:4 Discovery of Defendant Identities
18:5 Doctors as Defendants
18:6 Products Liability

18:1 Overview

Drawing the complaint for an action against a nursing home's responsible parties is not easy when the actual operators and owners are concealed behind a maze of interconnected entities.[1] Suing the named owner of the license, often a limited liability company or limited partnership of shell corporate entities, may not be sufficient to reach the deep pocket of the real owner.[2] In some cases the actual care delivery was subcontracted to a related entity.[3]

Of what value is a huge windfall verdict if the wrong defendant was named and that party can easily go bankrupt? Nursing home operators recognize the optimal ways to avoid liability threats.[4] The prudent plaintiff's counsel will first obtain the state registration forms

1. Christopher Cazin, *Personal Liability Exposure for Nursing Home Operators*, 85 Fla. Bar J. 46 (2011).

2. Charles Duhigg, *At Many Homes, More Profit and Less Nursing*, N.Y. Times, Sept. 23, 2007.

3. *Id.* (allowing abandonment of liability with a shell corporation that enters bankruptcy).

4. OliverWyman & Marsh, 2022 General and Professional Liability Benchmark Report: For Senior Living and Long-Term Care Providers (2023), https://info.marsh

that were filed to obtain the nursing home license, and then assert the Florida concept that nursing home health care is a nondelegable duty of the license holder[5] and so the license holder cannot hide behind a string of independent contractors.[6]

The individual low-wage worker will only rarely be named and then assessed damages as an individual defendant; the nursing home typically is liable under the doctrine of respondeat superior. In the regulatory administrative hearings context, unlike the tort damages situation, the civil penalties could be avoided if the defendant company showed that the employee's misconduct, though he violated the regulations, was not anticipated by or endorsed by the company.[7] The regulatory context often involves matters that did not produce serious injury, as tort cases would, but that would show a failure to protect against potential harms[8] even without a showing of specific victims.[9]

18:2 Interconnected Corporations

"Follow the money!" In the Watergate scandal, this message from "Deep Throat" to a journalist was the key to bringing out the true story. The scandal of nursing home ownership in recent years has been the reduction in the quality and frequency of competent nursing care for residents of nursing homes, for reasons of increased profitability.[10] A prudent litigator will do careful homework. The federal Centers for Medicare and Medicaid Services (CMS) requires the disclosure of owners' identities for homes receiving Medicare, as do most states.[11] A standard form should supply basic information about ownership of the home. But corporate lawyers are skilled at concealment, and

---

.com/1/395202/2023-02-28/cjdj81/395202/1677611146YHZ73UPd/2022_General_and_Professional_Liability_Benchmark_Report.pdf.

5. Fla. Stat. § 400.022.

6. NME Props. Inc. v. Rudich, 840 So. 2d 309 (Fla. App. 2003).

7. Cal. Ass'n of Health Facilities v. Dep't of Health Servs., 16 Cal. 4th 284, 940 P.2d 323 (1997).

8. Crestview Parke Care Ctr. v. Thompson, 373 F.3d 743 (2004).

9. Lake Cnty. Rehab. Ctr. v. Shalala, 854 F. Supp. 1329 (N.D. Ind. 1994).

10. Duhigg, *supra* note 2, at 1.

11. 42 C.F.R. § 483.75(p); *see* CMS Form 671.

nursing home ownership linkages are purposely obscured in some cases.[12] State ombudsmen urged Congress to remedy this abusive practice by requiring public notice of the true owners of the facilities.[13] Somehow, shareholders receive dividends, and tax write-offs are benefiting someone; tracing the "who" and "where" is possible, but not easy. The management agreements among the various corporate entities, LLCs, and limited partnerships should be sought in discovery, and shared with a forensic accountant, as one would do in a white collar crime situation.[14]

Sometimes the corporations are truly distinct companies at arm's length, such as a licensee running a nursing home in a building that is owned and (poorly) operated by a real estate investor. Are the two companies related by common owners or common directors, as shown at the state office that maintains corporate records? Critics have urged that the lease terms for nursing home ownership should be transparent, and that the public health need for safety protection should override the contrary terms of a private real estate lease.[15]

The issue of hidden corporate ownership and control has become such an issue that the Centers for Medicare and Medicaid Services recently enacted a new rules, requiring additional disclosures.[16]

In other cases, the corporate parent's decisions control what the operational managers can do for patient care. As a litigant against nursing homes has advised, cases are won at depositions with lower-level managers who explain the relatively close policy control that the

12. Nathan Carter, *Who's Really Running the Nursing Home?*, 43 Trial 50 (Nov. 2006) [hereinafter Carter, *Nursing Home*].

13. *Nursing Home Transparency and Improvement, Hearing before the U.S. Senate Comm. on Aging*, 110th Cong. (Nov. 15, 2007) (testimony of Sarah Slocum, Nat'l Ass'n of State Long-Term Care Ombudsman Programs), http://www.aging.senate.gov/hearing_detail.cfm?id=321325&.

14. An excellent guidance document available on Westlaw is Nathan Carter, 2 Ann. 2007 AAJ-CLE 2103 (2007) [hereinafter Carter, Guidance].

15. *Nursing Home Transparency and Improvement, Hearing before the U.S. Senate Comm. on Aging*, 110th Cong. 6 (Nov. 15, 2007) (testimony of Long Term Care Institute President David Zimmerman), http://www.aging.senate.gov/hearing_detail.cfm?id=321325&.

16. 42 C.F.R. pt. 424.516(g)(1); 42 C.F.R. pt. 455.101, .104. For a detailed discussion, see https://www.federalregister.gov/documents/2023/11/17/2023-25408/medicare-and-medicaid-programs-disclosures-of-ownership-and-additional-disclosable-parties. *See also* CMS Form 855A.

parent has maintained. Brilliant corporate law drafting into an intricate web of entities has been a feature of recent nursing home chain developments—but the deposition of one home's director of nursing may burst the bubble by describing the failure to have additional care staff as a directive that came from the corporate offices to all nursing homes: "Keep in mind that you are trying to show that the facility is part of a larger chain and that the critical decisions are made at a higher level by people who work outside the facility."[17] Because financial decisions made by remote chain-employed managers affect the daily lives of the patients, linking them to the staffing or care practices will expand the field of potential defendants.[18]

Structures aside, litigators should focus the jurors' attention on the humans involved at the caregiving level. These fact witnesses will know what influences affected their decisions and what shortcomings of staffing or equipping the facility had compromised their abilities to help the deceased or injured plaintiff. Study the documentation for the period of the incident. Study the last three state survey reports of violations. Reread the CMS Conditions of Participation to understand Medicare's expectations for the facility that was receiving funds, even if the individual plaintiff was a private-pay patient. Keep asking probing questions to the parade of individuals who had responsibility for the operations of the nursing home, and then ask them to help you to follow the decisions on costs "back up the ladder." What executive could and did veto the assignment of additional staff members to this task? When hurricane evacuation was planned, did the corporate main office veto the generator needed to save immobilized patients' lives?[19] The wall of corporate intricacy was expensive to construct; plaintiffs can avoid it by showing the structure and aiming their efforts to "pierce the corporate veil."[20]

---

17. Carter, Guidance, *supra* note 14.

18. *Id.*

19. *See, e.g.*, Howard Law Journal Symposium, *Katrina and the Rule of Law in the Time of Crisis*, 51 Howard L.J. 621 (2008).

20. Carter, Guidance, *supra* note 14.

The plaintiff in a nursing home case may be facing a very sophisticated liability-dispersal plan, under which the operation of a home has multiple corporate and contractor participants. The state corporation office registry may have information about the multiple corporations, but the field may be a national chain. The health care industry has undergone controversial changes as it has become more corporate and complex.[21]

Statistics show that the chain nursing homes tend to attract more litigation and, as with other for-profit nursing homes, were "less likely to meet the long-stay staffing ratios and had poorer quality indicators in comparison to nonprofit homes."[22]

A 2008 investigative report exposed in the news media a defensive tactic that had become well known to plaintiff's counsel. The defendant nursing home split its ownership and management into thinly capitalized corporate entities.[23] Private equity firms became major chain nursing home owners, and they cut costs. Analysis of data from 2003 to 2008 demonstrated that the nation's ten largest for-profit nursing home chains had a 36 percent higher number of deficiencies and a 41 percent higher number of serious deficiencies when compared to government facilities.[24]

A plaintiff's successful challenge to misconduct could be met with a jury award that leads to immediate bankruptcy of the "shell" corporation, in the hope that this would preserve the assets of the corporation that actually made decisions about staffing, patient care, and other important choices. News exposes in 2007 revealed these tactics.[25] A

21. JOHN GEYMAN, THE CORPORATE TRANSFORMATION OF HEALTH CARE: CAN THE PUBLIC INTEREST BE SERVED? (2004) (Medicare "policies have been the major stimuli of what has become an enormous corporate empire of diverse, inter-twined investor owned chains or hospitals or other health care facilities and service providers.").

22. Christopher Johnson et al., *Predicting Lawsuits against Nursing Homes in the United States 1997–2001*, 39(6) HEALTH SERVS. RES. 1713, 1724 (2004).

23. *Nursing Home Transparency and Improvement, Hearing before the U.S. Senate Comm. on Aging*, 110th Cong. (2007) (testimony of SEIU Asst. Dir. of Research Arvid Muller), https://www.aging.senate.gov/imo/media/doc/11152007.pdf.

24. Charlene Harrington, Brian Olney, Helen Carrillo & Taewoon Kang, *Nurse Staffing and Deficiencies in the Largest For-Profit Nursing Home Chains and Chains Owned by Private Equity Companies*, 47(1, pt. 1) HEALTH SERVS. RSCH. 106–28 (2012).

25. Duhigg, *supra* note 2, at 1.

2006 review in a magazine for trial lawyers observed that virtually all chains had "undergone extremely complex business transactions into which they were sold, merged, or parceled out into different entities—or otherwise drastically changed."[26] This means that a plaintiff may find the victory hollow; a million-dollar judgment against a shell limited liability company would bring its bankruptcy, and attempts to collect on the judgment would encounter a defensive posture by the true owner, a national chain or regional corporate owner.[27]

In the Delaplane case, a 2001 budget cut by corporate management resulted in short staffing at a Kentucky nursing home, and a terrible 2002 death by neglect case led to a $20 million verdict.[28]

If the plaintiff's counsel practices in a smaller community setting, it would be prudent to retain as an advisor a corporate law specialist who is familiar with the state's jurisprudence for "piercing the corporate veil." The shared liabilities among the corporations and owners[29] can be worked through by such a specialist, making careful and knowledgeable use of state corporate liability precedents that will facilitate the litigator's drafting efforts.[30]

18:3 Deposing Corporate Representatives

The cases of nursing home negligence are often won or lost in the depositions, a plaintiffs' lawyer has observed,[31] and this appears to be correct in light of the settlements that occur in nursing home litigation. The Rule 30(b)(6) deposition of the designated corporate representative is a crucial event for the plaintiffs. Is the plaintiff prepared with documents and interviews to be ready for the questioning of this official spokesperson? Has the plaintiff counsel dug deep into state records,

---

26. Carter, *Nursing Home, supra* note 12.

27. *Id.* at 54.

28. Delaplane v. Beverly, No. 02-CI-01119 (Franklin Cnty. Cir. Ct. Ky. 2006), *reported in* VERDICTS, SETTLEMENTS & TACTICS 264 (June 2006).

29. Christopher Cazin, *Personal Liability Exposure for Nursing Home Operators*, 85 FLA. B.J. 46 (2011).

30. A helpful analysis appears in Mark Kosieradzki & Joel Smith, ATLA's LITIGATING TORT CASES 63:16 (2006 Supp.).

31. Carter, Guidance, *supra* note 14.

Medicaid complaints, and the elements underlying the score assigned to this facility by the CMS website Nursing Home Compare?[32]

18:4 Discovery of Defendant Identities

Plaintiff's counsel is presumably familiar with state procedures for the identification of potential defendants. Typically, a corporations registry office within the Secretary of State's office has an online inquiry option. Nursing home cases are no different. The CMS Nursing Home Compare website and state department of health websites also aid in identifying related corporations. Discovery will be utilized to identify which aspect of the chain of companies is the proper defendant among the several interwoven links of the chain. The deposition of the corporate official representative under Rule 30(b)(6) should include an examination of the Medicare cost reports as well as relevant corporate agreements for the management of the nursing home. A skilled expert witness for the plaintiff who is a licensed nursing home administrator will be very valuable at this stage of the preparation of the suit.

18:5 Doctors as Defendants

Should the medical director and attending physician, if any, be included individually as defendants in the lawsuit? Probably not. There may be simpler ways to handle the lawsuit, outside of state laws that procedurally encumber a malpractice claim against a physician. The lawsuit could focus on negligence in nonmedical activities like a slip and fall on a waxed staircase. There may be reasons why the real proximate cause burden falls on the postphysician stage, for example, care of the feeding tube or mix-up of pill delivery. There may be other times when it is clearly the malpractice of the physician but all of the nursing staff had acted perfectly; these are relatively infrequent instances. Having the physician as a co-defendant complicates the case and allows the defense to invoke the state law shields for malpractice suits, so if the

32. http://www.medicare.gov/nursinghomecompare.

injury was mostly attributable to an activity of daily life, prudent counsel will prefer to have the doctor as a nonparty witness, to describe the care plan, if he or she is brought into the case at all.

Several questions should be asked: Was the injury something related to the patient's cognitive impairment by the known side effects of medication, thereby allowing a plaintiff's medical expert to reflect on the prescribing decisions of the doctor? Did the medical director conduct or supervise implementation of the care plan as the staff members performed work with the patient, for example, training them on feeding tube replacement or maintenance? Did the instruction and policy manual for the nursing home contain a description of the work that was to be expected from the medical director? If all of those steps had been followed properly by the physician, would the precautions have prevented this accident from occurring? And is the physician actually the one who made the crucial decision for this patient's health? Using the expert witnesses as advisors, counsel should focus on defining the duty of the medical director as a defendant, and then explaining in simple terms how that duty had been breached.

Beyond the physician are the nurses, aides, physical and occupational therapists, dieticians, and others. State laws and procedures may favor physicians but not other professionals; state medical malpractice laws will vary. Did the nurse do something that may have been professional negligence or malpractice? Was her or his action beyond their state-licensed scope of practice? Be sure to read the applicable state statutes before adding her or him into the lawsuit as a defendant.

18:6 Products Liability

If the case involves a particular product, such as a medical device, safety device for protection from falls, security alarm or pharmaceutical, the prudent counsel will consider making the manufacturer a co-defendant with the nursing home staff. This is especially important if the actual product had been retained or secured at the hospital at the time of acute treatment, or if the clinical chart and medications records indicate that the specific drug had been given to this patient.

Absent a clear record, or absent the actual unit of product alleged to have caused the harm, the nursing home liability case may be best left as the primary cause of action. Defenders of the large and deep pocketed medical device or drug company will run up thousands of dollars of costs and time expended by the contingent fee plaintiff's counsel, probably out of proportion to the contingent fee plaintiff's probable reward, especially in states with caps on damages in product liability lawsuits. So this sideways attack alongside a nursing home liability case is not a simple decision for the patient's advocate to make.

CHAPTER 19

Evaluating the Potential Plaintiff

19:1 Overview
19:2 Deterioration of Mental and Physical Condition
19:3 Testimony Issues
19:4 Peer Pressure
19:5 Actions after the Patient's Death
19:6 State Wrongful Death Actions
19:7 Standing and Family Representation
19:8 Practical Issues
19:9 Effects of Death of the Plaintiff
19:10 Questions to Ask Potential Clients

19:1 Overview

Although it may seem harsh to admit it, the most efficient screening tool to filter out weak cases is the skilled plaintiff lawyer's economic self-interest. The contingent fee lawyer tends to be brutally frank, even cynical, about the merits of a nursing home case offered by survivors, family members, and would-be representatives of the injured plaintiff. Like evolution, the fittest case selectors survive; the weakest case selectors cannot continue to fund their law practice, and move to other types of cases. Overly optimistic lawyers are not selective enough to survive in this economic climate of high up-front costs in tort litigation.

Realist lawyers who have fine trial skills and who select cases cautiously can prosper in the handling of nursing home litigation. The barriers to success tend to be highly case-specific, so the experience one gains from the first five cases one pursues may allow a fine discernment about whether the nursing home litigation field will be receptive to that lawyer's talents. Your authors and their colleagues who train law students recognize this gap between eager idealists championing the protection of the sick, ill, and frail, and the elite economically successful advocates who handle the more successful cases. A word to the wise is sufficient.

Proper plaintiff selection is critical. The injured or dead nursing home resident is very likely to be unavailable as a witness when the trial is eventually held. It is realistic, not merely morbid, to say that defense counsel and insurance companies have time on their side when they delay the opening of a trial. Fading memory, physical impairments, and the decline of health that follows injuries in one's later years combine to make the ailing resident's testimony less likely to occur and less likely to carry strong first-person persuasiveness with jurors. Additionally, though bleak to say the least, cases in which the plaintiff has died from his or her injuries may have a higher potential recovery due to the effects of tort caps in some states.

19:2 Deterioration of Mental and Physical Condition

A resident who suffers a fall or an assault to a degree of injury worthy of the consideration by a potential plaintiff's attorney is likely to have serious negative health consequences that are prolonged and multiphasic. Ideal trial witnesses have excellent recollection of facts and events several years before the date of their testimony, and they have the stamina to endure rigorous cross-examination without losing their attractive demeanor that convinces jurors of the worthiness of their cause. Although it is hard to generalize, persons over 80 whose health condition led them into a nursing home are not likely to be ideal witnesses.

"Co-morbidity" is the medical term signifying that a person has multiple medical conditions that interact to make him or her more negatively affected by the results of the particular injury. The injury that is manifest after a beating, a fall, or a drug error does not occur on a blank slate. Rather, the person is already ailing in ways that exacerbate the effect of an adverse reaction to a drug, or that slow the healing from a deep Stage IV pressure ulcer caused by neglect. The aphorism that the defendant "takes the plaintiff as he finds them" is true, but the defense will certainly seek to minimize damages by having jurors understand how many other deficits this plaintiff had before the event occurred. A prudent plaintiff's attorney will seek a jury instruction that explains the eggshell plaintiff rule to the jury and will reiterate that efforts to blame the nursing home resident's co-morbidities equate to blaming the elderly person for the neglect that he or she suffered.

19:3 Testimony Issues

Rules of civil procedure accommodate the circumstances of the elderly victim of a nursing home neglect or abuse case. The plaintiff may notice a deposition to preserve the testimony of the elder for trial. Video depositions of the individual resident will generally be admissible at trial if the witness becomes physically unable to appear in person.

19:4 Peer Pressure

One who sues a nursing home should have moved out of that home to some other location. If the injured person attempts to remain at the same nursing home where the abuse or neglect was claimed to occur, the fact of the lawsuit may make life socially intolerable, and the elder's continued presence at the home may be practically impossible. Also, it undercuts the charge that life at the home was so bad that compensation should be awarded. Discharge of the resident/plaintiff by management of the home is very likely, after service of the complaint upon the management, if the relatives or guardian have not already acted to remove him or her from the risk of further injuries. Of course, explaining this reality to the resident may remove the prospects of the suit, for a transfer has disruptive psychological effects, and some elders would not wish to make waves even at a home that was negligently operated.

19:5 Actions after the Patient's Death

This chapter addresses the damage actions that are specifically available after death of the nursing home patient. It has been estimated that less than one-fifth of malpractice cases involve a death, but more than one-half of nursing home cases involve a death. Probate appointment, wrongful death statutory designation of plaintiffs, and other complications must be factored into counsel's case planning.

The tort action against the nursing home may be brought by the personal representative of the decedent. The filing of the action by an estate must await appointment of that representative under procedures of the state probate laws.

19:6 State Wrongful Death Actions

State wrongful death laws serve as limitations on who can recover what damages in the nursing home litigation. These statutes spell out which persons can serve as plaintiffs in a wrongful death action. The inheritance status of the potential plaintiff is significant under these statutes.

Ethical issues may arise in representation under a wrongful death action. The lawyer who is approached to represent a client is usually unencumbered in doing so; but in the wrongful death action, the person retaining counsel must be told up front whether the wrongful death statute would allow that individual to be paid a share of recovery. The individual who sought legal advice should be given a clear warning that the recipients of the wrongful death award may be persons other than the individual who seeks to hire the lawyer. Any intrafamily conflict should be resolved before the lawyer invests time in preparing for possible litigation.

19:7 Standing and Family Representation

Unanimity within the family is a necessity before nursing home litigation can be sustained; the ability to present a united front in the depiction of the decedent's care will be essential.

Standing as proper parties under state law is another reason for careful selection of the named plaintiffs. Wrongful death statutes designate the persons in interest who may bring the case.[1]

A nursing home admissions packet may include a mandatory arbitration agreement. Chapter 29 addresses these issues. The arbitration alternative greatly favors the defense, as it precludes punitive damages and eliminates jury empathy as a factor in the award of damages. The later avoidance of the arbitration agreement after death of the nursing home resident would be very difficult if the family member who signed the agreement opposes the litigation and wishes to close the case quickly.

A very practical question to be asked of the family by the potential plaintiff's counsel is the level of support that the family provided to the decedent during his or her final years. Was the family actively supportive of keeping the person at home, and chose the nursing home only as a last resort when physical or mental challenges outgrew their ability to control the individual's problems? Or did the family members avoid bearing a sacrifice, and placed the elder into institutional care as a convenience to the younger members of the family? How would it play with jurors if the family never visited, or if they visited and did not notice the malnutrition or abuse? Either would assist the defense claims that no negligence had occurred.

Astute observation by the potential plaintiff's lawyer will be needed. After listening to the family, one should ask, what will be the likely perception by the jury about these persons when they are sitting at counsel table in the courtroom? Is the jury going to see a loving family, or disengaged, money-hungry survivors?

---

1. And these vary widely, see Wrongful Death Statutes, 12 Am. Jur. Trials § 317.

Disagreement among significant heirs regarding the desirability of the lawsuit may effectively block the filing of the litigation in some cases. A prudent counsel will ask if all agree; if not, a mass family meeting and multiple signatures on the engagement letters will be recommended.

19:8 Practical Issues

Insurance adjusters for the nursing home may respond to the claim by making a modest settlement offer, in lieu of litigation. The family may want to accept the accommodation to cover the burial or cremation costs.

Life insurance payment claims covering the death of the patient may be disputed by the company if, during the decedent's fading memory, the periodic payment for the life insurance policy has been allowed to lapse. Long-term care insurance contracts may contain a lien on tort awards for recovery of the insurer's costs; a later chapter addresses these liens.

19:9 Effects of Death of the Plaintiff

Claims for injury and abuse that were suffered before death will survive, as the representative continues the suit.[2] The named plaintiff in a wrongful death action will sue both for the deceased person's survivorship claims and on behalf of the deceased person's family members who have suffered injury from the death of the decedent. Drafters who choose to include a count for damages under the wrongful death statute should carefully establish the relationship so that the named plaintiff is properly identified.

The aspect of death that plaintiff's lawyers should inquire about immediately is the autopsy of the decedent. Proving abuse, assault, and the like may require the opinion of a pathologist. Autopsy results

2. Somberg v. Fla. Convalescent Ctr. Inc., 779 So. 2d 667 (Fla. App. 2001), *decision approved,* 640 So. 2d 998 (Fla. 2003).

are crucial to establishing liability in some cases. Evidence of causation should be specific and useful. Pathologists' specific attention to mode of death is needed.

19:10 Questions to Ask Potential Clients

Following are examples of questions that plaintiffs' attorneys may consider asking as part of the intake process when evaluating potential cases.

- Please provide your name, address, phone number, e-mail address, and date of birth.
- If you are contacting [the firm] on behalf of someone else, please provide that person's name and date of birth. Additionally, state your relationship to the injured party.
- Where did the issue you are complaining about occur?
- When did the issue you are complaining about occur? (If the events span multiple days, please provide the earliest date.)
- Whom do you believe to be at fault for your complaint? (Please give the person's name if known.)
- Please provide as detailed a description of events as possible, including the location of events, the names of persons involved (if known), and the dates of events. Please provide the dates of admissions to any hospitals or nursing homes.
- Is the injured person deceased? (If so, please state the date of death and the cause(s) of death as listed on the death certificate, if known.)
- If the injured person is deceased, please state whether or not the deceased person has a will.
- If the injured person is deceased, has an estate been opened with a probate court?
- Please describe any evidence that you have in your possession or are aware of (medical records, video recordings, photos, etc.).

CHAPTER 20

State Oversight and Regulation

20:1 Overview
20:2 State-Federal Funding
20:3 State Licensing
20:4 Ombudsman Roles

20:1 Overview

State legislators are receptive to caring for the needs of those who are most likely to vote in elections—the elderly. Legislators are prone to share the available funding for nursing care with the caregivers in their state. These policies intersect and sometimes collide with the policies of Medicaid[1] and other federal structures, which administer and contribute part of the funding for most long-term care patients.[2]

Litigators should understand motivations underlying state laws. Many state legislators have responded to scandals or news accounts of ill treatment and have adopted some form of nursing home resident protective statute. Plaintiff's counsel must study these texts and any interpretive appellate guidance. Protective laws are interpreted in various ways and have various operative terms used in their texts.[3]

1. Medicaid is a federally funded program that assists states; see www.cms.gov.
2. Cultural Change in Long Term Care 397 (Audrey Weiner ed., 2003).
3. Robin Miller, *Construction and Application of State Patient Bill of Rights Statutes*, 87 A.L.R.5th 277 (2001).

Other sources have compiled the separate state requirements, or the reader can find them through the particular state websites.[4] The state health regulators have a critically important role in the survey inspections and the prosecution of bad conditions; but the reader should note that having a dual-layer system means that delay is inevitable. For example, it took seven years for a nursing home penalty case concerning inadequate treatment of pressure sores on the skin of a patient to be finally affirmed, during which time the patient was probably no longer living at the facility (or anywhere).[5]

20:2 State-Federal Funding

The Fourth Circuit said best what many state officials already know: "There can be no doubt but that the statutes and provisions in question, involving the financing of Medicare and Medicaid, are among the most completely impenetrable texts within human experience. Indeed, one approaches them at the level of specificity herein demanded with dread, for not only are they dense reading of the most tortuous kind, but Congress also revisits the area frequently, generously cutting and pruning in the process and making any solid grasp of the matters addressed merely a passing phase."[6] (We who dare to author on this topic can heartily agree!)

This text addresses torts and compensation, not structures and fiscal matters. But counsel who finds the thicket of state requirements to be difficult in preparation of a tort case may come to sympathize with the state regulators and with some of the fiscal managers of the defendant nursing homes.

4. *See* 2 DAVID COUCH, LIBBY EDWARDS & DAVID HOEY, LITIGATING NURSING HOME ABUSE CASES (West 2007) (state compilation).

5. Windsor Place Nursing & Rehab. Ctr. v. U.S. Dep't of HHS, 649 F.3d 293 (5th Cir. 2011) (there was no need for negative outcome to occur for there to be a finding that service offered was insufficient) citing 42 C.F.R. § 483.25(a)(3).

6. Rehab. Ass'n of Va. v. Kozlowski, 42 F.3d 1444, 1450 (4th Cir. 1994).

20:3 State Licensing

All states license long-term care facilities. In each state, a set of rules is available from the state agency, often on its website. CMS has created a contract delegation of powers, empowering one state agency in each state to enforce its rules by means of periodic surveys and by responses to serious complaints. The CMS State Operations Manual and the Guidance to Surveyors, a colorful binder referred to as the "watermelon book" because of its green and yellow pages, are essential reference sources in this complex regulatory matrix.[7]

Most states enforce specific protective state laws as well as federal CMS requirements during the survey visits. Others simply enforce the CMS norms and interpretations of the federal regulatory norms. Legislators and regulators need to interact and understand each other's role in protecting patients.

The state has a nursing home survey team that usually spends three days at a facility, interviews selected patients, examines complaints, observes staff, and proceeds to make the inquiries directed by the CMS Manual for Surveyors in its set of inquiries.[8] As one lay commentator has observed: "The state wouldn't have to look hard to find reasons to severely penalize a nursing home, if it wanted to, or shut it down."[9] The inspectors arrive unannounced, but in practice the astute nursing home has clues to when they might arrive. Problems with "surprise" state inspections have been substantiated by a federal study that found serious weaknesses in state enforcement, easy awareness by operators of when the inspection would be held, and significant understatement of serious problems in patient care.[10]

---

7. *See* http://www.cms.hhs.gov/manuals.

8. No survey can ask all of the thousands of questions in the manual, but a representative sample is used.

9. Charlotte Digregorio, Everything You Need to Know About Nursing Homes 204 (2005).

10. U.S. Gov't Accountability Office, GAO-03-1016T, Nursing Homes: Prevalence of Serious Quality Problems Remains Unacceptably High, Despite Some Decline (July 17, 2003).

Did abuse occur? Mandatory reporting of elder abuse by physicians, nurses, and social workers is required in most states.[11] These reports are admissible in evidence, unless a statutory privilege applies. The state survey report on the nursing home's compliance with CMS and state rules is admissible in a subsequent tort case.[12]

States also license nursing home administrators and nurses, and this provides the state long-term care agency with marginal additional "leverage" to hold accountable those individuals who were in charge when serious violations or failures occurred.[13]

20:4 Ombudsman Roles

Virtually every local area has a long-term care ombudsman who visits nursing homes and aids in the resolution of disagreements. CMS rules attempt to assure uniform standards for ombuds service.[14] Often volunteer groups serve the ombuds role for a community. There are currently about 1,200 paid and 9,000 volunteer ombudsmen who resolve about 260,000 complaints each year, and who have statutory powers to review records and to report potential violations to state enforcement agencies.[15] Because of lack of resources, ombudsmen have been able to visit only about half of the facilities that have been assigned.[16]

The CMS rule tries to standardize the specific responsibilities of the ombudsman, which include (1) to identify, investigate, and resolve complaints that are made by, or on behalf of, residents; (2) to provide services to assist the residents in protecting the health, safety, welfare, and rights of the residents; (3) to inform residents about means of obtaining ombudsman services; (4) to ensure that the residents have regular and timely access to the services provided through the office

---

11. Kira Larson, *Nursing Homes: Standards of Care, Sources of Potential Liability, Defenses to Suit, and Reform*, 37 DRAKE L. REV. 699 (1987).
12. Montgomery Health Care Facility v. Ballard, 565 So. 2d 221 (Ala. 1990).
13. DOUGLAS SINGH, EFFECTIVE MANAGEMENT OF LONG-TERM CARE FACILITIES 47 (2005).
14. CMS Proposed Rules, 78 Fed. Reg. 36,449 (June 18, 2013).
15. *See* website, http://www.aoa.gov/eldfam/elder_rights/LTC/LTC.asp.
16. Press Release, Senate Comm. on Aging, Long Term Care Ombudsman Program (Nov. 15, 2007), http://www.aging.senate.gov.

of the ombudsman and that residents receive timely responses to complaints from representatives of the office; (5) to represent the interests of the residents before governmental agencies and seek administrative, legal, and other remedies to protect the health, safety, welfare, and rights of the residents; (6) to provide administrative and technical assistance to government agencies to assist the agencies in participating in the program; (7) to analyze, comment on, and monitor the development and implementation of federal, state, and local laws, regulations, and other governmental policies and actions relating to the health, safety, welfare, and rights of the long-term care residents; and (8) to provide for training of representatives of the office of ombudsman.[17]

Critics of nursing home operations urge that the complaints be taken to state central offices, rather than the voluntary ombudsmen, to get action.[18] The reports prepared by ombudsmen in response to complaints are generally privileged under state law; some states expressly allow them to be used in litigation.[19]

17. CMS Proposed Rules, 78 Fed. Reg. 36,449 (June 18, 2013).

18. Charlotte Digregorio, Everything You Need to Know About Nursing Homes 160 (2005).

19. Ga. Code Ann. § 31-8-58; Coastal Health Servs. v. Rozier, 335 S.E.2d 712 (Ga. Ct. App. 1985).

CHAPTER 21

Shared Facts, Multiple Defendants

21:1 Collective Responsibility and Group Coverage of Liability Insurance
21:2 Why Name Individual Defendants?
21:3 Nursing Liability
21:4 Physician Liability
21:5 Administrative Liability
21:6 Careful Use for State Corporation Law Research
21:7 The Role of Respondeat Superior Liabilities

21:1 Collective Responsibility and Group Coverage of Liability Insurance

Multiple participants impacting the safety or health of the resident should be considered for the punitive damage awards. In such a case, physician, therapist, nurse, and consulting pharmacist malpractice carriers may also need to be involved in the defense or settlement of their individual portions of the collective liability of the professionals working at the nursing home. Those cases of overlapping liability insurance policies will be the occasions when individuals should be named along with the listed corporate owner of the nursing home, the operating corporation that runs the actual resident care, the administrators of the home, and the parent company that holds the state license and is legally accountable for care violations.

21:2 Why Name Individual Defendants?

Adding defendants to the plaintiff's complaint allows defendants to cross-claim[1] and lightens the plaintiff's burden in proving liability of defendants as each defendant will likely produce evidence that points the finger at a co-defendant. Additional defendants allow the jury to place blame for the injury on some party, and precludes the defendants from using the "empty chair" defense by blaming some party who is not in the lawsuit.[2] Another tactical benefit of adding defendants is the "Mary Carter" agreement, in which individual defendants can settle with plaintiff after agreeing to testify in the case.[3]

Plaintiff's counsel should proceed with caution—or, at the least, low expectations—because it has been this author's personal experience that defendants, even those without any relation to one another, are rarely inclined to point the finger at one another. Rather, the general strategy in nursing home cases tends to be to point the finger at the resident by blaming the resident's injury on the resident's preexisting conditions, age, or conduct. Defense counsel can be creative in their excuses to avoid liability. And an attorney must be careful that the numerous defense theories do not overshadow the plaintiff's liability picture in the eyes of the jury. The risk of juror confusion is diminished when the defendants share the same defense counsel.

21:3 Nursing Liability

The nurse has certain liabilities as a professional, discussed in Chapter 4. She or he has accountability under state nursing statutes for the direct care of the resident.[4] The registered nurse may be promoted in the nursing home structure to the role of director of nursing, in charge

---

1. Rey v. Park View Nursing Home, Inc., 692 N.Y.S.2d 686, 688 (N.Y. App. Div. 2d Dep't 1999).

2. Defense against a Prima Facie Case § 13:38.50 (Daniel Jakala 1st ed 1982).

3. Laura Hunter Dietz et al., *Mary Carter Agreements*, 57B Am. Jur. 2d *Negligence* § 1057 (2013).

4. Nursing Home Litigation: Investigation and Case Preparation 78 (Patricia Iyer ed., 1999).

of supervision of employees, including staff and certified nursing assistants (CNAs). The nurse will be described in the typical nursing home documents as the person responsible for maintaining resident care plans.[5] For that reason, it is prudent to have the supervisory nurse included as an additional named defendant.

In the case of resident injury associated with actions of contract nurses and temporary nurses, only a limited amount of the liability insurance of the temporary agency may be available, so it will be important to discern early whether the injury occurred as a result of a contract employee's negligence.

21:4 Physician Liability

The physician who made the critical decisions causing injury to the resident may have been the attending physician selected by the resident, or may have been the medical director, as an employee or a contractor of the nursing home corporation.

Chapter 5 deals with the physician's substantive liabilities. State laws dealing with physician malpractice will establish the set of procedures that your client will have to follow. If the case involves inadequate care of the resident within the nursing home, then the physician who was the medical director may be named a defendant, along with his or her practice group, and the nursing home corporation may be sued under the legal doctrine of respondeat superior.

Claims of intentional harm asserted against physicians may not be covered by the nursing home through respondeat superior or by that physician's insurance.[6]Obligations of the professional person to the nursing home resident are likely to go beyond the grounds of the state versions of malpractice liability. Whether the medical issues can be compartmentalized and avoided will be a very fact-specific question;

---

5. Ctrs. for Medicare & Medicaid Servs., State Operations Manual, CMS Pub. No. 100-07, Appendix PP: Guidance to Surveyors for Long Term Care Facilities (2007 ed.). Also see the policy manual of the particular chain or individual nursing home.

6. Elashker v. Med. Liab. Mut. Ins. Co., 847 N.Y.S.2d 268, 269 (N.Y. App. Div. 3d Dep't 2007) (assault claim against physician was not covered by physician's insurance).

if medical negligence was in some way distinguishable from nursing home activities, the defendant home will seek to distance itself from accountability for harm to that patient.[7]

Attributing shared fault among multiple actors is complex. Nursing homes may find it difficult to distance themselves from claims of negligent hiring, training, and supervision by blaming the doctor for the negligent health care.[8]

These issues of when to name the physician in the complaint, and of how to deal with the dual role of the physician as medical advisor to the nursing home and as caring physician for the individual, need to be carefully worked out in the context of your state's malpractice jurisprudence.

Physicians who serve as medical directors and treat residents present another set of challenges for plaintiffs as standards of care for each role vary.[9] It may be best to name the practice group from which the doctor came, as the group probably signed the service contract with the nursing home corporation.

21:5 Administrative Liability

Depending on the particular statutory scheme, nursing home administrators may have a duty of care assigned to them. In the interests of bringing the maximum amount of defendants into the case, plaintiff's counsel should investigate statutes for nursing home administrators to determine if statutes can impose a duty of care. If so, negligence can be plead against the administrators. For example, Mississippi has

7. N.X. v. Cabrini Med. Ctr., 765 N.E.2d 844, 847 (N.Y. 2002) (defendant hospital escaped vicarious liability by proving doctor was not acting within the scope of his employment when he caused the injury).

8. Harris v. Extendicare Homes, Inc., 829 F. Supp. 2d 1023 (W.D. Wash. 2011) (Washington statute limited damages in cases of administration of health care. The fact that a physician developed a care plan did not preclude claims of negligent hiring, training, and supervision. Claims against the nursing home when the doctor implemented the care plan were not limited because of the statute.).

9. Satterwhite v. Reilly, 817 So. 2d 407, 412 (La. Ct. App. 2d Cir. 2002), *writ denied*, 825 So. 2d 1193 (La. 2002) (plaintiff could not prove standard of care).

a statute that sets out minimum standards for nursing home administrators.[10] Under this statute and related statutes,[11] administrators are liable for operations of the nursing home, and therefore can be liable for torts even though the administration may have no personal contact with the residents who are plaintiffs.[12]

21:6 Careful Use for State Corporation Law Research

Be careful in drafting the complaint, especially as to allocating liability challenges to certain corporate entities. You will never know as much from the outside as the chain's executives know about the structure that they have erected. Make certain that you have researched, through appropriate state agency filings and commercial databases, all of the registered corporate names and corporate relationships of each of the subsidiaries that are accountable. Publicly traded companies will show some of this in their SEC and state filings.

Your efforts in this regard will be helped by a requirement of the federal Patient Protection and Affordable Care Act requiring nursing homes to report a considerably expanded amount of information about the management and ownership of their facilities.

CMS collects this data in its Provider Enrollment and Chain Ownership System database. Although it is not a requirement of the Affordable Care Act to do so, CMS is developing scenarios under which some of this ownership information would be displayed on its Nursing Home Compare website.[13]

When initiating litigation, name the correct entities and use "John Doe Corp." for others. The physician may have established a professional service corporation under state law; the nursing home property will be owned by a corporation, typically a thin shell protected as a limited liability corporation; the nurses might be employed by a

10. Miss. Code Ann. § 73-17-3 (West).
11. Miss. Code Ann. § 43-11-13 (West).
12. Hill v. Beverly Enters.-Miss., Inc., 305 F. Supp. 2d 644, 651 (S.D. Miss. 2003).
13. Dep't of Health & Human Servs., CMS 2012 Nursing Home Action Plan 2–3 (2012), http://www.cms.gov/Medicare/Provider-Enrollment-and-Certification/Certificationand Complianc/Downloads/2012-Nursing-Home-Action-Plan.pdf.

separate corporation; dietary service might be obtained from a separate corporation; and so on.[14]

Some courts have pierced this web by allocating damages to each of several related entities.[15] In limited cases, the nursing home can be held liable for the actions of independent contractors,[16] but the case will turn on the amount of control the nursing home has over the contractors.[17]

Some courts have allocated damages to the parent corporation even though the parent corporation did nothing more than pay an independent contractor to run the nursing home.[18] If there is any suggestion of this multiple-participant arrangement, the plaintiff's counsel must act carefully. It will be prudent to avoid potential future claims of legal malpractice by naming each of the known corporate defendants, as well as the "John Doe" defendants who will be identified later in an amended complaint following discovery. Counsel should seek to name only those organizations that were involved in the care of the resident, and not any related corporate entity.[19] Careful drafting is recommended, since it would be very unfortunate to get past the point of the statute of limitations and then learn that an unnamed isolated entity controlled the person who had committed the offense.[20] The information that a separate corporation had been accountable for the actions that caused the harm to your client will undoubtedly complicate the attribution of liabilities.[21]

14. Charles Duhigg, *At Many Homes, More Profit and Less Nursing*, N.Y. Times, Sept. 23, 2007.

15. Smartt v. NHC, No. 2182 (Warren Cnty., Tenn. Cir. Ct., Feb. 22, 2007) (multiple entities named), *reported in* Verdicts, Settlements & Tactics 149 (Apr. 2007).

16. Restatement (Third) of Torts: Phys. & Emot. Harm § 55 (2012).

17. Restatement (Second) of Agency § 220 (1958).

18. "The contracting party remains liable for the negligent performance of the contract, whether it be performed for him by his employee or an independent contractor." NME Props., Inc. v. Rudich, 840 So. 2d 309, 312–13 (Fla. 4th Dist. Ct. App. 2003).

19. Price v. TLC Health Care, Inc., 2004 OK 8, 85 P.3d 838, 841 (plaintiff sued property owner (landlord) and landlord's property manager).

20. Morton v. Madison Cnty. Nursing Home Auxiliary, 761 N.E.2d 145, 153 (Ill. 2001) (service on correct entity did not relate back to original complaint because statute of limitations had expired at time of service).

21. Johnson v. Delmar Gardens W., Inc., 335 S.W.3d 83, 89 (Mo. Ct. App. E. Dist. 2011) (plaintiff failed to serve correct party, but was allowed to amend complaint to add correct party because incorrect party and correct party shared offices, directors, corporate headquarters, and attorneys, giving sufficient notice to correct party of impending litigation).

21:7 The Role of Respondeat Superior Liabilities

There are two vertical relationships to be considered. The worker acts for the benefit of the corporation; traditional state common law and corporate statutes will determine the relative relationships and liabilities of "agent and principal" in the implementation of nursing home policy. Of course, the corporation will deny that the negligent act of the CNA who dropped the heavy, immobile resident could be attributed to the corporation. But as a tactical matter, the individual worker may not be targeted as a defendant, as Chapter 18 explains.

A nursing home can be found directly liable for negligent hiring by failing to use reasonable care in doing background checks before hiring an abusive worker when a reasonable investigation would have disclosed a propensity to commit abuse. However, it is unlikely that a cause of action for the respondeat superior liability of the nursing home will be successful. An employer can be found liable under respondeat superior for the harmful acts of its employees that cause harm when those acts are committed within the scope of their employment.[22]

However, the intentional torts of employees, though committed while on the job, are not considered to be committed within the scope of employment.[23]Adding to the foregoing causes of action, the nursing home can be found directly liable for the failure to use reasonable care in training the employees in the appropriate interventions to deal with uncooperative or aggressive residents as well as what measures to avoid because these actions may rise to the level of being patient abuse.

Parent companies are likely to attempt to distance themselves from the employee's actions, but prudent counsel will introduce employee training records, employee criminal records, and oversight agency findings to refute the home's claims of proper training and diligent hiring practices.[24]

---

22. Heritage Hous. Dev., Inc. v. Carr, 199 S.W.3d 560, 565 (Tex. App.—Hous. [1st Dist.] 2006).

23. Elashker v. Med. Liab. Mut. Ins. Co., 847 N.Y.S.2d 268, 269 (N.Y. App. Div. 3d Dep't 2007) (assault claim against physician was not covered by physician's insurance).

24. Rodebush *ex rel.* Rodebush v. Okla. Nursing Homes, Ltd., 867 P.2d 1241, 1244 (Okla. 1993) (defendant home had failed to provide training or investigate the background of

The nursing home can also be held directly liable for failure to use reasonable care to provide a proper level of staffing that contributes to abuse. Under this theory, the use of the substantial factor test for causation will assist a lawyer in establishing liability.

One resource that is especially helpful during the preliminary investigation, before discovery of the actual nursing home records, is the information that CMS currently provides on the staffing levels of each licensed nursing home on its Nursing Home Compare database.[25] This information has become more accurate and comprehensive as CMS has undertaken a program to publish staffing information based on payroll data.[26]

Counsel in a patient-abuse case may find it tactically efficient to argue that the alter-ego doctrine applies to the parent corporate entity or that inequity would result from the parent corporation not being held liable.[27]

The second vertical relationship is a product of astute accountants and corporate transactional lawyers. The money that flows into the licensed nursing home's account from states, from insurers, and from residents goes up the chain to the parent company. The parent company has been structured in a way that seeks to bar attribution of liabilities to the parent, leaving the operating company to go bankrupt if a serious verdict is awarded in a tort case.[28]

A widely read *New York Times* investigative report in 2007 made the convincing case that shell companies, limited liability companies, and limited partnership arrangements had actually reduced the quality of care.[29] Identifying and then naming the correct parent companies will be a sophisticated adventure for the intrepid plaintiff's counsel.

---

employee who assaulted resident; nursing home was cited by Department of Human Services for training policy violation).

25. Ctrs. for Medicare & Medicaid Servs., Nursing Home Compare, http://www.medicare.gov/nursinghomecompare/.

26. Dep't of Health & Human Servs., CMS 2012 Nursing Home Action Plan 2–3 (2012), http://www.cms.gov/Medicare/Provider-Enrollment-and-Certification/CertificationandComplianc/Downloads/2012-Nursing-Home-Action-Plan.pdf.

27. Walsh v. Kindred Healthcare, 798 F. Supp. 2d 1073, 1082 (N.D. Cal. 2011).

28. Heritage Hous. Dev., Inc. v. Carr, 199 S.W.3d 560, 565 (Tex. App.—Hous. [1st Dist.] 2006).

29. Duhigg, *supra* note 14.

CHAPTER 22

Witnesses

22:1 Overview
22:2 When Are Experts Needed?
22:3 Case Evaluation and Nontestifying Experts
22:4 Current Administrators
22:5 Current Medical and Nursing Staff
22:6 Former Staff Members
22:7 Support Staff
22:8 Preparation and Document Review
22:9 *Daubert* Effects
22:10 Fact Witnesses
22:11 Deposing Management and Supervisory Employees
22:12 Deposing the Corporate Representative
22:13 Testimony of the Patient

22:1 Overview

Trial counsel must remember that trials involve people talking to people. Expert witnesses are a central part of most nursing home cases, yet experts are people first and foremost, and each will be slightly different in disposition and presentation. Experience as an expert witness brings the admonition for counsel to remember that every expert is an individual person, first. The process of modern litigation sometimes leads less experienced attorneys to think of the expert as an item to check off a list, a puzzle piece, or as a fungible acquisition of knowledge while assembling evidentiary support. The best outcomes with the use of an expert begin with the lawyer building a positive interpersonal connection of trust and reliance in the communications that one can have with that expert.

If the consultation is early enough, the plaintiff's counsel may be spared months of wasted effort or may find an angle that had not been considered. For example, an elderly woman fell in a nursing home bathroom while she was unattended; perhaps the employee responsible for toileting that woman resident during that shift was overworked and aiding others. The case settled before trial for $175,000.[1] A case of respondeat superior could be used for a negligence action. But the expert may demonstrate to counsel that the system was at fault, not just the aide, because a poor choice of prescription drugs was a big contributor to the instability of the patient; may show that the administrator had acted upon a corporate directive that cut the staff so severely that only one aide was available for 20 frail elders on that evening shift; and could help find that the director of nursing had written a policy memo that two workers would assist this type of patient in order to meet the minimums called for by the state long-term care agency.

Expert witness testimony about the workings of a properly managed and sufficiently staffed nursing home will aid the plaintiff's case greatly. This model or ideal set of performance conditions will mark the type of staffing, responsiveness, and protection that the expert found to be lacking in the defendant's nursing home.

This chapter anticipates that some lawyers will not wish to invest in expert testimony in the preparation of a nursing home case. Chapter 31 cautions that the case may be expensive if experts are needed. The best-experienced witnesses will offer a superior resume, a bright persona as a witness, tenacity in holding to the strength of their conclusions, and a willingness to listen and inquire as the family and any fact witnesses describe what they believe happened to the injured person. Should the attorney scrimp on expertise and hope to win a settlement cheaply? Should the attorney bet that the judge would treat this topical area as so commonly known that jurors do not need the guidance

1. Zorn v. Life Care Ctrs of Am., 2004 WL 5217647 (S.C. State Ct. 2004).

of an expert? "Penny wise, pound foolish" may be the right response; it would be a serious strategic error to lose a nursing home case that otherwise could have generated a six-figure recovery because the lawyer was hesitant to invest $10,000 in the best available expert. The negligence verdict that could be won with a sufficient expert showing might be exceptional if the case is both meritorious and well prepared.[2]

22:2 When Are Experts Needed?

Courts divide the evidentiary requirements in nursing home cases into those injuries that can be readily understood by the common experience of jurors and those for which expert testimony must establish the standard of due care. If the duty of reasonable care for the resident was within the common knowledge of the jury, then the plaintiff did not have to obtain expert witness testimony on that topic.[3] As a rule of thumb, the activities of daily living are customarily known to all; falling out of an unguarded bed is a hazard of daily living and guardrails are a method of protecting against this very common risk for infirm and elderly patients. But the standards of care as to medical and nursing behavior under specific patient needs are reserved for experts. Causation is presented by the medical expert; failure to meet the nursing standard of care is for the nursing expert.[4] Ulceration and medication cases are among those for which expert testimony will be essential to success.

---

2. For example, inadequate care of patient sores by overworked staff resulted in two 2006 major verdicts against nursing homes; these are the type of "standard of care" cases necessitating expert witness testimony. *See, e.g.*, Davis v. Pruitt Corp., 2006 WL 2641137 (Ga. Trial Ct. 2006) ($1.17 million award); Washington v. Nexion Health, 2006 WL 5347044 (La. Trial Ct. 2006) ($990,000 verdict).

3. Juhnke v. Evangelical Lutheran Good Samaritan Soc'y, 634 P.2d 1132 (Kan. Ct. App. 1981).

4. William Lawson & Elizabeth Capezuti, *Handling Witnesses: Working with Expert Witnesses, in* Nursing Home Litigation: Pretrial Practice and Trials 429, 448 (Ruben Krisztal ed., 2d ed. 2003).

22:3 Case Evaluation and Nontestifying Experts

Nursing home patient and family complaints are more common than any of us wish they were. Disappointment, anger, frustration, and some guilt underlay the family's response to the accident that causes harm, over and above the backdrop of past illness and incapacitation of a loved one within the nursing home. Counsel should be skeptical of the first reports received about the "how" and "why" of this accident. Not all cases unfold as the initial client interview had portrayed them.

Evaluating the standard of care in the nursing home is optimally done by a legal nurse consultant, working with a former nursing home administrator or former director of nursing. The consultant will advise the attorney about the records the attorney has obtained and will lay out the path for deciding whether the injury or death was related to a negligent act.[5]

The legal privilege for statements by nontestifying experts allows the counsel to obtain a frank evaluation of the merits of the case before the litigation reaches the more costly and intensive stages. No data exists on total claims and total possible claims; but reasonable guesstimates indicate that the vast majority of would-be litigants are declined and their claims do not become lawsuits. A key role in this is the expert evaluation of the factual assertions, used to separate the meritorious from the improbable claims.

22:4 Current Administrators

The critical decision to be made by the plaintiff's lawyer in approaching the selection of witnesses is to have defined a theory of the case, into which the selected witness would fit. The witnesses who are presented, in a persuasive and expanding sequence, will then impress upon the jurors that either the staff who provided the care to the injured person were negligent, and wished to do as little caregiving as possible; or

---

5. Nursing Home Litigation: Investigation and Case Preparation 415 (Patricia Iyer ed., 1999).

that they were nominally qualified persons, who simply were present in inadequate numbers to perform the risk-avoidance tasks that were assigned to them. The suit is not about the individual employee who caused the event, but about the system in place at the nursing home that had failed to adequately protect the resident.

The neglect of a nursing home patient may lead to the more frequent occurrence of serious skin ulcers, injurious falls, medication errors, or other sources of injury. The deposition of the persons who run the day-to-day operation of the nursing home will typically provide bland assertions of the seamless, flawless, and caring protection that every resident received. The last four or five state survey reports for this nursing home (as discussed in the following chapter) may undermine some of these assertions.

State licensing boards may have a detailed documentary file on the prior work of the defendant's manager, director of nursing, and medical director. With appropriate subpoenas or signed waivers of privacy rights, these state records should be examined for information that may be used for impeachment of the witness.

In virtually all cases, the nursing home administrator will be a defense witness, if he or she had been in that or a similar local role when the injury occurred. The current administrators of the nursing home are likely to have been promoted and selected by the company for their ability to satisfy the company's financial goals, and to meet those goals with the minimum amount of disruption. The ability to satisfy the corporate chain's cost requirements will be the most essential career element for the administrator. To the extent relevant, she or he may also have been wonderfully kind, supportive, and caring for patients; but counsel should view the person who is the chief of the nursing home as the principal agent for implementing the owner's corporate policies. The adversarial nature of the litigation process is such that the administrator will probably be cross-examined in deposition as a hostile witness, regarding budget, personnel assignments, and the like.

The administrator may have investigated the facts of a particular incident, and may have a personal point of view regarding the causation of this incident. But typically, the fall or other injury would have occurred outside the presence of that person. The administrator's role in the litigation is an adjunct defensive role, to aid the denial of responsibility by the corporate defendant. Counsel for the resident or survivors may expect to find in the files, after consultation with experts, a basis for criticism of the oversight, training, and the supervision responsibilities of the administrator as they were allowed to impact on the conditions of care for this injured resident.

A critical aspect of the administrator's role is the training of employees in the proper procedures for handling elderly patients. The adequacy of the training for certified nursing assistants (CNAs) that is provided should be excellent, at least on paper. The adequacy of the training as it is actually applied can be elicited from the defense witnesses by asking specific questions about the hours of training, the degree of intensity, the follow-up, and the continuing education programs. Although training time removes the person from availability for day-to-day work, in the long run it is necessary that the full staff training be done competently and with the active support of the persons being trained. This "active learning" imperative is especially true in nursing homes, because of the rapid turnover of staff, and of the complexity of the comprehensive care tasks. Training will be vital for protection of the interests of the resident. It must be performed well and supervised well and must be put into action and overseen by managers.

22:5 Current Medical and Nursing Staff

Turnover of staff and recruitment of new workers is a constant pattern in most skilled nursing facilities. By the time of trial, the current nursing home staff and the medical director will probably have a minimal recollection of the facts leading up to this particular incident. They will instead rely upon the chart, and so the plaintiff's representative should be careful to examine the chart in its original form, to discern whether any additions, changes, deletions, or later modifications were made to the chart record concerning this resident, before and after the first incident occurred. A back-dated or written-over entry or belated entry of what the writer might have recalled later should not be in the patient's chart, if the chart is to be deemed credible. For electronic health records, attention to the metadata showing when a record was initiated and when it was altered (and by whom) is especially helpful.

The persons who at the time of injury held the positions of medical director and director of nursing are typical witnesses.[6] The medical expert for the plaintiff will aid in preparations for these depositions.[7] Below the level of the director of nursing, high turnover of nurses and aides creates a continuing problem of finding the testimony needed to reconstruct the scene of injury. Persistence in tracking these people is essential since they have no allegiance to the nursing home and can be expected to be candid about deficiencies in working conditions that may have affected the patients.

22:6 Former Staff Members

Former employees can provide the best perspective on staffing shortages, since they can speak directly to the volume of patient care that they had borne at the time that the actual incident occurred. These former employees probably departed from the nursing home for reasons of low wages, dissatisfaction with management, clashes with residents, or more desirable types of work elsewhere. The departed employee has a perspective that will be instructive to the jury, especially if the witnesses for the plaintiff have more actual hands-on experience with this personal story, and can attest to the changes or deficiencies that were present at the time of the accident. The defense might argue that it is unethical to interview these witnesses outside of depositions, but the claims are not likely to survive close scrutiny, for interviews with

6. Gerald Taylor, *Handling Witnesses: Deposing the Medical Director, Director of Nursing, Attending Physician, Nursing Home Administrator and Upper Management*, *in* Nursing Home Litigation: Pretrial Practice and Trials, *supra* note 4, at 41.

7. Jeffrey Levine, *The Role of the Medical Expert in Evaluating Nursing Home Care*, *in* Nursing Home Litigation: Pretrial Practice and Trials, *id.* at 503.

former employees are customary and employee nondisclosure contracts are infrequent for these categories of workers.

Turnover by nursing home staff tends to be so frequent that, in a larger city, it may be impossible to locate the precise fact witnesses who were actively involved with the patient at the time that the accident occurred. Their mobility and frequent turnover makes it more difficult to authenticate claims by the family of the decedent that lower-level staff had acknowledged the problems that led to the injury. Was this item recorded in the chart? If not, some say it did not occur. The electronic records conversion may facilitate the search of patient records.

In some nursing homes, a turnover of lower staff members may exceed 80 percent in a year. The trial may occur four years after the event that caused the injury. The likelihood is that the ex-employee carries no lingering affection for the nursing home's pay and supervision of its employees. So it is feasible and ethical for plaintiff to locate and engage the cooperation of a former employee, who had some personal knowledge of the circumstances of the injury.[8]

From the defense viewpoint, this makes it difficult to defend a case in which the bare paper (or electronic) clinical record is the only source from which to find details—especially if the plaintiff's counsel had already located and noticed depositions of three former employees who had personal knowledge of the events in dispute.

The expert witness should be allowed to interact with the former employees and the other fact witnesses, so that the expert witness can have a sense of how his or her expectations would have been affected by the actual conditions, as they existed as of the date of the event that caused the harm.

22:7 Support Staff

If the injury is one of malnutrition and dehydration, these are chronic problems that result from a long pattern of inadequate action on the

8. J. Scott Myers, *Presenting Defense Witnesses for Deposition*, *in* NURSING HOME LITIGATION: PRETRIAL PRACTICE AND TRIALS, *id.* at 163–34.

part of the nursing home. To get an effective sense of the consequences of dehydration, please refer to Chapter 14.

22:8 Preparation and Document Review

The clinical records of the nursing home, and especially resident assessment and incident reports, will provide the basis for the expert witness report and subsequent testimony. The resident's chart for the day of the event will be examined; the prescription drug record may show what medications had contributed to the person's impairment. In a nutrition case, the longer-term plan and the notations on the dietary record for this patient will be important evidence. The records kept by the speech pathologist, for example, may show how the patient was determined to be unable to swallow, and therefore needed to be fed by tubes. Care plans when the patient was admitted were prepared by these separate disciplines and should be in the record. Review the CMS Guidance for Surveyors, the "watermelon book," for the regulators' expectations of documentation.[9] In each of these cases, the documents are available in discovery. The general principle of nursing home litigation is "What is not charted is assumed to not have been done."

22:9 Daubert *Effects*

The U.S. Supreme Court's standards for the establishment of expert witness qualifications in federal courts[10] are named for the *Daubert* decision,[11] in which federal courts were given five criteria for the evaluation of the relevance and reliability of expert witness testimony. Many but not all state supreme courts have adopted the full or a modified version of the *Daubert* standard. Many other sources expand on the

---

9. Ctrs. for Medicare & Medicaid Servs., State Operations Manual, CMS Pub. No. 100-07, Appendix PP: Guidance to Surveyors for Long Term Care Facilities (F-tag listings for specific requirements to be rated by the surveyors; the color-coded pages produced the informal name for the text).

10. Many but not all state courts have followed these norms; refer to your state common law and rules.

11. Daubert v. Merrell Dow Pharms., 509 U.S. 579 (1993).

topic, but in this context, counsel for the defense will argue before the trial that the proposed expert witness is bringing in material that is insufficiently relevant and not reliable.

22:10 Fact Witnesses

The difference between a fact witness and an expert witness is more significant than one might think. The expert may be needed to establish the baseline for standards of due care, so that the jury can understand the complex evaluation of nutritional needs, for example. Disputes over the relevance and reliability of the expert's views will continue up to and at the trial. The fact witness, such as a former CNA at the home, may testify about how a rush of time demands led to carelessness, and the patient was dropped on the floor after being lifted from the bath. By contrast, the expert describes the proper use of the Hoyer lift sling and the standards of due care for methods of lifting; the expert produces the Hoyer label and instruction that says the lift should not be used by fewer than two aides and that each should have had training before use. Counsel should use discovery to obtain copies of the nursing home personnel files, especially the background check performed on the former employee, and should verify whether the employee is on the list of persons who have been barred from future nursing home service.[12]

22:11 Deposing Management and Supervisory Employees

Decisions to cut costs by cutting staff have painful impacts on nursing home patients,[13] and the executive level managers should be deposed to elicit a pattern of decisions that contributed to this injury situation. Major

12. Kaitlyn Luther, *Who Watches the Watchmen?*, 20 Elder L.J. 161 (2012).
13. Mei Zhao & D. Rob Haley, *Nursing Home Quality, Staffing and Malpractice Risk-Losses*, 38 J. Health Care Fin. 1 (2011).

exposure to punitive damages can be attributed to some of the conscious management decisions to slash the staffing that serves patients.[14]

The nursing home managers should be deposed during discovery to verify the authenticity—or admit the forgery—of its clinical records about the plaintiff. The testimony of experienced care managers who were resistant to a corporate edict to reduce staff and pushed back against corporate budget cuts would be very helpful, if it can be elicited during the course of the depositions. Loyalty to the chain owner is probable, but professional pride is stronger than the short-term economic advantage of retaining a job by testifying as to the "acceptability" of the corporate staffing decision. Since mobility among experienced nursing home administrators and nurses is very open in many parts of the country, management has less compelling force to suppress an employee's honest responses if the employer were so inclined. Therefore the deposition questions may elicit honest responses that might not be tilted exclusively in the owner's preferred direction.

22:12 Deposing the Corporate Representative

The corporate nursing home chain or other management office will be deemed to have custody of its records. Under the rules of civil procedure in the state, there is likely to be an equivalent to Federal Rule of Civil Procedure 30(b)(6) on the designation of a corporate witness. The witness will present the views of the nursing home company and will presumably give an authentication of its records. The records and forms are expected to follow the state rules and the CMS requirements, so it would be surprising for a corporate representative not to have the complete set of documents that had been called for in the deposition notice.

---

14. Mark Schauerte, *Landmark Nursing Home Settlement Agreement of $50 Million*, 12 J. Health Care Compliance 55.

22:13 Testimony of the Patient

In some situations, the patient is competent and capable of recollection of the event. A videotaped deposition of the patient should be conducted, after extensive preparation and practice.[15] Defense counsel recommend careful attention to details with the deposition of the elderly resident[16] and with the family members.[17]

---

15. Julie Braun, *Dealing with the Older Witness, in* NURSING HOME LITIGATION: PRETRIAL PRACTICE AND TRIALS, *supra* note 4, at 41.

16. Thomas Rockwell, *Dealing with the Older Witness: The Defense Perspective, in* NURSING HOME LITIGATION: PRETRIAL PRACTICE AND TRIALS, *id.* at 81 ("The opposing side will have to exercise great care to not appear to be harassing or embarrassing the witness.").

17. J. Roslyn Lemmon & Pamela Lormand, *Handling Witnesses: Deposing Family Members, in* NURSING HOME LITIGATION: PRETRIAL PRACTICE AND TRIALS, *id.* at 83.

CHAPTER 23

Use of Regulatory Surveys of Nursing Homes

23:1 Use of Government Survey Findings
23:2 Utility of Survey Findings to Plaintiffs
23:3 Authentication and Admissibility
23:4 Penalties and Appeals

23:1 Use of Government Survey Findings

Government surveyors should visit each licensed nursing home every 15 months or less, but special for-cause visits in response to resident safety complaints may come at any time, as "complaint surveys" examine a specific aspect of the nursing home's operations.[1] The CMS sourcebook on surveys can be ordered,[2] and several references on the survey process are available.[3] The federal website for comparisons is available.[4]

Medicaid and Medicare pay for most nursing home beds in American nursing homes. The quality of the nursing home experience is

---

1. These may be initiated by an ombudsman's complaint or a credible complaint from a family member.

2. CTRS. FOR MEDICARE & MEDICAID SERVS., STATE OPERATIONS MANUAL, CMS PUB. NO. 100-07, APPENDIX PP: GUIDANCE TO SURVEYORS FOR LONG TERM CARE FACILITIES P-1 (Rev. 22, 2006) [hereinafter CMS SURVEY GUIDANCE].

3. *See, e.g.*, Ruth West, *The Survey Process, in* MEDICAL-LEGAL ASPECTS OF LONG-TERM CARE (Jeffrey Levine ed., 2003).

4. *Find & Compare Providers Near You,* MEDICARE.GOV, www.medicare.gov/care-compare (last visited Dec. 17, 2024).

maintained by the managers of the nursing home, whose stream of income is subject to penalties identified in inspections by a team of surveyors who are selected by the states and who implement the federal CMS guidance.[5]

States can adopt levels of reports. In Ohio, for example, these reports have included Inspection Reports, Facility Details Reports, Family Satisfaction Survey Scores, and Resident Satisfaction Survey Scores.[6]

At the end of the visit the state surveyors provide the nursing home management with a set of findings,[7] and the management then can respond. If the state imposes a penalty because of a deficiency, the penalty is based on the survey results. The penalty for noncompliance may be a cash civil penalty per day, or may be as severe as cutting off further Medicaid/Medicare admissions to the nursing home, a form of "death penalty" that is reserved for the chronically worst performing nursing homes.[8]

"Complaint surveys" are unannounced government inspections of nursing homes; these result from complaints by ombudsmen, patients, visitors, relatives, or local officials. These are very likely to result in findings against the nursing home, and potentially in civil penalties as well. In fiscal year 2007, there were an estimated 47,000 complaint related inspections.[9] There are also initial certification surveys for facilities and abbreviated standard surveys for homes under new management or for responses to certain serious complaints.

Surveys are done twice as frequently on nursing homes that are on the problems list, the CMS Special Focus Facility list.[10] These facili-

---

5. CMS SURVEY GUIDANCE, *supra* note 2.

6. *2022 Residential Care Facility Family Satisfaction Survey Results*, OHIO.GOV, https://ltc.ohio.gov/care-information/data-on-care-service/2022-residential-care-facility-family-satisfaction-survey-results (last visited Dec. 17, 2024).

7. CMS Form 2567.

8. The nursing home usually appeals the cutoff, and administrative hearings and appeals will follow.

9. Press Release, Senate Comm. on Aging, Kohl: We Need Greater Transparency and Stronger Enforcement of Nursing Home Quality (Nov. 15, 2007), http://www.aging.senate.gov.

10. *Lawmakers Demand CMS Release Full Special Focus Facility List*, INSIDE HEALTHCARE (Dec. 13, 2007).

ties are specially examined because they are like yo-yos, in and out of compliance with CMS and state rules rather than steadily improving.

23:2 Utility of Survey Findings to Plaintiffs

The best possible finding for a lawsuit is, sadly, the worst possible finding for a resident: violations of the Medicare-Medicaid regulations that pose an "imminent jeopardy" to the life and safety of the residents.

Survey findings of violations are getting worse each year, "imminent jeopardy" up 10.7 percent and all violations up by 13.8 percent from reporting years 2004 to 2006.[11]

The survey finding on a specific resident is usually masked by a code number or other protection of individual privacy. And the regular typical survey occurs every 15–18 months, so the event that caused the litigation might not have been anticipated or reported upon by a survey document that occurred at a different time.

But two parallel systems exist. Some regular surveys note significant deficiencies that should be followed up; a "partial extended survey" sends the surveyors back in to check on remedial activities.[12] And in the case of a death that was reported with a complaint, there may be a "complaint survey" which shows the government analyst's views on the specific facts that are being litigated in this case.

In one set of cases, the actual survey report may be admitted into evidence at the trial to show knowledge by the nursing home management of a deficiency in its systems, for example, nutrition or exit door security, which is related to the harm that this resident suffered, such as malnutrition or escape of a wandering resident.

In another case, the survey document may demonstrate a failure of the correction plan that the nursing home had communicated to the survey agency, following a finding of deficiencies. Here, the claim may be one of misrepresentation; the management had given a promise of

---

11. *Nursing Home Transparency and Improvement, Hearing before the U.S. Senate Comm. on Aging*, 110th Cong. (Nov. 15, 2007) (testimony of SEIU Asst. Dir. of Research Arvid Muller), http://www.aging.senate.gov/hearing_detail.cfm?id=321325&.

12. CMS Survey Guidance, *supra* note 2, at P-3 (Rev. 22 2006).

corrective actions that it then failed to execute. The government had relied on the nursing home administration to protect residents, but it failed both in its original omission and in its inadequate or absent "correction." This will be checked during the partial extended survey follow-up.[13]

Another case might be the specific event subject to this suit, with the official state survey report demonstrating the contemporaneous investigator's findings of how this death or serious injury had occurred, for example, a "complaint survey" of a burn incident that is investigated ten days after the death of the burned resident.

23:3 *Authentication and Admissibility*

Survey reports are routinely admitted into evidence in tort cases relating to the same facility during the same period as the alleged injury.[14] Hearsay exceptions permit admission into evidence of government investigatory documents prepared in the ordinary course of business,[15] so surveys prepared by the state agency will probably suffice for the admission of the report of the survey team, its underlying report segments, and the set of findings. Appeals from federal or state determinations may generate administrative law judge and Departmental Appeals Board findings,[16] and presumably these would be admitted as well if deemed relevant to conditions at the time of the injury.

23:4 *Penalties and Appeals*

Surveyors who find a deficiency can recommend that penalty action be taken by the agency, such as a state health department or long-term care agency. The central office review evaluates the findings and may

---

13. *Id.*

14. NURSING HOME LITIGATION: PRETRIAL PRACTICE AND TRIALS 41 (Ruben Krisztal ed., 2d ed. 2003).

15. FED. R. EVID. 803(8)(c), Beech Aircraft Co. v. Rainey, 488 U.S. 153, 170 (1988); Montiel v. City of Los Angeles, 2 F.3d 335, 341 (9th Cir. 1993).

16. U.S. Dep't of HHS, Departmental Appeals Bd., http://www.hhs.gov/dab.

issue letters or proposed penalty notices to the licensee. The licensee then can appeal for an administrative hearing.

The appeal of a civil penalty or suspension is adjudicated by an administrative law judge, and then by the Departmental Appeals Board of the Department of Health and Human Services.[17] Final decisions of the board then can be reviewed by the federal appellate circuit courts. This results in a final decision four to six years after the inspection. It is virtually certain that the person whose injury was the source of the finding will be dead before the lengthy adjudicative process is completed. So the question arises whether the penalty should be stayed, pending the outcome of the appeals. In the worst cases, immediate action is taken when there is an imminent threat to the health of the residents from continued operation of the nursing home.

17. *See id.*

CHAPTER 24

Documentation: Needs and Sources

24:1 Overview

24:2 Assembly of Records for Expert Review

24:3 Effect of Alteration or Destruction of Records

24:4 Patient Privacy Issues

24:5 Mandatory Reports

24:6 Informed Consent

24:7 DNR and Advance Directives

24:8 Patient Care Plans

24:9 License and Survey Data Regarding the Nursing Home

24:10 Medicare Cost Reports

24:11 HHS Office of Inspector General Reports

24:1 Overview

Paperwork and electronic records truly matter a great deal in the life (and death) of the nursing home patient. Paperwork fuels the state survey discussed in the preceding chapter, and it fuels the tort litigation possibilities. As the plaintiff's lawyer considers filing suit, a reconstruction of the chronology of the plaintiff's care will be needed, in order to locate several useful documents that are important to understand.

The papers start with admissions and proceed through to death or discharge.[1]

If the patient left the nursing home alive, there must be a discharge summary that relates his or her condition to the treatment provided.[2] Records of a death will be part of the file. There must be certain preadmission data in the nursing home's files, including a resident assessment that was prepared when the patient first entered the home, updated at least annually thereafter.[3] The patient's prior health status relevant to this claim is included in the minimum data set (MDS), a packet of evaluative and health data that accompanies the application for admission. The data will be drawn from questionnaires to the patient and, in some cases, the family; the MDS must be compiled for each admitted patient.[4]

State surveyors created some useful reports on this nursing home's patient conditions. Families or potential residents can use the federal website Nursing Home Compare for checking the recorded problems in a potential residence. Surveyors have been examining the file records on patients and in some cases, validating the data that is recorded there.[5] The state survey forms (including CMS Form 2567) for the past several years may be instructive and a source of insights. These are required to be available to representatives of residents at the home; they are public documents at state offices.

Attorneys considering a possible lawsuit against a nursing home should be cautious in crediting recollections by the family. Documentation of the decline in the plaintiff patient's condition should be carefully assembled with the use of nursing home records, which should be obtained after the meeting with the potential clients. CMS standards and state laws will typically provide rights of access to these records after a privacy waiver is obtained.[6] Even after the patient has left the nursing home, there are still rights of record access that can be asserted

---

1. 42 C.F.R. § 483.20.
2. *Id.* § 483.20(l).
3. *Id.* § 483.20.
4. *Id.*
5. *Id.* § 483.10(g).
6. *Id.* § 483.10(b).

by counsel, with the appropriate HIPAA releases signed by the legal representative of the patient, such as an executor or guardian.[7]

The accuracy of the information about care of the resident is an important responsibility for the nursing home administrator. The facility's systems for records accuracy and quality are required to meet CMS as well as state standards. For example, CMS can penalize a nursing home that fails to maintain documentation about an assault, a record that was prepared at the time, and that was needed for examination by the surveyor and perhaps by Medicaid enforcement officials.[8]

24:2 Assembly of Records for Expert Review

The lawyer who is retained for an injury or death of a nursing home patient should begin promptly with the representation of the new client. The prelitigation inquiry letter to the nursing home should be drafted with the help of an experienced nursing home veteran, who knows where the several files are likely to be retained and how they are likely to be described, including medication administration record (MAR), treatment administration record (TAR), care plan, physician orders, nurses' notes, dietary records, list of diagnoses, list of medications, records of weights and vitals, skin assessments, and other relevant files.[9] The request should be accompanied by a release, signed by the legal representative of the patient, which satisfies HIPAA privacy rules.[10] Exceptions to patient privacy rights should be invoked if needed.[11] In addition to the individual patient records, the representative also should ask for a copy of the most recent CMS/state statement of deficiencies, Form 2567, and patient care plan as these may intersect with the patterns of neglect that counsel believes may have affected the plaintiff.

---

7. A useful analysis appears in Mark Kosieradzki & Joel Smith, *Nursing Home Litigation* 63:10, *in* ATLA's Litigating Tort Cases (2006 Supp.).

8. Vandalia Park v. Leavitt, 157 F. App'x 858 (6th Cir. 2005).

9. A useful summary is J. Scott Myers, *A Practical Guide to the Defense*, *in* Nursing Home Litigation: Investigation and Case Preparation 404 (Patricia Iyer ed., 1999).

10. Health Information Portability and Accuracy Act, http://www.hhs.gov/ocr.

11. 42 C.F.R. § 164.524(b)(1).

The records should be gathered and tabbed for ease of review by the expert witness; this secretarial task will save time and money by speeding the expert, who is paid by the hour, through the paperwork review. In the case of an expert who is a nurse or nursing home administrator, this expert may be able to identify which additional forms may exist that were not released, and explain why they would be relevant to the assembly of the plaintiff's case.

24:3 Effect of Alteration or Destruction of Records

In the litigated nursing home cases, there have been numerous instances of records falsification and "retroactive additions" that appear to cover up what had actually occurred in patient care.[12] These mistakes by employees have helped to produce lucrative settlements and verdicts against owners.[13] Experienced trial lawyers understand immediately what the falsified records portend: a possible cover-up conspiracy within the nursing home to deny that a factual matter or event had occurred. But do not jump to an erroneous conclusion as a plaintiff's counsel. Dig deeper, get experts, consult reliable sources, and always make color copies of any hand-written journal record entries so as to help detect fraud. The best policy for plaintiff's counsel is to work with a legal nurse consultant to frame the request, and then to frame the evaluation of the records as they are received.

The best policy for defense counsel is to immediately caution the nursing home administrator to sequester the set of records that covers the patient's stay in the nursing home. The records should be copied and the originals must not be altered by any level of employee, and if corrections or amendments have already been made, defense counsel should begin immediately inquiring of the supervising staff and the director of nursing as to who did what and why. Of course, a policy against writing over or discarding properly recorded facts should be

12. Advocat Inc. v. Sauer, 353 Ark. 29, 111 S.W.3d 346 (2003); Moskovitz v. Mt. Sinai Med. Ctr., 69 Ohio St. 3d 638, 635 N.E.2d 331 (1994).

13. Ruben Krisztal, *Investigation and Pretrial Considerations*, *in* Nursing Home Litigation: Investigation and Case Preparation 361, 380 (Patricia Iyer ed., 1999).

in place and should be part of employee training. The simple change of records might seem to the novice nurse as an easy way to fill in the gaps for work that was not performed. But these records are a ticking time bomb for the defense case, because the plaintiff who can prove fraud can ask for an award of punitive damages and during the trial could seek a court ruling on spoliation, which could exclude the use of the altered records as defense evidence.

24:4 Patient Privacy Issues

Federal standards for medical records have a protection in the HIPAA privacy regulations against unauthorized disclosure.[14] This does not justify withholding records of an assaultive patient who committed an assault against plaintiff.[15] The privacy interests do not apply to shield the predator from public agency investigations.[16] Similarly, physician-patient privilege does not protect documentation of a nursing home patient's assaults on other patients.[17]

24:5 Mandatory Reports

The state statutes may require the mandatory submission of reports concerning nursing home abuse to a central state office supervising nursing homes. The defendant nursing home should have made a timely filing of these mandatory reports. In some cases, the filing of the report comes before the full facts are known, so a supplementary report may also have been filed. The reports are usually available under state open records laws after their investigation has been completed; a signed privacy release form may be needed for access to these individual patient records.

---

14. 45 C.F.R. pts. 160, 164; *see also* detailed HHS website coverage at U.S. Dep't of HHS, Office for Civil Rights, http://www.hhs.gov/ocr.
15. Goodyear v. Care Concepts, 625 N.W.2d 876 (Wis. 2001).
16. Oklahoma v. Thomason, 33 P.3d 930 (Okla. Civ. App. 2001).
17. Crawford v. Care Concepts Inc., 625 N.W.2d 876 (Wis. 2001).

Abuse-related reports are not simple forms; the fact of being reported as an offender will probably make the accused employee very angry. The content of the mandatory report may be privileged under state law against claims that the reporting person had libeled the nursing home or a person referred to in the report.[18]

24:6 Informed Consent

A mentally competent person in a nursing home should be allowed to have access to potential benefits that also carry risks of harms. A "right to smoke" may be asserted. Documentation signed upon admission, or later during site visits by the conservator or caregiver, may ask that the patient or guardian give consent to the use of restraints, with forms calling for advance consent to emergency surgery and so on.[19] The person giving consent has a right to be told about the risks, as well as the benefits, of participating in a clinical test if one is undertaken at the facility.

24:7 DNR and Advance Directives

As the end of life approaches, a patient's clinical chart marked "do not resuscitate" or a sworn statement disclaiming extraordinary measures to preserve life may be in the patient's health care records. The choice to die in a certain manner is a matter of individual freedoms protected by laws in most cases. These issues will not normally be found in tort cases, so we will direct the reader to bioethics texts for a further review on this narrow topic.

24:8 Patient Care Plans

CMS requires that a patient care plan be prepared for each new resident at the time of first admission and reviewed and updated annually. The

18. Hohlt v. Complete Health Care, 936 S.W.2d 223 (Mo. Ct. App. 1996).
19. Consult the CMS Survey Guidance for the expectations of regulators concerning the documentation of the consent.

plan sets forth significant goals (being able to walk or feed oneself, for example) and progress measurements.

A 2013 Inspector General report criticized CMS oversight:

> For 37 percent of stays, Skilled Nursing Facilities did not develop care plans that met requirements or did not provide services in accordance with care plans. For 31 percent of stays, SNFs did not meet discharge planning requirements. Medicare paid approximately $5.1 billion for stays in which SNFs did not meet these quality-of-care requirements. Additionally, reviewers found examples of poor quality care related to wound care, medication management, and therapy. These findings raise concerns about what Medicare is paying for. They also demonstrate that SNF oversight needs to be strengthened to ensure that SNFs perform appropriate care planning and discharge planning.[20]

Under the patient care plan, certain rehabilitation or special needs goals will be set. This plan is later useful to a plaintiff in establishing a claim for breach of the duty to assure proper care. The responsibility to act in accordance with the care plan falls on the nurses and therapists.

24:9 License and Survey Data Regarding the Nursing Home

Public access to the license record of the nursing home is routinely assured by state laws and CMS rules. A potential plaintiff will obtain discovery of the file and should also make a state freedom of information request or an open records request. However, these requests are titled in state law.[21] Certified copies will be admitted into evidence as official records.[22]

---

20. Feb. 2013 HHS Inspector Gen. report, https://oig.hhs.gov/oei/reports/oei-02-09-00201.asp.

21. *See* 2 James O'Reilly, State Laws, ch. 27 in Federal Information Disclosure (2008 Supp.).

22. Fed. R. Evid. 803(8).

The state may enforce its requirements through the survey process. Most do this as a matter of delegated authority from CMS as well as from state rules. The CMS Guidance for Surveyors, nicknamed the "watermelon book," provides some interesting approaches. Chapter 23 covers these matters.

The nursing home ombudsman also has data on the nursing home and may have resolved similar disputes;[23] these files should be sought during discovery.

24:10 Medicare Cost Reports

Each facility receiving federal funding will have a publicly available Medicare Cost Report available annually.[24] This will provide details of what had been spent on patient care. A malnutrition claim, for example, would be aided by showing the nursing home spent less than X dollars a day on food for residents; the jury would be asked, Can one feed an adult on X dollars a day?

24:11 HHS Office of Inspector General Reports

The Office of the Inspector General is the primary fraud preventive organization impacting on the operations of nursing homes.[25] Its reports contain valuable insights into the patterns of nursing home problems. A 2013 report is especially useful if the claim of injury relates to discharges of patients.[26]

---

23. Mildred Hogstel, Gerontology: Nursing Care of the Older Adult 398 (2001).
24. Form HCFA2540-96, available from http://www.cms.hhs.gov/cmsforms.
25. U.S. Dep't of HHS, Office of the Inspector General, https://oig.hhs.gov/.
26. HHS Office of Inspector Gen., No. OEI-02-09-00201, Skilled Nursing Facilities Often Fail to Meet Care Planning and Discharge Planning Requirements (Feb. 27, 2013).

CHAPTER 25

Product-Related Risk Issues

25:1 Overview

25:2 Assistive Devices

25:3 Medical Devices

25:4 Residential Products

25:5 Reporting Injuries to Government

25:1 Overview

Accidents involving equipment and devices in the nursing home can be fatal for vulnerable residents, and the incorrect use of special products is often the basis of the harm. Plaintiff's counsel should consider naming the nursing home as well as the product manufacturer and distributor as defendants. This may generate a settlement offer or access to similar product outcomes in the cases of other past users.

Instructions on a powered lift device may have called for two employees to operate the lifting steps, but the understaffing of the home may be responsible for the routine practice of that facility to have just one certified nurse assistant in the room, who had failed to follow instructions while attempting to perform the lift task. Or the death of the patient may have followed a fatal error with the pump used for drug administration; a busy pharmacist, an inattentive nurse's aide, and an inadequately labeled generic drug may result in a mix-up that has fatal consequences for the patient.

Counsel's task is to reconstruct the accidental injury, focus on the device and its instructions for use, and discern what product element or user behavior had proximately caused the problem.

25:2 Assistive Devices

This category of products includes specialized patient lifts, gurneys, mobility devices, and equipment used for caring for immobilized or impaired patients. A subsequent section deals with beneficial medical products that are labeled with the formal FDA regulatory controls upon "medical devices."

For these assistive devices, the mechanical attributes require study and design efforts to improve the daily life of the elder user. The manufacturer's premarket design and experimentation has probably demonstrated the normal safe uses of the product. If an accident occurs and harm results, there may be a lawsuit against the device maker as well as the device's nursing home user, for example, a certified nursing assistant, the employer, and the maker of a patient lifting device.

In a product failure case, the plaintiff's consulting engineer would seek access to the actual device under a discovery request directed to the defendant nursing home. Plaintiff may also rent a similar unit of the same manufacturer and model year and conduct engineering evaluation of the scenario as it had been described by the eyewitnesses. Third-party evidentiary subpoenas may seek manufacturer and distributor information on recalls, service visits, repairs, and similar incidents that had been reported to the FDA by the manufacturer.

By naming the equipment manufacturer and distributor as co-defendants in the complaint, the plaintiff gets several benefits:

- Access to data on similar accidents from the manufacturer's files;
- Records of the distributor's maintenance and repair logs, if any;
- Potential settlement by these parties who blame the nursing home operator and staff members for the accident, offering a small payment for dismissal; and
- Credible engineering testimony from the settling manufacturer

about the way in which there had been misuse of the assistive device by the staff of the nursing home.

It is also possible that state Medicaid survey instructions (see Chapter 23) contain precautions about the training and calibration needs for use of this assistive equipment, so the failure of the nursing home to properly manage this equipment according to instructions and warnings, may be cited by plaintiff as a violation of the government requirements as well as a common form of negligence.

The claims for products liability relating to injuries associated with assistive devices often include allegations of inadequate safety features in the design of the product, or product warnings that are inadequately phrased, inadequately covering the need for avoidance of the potential harms, or in some cases the poor quality of a key part that breaks during use. For software-driven devices, the harm might arise when the user inadequately connects the actual device to the patient, showing in retrospect that communication about the problem was not received by or acted upon by the end user. For example, the manufacturer of a complex patient bedside monitor may have delivered a thick product owner's manual with no Tag or label on the product concerning shock hazards. This labeling was inadequate, as the postaccident study of a user's electrocution would demonstrate.

Sometimes the assistive device postinjury claims are easily settled; after the accident, the local representative of the manufacturer obtains the failed product and returns it; the factory quality director finds that it had been assembled badly, with a miswiring or misassembly that had increased the risk of failure. Since no manufacturer wants to go through the publicity and expense of trial for an unintended and undesired "bad" unit, settling is the most likely response to a plaintiff's demand letter that includes some showing that the product failure was a result of deficient assembly.

The most difficult settlements are those that necessarily challenge a design that has been used across thousands of identical units of the same model of the product. If model A-200 has a defect, then a recall might be required. But the recall and the costs of replacing all 10,000 units would be so high that the company might choose to fight in court to rebut the "defective design" claim; in terms of efficient use of funds, this "litigate rather than remediate" approach is the proper course from the corporate perspective. Though recalls are more frequent with medical products like implantable joints, the consumer or occupational safety regulators are concerned when accident reports reveal that a product exposes users and patients to a higher-than-normal risk of unanticipated harm.

If the design of the assistive product had been reviewed by the Food and Drug Administration (FDA) before marketing, its design and warning will be laid out in files that may be requested under the Freedom of Information Act from the FDA or from commercial document services.[1]

Where the product design was believed by plaintiff's counsel to have been defective and had proximately caused the harm, then the counsel may have a basis for retaining experts in medical device review, some of them alumni of the FDA reviewing groups. These specialists in postaccident analysis are accustomed to digging into the appropriate federal regulatory agency files, reviewing the defendant company's complaint files, examining the state survey reports for nursing home injuries of the largest states that oversee nursing home injuries, and reading the applicable technical standards of the relevant trade association or other standards writing bodies.

Such expertise is not cheap; many of the design defect claims carry a very high cost in technical expertise from consultants who have this subspecialty. Some experts may simply decline to serve the occasional plaintiff's request. To do so might alienate future clients in the manufacturing community, a decision fraught with consequences.

Plaintiffs should consider:

1. To avoid long delays, review the commercial services such as foiservices.com for their library of already disclosed FDA reviews of medical devices.

1. To avoid long delays, review the commercial services such as foiservices.com for their library of already disclosed FDA reviews of the problems with particular medical devices.
2. Plaintiff may receive a far larger and steadier income payment stream from a settlement than from the fees to be paid by this one liability defendant. So it may take some research to find an available competent expert. Other defendants may be selected.

Prudent tort lawyers are already aware of the basic criteria for the design defect cases: proof of a "defect" in design and then proof that the defect made the unit that harmed this patient "unreasonably dangerous" even when the unit could have been used properly, in the intended manner, and with the same product form and contents (not modified by a local dealer, for example) as it was when the unit left the control of the manufacturer.[2] In most states, the risk/utility test is applied: did the risk of this feature or design element in this unit exceed the utility to the patient and user? If the risk exceeded the utility, then the state products liability law might deem the product to have been defective at the time of the injury. The jury could then determine whether the benefit of the product remained so high that it was not "unreasonably" dangerous to this plaintiff.

25:3 Medical Devices

What products can be challenged as a defective "medical device"? Assume that virtually everything in the nursing home patient's surroundings has some effect on the patient's stability or recovery or therapy. Then remove from the discussion common everyday items like pajamas, robes, chairs, and mattresses. And remove assistive devices that any person might need that do not impact on medical aspects of

---

2. *See generally* James O'Reilly, Product Warnings Defects & Hazards (2d ed.); Restatement of Torts § 402A (1965); Restatement of Products Liability 2(B) (1997).

the ordinary life of the patient. What remains will probably be regulated as "medical devices" by the FDA.[3]

Medical devices are a critically important area for plaintiff product liability lawyers to understand. A small portion of the tens of thousands of products in this medical device field undergo federal "premarket approval" as they are specifically tested, submitted, and approved for marketing by the FDA's Center for Devices and Radiological Health.[4] FDA oversight remains tight after the device's specific approval; these specifically approved medical device products have an extensive shield from products liability under the Supreme Court's *Lohr* and *Riegel decisions.*[5]

The logic of the Court's denial of state jury decisions about medical device safety was that the device, having undergone a specific demonstration of the proof of the device's safety, performed to the satisfaction of the federal agency scientists, is safe; and that it would conflict with federal norms, if a state trial jury were to find that the medical device was not safe, that is, it was "defective" in a products liability context.

A conflict might arise over whether the newly FDA-approved medical device product is properly considered "safe." The same set of technical and clinical studies is available to federal science and engineering reviewers, and to a lay person jury in a state court. The question is the classic tort issue of defect and risk. Either the state jury or the federal scientific expert agency would be correct about the safety of the product. Federal decisions under the Constitution[6] and federal laws should act as a protection of the device from a contrary state decision; so under principles of federal statutory preemption, the U.S. Supreme Court has virtually preempted all device design claims for the small category of "premarket approved" devices.[7]

But remember, 90 percent of medical devices did not go through this process, so do not drop the idea of a products liability count from

3. 21 U.S.C. § 321; *see* 1 James O'Reilly, Food & Drug Administration ch. 18 (4th ed. 2013).

4. 21 C.F.R. pts. 800–890.

5. Lohr v. Medtronic Inc., 518 U.S. 470 (1996); Riegel v. Medtronic, 552 U.S. 312 (2008).

6. U.S. Const. art. VI, cl. 2.

7. *Lohr*, 518 U.S. 470; *Riegel*, 552 U.S. 312.

your complaint; include it and let the defendant demonstrate that its formal FDA premarket approval applies.

Several scenarios arise. Was your client harmed by a medical device when the feeding tube to the stomach or the catheter or the breathing tube clogged? Was the electric shock that killed your decedent a predictable result of design problems with the model A-200 respirator? Look at the FDA's website for the index, enter the name of the device that had been in use at the time of the accident, and review what the FDA knows about the product type and about this specific brand of the device. Many thousands of reports are accessible.

If premarket approval for the specific device by the specific manufacturer had been given by the FDA, then this official device approval by the FDA may preempt a state design liability claim about that specific product feature. But one must look beyond the blueprint designs, examining the assembly and manufacture to determine what had gone wrong. Compare the plan to the product: Did the nursing home company have a risk manager or loss-prevention director or safety manager; did she or he study the actual device at the time of the accident; did their report blame the accident on device failure, or on personnel failure within the nursing home?

If it were a case of device failure, was the failure one of the manufacturer not properly assembling the device to be safe and secure for elders' use, or of the way the device was handled by a dealer, hooked up, linked in, or adjusted on site? If a government report of medical device adverse effects was filed (FDA Form FD-3500A, available online through fda.gov), the filing may require the reporting company to state whether it was the medical product that failed or the user error in utilizing the product that caused the harm. It may be intriguing to study how the regulatory context of companies' admissions to the FDA about causes may carry consequences in later litigation.

25:4 Residential Products

Falls among the elderly have the most risk of serious adverse effects. Residential rugs, flooring and related products that are safe for many types of use might pose special problems for the elderly. Consumer Product Safety Commission data about risks from residential products, found via cpsc.gov, may be useful.[8]

If the nursing home knows of vision, dark stairway, and agility problems affecting many of its residents, but makes no effort to protect them from dangerous floors or steps that cause slips and falls, plaintiff's counsel may be able to show that the danger had been unreasonable and avoidable in this particular setting. Outcomes of such cases are highly dependent upon state premises liability norms and state immunity laws for nonprofit entities. Jurors are quite likely to have had experience with elder family members' slips and falls. Could these harms have been avoided by the nursing home staff?[9]

25:5 Reporting Injuries to Government

The nursing home may choose to report to the FDA when a medical device, diagnostic or drug is causally related to a death or injury of a resident at the facility. Hospitals may be required to make these reports under a state statutory command. The FDA receives these adverse experience reports and it might follow up with an inspection to establish the basis of causation between the product and the injury. Plaintiffs should ask what the FDA found or why the FDA did not search for the cause to this reportable injury.

The Consumer Product Safety Commission (CPSC) hotline (saferproducts.gov) may be used by counsel for the injured resident to communicate about this product defect. The CPSC databases of complaints were expanded in the 2008 CPSC statutory amendments and are a valuable source of information for plaintiffs.[10]

---

8. Consumer Product Safety Comm'n, www.cpsc.gov.

9. Outcomes of such cases are highly dependent upon state premises liability norms and state immunity laws for nonprofit entities.

10. *See* James O'Reilly, Consumer Product Safety (PLI 2008).

CHAPTER 26

Causes of Action

26:1 Overview
26:2 Negligence
26:3 Use of Clinical Practice Guidelines or CMS Guidelines as Evidence of the Standard of Care
26:4 Negligence Per Se
26:5 Wrongful Death Statutes
26:6 Loss of Chance of Life
26:7 Statutory Causes of Action
26:8 Medical Malpractice
26:9 Intentional Torts
26:10 Wrongful Discharge of a Resident
26:11 Misrepresentation
26:12 False Claims Act
26:13 Infliction of Emotional Distress
26:14 Economic "Abuse" by Theft or Fraud
26:15 Breach of Contract
26:16 Class Actions

26:1 Overview

This chapter briefly recaps the principal causes of action that could be included in the complaint in a nursing home tort case. Separate chapters advise the reader concerning the drafting of the complaint and the selection of defendants and plaintiffs. In general, ample lobbying of nursing home owners in state capitals may have restricted the causes of action that are available under any particular state's laws. In addition, each state may have different capped damages in certain claims, so the reader must be attuned to the use and limitations of certain causes of action depending on the state in which the suit is brought.

26:2 Negligence

The classical elements of negligence play out in most of the nursing home liability cases:

- The nursing home had a duty of care to protect the resident from foreseeable harm, express duties from a care plan, state protective statutes, or common law;
- There was a breach of duty by negligent acts or omissions on the part of the nursing home;
- This breach was the cause-in-fact of the harm;
- The plaintiff and the risk of harm were both foreseeable; and
- The resident suffered legally cognizable damages.

The plaintiff has the burden to satisfy each of these prerequisites to recovery.[1] Typically the evidence will show that "but for" the acts or omissions by the nursing home,[2] the injury would not have occurred.[3] In the alternative, the plaintiff must prove that the defendant's negligent act was a substantial factor in bringing about the injury.[4] The connection of the event to the injury must meet state common law norms of both cause-in-fact and proximate cause.[5] Foreseeability issues often arise in the defendant's response.[6] The astute plaintiff's counsel

1. Estate of Hazleton v. Cain, 950 So. 2d 231 (Miss. Ct. App. 2007).
2. *See, e.g.*, Mast v. Magpusao, 225 Cal. Rptr. 689 (Cal. Ct. App. 1986).
3. Francis v. Lafon Nursing Home, 840 So. 2d 1281 (La. Ct. App. 2003).
4. Palermo v. Port of New Orleans, 951 So. 2d 425 (La. Ct. App. 2007); Busta v. Columbus Hosp. Corp. 916 P.2d 122 (Mont. 1996); RESTATEMENT (THIRD) OF TORTS: LIABILITY FOR PHYSICAL HARM § 27 (2009).
5. Kildron v. Shady Oaks Nursing Home, 549 So. 2d 395 (La. Ct. App. 1989).
6. K.L. v. Riverside Med. Ctr., 524 N.W.2d 300 (Minn. Ct. App. 1994); Shepard v. Mielke, P.2d 220 (Wash. Ct. App. 1994).

will be careful to coordinate the negligence claims with the state statutory remedies.[7]

The nature of the negligence claimed may make a cost difference to the presentation of the case. Expert witnesses are virtually always needed in professional negligence cases but are not necessary in many claims of ordinary negligence, for example, in care during activities of daily life.[8] Nursing homes take care of all activities of daily life, such as toileting and eating; ordinary human understanding of these daily activities means that no special expert knowledge will be needed for the jury to make its decision. In determining a cause of death, however, the courts still demand an expert opinion.[9]

26:3 Use of Clinical Practice Guidelines or CMS Guidelines as Evidence of the Standard of Care

In order to meet the standard of care in a medical malpractice case, a health care provider must "possess and use the care, skill and knowledge ordinarily possessed and used under like circumstances."[10] The scope of admissible evidence that may be used to define reasonable care in the majority of states is based on the "customary care rule."[11]

As a general matter, "customary care" is the type of care that is typically given by other health care providers under comparable circumstances. Customary care is subjective and is based on the predilections

---

7. Jeffrey Spitzer Resnick & Maya Krajcinovic, *Protecting the Rights of Nursing Home Residents: How Tort Liability Interacts with Statutory Protections*, 19 NOVA L. REV. 629 (1995).

8. Note the distinction drawn in case law, e.g., Mast v. Magpusao, 225 Cal. Rptr. 689 (Cal. Ct. App. 1986) (no expert needed where laymen's common knowledge will show injury would not occur but for negligent defendant); *accord*, Juhnke v. Evangelical Lutheran Good Samaritan Soc'y, 634 P.2d 1132 (Kan. Ct. App. 1981).

9. Barton v. United States, 2008 WL 872304 (S.D. Miss. March 27, 2008).

10. Burns v. Metz, 513 N.W.2d 505, 509 (Neb. 1994); Vergara v. Doan, 593 N.E.2d 185, 188 (Ind. 1992) (judging the physician's conduct by a "minimum standard of care for the particular practice"). For an excellent overview of medical malpractice law, see DAN B. DOBBS, THE LAW OF TORTS § 242, 631–34 (2000).

11. *See generally* Philip G. Peters Jr., *The Role of the Jury in Modern Malpractice Law*, 87 IOWA L. REV. 909 (2002) (discussing the merits of the role of custom as conclusive evidence of the standard of care in malpractice litigation and the movement by many states to use custom as only some evidence of the standard of care); Philip G. Peters, Jr., *The Quiet Demise of Deference to Custom: Malpractice Law at the Millennium*, 57 WASH. & LEE L. REV. 163, 170 (2000).

of particular physicians based upon tradition, opinion, or clinical experience and not on objective, scientific evidence.[12] The practice of providing customary care, also referred to by many as "eminence-based medicine," is the normative practice in the United States.[13]

The evidence-based model of medical practice is centered on empirical data created by comparative effectiveness research and outcomes analysis. In other words, custom is what practitioners *do*; empirical evidence is evidence of what a practitioner *ought to be doing*.

The good news for nursing home residents is that many state tort systems are slowly moving away from the current majority rule, which uses customary practice as conclusive evidence of the standard of care,[14] as judges and lawyers begin to recognize the problems with using custom (as discussed above) as the exclusive proxy for quality.[15] Instead of limiting the scope of admissible evidence in defining reasonable care to what is customarily done under the circumstances, some state tort systems are also allowing the introduction of risk-benefit analysis grounded in empirical science (in the form of scientific studies as well as clinical practice guidelines in malpractice cases) as evidence of what should be reasonable quality care under the circumstances. This transition away from the tort system's use of custom as the exclusive proxy for quality appears to benefit both the quality and cost of health care. Thus, the tort systems of some states are operating instrumentally to encourage the transition away from custom-based medical practice to evidence-based medical practice.

---

12. *See* IOWA CONSORTIUM FOR SUBSTANCE ABUSE RESEARCH & EVALUATION, EVIDENCE-BASED PRACTICES: AN IMPLEMENTATION GUIDE FOR COMMUNITY-BASED SUBSTANCE ABUSE TREATMENT AGENCIES 3 (2003), http://www.uiowa.edu/~iowapic/files/EBP%20Guide%20-%20Revised%205-03.pdf (The Iowa Consortium for Substance Abuse Research and Evaluation is based at the University of Iowa).

13. Katharine Van Tassel, *Using Clinical Practice Guidelines and Knowledge Translation Theory to Cure the Negative Impact of the National Hospital Peer Review Hearing System on Healthcare Quality, Cost, and Access*, 40 PEPPERDINE L. REV. 911, 937–38 (2013).

14. *See* Philip G. Peters, Jr., *The Quiet Demise of Deference to Custom: Malpractice Law at the Millennium*, 57 WASH. & LEE L. REV. 163, 170 (2000) (explaining that many states are moving away from custom as the exclusive proxy for quality).

15. Philip G. Peters, Jr., *The Role of the Jury in Modern Malpractice Law*, 87 IOWA L. REV. 909 (2002) (discussing the merits of the role of custom as conclusive evidence of the standard of care in malpractice litigation and the movement by many states to use custom as only some evidence of the standard of care).

So what does this mean to litigating a nursing home case? One way to explain the answer to their question is to show how this plays out using an example of a common subject of litigation, the development of an avoidable pressure ulcer. As the reader will quickly see, the transition in this country from customary care to evidence-based care can mean a great deal to both plaintiffs and defendants.

CMS regulations require that "[t]he services provided or arranged by the facility must . . . meet professional standards of care. . . ."[16] According to the interpretive guidelines, "'[p]rofessional standards of quality' means services that are provided according to accepted standards of clinical practice."[17] What will be considered to be "accepted standards of clinical practice"? The interpretive guidelines specifically allow for the use of standards published by a short list sources, including professional organizations, licensing boards, clinical literature, current professional journals, or the clinical practice guidelines published by the Agency of Health Care Policy and Research.[18] Importantly, the use of "customary care" is not on this short list of accepted standards of clinical practice.

What does this conflict between the state customary care standards and the CMS requirements mean to our example?

According to federal law, nursing homes must ensure that new residents who enter without pressure sores do not develop them "unless the individual's clinical condition demonstrates that they were unavoidable."[19] In addition, the home must ensure that a resident who has a pressure sore "receives necessary treatment and services to promote healing, prevent infection and prevent new sores from developing."[20]

In some ways, whether a nursing home will be found liable for the development of a pressure ulcer is straightforward. Empirical evidence has demonstrated that ulcers fall into two categories: avoidable and

16. 42 C.F.R. § 483.20(k)(3) (as revised on July 1, 2011) (relating to Tag F281).
17. 42 C.F.R. § 483.20(k)(3)(i) (as revised on July 1, 2011).
18. *Id.*
19. 42 C.F.R. § 483.25(c).
20. 42 C.F.R. § 483.25(c).

unavoidable. Nursing homes will be held responsible by CMS, the tort system or state abuse and neglect statutes only when an *avoidable* pressure ulcer develops. It will not be found responsible when an *unavoidable* pressure ulcer develops. Key to this dichotomy is that a pressure ulcer will be deemed unavoidable when the nursing home has instituted appropriate measures to prevent the wound and the pressure ulcer develops in spite of these efforts, or, if a wound develops, whether the home instituted appropriate measures to treat the wound and it either fails to heal or grows worse.

What are the appropriate measures? CMS has identified several organizations that have created CPGs that CMS finds acceptable.[21] A nursing home will do well to adopt the CPGs of one of these specifically listed groups, as well as paying special attention to the section of CMS's State Operations Manual, Appendix PP, Guidance to Surveyors that deals specifically with pressure ulcers.[22] The home should then carefully document compliance with these adopted CPGs and the requirements listed in the State Operations Manual.

21. According to 42 C.F.R. § 483.25(c):

> There are many recognized clinical resources regarding the prevention and management of pressure ulcers (including wound care, and complications such as infections and pain). Some of these resources include: [1] The Clinical Practice Guidelines from the Agency for Healthcare Research and Quality (AHRQ) www.ahrq.gov (Guideline No. 15: Treatment of Pressure Ulcers and Guideline No. 3: Pressure Ulcers in Adults: Prediction and Prevention) (AHRQ was previously known as the Agency for Health Care Policy and Research [AHCPR]); [2] The National Pressure Ulcer Advisory Panel (NPUAP) www.npuap.org; [3] The American Medical Directors Association (AMDA) www.amda.com (Clinical Practice Guidelines: Pressure Ulcers, 1996 and Pressure Ulcer Therapy Companion, 1999); [4] The Quality Improvement Organizations, Medicare Quality Improvement Community Initiatives site at www.medqic.org; [5] The Wound, Ostomy, and Continence Nurses Society (WOCN) www.wocn.org; and; [6] The American Geriatrics Society guideline "The Management of Persistent Pain in Older Persons," www.healthinaging.org.

42 C.F.R. § 483.25(c)(2006); *see* CTRS. FOR MEDICARE & MEDICAID SERVS., STATE OPERATIONS MANUAL, CMS PUB. NO. 100-07, APPENDIX PP: GUIDANCE TO SURVEYORS FOR LONG TERM CARE FACILITIES 111–32 (2011) ("Overview").

22. CTRS. FOR MEDICARE & MEDICAID SERVS., STATE OPERATIONS MANUAL, CMS PUB. NO. 100-07, APPENDIX PP: GUIDANCE TO SURVEYORS FOR LONG TERM CARE FACILITIES 211 (2023).

For example, the CPGs of all of these groups, as well as the CMS regulations,[23] point out that the reduction of the risk of pressure ulcers entails an individualized, multifactorial, multidisciplinary intervention contributed to by a team consisting of medical, nursing, nutrition, physical therapists, aides and other disciplines.[24] The risk factors for each elder resident should be considered as the group identifies the types of interventions that are most likely to be effective.[25] These interventions must be continuously evaluated for effectiveness and modified as needed.[26] The risk evaluation, the chosen interventions, and the application of the interventions should all be well documented. The home should then provide continuous training on the chosen CPGs and their updates.[27] Through this avenue, the nursing home will be applying "best practices."

This use of "best practices" puts the nursing home in a good position to defend a pressure ulcer case. For the purposes of defending a case for malpractice in a state that follows the customary care rule, the first way that the CPGs can be used is for the nursing home to argue that the custom in the community, a same or similar community or the nation, depending on which version of the customary care rule the state applies,[28] is for nursing homes to comply with the standard of care as prescribed by CMS.[29] The nursing home can then introduce its carefully kept records that reflect the CMS recognized CPGs and

23. *Id.*
24. *Id.*
25. *Id.*
26. *Id.*
27. *Id.*

28. The majority rule is that conclusive evidence of this failure occurs when the physician does not take the same actions customarily taken by other physicians in similar circumstances. The medical malpractice law of the different states varies with regard to the locality from which they draw their customary practices. States have chosen to apply the customs followed by the practitioners in the local community under the "same locality rule, or another community under the "similar community rule, or customary care on a national level under the "national rule." *See generally* Katharine Van Tassel, *Hospital Peer Review Standards and Due Process: Moving from Tort Theories to Contract Principles Based on Clinical Practice Guidelines*, 36 Seton Hall L. Rev. 1179–1256 (2006).

29. Brogdon *ex rel.* Cline v. Nat'l Healthcare Corp., 103 F. Supp. 2d 1322 (N.D. Ga. 2000); McCain v. Beverly Health & Rehab. Servs., 202 WL 1565526 (E.D. Pa. 2002); Hayward v. Jack's Pharmacy, Inc., 115 P.3d 713 (Idaho 2005); Morisette v. Terence Cardinal Cooke Health Care Ctr., 797 N.Y.S.2d 856 (Sup. 2005).

that these CPGs were followed.[30] It will be interesting to follow any possible arguments that the customary care standard has been preempted by the federal standard that requires evidence-based care.[31] In many cases, it will not be possible for the practitioner to comply with both the customary care rule and the evidence-based care rule as what is required by these rules can directly conflict.

The good news for the plaintiff's lawyer is that these clear protocols make the gaps in the provision of care easy to spot. If these gaps in care resulted in harm to the resident, liability will likely follow. In addition to improving the quality of care, this use of evidence-based health care and CPGs benefits the system as a whole as substandard care is more easily identifiable, leading to more rapid settlements and decreasing the cost of litigation. Refocusing the legal system to encourage evidence-based practice rather than custom-based practice will likely provide greater clarity to nursing homes on how to invest in quality of care improvements.

26:4 Negligence Per Se

In the spring of 2013, the Office of the Inspector General (OIG) released a study called *Skilled Nursing Facilities Often Fail to Meet Care Planning and Discharge Planning Requirements.*[32] This report revealed that 37 percent of skilled nursing facilities failed to prepare care plans that met requirements or did not provide care in accord with those care plans that were prepared. This study implicates one-third of skilled nursing homes and suggests that a negligence per se claim should be high on the plaintiff's list of possible causes of action. In order to place the

30. Frakes v. Cardiology Consultants, P.C., 1997 WL 536949 (Tenn. Ct. App. August 29, 1997); Levine v. Rosen, 616 A.2d 623 (Pa. 1992); Washington v. Wash. Hosp. Ctr., 627 A.2d 177 (D.C. 1990).

31. *See generally* JAMES T. O'REILLY, FEDERAL PREEMPTION OF STATE AND LOCAL LAW: LEGISLATION, REGULATION, AND LITIGATION (2006).

32. U.S. Dep't of HHS, Office of the Inspector General, Skilled Nursing Facilities Often Fail to Meet Care Planning and Discharge Planning Requirements, 2013, http://oig.hhs.gov/oei/reports/oei-02-09-00201.asp.

role of negligence per se in proper perspective for the lawyer new to litigating a nursing home case, a very pithy review of the mechanics of a cause of action for negligence is in order. A cause of action for negligence involves an allegation that a duty of care to avoid inflicting harm on the plaintiff has been violated by the defendant and that the plaintiff has been harmed by that violation. The duty of care that the defendant owes the plaintiff is always the same—reasonable care under the circumstances. The question that is generally for the jury to determine is *what amount of care* meets that duty of reasonable care. To make this determination, the jury is asked to resolve two questions: first, what risks would a reasonable person identify under the circumstances and, second, what steps would a reasonable person take to avoid those risks. If the person has failed to take those steps that a reasonable person would have taken, that person will have committed a negligent act. Of course, to make out the cause of action for negligence, the plaintiff must also prove that the negligent act is both the cause-in-fact and the proximate cause of legally cognizable damages.

The idea behind negligence per se is that the legislature has already done a fact-finding investigation (far broader and more extensive than that which could be undertaken in a single trial with very limited resources) into a particular risk of harm that is inherent in a particular circumstance, has found that the risk and degree of that particular harm is high, and has made a determination of what steps a reasonable person should take to avoid that particular harm. The legislature has then, through the democratic process, passed a statute or regulation that mandates that these steps be taken under certain described circumstances to avoid harm. The failure of an individual to take those steps under the described circumstances means that that person has violated that statute or regulation. By recognizing a cause of action for negligence per se, a court is giving deference to the legislative finding of what steps a reasonable person should take to avoid a particular risk inherent in certain situations, basically supplanting the role of the jury on this issue. If the statute applies (see the two steps below), then the only remaining question that a jury must answer before finding that the defendant has committed a negligent act is whether the defendant's conduct violated the statute. Thus, a violation of a federal regulation can be negligence per se.[33]

In order to qualify to bring a cause of action for negligence per se, the plaintiff must prove the facts in support of two elements: first, the plaintiff must be within the class of individuals the statute is designed to protect and, second, the risk of harm must be within the class of risks of harm that the statute is designed to protect against. The case of the injured nursing home resident fits squarely within this doctrine, as the CMS regulations located in 42 C.F.R. Part 483, Subpart B are designed to protect this particular class of people, residents in nursing homes, against a long laundry list of risks of harm, one of which the plaintiff claims came to fruition.[34] More particularly, the residents of nursing homes are exactly the persons the CMS regulation § 483.25(b), regarding pressure ulcers, is designed to protect and the risk of developing a pressure ulcer is exactly the kind of risk the statute is designed to protect against.[35] For a lawyer new to litigating the nursing home case, the brief discussion of the survey system, nomenclature, and use of Tags contained in Chapter 8 and the description of the resident assessment instrument contained in Chapter 9 may be of help.

Understanding what is actually happening in a negligence per se case explains why a handful of courts are misguided in finding negligence per se inapplicable in a nursing home case based on the reasoning that the CMS regulations do not create a private cause of action.[36] It is worth noting that while some courts may be reluctant to recognize federal or state statutory schemes as sufficient grounds to establish a negligence per se theory, most courts will recognize violation of these statutes as admissible evidence of negligence.[37]

---

33. Lowe v. Gen. Motors Corp., 624 F.2d 1373 (5th Cir. 1980).

34. Negligence Per Se—Federal Regulations, 755 AM. JUR. § 755 (2013); McClain v. Mariner Health, Inc., 279 Ga. App.410 631 S.E. 2d 435 (Ga. Ct. App. 2006); *cf.* Satterwhite v. Reilly, 817 So. 2d 407 (La. Ct. App. 2d Cir. 2002), *writ denied*, 825 So. 2d 1193 (La. 2002).

35. *See* CTRS. FOR MEDICARE & MEDICAID SERVS., STATE OPERATIONS MANUAL, CMS PUB. NO. 100-07, APPENDIX PP: GUIDANCE TO SURVEYORS FOR LONG TERM CARE FACILITIES 111–32 (2011).

36. *See, e.g.*, *Satterwhite*, 817 So. 2d 407.

37. Fal-Meridian, Inc. v. U.S. Dep't of HHS, 604 F.3d 445 (7th Cir. 2010).

Violations of norms may arguably be negligence per se, but in order to move from negligence to a verdict, there must also be a further showing that the negligent act that violated the rule was the cause-in-fact of the injury.[38] And negligence per se claims that are solely based on CMS rules must be very carefully drafted in order to avoid the state malpractice defense requirements.[39]

26:5 Wrongful Death Statutes

Many states have adopted legislation that creates a limited right of recovery for designated family members after the death of a relative, where the death was wrongly caused by the acts of the defendant. There are important variations in the terms of state wrongful death laws. But the typical statute is necessary in a nursing home death case as, under common law, a cause of action personal to an individual, does not survive the death of that individual.[40] The state law lists the persons who can act as the representative of the decedent, for example, Florida's limitation to surviving spouses and to the decedent's children under age 25.[41] A cap on damage awards may apply;[42] some states bar punitive damages in wrongful death actions.[43] The statute of limitations for these actions also varies from state to state.[44] A wrongful death action can be a powerful additional cause of action alongside the negligence and state statutory causes of action. Alternatively, the executor of the estate of a deceased resident may bring a survival action against the facility as if the decedent were himself bringing the action and benefiting from its disposition, with the proceeds of the action being attributed to the estate and so preserving claims to punitive damage awards.[45]

---

38. Long v. Brookside Manor, 885 S.W.2d 70 (1994).
39. Conley v. Life Care Ctrs., 236 S.W.2d 713 (Tenn. Ct. App. 2007).
40. *See, e.g.*, Denton v. Super. Ct., 945 P.2d 1283 (Ariz. 1997).
41. Fla. Stat. § 768.16-26 (1972).
42. Kan. Stat. Ann. § 60-1903 (1998).
43. Cal. Civ. Code § 3294 (1992), *In re* Paris Air Crash, 622 F.2d 1325 (9th Cir. 1980).
44. Crockett v. Medicalodges Inc., 799 P.2d 1022 (Kan. 1990).
45. Stuart M. Speiser et al., Recovery for Wrongful Death § 8:11 (4th ed. 2005).

26:6 Loss of Chance of Life

Unless survival was more likely than not, the traditional rule did not allow the plaintiff any recovery. This meant that an individual who causes the death of a plaintiff through a negligent act will not be found liable when the plaintiff had a less than 51 percent chance of survival before the negligent act. On the other hand, a plaintiff who proves that he or she had a greater than 51 percent chance of survival will recover for the negligent act that causes death. In May of 2013, the Supreme Court of Minnesota, in *Dickhoff v. Green*, followed a short line of cases recognizing as actionable a resident's increased risk of dying resulting from her doctor's negligent failure to secure timely diagnosis and treatment of cancer.[46] In *Dickhoff*, a physician failed to diagnose a lump on a baby as cancer for over a year. The baby was then diagnosed by another physician with a rare and aggressive cancer. The baby subsequently underwent a tumor-removal surgery, chemotherapy, and radiotherapy, but remained dangerously ill. A timely referral would have given the baby, at a minimum, a 60 percent chance of survival. The delay in diagnosis decreased this chance to 40 percent. Thus, the plaintiff made out a prima facie case for a 20 percent reduction in her chances to stay alive.

Following other state courts,[47] the Minnesota Supreme Court ruled that this reduction constitutes actionable damage in and of itself and held that a resident can successfully sue her doctor for an increased risk of the underlying illness's recurrence and a decreased life expectancy as stand-alone damage. The only limitation that the court placed on this cause of action is that the plaintiff's increased risk and decreased life expectancy must be substantial.

---

46. Dickhoff v. Green, __N.W.2d__, 2013 WL 2363550 (Minn. September 9, 2013).

47. Hesrkovitz v. Group Health Coop. of Puget Sound, 664 P.2d 474 (Wash. 1983); DeBurkarte v. Louvare, 393 N.W.2d 131 (Iowa 1986); Roberts v. Ohio Permanente Med. Grp., Inc., 668 N.E.2d 480 (Ohio 1996); Jorgenson v. Vener, 616 N.W.2d 366 (S.D. 2000).

26:7 Statutory Causes of Action

Scandals concerning nursing home abuse have provoked some states to adopt specific legislation that creates private causes of action against the nursing home operators.[48] A complaint may assert that the rights protected by this statute had been violated in the nursing home's treatment of the resident. The remedial purpose of the statutes is important; nursing home lobbyists seek to prevent their adoption in other states, or to slant them in favor of the home's management.[49] Some of these laws allow punitive damages with a lower-than-normal threshold of proof than classic punitive damages allowed in common law negligence.[50] These statutes are usually employed parallel with, and do not displace, the common law negligence actions.[51] The presence of a wrongful death action does not preclude a private statutory remedy.[52] One of their attractive features could be an award of attorney's fees along with the statutory remedy.[53]

The statutory cause of action usually has terms of coverage that require careful examination; not all of the fact situations in the nursing home injury case will fit within the statutory terms. For example, failure of a nursing home to protect against the sexual assault of a resident falls outside the Connecticut statute's term "care and services" for the resident.[54] Florida adopted a law that was very protective of residents,[55] but later modified the law to reduce advantages that plaintiffs had enjoyed.

---

48. *See, e.g.*, Stiffelman v. Abrams, 655 S.W.2d 522 (Mo. 1983); George Ingalls et al., *Elder Abuse Originating in the Institutional Setting*, 74 N.D. L. Rev. 313 (1998).

49. Carol Nixon, *Health Law: The Arkansas Resident's Rights Statute*, 29 U. Ark. Little Rock L. Rev. 597 (2007).

50. Sprosty v. Pearlview Inc., 1666 N.E.2d 1180 (Ohio Ct. App. 1995) (overruled by statute).

51. Jeffrey Spitzer Resnick & Maya Krajcinovic, *Protecting the Rights of Nursing Home Residents: How Tort Liability Interacts with Statutory Protections*, 19 Nova L. Rev. 629 (1995).

52. Stiffelman v. Abrams, 655 S.W.2d 522 (Mo. 1983).

53. Morgan v. Galilean Health Enters., 977 P.2d 357 (Okla. 1998).

54. Doe v. Advisors Healthcare Inc., No. X01CV020170300S, 2005 Conn. Super. LEXIS 1036 (Conn. Super. Mar. 24, 2005).

55. Fla. Stat. § 400.22; Jennifer Williamson, *The Siren Song of the Elderly*, 25 Am. J. Law & Med. 423 (1999).

The defense may assert that the claim against the nursing home under a statutory cause of action must first be exhausted by complaining to state officials, but tort cases need not follow the rule of administrative exhaustion.[56]

26:8 Medical Malpractice

The medical malpractice count in the complaint, if there is one, should include a showing of the reasonable standard of care, as required under that state's particular law; then the deviation from the standard; and then that the negligent act was the cause-in-fact and proximate cause of the injury[57] Proximate cause has many layers, including establishing that the plaintiff was a foreseeable plaintiff, that the risk of injury was a foreseeable risk, (in some states, that the manner in which the risk came to fruition was foreseeable), and that any intervening causes were foreseeable and not superseding.[58] Significantly, more than half of the nursing home cases involve death, while less than one-fifth of malpractice cases involve death.[59]

Inconsistencies among the states' many different medical malpractice statutes make it impossible to generalize about the coverage of traditional nursing home "premises liability" and state "medical malpractice." Some states do not recognize a nursing home malpractice claim, apart from negligence, but would allow such a claim against a hospital.[60] Where a plausible claim can be made regarding deficient health service, as opposed to cases of assault, the defense will assert the partial shield that the medical malpractice legislation affords.[61] Where the nursing home staff has engaged in reckless neglect, the medical malpractice laws of the state may not be applicable. The lines are

---

56. Salas v. Grancare, 22 P.3d 568 (Colo. Ct. App. 2001).

57. McDaniel v. Ong, 724 N.E.2d 38 (Ill. App. Ct. 1999).

58. Dann B. Dobbs et al., Torts and Compensation 218–49 (2009); *see also* Marshall S. Shapo, Principles of Tort Law (2005).

59. David Studdert & David Stevenson, *Nursing Home Litigation and Tort Reform: A Case for Exceptionalism*, 44 Gerontologist 588 (2004).

60. Morris v. Monterey Yorkshire Nursing Inn Inc., 278 N.E.2d 686 (Ohio Ct. App. 1981).

61. Conley v. Life Care Ctrs. of Am., 236 S.W.3d 713 (Tenn. Ct. App. 2007).

drawn between pro-defense and pro-plaintiff jurists in some states; for example, the defense strongly urged the Texas courts to push nursing home liability cases into the narrower channel of medical malpractice statutory liability and the Texas Supreme Court agreed, in a split decision in the *Diversicare* case in 2005.[62]

Does the nursing home staff commit malpractice when it does what the prescribing physician orders? No, according to one court; it has a duty to communicate with the prescriber, but it is not accountable for the errors or omissions by that physician, so long as it took reasonable care to insure the safety of its residents.[63]

Allegations against a nursing home for failure to provide adequate medication and medical care fit within the ambit of medical malpractice actions under some states' relevant medical malpractice statutes.[64]

A typical state nursing home bill of rights may encompass nearly two dozen rights afforded residents in all nursing homes, but state malpractice law relates only to "malpractice" claims against qualified nursing homes. There are many claims that a person can assert under the bill of rights that would not fall within the definition of medical malpractice and would, therefore, not be subject to review before a medical review panel; but state law directs that any claim of medical malpractice against a qualified health care provider is encompassed within the ambit of the medical malpractice law, and so it must be reviewed by a medical review panel prior to suit.[65]

Medical malpractice claims are subject to the general rules of proof applicable to any negligence action: the plaintiff must prove the standard of care, a breach of that standard, causation, and damages. Whether alleged malpractice constitutes negligence is a question for the jury.[66]

62. Diversicare v. Rubio, 185 S.W.3d 842 (Tex. 2005) (note the strong dissents).

63. Stogsdill v. Manor Convalescent Home Inc., 343 N.E.2d 589 (Ill. App. Ct. 1976).

64. Jaquith Nursing Home v. Yarbrough, 99 So. 3d 745 (La. 2013) (citing Mineo v. Underwriters at Lloyds, London, 2007-0514, p.6 (La. App. 4 Cir. Oct. 22, 2008), 997 So.2d 187, 192).

65. Hendrix v. Maison Orleans I, L.L.C., 101 So. 3d 1013 (La. App. 4 Cir. 2012).

66. Jaquith Nursing Home v. Yarbrough, 99 So. 3d 745 (La. 2013).

A nursing home that is a "qualified healthcare provider" can be sued for medical malpractice if it meets state court tests to determine whether alleged acts are governed by the state medical malpractice statute:

> [1] Whether the particular wrong is 'treatment related' or caused by a dereliction of professional skill;
>
> [2] Whether the wrong requires expert medical evidence to determine whether the appropriate standard of care was breached;
>
> [3] Whether the act or omission involved assessment of the patient's condition;
>
> [4] Whether the incident occurred in the context of a physician-patient relationship, or was within the scope of activities which a hospital is licensed to perform;
>
> [5] Whether the injury would have occurred had the patient not sought treatment; and
>
> [6] Whether the tort was intentional.[67]

Claims involving the handling of a patient, including loading and unloading, are covered by the state laws dealing with medical malpractice, and must be submitted to a medical review panel.

Hurricane Katrina devastated portions of New Orleans and caused deaths at a nursing home. The failure to safely evacuate patients was not subject to state "medical malpractice" limitations of liability because (1) any failure to evacuate the nursing home facility prior to the hurricane was not related to medical treatment; (2) a determination of whether the nursing home failed to evacuate or have an adequate evacuation plan did not require expert medical evidence; (3) the decision not to evacuate residents did not involve assessment of residents'

67. *Hendrix*, 101 So. 3d 1013.

condition; and (4) the decision not to evacuate residents did not occur in the context of a physician-patient relationship.[68]

A claim regarding the failure of a hospice to notify the family of a significant change in the patient's condition is not medical malpractice; this alleged negligent inaction on the part of the nursing home was not related to the patient's medical treatment.[69]

Nursing home liability claims are likely to fall within state tort law constraints on medical malpractice lawsuits. Issues of patient hydration and informed consent in the hospice category are related to medical treatment, and state malpractice law requires that the negligent act must be related to medical treatment. Some courts have followed a six-part test to determine whether a negligent act by a health care provider is covered under the state medical malpractice law:

1. Whether the particular wrong is "treatment related" or caused by a dereliction of professional skill;
2. Whether the wrong requires expert medical evidence to determine whether the appropriate standard of care was breached;
3. Whether the pertinent act or omission involved assessment of the patient's condition;
4. Whether an incident occurred in the context of a physician-patient relationship, or was within the scope of activities that a hospital is licensed to perform;
5. Whether the injury would have occurred if the patient had not sought treatment; and
6. Whether the tort alleged was intentional.[70]

26:9 Intentional Torts

Unlike the great majority of tort cases against negligent nursing homes, the intentional harm of a resident by an employee is an intentional tort and can include, for example, assault, battery, false imprisonment,

68. Montalbano v. Buffman, Inc., 90 So. 3d 503 (La. App. 4 Cir. 2012).
69. *Hendrix*, 101 So. 3d 1013.
70. *Jaquith*, 99 So. 3d 745.

intentional infliction of emotional distress, conversion of property, and trespass to chattels. Chapter 12 addresses the cause of action based upon intentional harm. The intentional harm will be denounced by defense counsel as having been wholly unauthorized, and liability will surely be disclaimed, but the nursing home may still be held liable under several theories: failure to protect the vulnerable resident; negligence in hiring, training and supervision; or a management ratification of the assault that is implicit (failure to discipline) or explicit (e.g., the Connecticut female nurse supervisor who told aides when they reported a male resident's imminent sexual assault upon a female resident, "Let him finish," and had her license revoked as a result[71]). Claims for false imprisonment should be considered when harm results from the improper use of physical or chemical restraints. It also should be pled when a resident is confined by virtue of threats that the resident was afraid to ignore.[72] In situations where a resident's personal property has been harmed, destroyed, or taken, a claim can be filed for either trespass to chattels[73] or conversion.[74]

71. Yaw v. Dep't of Health Servs., No. 703447, 1993 Conn. Super. LEXIS 1263 (Conn. Super. Ct. May 12, 1993).

72. There is liability for false imprisonment when a person confines another intentionally, without lawful privilege, and against the confined person's consent, within a limited space for any appreciable period of time, however short. The confined plaintiff must be aware of the confinement at the time, unless there are actual damages. The confined person may be restrained by acts or by words which he fears to disregard. RESTATEMENT (SECOND) OF TORTS §§ 35, 36.

73. "Ways of Committing Trespass to Chattel: (1). A trespass to chattel may be committed by intentionally: (a). dispossessing another of the chattel; or (b). using or intermeddling with the possession of the chattel in the possession of another. (2). One is liable for Trespass to Chattels if: (a). he dispossesses the other of the chattel; or, (b). the chattel is impaired as to its condition, quality or value; or, (c). the possessor is deprived of the use of the chattel for a substantial period of time." RESTATEMENT (SECOND) OF TORTS §§ 217, 218.

74. "What Constitutes Conversion: (1) Conversion is an intentional exercise of dominion or control over a chattel which so seriously interferes with the right of another to control it that the actor may justly be required to pay the other the full value of the chattel. (2) In determining the seriousness of the interference and the justice of requiring the actor to pay the full value, the following factors are important: (a) the extent and duration of the actor's exercise of dominion or control; (b) the actor's intent to assert a right in fact inconsistent with the other's right of control; (c) the actor's good faith; (d) the extent and duration of the resulting interference with the other's right of control; (e) the harm done to the chattel; (f) the inconvenience and expense caused to the other." RESTATEMENT (SECOND) OF TORTS § 222A.

26:10 Wrongful Discharge of a Resident

This cause of action relates to violation of rights recognized under CMS regulations that protect the rights of federally funded residents. Chapter 16 covers these issues in detail. A private nursing home that receives no Medicaid or Medicare funding is able to discharge residents, subject to its contractual agreements with each resident and subject to state laws that may protect against some forms of discrimination or unfair treatment. There is no constitutional right to continued residence in a home of the person's choice.[75] If a nursing home drops out of the federal funding programs, it cannot evict the federally subsidized residents, because of the 1999 Nursing Home Resident Protection Amendments.[76] This limits options once the Medicaid resident is accepted. The effect of these economic constraints has worried the operators of nursing homes who seek to make Medicaid status a reason for discharge of the resident who lacks private funding.[77]

The nursing homes that receive CMS funding often are losing money on the actual cost of delivering services. So instead of becoming totally dependent on the often variable budget of the federal CMS, the prudent nursing home will "certify beds" of a certain number to be Medicaid beds, while other beds are designated as "private pay" spaces. If a resident spends all of his assets and has no further funds available, then the nursing home may decline to keep him unless it has a "certified" federally subsidized bed into which to transfer him.

Most threats of lawsuits to stop a resident's eviction are negotiated and do not ripen into litigation. These are not easy cases in which to win damages, and retention under court order would be uncomfortable at best. In recent years the nursing home chains and their smaller brethren have written tight conditions into their contracts of admission that make for a tough challenge to a plaintiff's counsel if the resident or the family wants to pursue legal action to enjoin a resident discharge.

---

75. O'Bannon v. Town Court Nursing Ctr., 447 U.S. 773 (1980).

76. 113 Stat. 7, 42 U.S.C. § 1305 (1999).

77. Cori Brown, *Nursing Homes: Status-Based Evictions and the Medicaid Crisis*, 12 ELDER L.J. 355 (2004).

If the elderly resident is being sent to a hospital, the hospitals that have received some federal funds (i.e., virtually all) must comply with the Emergency Medical Treatment and Active Labor Act (EMTALA).[78] The law requires hospitals to care for emergency residents. These rights are limited and would apply only to the emergency situation, not as a chronic-illness solution for a particular resident.[79] The EMTALA issues are complex and are beyond the scope of this text.[80]

Sometimes the entire nursing home is being terminated from federal programs. An administrative appeal process can lead to federal court review.[81] The due process rights of the nursing homes have been recognized by the courts,[82] and appeal processes have been built into the various systems.[83]

Senior housing that is not a nursing or health care facility is governed by antidiscrimination legislation protecting persons with a "disability," as is other federally assisted housing.[84] The assisted living facilities have great variability in the means of complaint resolution[85] and have some specific norms of regulation that distinguish them from conventional nursing homes.[86]

There may not be a valid claim if the would-be resident's medical records indicate that he or she needs a level of medical care that exceeds the capabilities of the defendant nursing home. State rules may bar an assisted living facility from admitting a person who needs a higher

---

78. Pub. L. No. 99-272, 100 Stat. 82, 42 U.S.C. § 1395dd (1994).

79. Burditt v. U.S. Dep't of HHS, 934 F.2d 1362 (5th Cir. 1991).

80. For background see, for example, George Smith, *Patient Dumping: Implications for the Elderly*, 6 Elder L.J. 165 (1998).

81. The administrative appeals end up in a Departmental Appeals Board decision at the U.S. Department of Health & Human Services, http://www.hhs.gov/dab.

82. Caton Ridge Nursing Home v. Califano, 596 F.2d 608 (3d Cir. 1978); Hathaway v. Mathews, 546 F.2d 227 (7th Cir. 1976).

83. *See, e.g.*, 42 C.F.R. § 402.5 (2008).

84. Robert Schwemm & Michael Allen, *For the Rest of Their Lives: Seniors and the Fair Housing Act*, 90 Iowa L. Rev. 121 (2004).

85. U.S. Gov't Accountability Office, GAO-04-684, Assisted Living: Examples of State Efforts to Improve Consumer Protections (Apr. 30, 2004), http://www.gao.gov/new.items/d04684.pdf.

86. Marie-Therese Connolly, *Federal Law Enforcement in Long-Term Care*, 4 J. Health Care L. & Pol'y 230 (2001); Christine Williams, *The Nursing Home Dilemma in America Today*, 41 Santa Clara L. Rev. 867 (2001).

level of medical care.[87] Litigation about nonadmission is not easy for plaintiffs; it may be best to continue seeking alternative placements rather than suing over the failure to accept the resident.

26:11 Misrepresentation

The resident or his or her representative generally signs an agreement on admission to the nursing home. Some states will allow a claim for breach of contract to proceed separately from statutory and negligence claims, while others do not allow separation.[88]

Misrepresentation is grounds for action where the injured person relied reasonably upon an express statement by the defendant, concerning an action that the defendant would take to benefit the person who enrolls as a resident, and the statement was false. This count responds to admissions brochures and booklets about the nursing home that portray a safe and secure facility:[89] assaults by other residents, visitors, or intruders breach this "representation" of safety.[90]

26:12 False Claims Act

Nursing home fraud on the Medicare/Medicaid system is said to be a significant fiscal concern for the Department of Health and Human Services' Office of the Inspector General (OIG). Nursing homes file detailed cost reports as part of their requests for federal reimbursement.[91] OIG monitors and enforces against reimbursement claims that are fraudulent or excessive. But the enforcers all recognize that public resources for investigation are limited, so there needs to be an inducement for private individuals to come forward and expose the misuse of federal funds or the nondelivery of services paid for by

87. *See, e.g.*, 210 Ill. Comp. Stat. 9/75.

88. Hodgdon v. Beatrice D. Weeks Mem'l Hosp., 445 A.2d 1116 (N.H. 1982); Crockett v. Medicalodges, 799 P.2d 1022 (Kan. 1990).

89. Brochures can be potent evidence. *See* Corley v. Rosewood Care Ctr., 142 F.3d 1041 (11th Cir. 1998).

90. See Chapter 12, *supra*, for more case law on assaults.

91. 42 C.F.R. §§ 413.20, 413.24 (2008).

federal funding. Nursing homes and hospitals have become prime targets of qui tam actions.[92]

The Federal False Claims Act (FCA) affords the government an opportunity to recoup its funds, and for the "relator" who informs the government of the fraud there is an opportunity to be awarded a "bounty" in the form of a percentage of the money recovered by the federal agency.[93] Inadequate care provided to residents for which the federal government was billed can be a basis for FCA recoveries.[94] Investigators have praised the FCA remedy as it augments the limited funds for governmental enforcement.[95] There are opportunities for FCA and criminal remedies to be used.[96] But some opponents have criticized FCA use as inappropriate for the nursing home setting.[97] The prudent litigator realizes that the complexities and delays that arise in FCA cases make them a mixed blessing. These are procedurally complex.[98] The best advice one can give is to locate an experienced FCA litigator with whom to associate in the evaluation of the potential FCA lawsuit. Mixing an FCA count into a conventional tort recovery should be undertaken only after careful consultation with a very experienced lawyer who can evaluate the case objectively and warn of its FCA shortcomings. For counsel in localities remote from a federal courthouse, or those uncomfortable with federal court processes, FCA may be inadvisable because this count increases the likelihood

---

92. John Parisi, *Fighting Fraud in Long-Term Care*, *in* NURSING HOME LITIGATION: PRETRIAL PRACTICE AND TRIALS 249, 265 (Ruben Krisztal ed., 2d ed. 2003).

93. 31 U.S.C. §§ 3729–3731.

94. Kathleen Peterson, *First Nursing Homes, Now Managed Care?*, 26 AM. J. L. & MED. 69 (2000).

95. *Listening Session: Abuse of Our Elders: How We Can Stop It, Hearing before the U.S. Senate Special Comm. on Aging*, 10th Cong. (July 18, 2007) (testimony of Gregory Demske, Assistant Inspector for Legal Affairs, Office of Inspector Gen., U.S. Dep't of Health and Human Servs.), http://www.aging.senate.gov/hearing_detail.cfm?id=279115& [hereinafter Demske testimony].

96. Michael Davidson, *Governmental Responses to Elder Abuse and Neglect in Nursing Homes*, 12 ELDER L.J. 327 (2004).

97. James Utterback, *Substituting an Iron Fist for the Invisible Hand: The False Claims Act and Nursing Home Quality of Care—A Legal and Economic Perspective*, 10 QUINNIPIAC HEALTH L.J. 113 (2007).

98. 31 U.S.C. §§ 3731–3732.

of a successful motion for removal of your local case to federal court, especially in cases against multistate nursing home chains.

26:13 Infliction of Emotional Distress

Infrequently, a plaintiff, who is a relative or survivor of a nursing home resident, sues for the defendants' infliction of emotional distress upon either the resident or the nonresident representative plaintiff. In terms of intentional infliction of emotional distress, these state law claims are difficult to generalize, but "malice" is a frequently required element of proof. Terms like "repugnant" conduct that "shocks the conscience" are used in these cases; embarrassment or hurt feelings are not sufficient injuries to sustain this count of a complaint.[99] On the other hand, in a cause of action for negligent infliction of emotional distress, the courts recognize that a person's interest in freedom from serious emotional distress is entitled to legal protection.[100] Serious mental distress may be found where a reasonable person, normally constituted, would be unable to adequately cope with the mental stress engendered by the circumstances of the case. Normally, a plaintiff needs to show that there has been some contemporaneous physical injury. One of the exceptions to this physical impact rule is when the nature of the relationship between the parties is such that a duty arises to exercise ordinary care to avoid causing emotional harm. "Such claims have been recognized in the negligent performance of contractual services that carry with them deeply emotional responses in the event of breach as, for example, in the transmission and delivery of telegrams announcing the death of

---

99. Hout v. City of Mansfield, 550 F. Supp. 2d 701 (N.D. Ohio 2008).

Intentional Infliction of Emotional Distress: "One who by extreme and outrageous conduct intentionally causes severe emotional distress to another is subject to liability for that emotional distress, and if bodily harm comes from it is liable for that bodily harm." Of note is that "liability does not extend to mere insults, indignities, threats, annoyances, petty oppressions, or other trivialities. The rough edges of our society are still in need of a good deal of filing down, and in the mean time, plaintiffs must necessarily be expected to be hardened to a certain amount of rough language and to occasional acts that are inconsiderate or unkind."

Restatement (Second) of Torts § 46.

100. Oswald v. LeGrand, 453 N.W.2d 634 (Iowa 1990).

a close relative and the services incident to funeral and burial."[101] In *Oswald v. LeGrand*, the court held that "the birth of a child involves a matter of life and death evoking such 'mental concern and solicitude' that the breach of a contract incident thereto 'will inevitably result in mental anguish, pain and suffering.'"[102] The *Oswald* court found two preconditions that must be met before liability could be found. First, there must be a special relationship: and, second, there must be extremely rude behavior or crass insensitivity. Other exceptions to the physical harm precondition include the whole range of bystander-type rules.[103] Generally, this type of emotional distress claim falls within the knowledge and understanding of the jury and no expert testimony is required.[104]

The child of the victim cannot receive damages for her emotional distress concerning assault on her mother by an aggressive male resident.[105] A nonresident-plaintiff, however, may be entitled to damages for her own emotional distress where the resident was actively hidden from the plaintiff whenever the plaintiff came to visit the resident.[106]

But many nursing home cases will be emotionally traumatic to the child of the abused elder, to varying degrees. The claim may be asserted as part of a complaint with multiple counts, some of which may be dismissed on motions while others will merit attention if and when a trial occurs.

26:14 Economic "Abuse" by Theft or Fraud

There are a small number of elder "abuse" cases in which economic fraud or abuse has occurred. These tend to be criminally prosecuted as fraud cases against the thief and are not usually civil tort matters.[107]

101. *Id.*
102. *Id.*
103. Strasel v. Seven Hills, 170 Ohio App. 3d 98, 866 N.E.2d 48 (2007); Barry R. Furro et al., Liability and Quality Issues in Health Care 326–27 (6th ed. (2004).
104. Oswald v. LeGrand, 483 N.W.2d 634 (1990); Strasel v. Seven Hills, 170 Ohio App. 3d 98, 866 N.E.2d 48 (2007).
105. Dupree v. Plantation Pointe LP, 892 So. 2d 228 (Miss. 2004).
106. Miller v. Currie, 50 F.3d 373 (6th Cir. 1995).
107. State v. Janssen, 584 N.W.2d 27 (Neb. Ct. App. 1998).

But the pressures on nursing home caregivers sometimes lead to mistakes in judgment about the elder's permission for the caregiver to take advantage of the incompetent resident. In California, litigation claiming economic fraud or abuse of elders went up 98 percent from 2001 to 2006.[108]

A direct claim of recovery for funds spent where the nursing home provided inadequate care could be sustained with proper evidence, and Medicare administrative remedies need not be exhausted.[109] The claim that fraud was organized enough to support a civil RICO charge may be sustainable in a proper case with a pattern of wrongful activity.[110]

26:15 Breach of Contract

If the language of the admission contract has not been artfully drafted, the plaintiff may be able to sustain a claim that the harm was a breach of contract; but in some cases, the contract claims are deemed to be for "health care" and will be required to go through the state's medical malpractice channel of limited remedies.[111] Counsel for a plaintiff arguing for a breach of contract should focus on the obligations set forth in the resident care plan. Presumably the plaintiff will educate the court about the "activities of daily life" that occur in nursing home care, and why these activities are distinct from "medical care" for the ailment. Then the plaintiff will assert that the breach relates to toileting, walking, feeding, and so on, conditions that are not related to health care.

26:16 Class Actions

Class actions are used for mass torts, typically among groups of plaintiffs who suffered the same injury from the same product, such as Vioxx or a similarly mass-marketed product. The nursing home population

---

108. Charles Duhigg, *Shielding Money Clashes with Elders' Free Will*, N.Y. Times, Dec. 24, 2007, at 1.

109. Salas v. Grancare Inc., 22 P.3d 568 (Colo. Ct. App. 2001).

110. Corley v. Rosewood Care Ctr., 142 F.3d 1041 (11th Cir. 1998).

111. Brown v. Sun Healthcare Group Inc., 476 F. Supp. 2d 848 (E.D. Tenn. 2007).

does not usually have identical tort exposures, so the "typicality" requirement would not be met. It is possible that an economic class could be formed among those who felt economically wronged, but individual factors in the nursing home cases predominate over class wide circumstances. One class action for four residents representing 175 at a Lakewood, Colorado, home alleged that the staff lacked certification and some had criminal records.[112]

The one small subset of class actions in this field has involved the class of residents at a nursing home who have opposed the cessation of federal funding, because that funding decision would result in their being involuntarily transferred elsewhere.[113] Another class was allowed to pursue an action for refunds, without being forced to exhaust remedies at CMS because CMS could not award damages to residents.[114]

---

112. Rose Clifford & Mary Leverock, *Investigation of Billing Fraud*, *in* NURSING HOME LITIGATION: INVESTIGATION AND CASE PREPARATION 295, 342 (Patricia Iyer ed., 1999).

113. Klein v. Califano, 586 F.2d 250 (3d Cir. 1978); Klein v. Mathews, 430 F. Supp. 1005 (D.N.J. 1977); Wash. Nursing Ctr., Inc. v. Quern, 442 F. Supp. 23 (S.D. Ill. 1977); 37 A.L.R. FED. 683 (1978).

114. Salas v. Grancare Inc., 22 P.3d 568 (Colo. Ct. App. 2001).

CHAPTER 27

Damages

27:1 Elders Tend to Have Low Economic Damages
27:2 Noneconomic Damages or "Specials"
27:3 Calculating Damages
27:4 Allocating Liability
27:5 Death Effects
27:6 Effects of Tort Reform
27:7 Punitive Damages
27:8 Statutory Damage Provisions
27:9 Caps as Deterrence to Litigation
27:10 Consequences of Large Awards for Medicaid Eligibility

27:1 Elders Tend to Have Low Economic Damages

Conventional wisdom among contingent fee lawyers works against the elderly when it comes to "actual" damages and what are called "special" damages. Two measures of actual damages—loss of wages and medical expenses—are, arguably, not present in nursing home cases. Persons who have no employment have no element of compensatory damages for wage losses. And persons whose medical costs are paid by government insurance programs have minimal out-of-pocket costs to be considered as a basis for compensatory damage awards.

27:2 Noneconomic Damages or "Specials"

Damages for pain and suffering, mental aggravation and worry, emotional distress, loss of consortium, and inconvenience, also referred to as special damages or "specials," are not directly counted in the way that wages and medical bills are counted. These "noneconomic" aspects are no less real and troubling to the nursing home resident, but some worry that, unlike an average case, they are not quantifiable by direct evidence of a specific loss.

In fact, nursing home cases should be treated no differently than average tort cases. In an average case, medical expenses generated in the medical treatment of the plaintiff are evidence of the actual out-of-pocket costs that a jury can use for the purposes of determining an award of actual damages. This amount of actual damages will be used to award an amount to account for the special damages. For example, in the context of settling a case, lawyers follow the heuristic that the specials are anywhere from three to five to seven times the amount of the "actuals," depending on the severity of the circumstances involved in the case. Different regions in the country will have different heuristics. The private insurance company that actually paid the medical bills will have a lien on the proceeds of any award and will recoup their payments out of this award.

The same situation occurs in a nursing home case. The medical bills generated to treat the harm that was caused to the nursing home resident are evidence of the actual out-of-pocket costs that a jury can use for the purposes of determining an award of actual damages. Just like in the average case, Medicare or Medicaid is the insurance "company" that actually paid the medical bills and CMS will have a lien on the proceeds of any award and may try to recoup its payments out of this award. State "tort reform" laws often seek to restrict the amount of these larger damage awards.

27:3 Calculating Damages

Economic damages can be added up from specific wage records, medical bills, and so on. For noneconomic losses, evidence usually consists of arguments about the "comparable" awards of damages by other juries in the same state. Jury verdict research is readily available from Westlaw and other electronic services tailored to particular categories; the Westlaw newsletter *Verdicts, Settlements & Tactics* provides monthly updates on nursing home and other liability outcomes.

Percentage estimates are sometimes made by advocates—that is, that noneconomic damage awards should be X percent over and above the economic damage awards. Assume that a steelworker is off work for a month with great pain, and lost wages are $5,000, so the noneconomic damage award could be three, five, or even seven times that, or from $15,000 to $35,000 above the base economic damage award depending upon the severity of the circumstances. These estimates do not work in cases involving a nursing home resident, since no wages are present as the baseline of calculation. Particularly for elders with impaired communication skills relating to the experience of pain, noneconomic harm exists but estimation of it is very subjective.

Some injuries have an immediate impact; others have a chronic and recurring effect over the remaining years of life. Assertions about the years of life reduced by a serious injury usually are inapposite in nursing home cases, since the actuarial chart for life length may already have been exceeded by the individual plaintiff. A careless nurse drops an 85-year-old woman; her hip fractures and she suffers a concussion; the conventional calculations cannot capture the noneconomic harm of diminishing her probable future mobility, future enjoyment of life, and her (even further) reduced cognitive ability.

"Hedonic" damages, for loss of enjoyment of lifestyle, are sometimes argued in the elderly person's case when the person had an active and positive lifestyle that can no longer be enjoyed. States vary in their courts' receptivity to lifestyle as a consideration in damages. But the active, well-engaged community volunteer who was 78 when she entered the nursing home and then at age 79 is hampered by dehydration, immobilized by limb contractures, and subject to terrible pressure ulcers is hurting. She arguably would deserve the compensation jurors award for the consequences of inadequate feeding, injuries from falls, or other care that was not given properly by the facility.

The trial judge should not reject the jury's award of damages unless it is apparent to a reasonable trier of fact that the amount of the award is excessive and out of line.[1]

---

1. Mitter v. Touro Infirmary, 874 So. 2d 265 (La. Ct. App. 2004).

General damages involve "physical and mental suffering, inconvenience, loss of intellectual gratification or physical enjoyment, and other factors that affect the victim's life."[2]

Impairment of the mental capacity or ability to express feelings is a limitation on the ability to calculate harm, but harm can be routinely found from the observation of the non–nursing home victim during and after a criminal assault, for example.[3]

Testimony about the preassault and postevent conditions should be admissible from family and friends who had personal knowledge of the posttraumatic effects of the rape on the elderly resident.

27:4 Allocating Liability

The facts of the case will lead to an allocation of damages among the responsible defendants. In many cases there is one corporate entity to which the ultimate liability for employee misconduct is assigned, "respondeat superior," as the great majority of lower-paid workers are deemed "judgment-proof" by their low income.

The chain of nursing homes may have organized as a contractual maze to avoid liability,[4] but that evasion maneuver may not work. Mapping out this maze was made easier as the result of a requirement of the Patient Protection and Affordable Care Act that required nursing homes to report a considerably expanded amount of information about the management and ownership of their facilities. CMS collects this data in the Provider Enrollment and Chain Ownership System database. Although it is not a requirement of the Affordable Care Act, CMS has developed scenarios under which some of this ownership information would be displayed on the website "Nursing Home Compare."[5]

---

2. Guernsey v. Country Living Pers. Care Home, Civ. No. A.3:CV-04-0423, 2006 U.S. Dist. LEXIS 31450 (M.D. Pa. May 19, 2006).

3. Charles Duhigg, *At Many Homes, More Profit and Less Nursing*, N.Y. TIMES, Sept. 23, 2007, at 1.

4. Smartt v. NHC, No. 2182 (Warren Cnty., Tenn. Cir. Ct., Feb. 22, 2007) (multiple entities named), *reported in* VERDICTS, SETTLEMENTS & TACTICS 149 (Apr. 2007).

5. DEP'T OF HEALTH & HUMAN SERVS., CMS 2012 NURSING HOME ACTION PLAN 2–3 (2012), http://www.cms.gov/Medicare/Provider-Enrollment-and-Certification/CertificationandComplianc/Downloads/2012-Nursing-Home-Action-Plan.pdf.

Awards attributing liability to several corporate entities will be sought and achieved if the correct parties were initially selected for suit.[6]

The nursing home itself can be found directly liable for negligent hiring, training or supervision of an employee who had an undiscovered history of violence or negligence that was discoverable using reasonable care. The corporate entity that owns the nursing home chain may then become liable under the doctrine of respondeat superior. In *Boudreaux,* the court held that, in cases where an employee's negligence and/or willful torts result in death of a resident, a corporation may be held liable for all damages, including punitive damages, and that this in no way violates the due process of law.[7] In a 2006 Pennsylvania case, the wanton and reckless conduct of a defendant facility in a sexual assault case led to a $300,000 general damage and $800,000 punitive damage award.[8]

The award of damages may be joint and several, against the nursing home and its parent company and against the employee or contract entity that was responsible for the harm. For injuries that result from a defective product, the product's manufacturer can be pursued using strict liability and can be held jointly and severally liable under the substantial factor test for causation when the negligent acts of the nursing home, in conjunction with the use of the defective product, join together to produce the resident's injuries.

27:5 Death Effects

Death cuts off some implicit jury sympathy for the effects of pain and suffering, as the elderly person who survived the injury will not be sitting at the table with plaintiff's counsel. But the explicit statute on protection of nursing home residents may show, or the total statutory context may imply, that the estate or survivor of the deceased resident can receive compensation for pain and suffering.[9]

---

6. *Guernsey*, 2006 U.S. Dist. LEXIS 31450.
7. Boudreaux v. Pettaway, 108 So. 3d 486, 498 (Ala. 2012).
8. *See, e.g.*, Limbaugh v. Coffee Med. Ctr., 59 S.W.2d 73 (2001).
9. Guardianship/Conservatorship of Denton, 190 Ariz. 152, 945 P.2d 1283 (1997).

27:6 Effects of Tort Reform

The lobbying strength of the nursing home chain corporations has concentrated like a laser on a handful of elected state officeholders. The key elected majority members in the key congressional and state legislative committees are likely to profit greatly from the allegiance and friendship of the nursing home owners.[10]

"Tort reform" is the euphemism presented for the industry's effort to reform the damage awards process, so as to be spared from significant damage awards.[11] The use in tort reform statutes of a baseline of economic loss, with multiples allowed narrowly for noneconomic and punitive damage awards, puts at a great disadvantage any injured plaintiff who was not employed and whose medical care had been paid by state or federal funds.

On the other hand, California's legislature recognized "that elders and dependent adults may be subject to abuse, neglect, or abandonment and that this state has a responsibility to protect these persons."[12] To that end, California passed a statute that states that "a health care service plan or managed care entity . . . shall be liable for any and all harm legally caused by its failure to exercise that ordinary care."[13]

The nursing home industry's effort to protect its profitability in the face of public and media calls for greater accountability for injuries caused by conscious neglect[14] is very controversial politically. This is no surprise; it is an economic struggle between well-organized and constant players who own the defendant facilities and the episodic or occasional litigation advocates who benefit from prevailing in some of their nursing home damage cases.[15] If you were an elected official

10. State campaign contribution data is often posted on official disclosure websites and can be readily matched with executives and administrators of the state's nursing home industry.

11. *See, e.g.*, James T. O'Reilly, 2005 Ohio Tort Reform Legislation: An Analysis of Senate Bill 80, Effective Apr. 7, 2005 (2005).

12. Cal. Welf. & Inst. Code § 15600.

13. Cal. Civ. Code § 3428 (1999).

14. Duhigg, *supra* note 3.

15. Michael Rustad, *Heart of Stone*, 35 N.M. L. Rev. 337 (2005); David Studdert et al., *Nursing Home Litigation and Tort Reform: A Case for Exceptionalism*, 44 Gerontologist 588 (2004).

who saw the industry lobbyist visiting weekly or daily, and the citizen-advocate once a year, to whom would you be likely to listen?

27:7 Punitive Damages

Counsel should consider the elements and constraints of statutory provisions for punitive damages under state law.[16] First, it is important to note that some states draw a distinction between medical malpractice cases and cases resulting from failure to provide adequate custodial care. As a result of this distinction, some courts faced with the latter provisions have refused to follow damage limitations applicable to medical malpractice cases.[17]

Second, when it comes to the constitutional limitation on the relationship between the amount of damages and a punitive damages award, the U.S. Supreme Court in *BMW v. Gore*,[18] applied a three-part analysis to determine if a punitive damages award is excessive. This three-part test balances the following factors: "(1) 'the degree of reprehensibility of the defendant's conduct'; (2) the ratio between actual and punitive damages; and (3) the potential 'civil or criminal penalties that could be imposed for comparable misconduct.'"[19] The Court went on to explain that "low awards of compensatory damages may properly support a higher ratio than high compensatory awards, if, for example, a particularly egregious act has resulted in only a small amount of economic damages. A higher ratio may also be justified in cases in which the injury is hard to detect or the monetary value of

16. In a study on data from 1963 to 1993, it was revealed that an increasing number of verdicts resulting in punitive damages were against nursing homes. Michael Rustad & Thomas Koenig, *Reconceptualizing Punitive Damages in Medical Malpractice: Targeting Amoral Corporations, Not "Moral Monsters,"* 47 Rutgers L. Rev. 975 (1995). Approximately 20 percent of all nursing home cases resulted in punitive damages, five times more likely than other types of personal injury cases. Patricia Sievers Harris, *Defense Perspective: Litigating Nursing Home Cases*, 36 Ark. Law 15 (2001).

17. *See* Mark P. Robinson et al., § 28 *Punitive Damages, in* Litigating Tort Cases (2013).

18. BMW of N. Am., Inc. v. Gore, 517 U.S. 559, 582 (1996).

19. Richard H. Tilghman IV, *Rethinking Constitutional Limitations on Punitive Damages: Providing Economically Efficient Incentives to Prevent Nursing Home Abuse*, 54 DePaul L. Rev. 1007, 1017–18 (2005).

noneconomic harm might have been difficult to determine."[20] Would nursing home employee abuse of an elder be a "particularly egregious act"?

Nursing homes cases fit well within the Supreme Court's description of possible reasons to allow for greater punitive awards. With diminished mental and physical capabilities, the elderly may not be able to report abuses making them hard cases to detect. In addition, preexisting conditions, vulnerability to falls, disease, and other deteriorating conditions may make it difficult for juries to separate defendant caused injuries and the aging process.[21] For these reasons, an increased factor in punitive awards in nursing home cases are a possibility that would require the courts to develop a new standard.

A wrongful death case may fall within this exception. For example, in *Boudreaux*, the Alabama Supreme Court held that the *Gore* formula does not apply to wrongful death cases.[22] In *McLemore*, the court held that a punitive damage award of $4.25 million and a compensatory damage award of $500,000 was not excessive.[23] The Texas Supreme Court in the *Horizon* case interpreted "damages" to mean "compensation in money imposed by law for loss or injury."[24] Since punitive damages are meant to act not as compensation for the injury or loss but as punishment for the offender, these types of damages cannot be capped, except under constitutional considerations.

The state statutes' varying degrees of generic limitations on damages in tort cases may or may not also limit the punitive damages that are expressly allowed in some states' nursing home protective statutes.[25] Economists and scholars have argued the merits of punitive damage awards in the health care field.[26] This is a very complex issue to be debated in state legislatures and in election campaigns for

---

20. *BMW of N. Am.*, 517 U.S. at 582.
21. Tilghman, *supra* note 19, at 1030.
22. Boudreaux v. Pettaway, 108 So. 3d 486, 498 (Ala. 2012).
23. McLemore *ex rel.* McLemore v. Elizabethton Med. Investors, Ltd. P'ship, 389 S.W.3d 764 (Tenn. Ct. App. 2012).
24. Horizon/CMS Healthcare Corp. v. Auld, 34 S.W.2d 887 (Tex. 2000).
25. *See, e.g.*, Rodebush v. Okla. Nursing Homes, 867 P.2d 1241 (Okla. 1993).
26. Robert Shaw, *Punitive Damages in Medical Malpractice: An Economic Evaluation*, 81 N.C. L. Rev. 2371 (2003).

state appellate judges.[27] Plaintiffs' counsel must pay attention to the state records of election campaign spending by nursing home owners.

It is difficult to win punitive damages; plaintiff must show the actions were reckless[28] or willful and wanton (or intentional or based on malice, depending on the words of the state law).[29] The defendants may stonewall to obstruct and conceal the conduct that they recognize will be hard to defend.[30]

In an appropriate case, an award of punitive damages can flow directly from failure to furnish the "adequate and appropriate care" required by CMS regulations.[31]

In Oklahoma, punitive damages against a nursing home require a showing of clear and convincing evidence of wanton or reckless conduct; $1.2 million was upheld as an award against an employee who assaulted a resident.[32]

Vulnerability of the resident to the abuse is a predicate for the courts' discussion of punitive damages.[33] The facts in the patients' decubitus ulcer cases against large for-profit nursing home chains should not be read soon after a meal, as they are grossly disgusting.[34] Frankly, these court decisions on punitive damages for neglect and abuse describe fact patterns that are difficult to stomach; the jury award of punishment reflects outrage at the lack of adequate supervision by the corporate defendant of the actual treatment within its facilities.[35]

Of special interest are the cases with cover-up attempts, fraudulent or deceptive statements that attempt to hide the real conditions

---

27. Ellen Scott, *Punitive Damages in Lawsuits Against Nursing Homes*, 23 J. LEG. MED. 115 (2002).

28. *McLemore*, 389 S.W.3d 764.

29. Stogsdill v. Manor Convalescent Home Inc. 443 N.E.2d 589 (Ill. App. Ct. 1976).

30. First Healthcare Corp v. Hamilton, 740 So. 2d 1189, 1200 (Fla. Dist. Ct. App. 1999).

31. Sprosty v. Pearlview Inc. 666 N.E.2d 1180 (Ohio Ct. App. 1995).

32. Rodebush v. Okla. Nursing Homes Ltd., 867 P.2d 1241 (Okla. 1993).

33. Convalescent Servs. Inc. v. Schultz, 921 S.W.2d 731 (Tex. App. 1996).

34. Covenant Care v. Super. Ct., 86 P.3d 290, 293 (Cal. 2004); Beverly Enters.-Fla. Inc. v. Spilman, 661 So. 2d 867 (Fla. Dist. Ct. App. 1995); Payton Health Care Facilities v. Estate of Campbell, 497 So. 2d 1233 (Fla. Dist. Ct. App. 1986).

35. Counsel should watch for defense arguments that any punitive amount greater than nine times actual compensatory damages may be unconstitutional. State Farm Mut. Auto. Ins. Co. v. Campbell, 538 U.S. 408 (2003).

in which the injury occurred; these cases tend to increase the punitive damage award and to increase the odds of its being affirmed on appeal.[36] Appellate courts are very direct in expressing disfavor for a defendant's effort to conceal its poor care for the resident who suffered injuries.[37]

27:8 Statutory Damage Provisions

Counsel should carefully examine the damage provisions in wrongful death statutes and in specific nursing home remedial statutes. These may be a limitation on the size of the demand to be included in the complaint. Plaintiff's counsel should consider web-based reference sources for forms, checklists, and other drafting tasks, but must remember that the state of venue may have a damages limitation within its civil practice codes.

27:9 Caps as Deterrence to Litigation

State statutory caps on the maximum amount of damages in tort actions will require very careful examination. These were highly controversial political decisions pushed by the industry's lobbyists.[38]

Detailed study by scholars found that ineffective reforms would "fail to alleviate the burden of litigation," while inappropriately obstructing compensation for the relatives of the injured elder.[39] In a nursing home case, the cap that was in effect when the claim accrued will be the maximum that can be imposed.[40] However, a cap on damages may not limit a plaintiff's ability to receive punitive damage awards.

---

36. A useful fact pattern is the $63 million punitive verdict in Advocat Inc. v. Sauer, 111 S.W.3d 346, 361 (Ark. 2003), *cert. denied*, 540 U.S. 1012 (2003); *see also* First Healthcare Corp. v. Hamilton, 740 So. 2d 1189, 1200 (Fla. Dist. Ct. App. 1999).

37. Moskovitz v. Mt. Sinai Med. Ctr., 635 N.E.2d 331 (Ohio 1994).

38. Michael Rustad, Heart of Stone, 35 N.M.L.Rev. 337 (2005).

39. David M. Studdert & David G. Stevenson, Nursing Home Litigation and Tort Reform: A Case for Exceptionalism, 44 Gerontologist 588 (2004).

40. Horizon/CMS Healthcare Corp. v. Auld, 34 S.W.2d 887 (Tex. 2000).

The Texas Supreme Court in *Horizon* interpreted "damages" to mean "compensation in money imposed by law for loss or injury."[41] Since punitive damages are not meant to act as compensation for the injury or loss, but as punishment for the offender, these types of damages cannot be capped, except when under constitutional considerations.

27:10 Consequences of Large Awards for Medicaid Eligibility

Receipt of damage awards or settlements may adversely affect the nursing home resident's entitlement to Medicaid benefits, so the advice of a special needs trust attorney is essential. Use one of these specialists to navigate the barriers that will affect Medicaid eligibility. The preservation of the individual resident's Medicaid financial status may affect the client's satisfaction with the outcome of this litigation. This ties in to the issue of recovery by Medicare pursuant to a lien discussed in Chapter 34 of this text dealing with subrogation and lien recovery of public assistance funds from the successful plaintiff's award.

41. Geters v. Eagle Ins. Co., 834 S.W.2d 49, 50 (Tex. 1992).

CHAPTER 28

Defenses

28:1 Overview
28:2 Defenses Related to Residents
28:3 Defenses Related to Families
28:4 Defenses Related to Regulators
28:5 State Charitable Immunity

28:1 Overview

"The best defense is a good offense," a Civil War general once said, but is that really true in the case of nursing home abuse trials? Does it make sense for a corporation's lawyer to come before a jury as an aggressive, hostile opponent of a feeble elderly Alzheimer's resident or the survivors of a deceased 92-year-old incontinent and demented woman?

Hostility of counsel and assertions of arrogant corporate power, when combined, might aid the plaintiff's claim for punitive damages. Sophisticated advocates carefully modulate their presentations so as to avoid jury trials altogether, and, if necessary, to be perceived by jurors as benign caregivers.[1]

The trap into which litigators may fall is the perceptional conundrum: the more forcefulness with which defense counsel repels the

1. John Petrullo & Sunny Kim, *Voir Dire, Opening Statement and Closing Argument—From the Defense Perspective, in* Nursing Home Litigation: Pretrial Practice and Trials 349, 354 (Ruben Krisztal ed., 2d ed. 2003) ("You will be able to show the jurors the way out of the cloud of suspicion that will hover over the courtroom at the start of trial.").

claimants in these cases, the less attractive their client becomes in the eyes of jurors. No individual juror can foresee himself or herself becoming a *Fortune* 500 corporation, but each one will empathize with the nursing home resident, and identify with the resident's plight. Never forget that the subjective imbalance of juror perceptions may have a greater impact than the objective imbalance of corporate versus resident power.

A common technique to blunt this effect is to have a visibly friendly and likable member of the nursing home administration's staff, instead of a corporate representative, appear at the defense table with defense counsel and testify in the case. The goal is to personalize the corporate owner chain defendant and to identify the "nice guy" persona of the witness as a disguise for the corporation, in order to escape liability.

Thus, the challenge faced by the defense is to win on motions that dispose of the case before it reaches the sympathetic jurors.

The first line of defense is a motion to dismiss under Federal Rule of Civil Procedure 12(b)(6), for which a court may dismiss a plaintiff's complaint for "failure to state a claim for which relief can be granted." The long-followed standard was that all a well-pled complaint need provide is "a short and plain statement of the claim showing that the pleader is entitled to relief."[2]

Two Supreme Court cases, *Bell Atlantic Corp. v. Twombly*[3] and *Ashcroft v. Iqbal*,[4] act together to create a far stricter pleading requirement than Federal Rules of Civil Procedure Rule 8 traditionally required. In *Twombly*, the Supreme Court explained, "factual allegations must be enough to rise above the speculative level."[5] In *Iqbal*, the Supreme Court developed a two-step approach that federal district courts are to apply when considering motions to dismiss and that state courts are starting to follow. First, the court must accept as true all well-pled factual allegations in the complaint. However, legal conclusions are not entitled

2. Fed. R. Civ. P. 8(a) (2).
3. 550 U.S. 544, 555 (2007).
4. 556 U.S. 662 (2009).
5. 550 U.S. at 555.

to the assumption of truth. Mere recitals of the elements of a cause of action, supported only by conclusory statements, do not suffice.

Second, the court must consider whether the factual allegations in the complaint allege a plausible claim for relief. A claim is factually plausible when the plaintiff's complaint alleges facts that allow the court to draw a reasonable inference that the defendant is liable for the alleged misconduct.[6] This modern standard for the Rule 12(b)(6) motion is ideal for defendants when the claims in a complaint have not crossed the line from conceivable to plausible.

The second line of defense is a motion for summary judgment. Many nursing home cases involve such factual issues about multifactorial causation that Rule 56 norms for summary judgment were, until recently, hard to satisfy. The current version of Rule 56, in conjunction with the U.S. Supreme Court case *Celotex Corp. v. Catrett*,[7] makes proving out a motion for summary judgment far easier for defense counsel.[8] Right from the start, defense counsel needs to keep an eye on what the plaintiff needs to prove so as to structure a defense to take advantage of the *Celotex* ruling and current Rule 56. Based on *Celotex*, all the defendant has to accomplish in the motion for summary judgment is show that the plaintiff has failed to produce facts in support of one element necessary to prove the case.[9]

The benefit of the line of cases that follow the *Celotex* decision is that it holds that a defendant does not have to disprove the plaintiff's case. The role of the defendant is to point out a gap in the plaintiff's

---

6. 556 U.S. 662 (2009).

7. 477 U.S. 317 (1986).

8. Fed. R. Civ. P. 56(A) reads: "A party may move for summary judgment, identifying each claim or defense—or the party of each claim or defense—on which summary judgment is sought. The court shall grant summary judgment if the movant shows that there is no genuine dispute as to any material fact and the movant is entitled to judgment as a matter of law. . . ."

9. According to new Rule 56, "[a] party asserting that a fact cannot be or is genuinely disputed must support the assertion by: (A) citing to particular parts of materials in the record." The Advisory Committee explains that subdivision (c)(1)(B) "recognizes . . . a party who does not have the trial burden of production may rely on a showing that a party who does have the trial burden cannot produce admissible evidence to carry its burden as to the fact." Committee Notes on Rules—2010 Amendment, Fed. R. Civ. P. 56(c)(1)(B) (2010), http://www.law.cornell.edu/rules/frcp/rule_56.

evidence that, unless filled, will result in granting of defendant nursing home's motion for summary judgment.

Deferral to arbitration would evade this jury problem; but "unconscionable" clauses compelling arbitration have not fared well, in light of the context in which the nursing home admission papers had been signed.[10]

Exclusion of the plaintiff's experts with a pretrial hearing under either the more recent *Daubert*[11] test or the *Frye*[12] test may foreclose most of the esoteric portions of the plaintiff's case, but a well-pleaded set of claims will include some for which common experience would allow jurors to make findings, so the case could proceed to a jury with a narrower set of claims. Pro-defense lobbyists may succeed with adoption of state legislation that can foreclose the plaintiff's chance of getting before a sympathetic jury.

Caps on recovery amounts and legislation channeling all nursing home cases to the alternate dispute resolution favored by medical malpractice defenders are two statutory vehicles preferred by the nursing home lobby. The former is unlikely in a legislature that listens to elder advocacy groups; the latter is less likely where trial lawyers can band together against the mandatory malpractice treatment of the nursing home cases.

---

10. See Chapter 29.

11. The relevance and reliability of the proposed testimony by the expert witness can be tested under the U.S. Supreme Court's five criteria in *Daubert v. Merrell Dow Pharmaceuticals*, 509 U.S. 579 (1993); many states have followed this test in their own expert witness screening procedures.

12. This standard comes from *Frye v. United States*, 293 F. 1013 (D.C. Cir. 1923), a case discussing the admissibility of a polygraph test as evidence. The court in Frye held that expert testimony must be based on scientific methods that are sufficiently established and accepted. The court opined:

> Just when a scientific principle or discovery crosses the line between the experimental and demonstrable stages is difficult to define. Somewhere in this twilight zone the evidential force of the principle must be recognized, and while the courts will go a long way in admitting experimental testimony deduced from a well-recognized scientific principle or discovery, the thing from which the deduction is made must be sufficiently established to have gained general acceptance in the particular field in which it belongs.

Id.

The relevance and reliability of the proposed testimony by the expert witness can be tested under the U.S. Supreme Court's five criteria in *Daubert*, and many states have followed this test in their own expert witness screening procedures.[13] This standard comes from *Frye v. United States*, a case discussing the admissibility of a polygraph test as evidence.[14] The court in *Frye* held that expert testimony must be based on scientific methods that are sufficiently established and accepted. The court opined:

> Just when a scientific principle or discovery would be deemed to cross the line between the experimental and demonstrable stages is difficult to define. Somewhere in this twilight zone the evidential force of the principle must be recognized, and while the courts will go a long way in admitting experimental testimony deduced from a well-recognized scientific principle or discovery, the thing from which the deduction is made must be sufficiently established to have gained general acceptance in the particular field in which it belongs.[15]

28:2 Defenses Related to Residents

The cause-in-fact[16] of a person's death is determined by autopsy or medical opinion, together with expert evaluation of the context in which the death had occurred. "The resident would have died anyway!" is a defendant's claim that the negligent act did not cause the harm asserted from the fall or other event. The nursing home bathroom

---

13. Daubert v. Merrell Dow Pharms., 509 U.S. 579 (1993).

14. Frye v. United States, 293 F. 1013 (D.C. Cir. 1923).

15. *Id.*

16. The actor's negligent conduct is a cause-in-fact of harm to another if "his conduct is a substantial factor in bringing about the harm." RESTATEMENT (SECOND) OF TORTS § 431. The substantial factor test is used where there are multiple actors and "either's act would suffice to cause the plaintiff's' injury." *Id.* In this instance, the substantial factor test is used. *Id.* § 431(a). In situations with multiple actors a diligent lawyer will always assert substantial factor because the "but for" test allows the defendant to escape liability by asserting "but for" the defendant›s conduct, the harm would still have occurred. This test for causation is also used when the negligence of the defendant and nonnegligent causes combine to bring about the injury. *See, e.g.*, Anderson v. Minneapolis, St. P. & S. S. M. Ry. Co., 179 N.W. 45 (1920).

fall is a prime example; did the resident have a condition, for example a bone disease, predisposing her to injury, so that her hip spontaneously fractured; or was she mishandled by an aide who dropped her?

This is where a savvy plaintiff's lawyer will turn to the substantial factor test, which asks whether the defendant's negligent conduct was a substantial factor in bringing about the harm.[17]

If this resident is the classic "thin-skulled plaintiff" whose preexisting fragile but uninjured condition made her more susceptible to injury, the defendant takes the *uninjured* but fragile plaintiff as they find her or him.

In this situation, the defendant will be liable for the full extent of the plaintiff's injuries, even if that extent was unforeseeable. On the other hand, if the plaintiff already has a preexisting injury, the appropriate defense is that the defendant is liable only for the aggravation of that preexisting injury. If this is a situation where a form of harm is already likely to occur, the appropriate defense is that the defendant is only liable for the acceleration of an injury that was already likely to occur.

Of course, there are simply some injuries that are unforeseeable. The defense should take care to examine the plaintiff's proof on each of the many layers of proximate cause to ascertain whether the plaintiff has produced sufficient facts to establish that the plaintiff was a foreseeable plaintiff, that the risk of injury was a foreseeable risk, and that the actor's negligent conduct is a cause-in-fact of harm to another if "his conduct is a substantial factor in bringing about the harm."[18] The substantial factor test is used where there are multiple actors and "either's act would suffice to cause the plaintiff's injury."[19] In this instance, the substantial factor test can be used to excuse liability for a bathroom slip and fall.

In situations with multiple actors, a diligent lawyer will always assert substantial factor claims, because the "but for" test allows the

---

17. Palermo v. Port of New Orleans, 951 So. 2d 425 (La. Ct. App. 2007); Busta v. Columbus Hosp. Corp., 916 P.2d 122 (Mont. 1996); RESTATEMENT (THIRD) OF TORTS: LIABILITY FOR PHYSICAL HARM § 27 (2009).

18. DANN B. DOBBS ET AL., TORTS AND COMPENSATION 218–49 (2009); *see also* MARSHALL S. SHAPO, PRINCIPLES OF TORT LAW (2005).

19. *Id.*

defendant to escape liability by asserting that "but for" the defendant's conduct, the harm would still have occurred. This test for causation is also used when the negligence of the defendant and nonnegligent causes combine to bring about the injury. In some states, the manner in which the risk came to fruition must be foreseeable, and any intervening causes must be foreseeable and not superseding.

One caveat is that medical malpractice is not always foreseeable. For example, if a negligent act on the part of the nursing home means that a resident must be hospitalized for treatment, and then the hospital aggravates the injuries though negligent treatment, the negligent acts of the hospital will not cut off the liability of the nursing home under proximate cause as medical malpractice is always foreseeable. If the injury is indivisible through the use of reasonable means, then both the nursing home and the hospital will be held jointly and severally liable.[20] Contributory negligence[21] by the person who was injured is much less likely to be a successful argument in nursing home cases, because the individual impairment of mental or physical condition will typically prevent the court from treating a negligent act as a voluntary choice of a competent adult. "Where a resident suffering from diabetes, arthritis, and chronic brain syndrome had placed himself in the care of the hospital for the very purpose of protecting himself against the effects of these conditions, the court refused to allow the hospital to raise the defense of contributory negligence."[22]

For example, an escape by a nursing home resident whose outdoor wandering leads to a death on the adjacent highway is sometimes excused if the escaping resident had active dementia. "When a nursing home resident is unable to physically and mentally care for himself

---

20. Dobbs et al., *supra* note 18; *see also* Shapo, *supra* note 18.

21. Contributory negligence is conduct on the part of the plaintiff that falls below the standard to which he should conform for his own protection, and that is a legally contributing cause cooperating with the negligence of the defendant in bringing about the plaintiff's harm. Restatement (Second) of Torts § 463 (1965). The burden of establishing the plaintiff's contributory negligence rests upon the defendant. Restatement (Second) of Torts § 477 (1965).

22. Kent v. Cnty. of Hudson, 102 N.J. Super. 208, 245 A.2d 747, *aff'd*, 53 N.J. 546, 251 A.2d 760 (1968).

or herself, it may be argued that the resident should not be held to the same degree of accountability as a normal and healthy person."[23]

The burden of establishing the plaintiff's contributory negligence rests upon the defendant.

28:3 Defenses Related to Families

The defense counsel is likely to challenge the indifference of the resident's family as a reason why damage recovery should be denied. The condition of the resident would have been evident to the family, it is argued, if they visited often; if conditions were as bad as hindsight now asserts, the family could have protested; but for their inactivity, it would be asserted, the staff would have been more attentive to her or his needs. The argument is fine for in-home care; it misses the mark where the nursing home is the sole source of nursing, nutrition, hydration, and so on for an elderly resident.

28:4 Defenses Related to Regulators

Regulators compel some actions and proscribe other actions,[24] and the licensed nursing home administrators will comply. If they do not comply, the state surveyors will find a violation.[25] But the surveys are not infallible and are not omniscient. It would be likely that a court would accept the argument that no malnutrition occurred, where the survey team had visited the nursing home's dietary office and examined 100 resident charts and had not detected any. State surveyors have guidance books listing hundreds of possible problem situations[26] and cannot reasonably be expected to detect or act against all of them. The

---

23. Stogsdill v. Manor Convalescent Home, Inc., 35 Ill. App. 3d 634, 343 N.E.2d 589 (2d Dist. 1976).

24. *See, e.g.*, 42 C.F.R. pt. 483 (2008).

25. Ctrs. for Medicare & Medicaid Servs., State Operations Manual, CMS Pub. No. 100-07, Appendix PP: Guidance to Surveyors for Long Term Care Facilities.

26. *Id.*

state rules[27] and CMS regulations[28] act as a minimum for purposes of tort liability, and as a black-letter principle of tort law, one's compliance with a regulatory minimum is not a legally valid reason for excusing omissions of due care that had proximately caused harm.

28:5 State Charitable Immunity

In some states, charitable immunity is an affirmative defense. An affirmative defense must be set forth in the defendant's responsive pleading. The burden of pleading and proving an affirmative defense is on the party asserting it. Where the defense did not affirmatively plead the defense of charitable immunity in its answer, and failed to amend its answer to include the defense, as suggested by the trial court at the hearing on the motion to dismiss, the defense was barred. The mere statement in its answer that it is a not-for-profit organization that has received 501(c)(3) status is held not to be sufficient to raise the defense. The raising of the defense in the motion to dismiss is not sufficient to satisfy the requirement that an affirmative defense be specifically pled.[29]

---

27. A useful compendium of state requirements is found in 2 David Couch, Libby Edwards & David Hoey, Litigating Nursing Home Abuse Cases (West 2007).

28. 42 C.F.R. pt. 483 (2008).

29. McMullen v. Ark. Elder Outreach of Little Rock, Inc., 2011 WL 715014 (Ark. App. March 2, 2011).

CHAPTER 29

Arbitration

29:1 Overview
29:2 The Case for Requiring Arbitration by Contract
29:3 Criticism of the Use of Arbitration
29:4 Costs and Award Limitations
29:5 Procedures
29:6 Defenses against Arbitration

29:1 Overview

Resolving nursing home disputes through arbitration is likely to reduce the costs for nursing home owners, dissuade attorneys from involvement with nursing home claims, eliminate the risk of punitive damage awards, and drastically diminish the financial incentives for plaintiff's lawyers to take on these cases.[1]

It would be a great victory for the industry if arbitration swept away tort claims and replaced them with a modest rate of compensation payments in arbitrated cases. But the trend of nursing homes forcing arbitration clauses on new residents has been controversial.[2] The gen-

1. Marjorie A. Shields, *Validity, Construction, and Application of Arbitration Agreement in Contract for Admission to Nursing Home*, 50 A.L.R. 6th 187 (2010); Eleanor L. Grossman, Glenda K. Harnad & Jeffrey J. Shampo, *Arbitration Agreements-Requisites, Validity, and Effect*, 4 Am. Jur. 2d *Alternative Dispute Resolution* § 46 (2010); Robert J. Rice, *Nursing Home Liability*, 24 Am. Jur. *Proof of Facts 3d* 73 (2011); Daniel J. Penofsky, *Litigating Nursing Home Negligence and Wrongful Death Cases*, 110 Am. Jur. *Trials* 1 (2011).

2. Stacey Burling, *Arbitration a Growing Trend in Health Care*, Phila. Inquirer, Feb. 10, 2008.

eral public is unaware of how one-sided the process is and how little compensation will be available to the resident or survivors. Voters who elect legislators and judges in many states are not likely to embrace this loss of judicial remedies, if the reality becomes widely apparent to voters who have family members in nursing homes.

Legislators adopt certain remedies specifically to allow deterrence of future tortious behavior.[3] The Centers for Medicaid and Medicare Services (CMS) is expressly neutral on whether the nursing home can compel arbitration of disputes; a 2003 policy statement said it would not object, so long as the then-current residents were not compelled to retroactively agree to arbitrate.[4] The law forbids a nursing home from requiring a payment "or other consideration" as a precondition for admission,[5] and it can be asserted that the waiver of trial rights is to be a "consideration" precedent to admission.[6]

The Federal Arbitration Act (FAA) governs arbitration clauses[7] Arbitration clauses are presumed valid, irrevocable, and enforceable by section 2 of the FAA.[8] State laws that govern arbitration clauses that conflict with the FAA are preempted by the FAA.[9] Arbitration procedures are dictated by the FAA as well, but contracting parties have authority within those statutes to design procedures fitting their interests.[10]

29:2 The Case for Requiring Arbitration by Contract

The best case in favor of arbitration clause enforcement, when the survivors or guardians sue for compensation after an alleged abuse

3. Romano *ex rel.* Romano v. Manor Care, Inc., 861 So. 2d 59, 63 (Fla. 4th Dist. Ct. App. 2003).

4. Memorandum from Dir. of Survey and Certification Group, Ctrs. for Medicare & Medicaid Servs., *quoted in* Amy DeLaney, *Maneuvering the Labyrinth of Long Term Care Admissions Contracts*, 4 NAT'L ACAD. ELDER LAW ATT'YS J. 35, 57 (2008).

5. 42 U.S.C. § 1396r(c)(5)(A)(iii) (2000).

6. Sanford v. Castleton Health Care Ctr., LLC, 813 N.E.2d 411, 419 (Ind. Ct. App. 2004).

7. Perry v. Thomas, 482 U.S. 483, 489 (1987).

8. 9 U.S.C.A. § 2 (West).

9. AT&T Mobility LLC v. Concepcion, 131 S. Ct. 1740, 1747 (2011); Marmet Health Care Ctr., Inc. v. Brown, 132 S. Ct. 1201, 1204 (2012).

10. Gilmer v. Interstate/Johnson Lane Corp., 500 U.S. 20, 21 (1991).

to the nursing home resident, is based on an economic predicate.[11] Overhead costs to for-profit nursing homes detract from the funding available for resident service. Litigation costs of discovery, motions, experts, and trials have risen rapidly in recent years. Verdicts and punitive damage claims have driven up insurance costs. Costs for liability insurance and direct legal billings are an increasing burden on the expense side of the ledger. If arbitration supplanted litigation, confidentiality about claims and outcomes would diminish the attraction of this work for prospective attorney entrants into the field. "A cheaper, more efficient forum could potentially reduce the outcome-determinative quality arising out of the financial disparity between plaintiffs and defendant corporations by making the pursuit of claims more affordable and accessible."[12]

29:3 Criticism of the Use of Arbitration

The use of arbitration clauses in contracts of admission to nursing homes has been extensively criticized, because the level of resident and family awareness about these limitations is low, and the power of relatives to bind the elder to waive litigation remedies is debatable in postinjury cases.[13]

For example, Illinois expressly prohibits the use of arbitration clauses in admissions contracts.[14] Other state laws impose specific requirements on the arbitration terms that can be used in these contracts.[15] The context of forming the contractual agreement is crucial to understanding the conflicts over enforcement of the arbitration command.[16]

11. Katherine Palm, *Arbitration Clauses in Nursing Home Admission Agreements*, 14 ELDER L.J. 453 (2006).

12. *Id.* at 476.

13. Laura Owings & Mark Geller, *The Inherent Unfairness of Arbitration Agreements in Nursing Home Admission Contracts*, 43 TENN. BAR J. 20 (2007).

14. 210 ILL. COMP. STAT. 45/3-607 (1980).

15. Illinois, 710 ILL. COMP. STAT. 15/5 (1977); OKLAHOMA, OKLA. STAT. tit. 63, § 1-1939(E) (2001).

16. Ann Krasuski, *Mandatory Arbitration Agreements Do Not Belong in Nursing Home Contracts with Residents*, 8 DEPAUL J. HEALTH CARE L. 263 (2004); W. TODD HARVEY, *Arbitration Agreements in Nursing Home Admissions Contracts*, 39 TRIAL 72 (May 2003).

One way to pose the question would be: Did a lucid and rational applicant read and understand the degree to which this contract language would extinguish his or her rights?

The critics charge that these arbitration agreements are contracts of adhesion, with the weaker side totally unable to bargain with those who control the needed room or bed for that ailing relative.[17] The hospital discharge planner or doctor announces: "A bed is available for your aunt in the local nursing home and we need to discharge her from our hospital's intensive care unit tomorrow morning. Shall I call the nursing home now?"

In Alabama, hospital patients who are admitted into the nursing home as residents directly from a hospital and have not signed an admissions contract containing an arbitration clause cannot be bound by such a clause, but signed contracts are generally binding.[18]

This is not Boeing and Microsoft making an arbitration agreement at arm's length for aircraft equipment, where two sophisticated negotiators understand the context of an arbitration agreement.

Fairness concerns lead critics to assert that these arbitration clauses signed by relatives are unconscionable; that the agreements are inapplicable to the nonparty who did not sign them; and that these demands would arguably run afoul of the barrier to a nursing home requiring a cash donation or "other consideration" for admission in violation of federal Medicaid law.[19]

The courts have had extensive dealings with these contracts, and because the state courts vary so widely,[20] there is no one nationwide answer as to their enforceability.

Arbitration in nursing home admissions contracts has been widely attacked in state courts. The U.S. Supreme Court in the *Marmet* case[21] summarily rejected a West Virginia Supreme Court decision that held the arbitration clause unenforceable on two alternative bases: the first

17. Palm, *supra* note 11.
18. Springhill Nursing Homes, Inc. v. McCurdy, 898 So. 2d 694, 698 (Ala. 2004).
19. *Id.; contra* Owens v. Coosa Valley Health Care, 890 So. 2d 983 (Ala. 2004).
20. DeLaney, *supra* note 4.
21. Marmet Health Care Ctr., Inc. v. Brown, 132 S. Ct. 1201 (2012).

was a West Virginia statute that declared "null and void as contrary to public policy" any waiver by nursing home residents of their right to sue the nursing home operator for injuries sustained on the premises. The second basis was the common law doctrine of unconscionability. The U.S. Supreme Court vacated, rebuking the West Virginia court for "misreading and disregarding the precedents of this Court interpreting the FAA." West Virginia's interpretation of the FAA was "both incorrect and inconsistent with clear instruction in the precedents of this Court," because the FAA "requires courts to enforce the bargain of the parties to arbitrate" and "includes no exception for personal-injury or wrongful-death claims." West Virginia statutes that prohibit outright the arbitration of a particular type of claim is "a categorical rule prohibiting arbitration of a particular type of claim, and that rule is contrary to the terms and coverage of the FAA" so it must be "displaced by the FAA."[22]

In early 2013, a nursing home operator filed a writ of certiorari asking the U.S. Supreme Court to determine whether state courts can refuse to enforce an arbitration agreement signed by the resident in a wrongful death action brought by a resident's survivors under the FAA.[23] In its petition, SSC Odin Operating Co. asserted that there is a conflict among the highest state courts over whether wrongful death plaintiffs are bound by arbitration agreements signed by their decedents. In the case involving Odin, the Illinois Supreme Court did not enforce an arbitration agreement between a nursing home and a deceased resident to require arbitration of wrongful death claims asserted by the third-party resident's family members.[24]

The Kentucky Supreme Court[25] also held that wrongful death plaintiffs cannot be compelled to arbitrate claims. According to the court, under Kentucky law wrongful death claims are not derivative, but accrue separately to the beneficiaries and are meant to compensate

---

22. *Id.*
23. SSC Odin Operating Co. v. Carter, U.S., No. 12-1015 (petition for review filed Feb. 15, 2013).
24. Carter v. SSC Odin Operating Co., 976 N.E.2d 344 (Ill. 2012).
25. Ping v. Beverly Enters. Inc., 376 S.W.3d 581 (Ky. 2012).

them for their loss. Courts in four other states, Missouri, Utah, Ohio, and Washington, have ruled similarly.[26]

In contrast, the Texas Supreme Court held that the FAA preempts a state rule of law treating arbitration agreements signed by decedents differently than other types of contracts signed by decedents.[27] The court held that contracts signed by decedents generally are enforceable against their estates. To hold otherwise would create an anomaly as the estate would be bound by a contract in which the decedent completely disposed of the claim, but would then not be bound by an agreement that changed the forum in which the claim would be resolved.

The Florida Supreme Court used similar reasoning to declare an arbitration agreement enforceable against wrongful death plaintiffs.[28] The court found that a survivors' right to recover damages under the state's wrongful death act is predicated on the decedent's right to recover in a personal injury action. As a result, survivors cannot recover in actions where the decedent previously won damages or settled an action based on the same injuries that caused his or her death, or signed a document releasing the tortfeasor from liability.

In Pennsylvania, an arbitration clause in a nursing home admission contract was not broad enough to encompass a claim for wrongful death.[29]

In another case, the Florida Supreme Court declared that a provision in a doctor-resident arbitration agreement that limited resident's noneconomic damages to $250,000, but did not provide incentives included in the statutory arbitration scheme, including doctor's concession of liability, is void as against Florida public policy.[30]

---

26. Mary Anne Pazanowski, *Nursing Home Asks Supreme Court to Review States' Treatment of Wrongful Death Claims*, 22 Health L. Rep. 341 (2013), http://healthlawrc.bna.com/hlrc/4237/split_display.adp?fedfid=29858437&vname=hlrnotallissues&fcn=5&wsn=491410000&fn=29858437&split=0.

27. *In re* Labatt Food Serv. LP, 279 S.W.3d 640 (Tex. 2009).

28. Laizure v. Avante at Leesburg Inc., 2013 Fla. LEXIS 249 (Fla. Feb. 14, 2013).

29. Setlock v. Pinebrook Pers. Care, 2012 Pa. Super. LEXIS 3446 (Pa. Super. Ct. Oct. 23, 2012).

30. Franks v. Bowers, No. SC11-1258 (Fla. Sp. Ct. June, 20, 2013).

In the 11th Circuit, a federal trial court was reversed and arbitration was ordered, applying Alabama law concerning the FAA and its enforceability.[31]

29:4 Costs and Award Limitations

In arbitration, parties pay the costs, discovery is limited, and times are shortened. There is no "free" arbitration; there must be an up-front payment by the survivor or guardian of the arbitration filing costs, and agreement to pay the final bill for the arbitrator's time. And there are no punitive damages available, so the best case that a plaintiff's attorney can make is a "pain and suffering" damage award comparable to what civil juries have made in other jurisdictions for a similar injury.

29:5 Procedures

An arbitration claim begins with notice to the nursing home by the attorney for the personal representative of the resident. The local office of the designated arbitration association will send the packet to the claimant's attorney. Many nursing home arbitration contracts include a requirement that the arbitrators be members of the American Health Lawyers Association (AHLA) instead of the well-recognized neutral bodies that conduct most U.S. arbitration hearings. The number of arbitrators is determined by the contract, and if the number of arbitrators has not been listed in the contract the court shall designate one arbitrator or a panel.[32] Using AHLA has been deemed to be conscionable in Alabama,[33] but unconscionable in Florida because some of the rules of arbitration procedure for the AHLA had the effect of superseding or dismantling the protections afforded to residents in Florida's Nursing Home Resident's Act.[34] An interesting question for

31. Entrekin v. Internal Med. Assoc. of Dothan, P.A., 689 F.3d 1248 (11th Cir. 2012).

32. 9 U.S.C.A. § 5 (West); Ore & Chem. Corp. v. Stinnes Interoil, Inc., 611 F. Supp. 237, 241 (S.D.N.Y. 1985).

33. Briarcliff Nursing Home, Inc. v. Turcotte, 894 So. 2d 661, 665 (Ala. 2004).

34. Fletcher v. Huntington Place Ltd. P'ship, 952 So. 2d 1225, 1226 (Fla. 5th Dist. Ct. App. 2007).

a bit of empirical evidence is to determine who AHLA member lawyers represent in their day-to-day practice.

Financially, the person seeking to press a claim must come up with substantial cash up front. The claimant has to pay the filing fee and pay for the cost of the arbitrator. The attorneys meet with the arbitrator for an initial consultation. After a brief period for the exchange of records requested, the arbitrator sets a date for the hearing. Witnesses can testify and rebuttal witnesses can be put on, with none of the formalities of the civil trial. The hearing ends with closing statements. The arbitrator then departs and issues a ruling several weeks later. The arbitrator's findings of fact and conclusions are deemed to be final. The grounds for a court appeal of an arbitrator's decision are narrow and courts dislike rehearing cases that have already been decided through arbitration.

In one author's experience as an arbitrator, the side with the best documentation wins. Arbitration is "dispassionate," evaluating the merits with no heartstrings, looking at dollar amounts of awards in similar cases, and applying skeptical discounts to the amounts of compensation sought. Since the paper trail is examined closely, plaintiff's counsel should take color copies of the original records and discern alterations, backdating of care that was claimed to have taken place, and dubious recordings of care given while the resident was unavailable, for example, visiting a doctor's office while the record shows she was being bathed. Fraud or altered records catch the arbitrator's attention and plaintiffs should look very carefully for either.

29:6 Defenses against Arbitration

While it is not entirely surprising that a judge with an already overburdened docket might be inclined to grant a motion to compel arbitration that, on its face, appears to arise from a valid contract, residents facing efforts by nursing homes to compel arbitration are not without defenses.

The tests for substantive and procedural unconscionability[35] measure the bargaining power of the parties and the commercial reasonableness

35. THI of N.M. at Hobbs Ctr., LLC v. Spradlin, 893 F. Supp. 2d 1172, 1185 (D.N.M. 2012).

of the arbitration clause; in nursing home cases, courts are likely to apply these norms and to reject the "bargain" that led to this nursing home admission being subjected to arbitration rather than to litigation.[36]

Courts have refused to enforce arbitration clauses for various reasons. The circumstances of the resident's admission are often exigent and the terms of the clause are buried in the fine print of a lengthy "take it or leave it" contract.[37] There is no negotiation possible for the family of the ailing elder, and this diminishes the traditional theory that arbitration arises from careful negotiation.[38] The elderly resident-to-be does not usually sign the contract, so there is a lack of actual or apparent authority for the signatory person that undercuts the judicial acceptance of the agreement.[39] Another person signing the contract can present an advantage to plaintiff's attorney for claims brought by the persons who signed the document. In California, an arbitration clause was not enforced against the signer because the signer did not sign the agreement for herself, or as agent for the resident; she signed the agreement as representative of the resident and therefore she was not bound by the clause.[40]

Basically, if the contract is signed by a person that has no agency rights, the arbitration clause cannot bind the parties.[41]

Florida courts found that the arbitration clause in a nursing home contract was against public policy, as expressed in that state's nursing home rights statute; restricting rights created by statute made the contract void as against public policy.[42] Other Florida courts have found arbitration clauses conscionable and allowed a motion to compel arbitration on any controversy or claim arising out of the care in the nursing home.[43]

---

36. Hayes v. Oakridge Home, No. 89400, 2008 WL 525411 (Ohio Ct. App. Feb. 28, 2008).
37. Howell v. NHC Healthcare-Fort Sanders Inc., 109 S.W.2d 731 (Tenn. Ct. App. 2003).
38. Buracynski v. Eyring, 919 S.W.2d 314 (Tenn. 1996).
39. Raiteri v. NHC Healthcare Knoxville, E2003-00068-COA-R9-CV, 2003 WL 23094413 (Tenn. Ct. App. Dec. 30, 2003).
40. Goliger v. AMS Props., Inc., 19 Cal. Rptr. 3d 819, 821 (Cal. Ct. App. 2d Dist. 2004).
41. Gentry v. Beverly Enters.-Ga., Inc., 714 F. Supp. 2d 1225, 1230 (S.D. Ga. 2009).
42. Blankfeld v. Richmond Health Care Inc., 902 So. 2d 296 (Fla. Dist. Ct. App. 2005).
43. Five Points Health Care Ltd. v. Alberts, 867 So. 2d 520, 521 (Fla. 1st Dist. Ct. App. 2004).

Ohio courts have been hostile to the arbitration motions presented by nursing home defenders in some cases, on grounds of fairness,[44] and have been holding them strictly to procedures that allow a process for the assertion of the affirmative defense that arbitration must be undertaken.[45]

Finally, plaintiffs' counsel must remain cognizant of the nursing home's duty as the moving party. The nursing home must demonstrate that an arbitration agreement exists. In instances where the nursing home fails to abide by the rules of evidence and does not authenticate the purported agreement, courts will not compel arbitration.[46]

44. *See, e.g.*, Manley v. Personacare, 2007 WL 210583, 2007-Ohio-343 (Ohio Ct. App. Jan. 26, 2007).

45. Barnes v. Andover Vill. Ret. Cmty., Ltd., 2007 WL 2296459, 2007-Ohio-4112 (Ohio Ct. App. Aug. 10, 2007) (O.R.C. §2711,03(a) does not require an oral hearing—a submission of authority, arguments and affidavits will suffice); *compare with* Barr v. HCF, 2005 WL 3031723, 2005-Ohio-6040 (Ohio Ct. App. Nov. 14, 2005) (interpreting O.R.C. §2711.03(a) and holding that a court shall hear parties before compelling arbitration because it is statutorily mandated).

46. Carter v. Takoda Trails, Case No. C-230329, 2024 Ohio 911 (Ct. App. Mar. 13, 2024).

CHAPTER 30

Motion Practice

30:1 Discovery Motions
30:2 Failure to State a Claim
30:3 Summary Judgment
30:4 Removal to Federal Court
30:5 Motions after Verdict
30:6 Remittitur

30:1 Discovery Motions

"Seek first to understand, then to be understood," the proverb says. The prudent advocate invests in understanding the context of this particular injury, and discovery is the process to achieve more insights. Counsel should recognize the importance of winning discovery motions, like motions to compel, in the assembly of key evidence. The trial and the overall case may turn upon the outcome of the disputes over access to certain records of the nursing home.[1] An experienced plaintiff's litigator has remarked that defense tactics extend these cases by about two years: "Ironically, the defense philosophy of extended litigation persists, even though nursing homes [cases] generally get better for the plaintiff with additional discovery."[2]

1. Briana Rivera, *Discovery Motions, in* Nursing Home Litigation: Pretrial Practice and Trials 231 (Ruben Krisztal ed., 2d ed. 2003).
2. Allen Fuller, *Settlement Strategies, in* Nursing Home Litigation: Pretrial Practice and Trials, *id.* at 581.

Discovery disputes typically involve defense claims of evidentiary privilege. Privileges for medical records are not available to prevent plaintiff from access to the file of an assaultive patient who attacked plaintiff in a nursing home.[3]

Sanctions for discovery abuse can be imposed against a nursing home that acted improperly in handling a demand for records.[4]

Often initial discovery productions from nursing homes may be limited to the resident's medical records. However, due to various state and federal regulations, the actual breadth of discoverable information is far more voluminous. For example, a facility's policies and procedures can be foundational in establishing what the facility's own position on its "duty" is. If these policies and procedures are in place in numerous facilities, they can be used to establish the corporate parent's duty. Likewise, in an infectious disease case, the facility's infection control logs can tell the plaintiff's counsel whether a potential outbreak was being ignored or whether poor infection control practices resulted in infectious diseases not being recorded. Such pivotal documents must be requested in discovery and, more importantly, must be fought for when not produced.

30:2 Failure to State a Claim

These motions more often take the form of attacking technical defects in a complaint. For example, if a poorly drafted complaint seeks punitive damages for wrongful death in a state where such damages are not permissible by statute, a Rule 12(b)(6) motion may be expected. Generally, though, when complaints are carefully drafted, such motions are uncommon.

An example of this Rule 12(b)(6) motion is seen in a Missouri case of severe assaults on a nursing home resident by staff members; the appellate court reversed and remanded a dismissal for failure to state a claim, as the court held that the statutory cause of action was sufficient

3. Goodyear v. Care Concepts, 625 N.W.2d 876 (Wis. 2001).
4. *In re* Lavernia Nursing Facility Inc. 12 S.W.3d 566 (Tex. App. 1999).

to take the case to the jury.[5] A Tennessee court dismissed an action predicated on a private cause of action to enforce CMS Medicaid rules, for inadequate care of skin ulcers and malnutrition, as the court decided no private action was created by the federal legislation.[6]

30:3 Summary Judgment

The moving party who seeks summary judgment bears the burden to prove that no issues of fact remain for the jury to decide.[7] The defendant nursing home must "affirmatively negate an essential element of the nonmoving party's claim or establish an affirmative defense that conclusively defeats the nonmoving party's claim."[8]

30:4 Removal to Federal Court

The multistate chain nursing home corporation may wish to avoid local jury sentiment against their local home. The tactic of removing a plaintiff's case to a (probably) more distant federal courthouse with a wider jury pool may be a wise choice. The federal court also shields the defendant by forcing plaintiff witnesses to get through the *Daubert*[9] screening standards, while some states retain the easier approach of another evidentiary admission standard. Additionally, defendants may seek federal courts due to the requirement of a unanimous jury verdict. Some state courts permit verdicts that are not unanimous.

The other federal court, bankruptcy court, may become the court with the most control over outcomes, if the thinly capitalized corporation facing a huge liability verdict files for bankruptcy in order to avoid its potential damage awards.

---

5. Stiffelman v. Abrams, 655 S.W.2d 522 (Mo. 1983).
6. Brown v. Sun Healthcare Group Inc., 476 F. Supp. 2d 848 (E.D. Tenn. 2007).
7. Fed. R. Civ. P. 56 and state law equivalents.
8. Conley v. Life Care Ctrs. 236 S.W.2d 713 (2007).
9. Daubert v. Merrell Dow Pharms., 509 U.S. 579 (1993).

30:5 Motions after Verdict

Nursing home cases can be subjected to substantial postjudgment motion practice. Such practice can both extend the time for the nursing home to file an appeal in an attempt to avoid the judgment and create additional grounds for such an appeal. For plaintiffs' counsel, defending a verdict can be more arduous than obtaining it.

Motions for a new trial, for example, are allowed in the discretion of the trial judge where the verdict was contrary to the substantial weight of the evidence. But the denial of these motions will be difficult to overcome.[10]

30:6 Remittitur

The trial court may grant a motion for reduction of a jury's verdict that the judge considers to be excessive.[11] The defendant may be contesting the award for suffering incurred between the time of the negligent act and the death.[12] Or on appeal, the plaintiff may be forced to consider either the delay and cost of a new trial, or giving up a portion of the damage award by "remittitur."[13] In a 2003 case, a two-thirds reduction was ordered in a $63 million award of punitive damages.[14] These can be very substantial rollbacks from liability judgment awards.[15]

---

10. Dupree v. Plantation Pointe LP, 892 So. 2d 228 (Miss. 2004).
11. Richardson v. Abbey Nursing Home, 1983 Westlaw 2867 (Ohio App. 1983).
12. Living Ctrs. of Tex. v. Penalver, 2010 WL 1708333 (Tex. App. 4/28/2010).
13. *See, e.g.*, Bentley v. Abbey Nursing Home Inc., 1983 Ohio App. LEXIS 12777 (Ohio Ct. App. 1983).
14. Advocat Inc. v. Sauer, 111 S.W.3d 346 (Ark. 2003).
15. Note, Nursing Homes, 56 Ark. L. Rev. 497, 504 (2004).

CHAPTER 31

Trial Procedure Issues

31:1 Voir Dire—The "Ideal" Juror
31:2 Presentations and Demonstrative Evidence
31:3 Decisions on Evidence
31:4 Impeachment and Response

31:1 Voir Dire—The "Ideal" Juror

Most nursing home cases settle. If the case is not settled, the focal point of attention for defense counsel's preparation may become the survey of perceptions of potential jurors about the nursing home industry. The individuals in the jury pool in a smaller community may be inclined to support the plaintiff's advocates, as the jurors are related to a current or former resident of this nursing home, or may know workers at this nursing home. This familiarity is not a disqualification from jury service, so long as the person's mind is not made up concerning the conditions at that facility. Searching the jury pool for the person who is likely to lean to one side or the other is a learned art among experienced trial counsel.[1] If you can collect enough sympathetic jurors, the case may settle during trial as the defense considers the facial and body language of the jurors, especially during witness cross-examination of the corporate executives of the nursing home chain.

1. Roger Rider & Ruben Krisztal, *Voir Dire, Opening Statement and Closing Argument: The Plaintiff's Perspective, in* Nursing Home Litigation: Pretrial Practice and Trials 311 (Ruben Krisztal ed., 2d ed. 2003).

Is the plaintiff vulnerable to a backlash? Bias and predisposition among the jurors against elders, against increasing the costs of the nursing home to Medicaid, and even against "greedy" plaintiffs' lawyers should be probed. The heirs of the decedent may be portrayed as avaricious offspring seeking to make a windfall from the tragic death of an indigent parent. The nursing home administrator may be portrayed as a cruel profiteer oblivious to gross suffering all around him or her. Neither portrait is likely to be correct, but the perceptions of the juror are "up for grabs" when the questionnaire responses from jurors are received and evaluated. A professional jury consultant may be very valuable to the defense's choice of strategies or settlement offers.

31:2 Presentations and Demonstrative Evidence

Expert witness testimony will be heard in many nursing home tort trials, as Chapter 22 explains. For example, expert witnesses will explain the plaintiff's view that the short staffing of a nursing home's late shift with too few CNA aides was a cause of the untimely death of a neglected plaintiff.[2] An experienced nurse could so testify as an expert.[3] The expert will bring a visual aid or set of photographic evidence. Its admissibility may be challenged. For example, photographs of the skin ulcer process and models of the skin showing the erosion that can occur would be useful illustrations. An accident reconstruction of a bathroom fall incident may be offered in evidence. Excellent service companies can provide these exhibits. A valuable descriptive primer on how the demonstrative evidence is best assembled and presented is available.[4]

Records will be introduced into evidence in most cases, including patient charts. State surveyors may already have examined the charts. The normal privacy protection for patient records under federal HIPAA

2. Sunbridge Healthcare Corp. v. Penny, 160 S.W.3d 230 (Tex. App. 2006).
3. Cornerstone Hosp. of S.E. Ariz. v. Marner, 231 Ariz. 67 (Ariz. Ct. App. 2012).
4. Stephen Applebaum et al., *The Preparation and Use of Demonstrative Evidence in Nursing Home Cases, in* NURSING HOME LITIGATION: PRETRIAL PRACTICE AND TRIALS, *supra* note 1, at 176.

does not act as a barrier to the access of nursing home patient files by the state. The purpose of the evidentiary privilege is to advance patient welfare, not to protect a predator.[5]

31:3 Decisions on Evidence

The plaintiff's expert witness testimony about conditions in the nursing home and the standard of due care may be absolutely central to the plaintiff's case.[6] Indeed, a major self-limiting concern for the plaintiff's lawyer is the cost of expert witness testimony to establish the breach of duty that is at the core of the negligence claims. Assembling the set of experts can cost $25,000 and up. This barrier limits the ability of contingent fee counsel to accept a case in which the negligence or assault did not cause death, and the damages are likely to be moderate relative to other physical problems of the plaintiff patient.

Testimony about the incidence of injuries in nursing homes and about the risks posed by actions of the staff create the perception with the jurors that something in the system was ultimately at fault in this incident. Jurors learn about the proper workings of a nursing home and why this facility was deficient. Faced with that basis for the negligence charge, the defense will try to knock out that witness, using the *Daubert criteria*[7] that are discussed in Chapter 22.

As with any trial, the party asking for jury instructions must have established a foundation in the evidence that supports the assumptions presented in the instruction, or it will not be given.[8]

31:4 Impeachment and Response

The jury will be shocked, perhaps horrified by the direct evidence of what happened inside the nursing home. Records compiled by

---

5. Oklahoma v. Thomason. 33 P.3d 930 (Okla. Civ. App. 2001).

6. *See, e.g.*, Sunbridge Healthcare Corp. v. Penny, 160 S.W.3d 230 (Tex. App. 2006) (expert testimony re adequacy of staffing).

7. Fed. R. Evid. 702, adopted following Daubert v. Merrell Dow Pharms., 509 U.S. 579 (1993).

8. May v. Triple C Convalescent Ctrs., 19 Wash. App. 794, 578 P.2d 541 (1978).

state "survey" inspectors will be admissible as routine governmental records.[9] The pathology, surgery, and hospital records about the injuries observed when the nursing home patient came to the hospital will be admissible. The defense will respond with its own experts, and with rebuttal testimony of the normalcy of the conditions inside the nursing home. The tone and sensitivity of the defense case must be carefully calibrated to the context, so that the jury is induced to treat both sides with true impartiality as the facts of the case unfold.

9. Montgomery Health Care Facility v. Ballard, 565 So. 2d 221 (Ala. 1999).

CHAPTER 32

Insurance

32:1 Coverage of Nursing Home Liability Cases
32:2 Settlement Authority at "Policy Limits"
32:3 Bad-Faith Litigation
32:4 Beneficial Role of Insurers

32:1 Coverage of Nursing Home Liability Cases

Liability insurance for nursing homes would seem to be a practical necessity when trends in the claims for falls, skin ulcers, or malnutrition arise. Most claims are settled and "only a very small percentage of these cases actually go to trial, verdict and final disposition."[1] Premiums for liability insurance have risen sharply for nursing homes in recent years; this has had a disciplining effect on the risk-avoidance practices of some chains and nursing home groups.[2] Disputes among insurers about coverage are not unusual.[3]

Which operating subsidiary of the nursing home chain had carried what type of insurance during what period? There may be disputes concerning whether malpractice coverage policies were in force and

1. Paul Hamlin, *Claims Management: From Report to Resolution*, Nursing Homes (July 2007).

2. Marshall Kapp, *Legal Anxieties and End of Life Care in Nursing Homes*, 19 Issues in Law & Med. 111, 130 (2003) ("liability insurance premiums exert a tremendous influence on provider perceptions and conduct, both because of the actual dollars involved and the symbolic importance attached to them").

3. *See, e.g.*, Progressive Preferred Ins. Co. v. Certain Underwriters at Lloyds, 2008 WL 2069404 (Ohio Ct. App. 5/28/2008).

could be invoked for injuries as of the specific time when an accident occurred, if that can be identified;[4] the general premises liability insurance carrier may disagree regarding which policy should pay for which type of negligence within the nursing home.[5]

Despite the apparent necessity for a nursing home to pay for this liability insurance, some chains have placed their individual-home corporate structures into thinly capitalized entities that "go bare" without liability insurance.[6] If a claimant wins a large damage award, the nursing home limited liability company simply declares bankruptcy,[7] and the claimant fails to collect.[8] Insurance carriers are wary of relying on caps legislation for all nursing home companies, since the absence of state licensing for one of the companies involved may leave that company vulnerable to uncapped damage awards.[9]

This pattern of corporate strategic behavior recognizes that nursing home malpractice "remains a difficult class of litigation," because these cases "can be explosive in the courtroom, and no jurisdiction is immune from them."[10] As discussed earlier, it is likely that factual disputes will linger and the cases will get past summary judgment, so a jury issue may pose real concerns to the insurance carrier, for example, in a death or serious injury case with some records alteration issues. Fear of the "runaway jury" like the Arkansas trial jury that awarded $63 million in punitive damages[11] led nursing homes to lobby heavily for caps and restrictions against recovery of damages by patients. Even then, state licensure lapses or omissions by one of the maze of subsidiary companies may have left that company exposed to uncapped risks of liabilities.[12]

---

4. La. Extended Care Ctrs. v. Miss. Ins. Guar. Ass'n, 87 So. 3d 1030 (Miss. 2012).
5. *See, e.g.*, U.S. Fire Ins. Co. v. Scottsdale Ins. Co., 264 S.W.3d 160 (Tex. App. 2009).
6. Sara Jurand, *Lack of Insurance Hinders Recovery in Nursing Home Cases*, 42 TRIAL 14 (2006).
7. Brashear v. Victoria Gardens, 302 S.W.3d 542 (Tex. App. 2009).
8. Charles Duhigg, *In Nursing Homes, More Profit, Less Care*, N.Y. TIMES, Sept. 23, 2007, at 1.
9. Casas v. Paradez, 267 S.W.3d 170 (Tex. App. 2008).
10. Paul Hamlin, *Claims Management: From Report to Resolution*, NURSING HOMES (July 2007).
11. Advocat Inc. v. Sauer, 353 Ark. 29, 111 S.W.3d 346 (2003).
12. Casas v. Paradez, 267 S.W.3d 170 (Tex. App. 2008).

Policy exclusions are sometimes litigated as coverage disputes under contract law. Staff assaults on patients may be covered by a liability policy.[13] A patient's assault on another nursing home patient did not merit exclusion from a liability policy that excluded physical or sexual abuse, since the assault was not done for or by employees of the insured home.[14] The individual policies for professional liability do not cover the cases in which the individual insured professional commits a sexual assault, as that is not a "professional service."[15] It is in the insurer's interest to negotiate on smaller claims but to decline the larger claims, so a reservation of rights letter may be the insurance carrier's response to the notice of claim.

Coverage terms are drafted by the insurance carrier, so they are later construed strictly against the carrier. For example, coverage in a liability policy for a "personal injury offense" included the liability of the nursing home for retaliating against a whistleblower.[16]

Finally, the issue of insurance coverage is further complicated by "eroding" or "wasting" policies. Such policies are written in such a way that the costs of defending the case are subtracted from the total liability coverage. In practice, such policies can be used by defense counsel to pressure plaintiffs into settling for less than adequate value because the longer the plaintiff litigates the case, the less insurance money there is to collect. A plaintiff is then placed in the awkward position of either persevering in the hopes of a settlement or judgment that includes funds from the nursing home's corporate coffers or walking away with whatever money remains from the policy.

32:2 Settlement Authority at "Policy Limits"

The insurer has a fixed dollar exposure to risk when the contract is written. If the facts of the case are bad, then there may be an interest

---

13. Limbaugh v. Coffee Med. Ctr., 59 S.W.3d 73 (Tenn. 2001).

14. Riley v. Maison Orleans II Inc. 829 So. 2d 479 (La. Ct. App. 2002). Also, note that in the event that a sexual assault was committed by an employee, coverage may be difficult to find because most insurance policies include exclusions for liability from intentional torts.

15. St. Paul Fire & Marine Ins. Co. v. Alderman, 455 S.E.2d 852 (Ga. Ct. App. 1995).

16. St. Paul Fire & Marine Ins. Co. v. Hausman, 604 N.W.2d 908 (Wis. Ct. App. 1999).

in settling for the policy limits,[17] while the nursing home and individual defendants might not wish them to be settled. The insurer whose policy covers a maximum amount for claims of negligent hiring and training, for example, is not required to pay any more in a resident sexual abuse claim.[18]

32:3 Bad-Faith Litigation

It is possible that a denial of coverage to a nursing home might give rise to litigation against the insurer or the excess coverage insurer, and these become complex contractual disputes.[19] The nursing home that is denied coverage will assert that it was properly covered by an applicable policy but the insurer failed to pay, in bad faith. These denials of coverage may be of such a sizeable amount that they are litigated.

32:4 Beneficial Role of Insurers

The nursing home insurer can be a great help to the residents of the nursing home by acting as an additional outside observer and as a source of improvement incentives for additional safety. The nursing home insurance firm's claims prevention role is overlooked, but the home gets the benefit of that insurer's past experience with flaws in other homes that have caused substantial losses to the insurance carrier. The learning from others' mistakes is crucial as the nursing home seeks to remain profitable; as an expert on nursing home law has written, "insurers are concerned enough about legal risks" that a review of practices and procedures is done, and "if a deficiency or possible future problem is found, the insurer works with the facility, either on a one-time basis or in a continuing collaboration, to correct the situation."[20] So the presence of a knowledgeable loss-prevention auditor may sharpen the performance of the nursing home staff, or at least result in expanded training and follow-up efforts.

---

17. *See, e.g.*, Westchester Fire Ins. Co. v. Admiral Ins. Co., 152 S.W.3d 172 (Tex. App. 2004).
18. Lexington Ins. Co. v. Educare Cmty. Living Corp., 149 F. App'x 326 (5th Cir. 2005).
19. *See, e.g.*, Westchester Fire Ins. Co. v. Admiral Ins. Co., 152 S.W.3d 172 (Tex. App. 2004).
20. Marshall Kapp, *Legal Anxieties and End of Life Care in Nursing Homes*, 19 ISSUES IN LAW & MED. 111, 125 (2003).

CHAPTER 33

Verdicts and Settlements

33:1 Overview
33:2 Settlement Influences
33:3 Effects of Settlement and Release
33:4 Verdicts Allocating Percentage Fault
33:5 Special Verdicts and Interrogatories
33:6 Verdicts against Individual Actors
33:7 Partial Settlements with Selected Defendants
33:8 Releases of Selected Defendants
33:9 Threats of Bankruptcy

33:1 Overview

The end point of the nursing home lawsuit traditionally was a verdict by a jury that awards a certain amount of damages to the plaintiff. Today's cases are far more likely to be settlements, with complex divisions among the multiple co-defendant parties and a confidentiality promise by the settling plaintiff. In some states, the damage awards come with prejudgment interest awards; in some states, attorney fees and costs are included as additional elements, over and above the damage awards. Caps may exist that reduce the potential recovery against those defendants who qualify for coverage of the caps,[1] but proponents of "tort reform" have often tailored the caps so that the jury

1. Casas v. Paradez, 267 S.W.3d 170 (Tex. App. 2008).

is not told of their existence, and the judge later reduces the amount of the final judgment to match the state cap.[2]

33:2 Settlement Influences

Why settle a nursing home abuse case? Death is final; putting closure on the litigation that arose from abuse prior to the patient's death, is an implicit psychological element of the family's desire to settle the case against a nursing home. "From the plaintiff's point of view," observed one veteran litigator, "most families are not in a position to roll the dice and will accept a reasonable settlement if promptly offered."[3]

One important influence on settlement is the state statutory cap on damages; another is the state court enforcement of admission contracts that contain arbitration clauses. The first puts a potential ceiling on recoveries against qualified entities[4] that makes the potential amount of the winning verdict unattractive (after liens are satisfied), while the former may cut off punitive damages and dramatically reduce the likely payout from a meritorious claim.[5]

Another influence point is fraudulent conduct by the nursing home managers and staff, to the detriment of the resident. The exposure of the fraudulent concealment creates an impression of misconduct that is likely to generate substantial jury interest; "if they weren't doing anything wrong, why would they need to conceal it?"

33:3 Effects of Settlement and Release

Settlement of a nursing home tort case may trigger repayment of a lien to Medicaid or Medicare; this "recoupment" is addressed in Chapter 34.

---

2. *See* JAMES O'REILLY, OHIO TORT REFORM LEGISLATION 2005 (Lexis/Bender 2005).
3. Allen Fuller, *Settlement Strategies, in* NURSING HOME LITIGATION: PRETRIAL PRACTICE AND TRIALS 88 (Ruben Krisztal ed., 2d ed. 2003).
4. Casas v. Paradez, 267 S.W.3d 170 (Tex. App. 2008) (if it is not a state-licensed facility, might not be eligible to claim protection of a cap statute).
5. Fuller, *supra* note 3, at 585.

Settlement and release with one individual defendant, such as a medical practice group's physician that had inadequately served the treatment needs of the patient, may leave the co-defendant nursing home with all of the exposure to tort liability. The effect will be to intensify the pressure to settle in a jury-attractive case.

33:4 Verdicts Allocating Percentage Fault

Sometimes the tort case ends with a jury verdict of $X and a jury allocation of that amount by percentage shares that are allocated to three or four entities, e.g., the medical director, the nursing home parent company, the subsidiary that provided the specific failed service, and so on. The persons who are employees of the home will typically be deemed to be part of its percent allocation of amounts due. The home is ultimately responsible. It is rare, but possible, that an incompetent elderly person could be allocated part of the legal obligation for negligence or for assault. But for obvious reasons, this is distasteful as an argument at trial by defense counsel for a profitable corporation that had lapses in the oversight of patients' behaviors.

33:5 Special Verdicts and Interrogatories

Counsel should consider asking the jury to allocate the percentage of fault among the companies responsible, in a manner that distributes most of the verdict to hit the parent company whose fiscal decisions made the most impact on a short-staffed facility. It is predictable that the defense will seek to build its case for appeal by asking jury interrogatories that may reveal inconsistency to be used as a basis for appellate review.

33:6 Verdicts against Individual Actors

Nursing home employees who act callously or carelessly against the resident are not likely to have substantial personal assets with which to satisfy a judgment. It may be better to rely on respondeat superior theories of recovery under which the nursing home parent corporation will pay for the lack of training, lack of supervision, or lack of personal care time that the budget for this nursing home had produced.

33:7 Partial Settlements with Selected Defendants

The use of a "Mary Carter" agreement to settle litigation early, with payments allocated between plaintiff and one defendant party, occurs in some multidefendant cases. They are economic bargains for the less culpable co-defendant, and they are controversial. The agreement is an undisclosed side agreement of prospective settlement terms between the plaintiff and one of the several defendants. The defendant will be paying a fixed amount; the plaintiff agrees that it will not demand to collect more, even if the jury awards a larger amount. So a physician who is a medical director may be a co-defendant with the nursing home; for a commitment to pay the plaintiff a certain amount, the plaintiff agrees not to enforce whatever judgment the jury may allocate to the percentage of responsibility borne by the settling defendant. The jury sees all the defendants and can allocate percentages of its verdict for the parties deemed to be most accountable for the misconduct.

33:8 Releases of Selected Defendants

Potentially, some defendants (and their insurers) may wish to avoid standing trial more than others, especially if a co-defendant's bad conduct may potentially enflame a jury against all of the defendants. For example, the malpractice insurance carrier for the attending physician may to want to save itself from the vagaries of a malpractice trial by negotiating an early settlement with release of the physician's liability. Such a release is less likely for the physician who was an employee of the nursing home as its medical director. There may also be contract nursing employees and contractor therapists or dieticians who are partially responsible for the failings that harmed the plaintiff. Their insurance carriers will also be seeking to avoid the jury through an early settlement.

Likewise, the opposite can sometimes be true: one defendant holds out, preventing a global resolution of all claims. Absent a global resolution, plaintiff's counsel may not wish to settle the case with other defendants due to the possibility of the jury seeing an incomplete story or the trial defendant pointing fingers at a co-defendant. Doctors can often cause such an issue because settlement of a malpractice claim against a physician generally requires the physician's personal consent. While a nursing home may wish to resolve a case early due to the potential expense and liability down the road, a doctor may not wish to settle the case due to its effect on her or his name and professional credibility.

33:9 Threats of Bankruptcy

A 2007 *New York Times* investigative reporting article exposed the recent tactic of having shell companies with few assets be the licensee of the nursing home, sometimes without liability insurance, so that the company can readily go bankrupt if a jury awards large damages for its misconduct.[6] An attitude that inspires such corporate gamesmanship is likely to pervade the other decisions about actual care for patients.

Counsel for the injured plaintiff should include in the pleadings as many related corporations as may have been involved, and should include "John Doe Corporations" in order to prepare for discovery of the network within which money flowed and care choices were actually made. This complicates the taking of an official corporate representative's deposition under Rule 30(b)(6), as there may be multiple shells over one peanut in the game.

---

6. Charles Duhigg, *In Nursing Homes, More Profit, Less Care*, N.Y. Times, Sept. 23, 2007, at 1.

CHAPTER 34

After-Verdict Liens and Offsets

34:1 Subrogation and the Effect of Repayment of Liens
34:2 Specific Steps for the Prudent Plaintiff's Counsel
34:3 Informing the Client Early
34:4 Continued Eligibility
34:5 Payment of Private Insurer Liens

34:1 Subrogation and the Effect of Repayment of Liens

"Subrogation" is an alien, strange word to the average plaintiff. It may sound odd, and will certainly sound troubling to the prospective client, when counsel advises the would-be plaintiff that he or she may win, but then may collect a far smaller amount of net damages than the amount of the jury verdict. The size of the jury award will be celebrated with joy as a vindication of the patient, a size that "sends a message" to other bad actors. One person's "lesson" is seen by another person as a "random windfall by a runaway jury." But the award then would be reduced in net amount, as plaintiff may have to pay a large portion of that money back to Medicaid, which has a statutory lien that is to be satisfied from the award.

The lien recovering benefit payments exists under federal law[1] because Medicaid had routinely paid the defendant corporation that had provided the nursing home services.[2] Because Medicaid eligibil-

1. 42 U.S.C. § 1396p.
2. Benjamin Glass, *The Medicare "Super Lien," in* Nursing Home Litigation: Pretrial Practice and Trials 567 (Ruben Krisztal ed., 2d ed. 2003).

ity had been premised on lack of financial resources of the patient, any windfall in the form of a tort award triggers a duty to repay the Medicaid pool of funds.

This is a sobering and very real message delivered at the point of the client's anger and hope for a big damages award. Some clients will hear this erroneously as, "If we win the money from the nursing home, we then have to pay it back to the nursing home." Liens are held by, and satisfied by payments to, the state Medicaid (or in some cases, Medicare) authorities. The money derived from collecting subrogation payments from tort verdicts goes into the pool from which future groups of injured patients will benefit.

The concept of a legally enforceable lien on the proceeds of the tort action is completely logical and defensible; the duty of the indigent Medicaid recipient to repay public funds spent on his or her behalf is statutory and is quite foreseeable. But this legally sound outcome is no less difficult for the lay person to accept. The state government's Medicaid program, and the federal government for those patients with Medicare, has funded the treatment of the person who has a need for nursing home care, as of the time she or he sustained this injury at the nursing home. Congress wants to get the expended funds back so the dollars can be spent on others, and the statute so provides.[3] Changes to the reporting and repayment provisions of the law have been quite complex.[4] However, institution of the Medicare Secondary Payer Recovery Portal has eased the attorney's role in resolving Medicare subrogation interests.[5]

The treatment of that nursing home resident's injury, and the reimbursement of costs of treatment out of the jury's award of compensation, poses a quandary. The survivors or representatives of the

---

3. 42 U.S.C. § 1395y(b), 42 C.F.R. § 411.20, Pub. L. No. 112-242 (2013).

4. Counsel for plaintiffs should be aware that amounts paid to Medicaid and Medicare beneficiaries will become known to federal agencies. Insurers and other Responsible Reporting Entities (RREs) are affected by the Medicare Secondary Payer (MSP) reporting that had been mandated by section 111 of the Medicare, Medicaid and SCHIP Extension Act (MMSEA) of 2007 (Pub. L. No. 110-173).

5. *Medicare Secondary Payer Recovery Portal*, CTRS. FOR MEDICARE & MEDICAID SERVS., https://www.cob.cms.hhs.gov/MSPRP/ (last visited Dec. 17, 2024).

individual who wins a verdict or settlement will have to pay back to the government a portion or all of the amounts that Medicare and Medicaid paid to the nursing home.[6] Delaying the payment of those funds to the government does not make the debt go away. Overlooking subrogation debt is never a sound strategy. The plaintiff's counsel has three reasons to explain subrogation up front: first, it is the right thing to do; second, it avoids belated ethics grievance claims to the Bar; and third, any money paid to an attorney from a verdict or settlement that represents the government's payment for health care for that patient/plaintiff, can be collected by the government from the attorney's funds, if the recipient of the windfall proceeds of the award has not paid and the lien has not been satisfied.[7]

The policies and rules of the Medicare and Medicaid system are exceedingly difficult for lay people to understand, and difficult for most lawyers to fully understand. There is ample room for legal malpractice, if the lawyer counseling the client about possible large dollar recoveries is not well prepared on the subject and glibly gives a vision of the large windfall without mentioning the lien. Bad feelings, grievances, and malpractice claims tend to follow these surprises. Reducing the surprise up front requires an expertise that many litigators will not have at the outset of the nursing home patient's case.[8] That is because a focus on case intake and a sense of a potential big dollar verdict may distract the attorney from giving early notice of the existence of a Medicaid subrogation lien.

In this specialized field of subrogation, the lawyer representing the plaintiff should gather information about prior payments from Medicaid and Medicare on the patient's behalf. As Medicaid paid $75,000 for the year of nursing home residence for the indigent elder, and Medicare paid $25,000 for hospital and surgical responses to the accidental injury, there is an overhanging amount that would need to be paid back out of the settlement or jury verdict. Perhaps the most prudent course of action would be to obtain an opinion from a "special needs" lawyer

---

6. 42 C.F.R. § 411.26.
7. 42 C.F.R. § 411.24(g).
8. Norma Schmidt, *King Kong Contingent*, 68 U. Pitt. L. Rev. 467 (2006).

familiar with these kinds of third-party subrogation cases, who can advise the lawyer, and through the lawyer advise the guardian of the elder, about these limitations and restrictions. If $150,000 is received in settlement, the money should go into the attorney trust account.

Getting the "Medicare release" letter before disbursing the proceeds from the lawyer's trust account is the ideal way to be protected, but holding cash for months will frustrate the client who perceived that she or he had "won big" against the nursing home. For this highly specialized work, the litigator should consider retaining a specialist in Medicare trust issues.

The private insurer's claims of contractual rights of subrogation are more complex as parts of a private group health insurance or group long-term care contract, typically a private contract between the carrier writing the insurance policy and the employer or group owner for the group policy. The private insurer has undoubtedly written a very strong subrogation clause, which allows that company to get its money back from a tort compensation verdict, when it has expended funds for nursing home service, and a jury determines that the service was negligently provided and awards damages against the nursing home.

Counsel who advise the client regarding the potential recoupment of these expenditures should be very careful to engage an experienced professional advisor when drafting a notice to the insurance carrier. The insurance carrier, in turn, will be very careful in writing its notification to your client regarding its expectations for reimbursement. This also may entail a delay in disbursement from the trust account, so the client should be forewarned.

Reform proposals include suggestions that the Medicaid eligibility not be lost where the award of damages to the patient comes as a result of suits challenging abuse of the patient.[9]

Examples from the case law include a 2007 Ohio case in which the Medicaid entity intervened as a party to protect its right to recover

9. *See, e.g.*, N.Y. PUB. HEALTH L. 2801-d(5); Kevin Dreher, *Enforcement of Standards of Care in the Long Term Care Industry*, 10 ELDER L.J. 119, 148 (2002).

costs, where the nursing home patient's survivors sued for wrongful death of the resident.[10]

34:2 Specific Steps for the Prudent Plaintiff's Counsel

Counsel should ask in the initial interview whether the prospective plaintiff is a Medicare beneficiary, and if so, the claim should be reported to Medicare at the outset of representation. It takes time to resolve the Medicare reimbursement claim if the case is settled or a jury verdict is obtained. Counsel who reports the claim should immediately request a conditional payment letter in which Medicare will itemize the charges for which it seeks reimbursement. Counsel should review the conditional payment letter for accuracy. One should look for "related" charges, those that were paid as a result of the injuries addressed in the claim. If some charges were not related, counsel should ask Medicare to remove these charges from the claim. Once the settlement or verdict is reached, counsel should contact Medicare and request a final itemization of the lien amount.[11]

34:3 Informing the Client Early

Particular consideration should be given to calculating the actual remainder amount that will be left for the plaintiff, after the Medicaid or Medicare liens are paid off. Experienced lawyers know that any surprise to the client can have a dark side; grievances, more suits, and ethics charges tend to complicate life very severely. Do *not* surprise the client by postponing the discussion of liens; the client's role as heir to the estate may cloud his or her later judgment. Discuss the probabilities based on current data, but be certain that a letter or minutes of a meeting is sent to the client that recaps the discussion about the liens and cautions that an approximate amount will have to be paid out of any settlement or verdict.

---

10. Barnes v. Andover Vill. Ret. Cmty., 2007 WL 2296459 (Ohio Ct. App. 2007).
11. Staci Yandle, *Protect the Innocent: Establish Elopement Liability*, 49 TRIAL 36 (Mar. 2013).

34:4 Continued Eligibility

The verdict favoring a living nursing home resident that exceeds the lien for that resident's costs may be counted by state Medicaid eligibility screeners as being an asset, the receipt of which could trigger a recalculation of indigent status and a loss of coverage by Medicaid.[12] But losing Medicaid would be a blow to the family of the institutional resident; they now must pay full costs of continuing care from the proceeds of the one-time net cash of the settlement. Interpersonal family conflict situations abound. For the heirs of those patients whose death from abuse is being litigated and then compensated, the lengthy delays in bringing closure to the case of a deceased relative's past abuse (while the estate awaits a Medicaid release following the estate's payment) will seem intolerably long.

To assure that the living Medicaid recipient does not lose government benefits upon receipt of the net settlement, prudent counsel will engage separate counsel for a "structured settlement" arrangement. The trust created by the plaintiff for the benefit of the elder must comply with complex rules in order to maintain the desired Medicaid eligibility. Get experienced advisors early and follow their expert advice.

34:5 Payment of Private Insurer Liens

Just because Medicaid has not paid for the elder's care does not mean that subrogation issues are removed. Tens of thousands of private health insurance contracts exist that provide for some "claw back" by the long-term care insurance carrier, taking back to the insurance firm a portion of the money that was received by an insured patient, as damages paid from the entity that was responsible for the injury. This recovery has been quite controversial when employer-paid health insurance is involved in later tort recovery situations.[13] This form of

12. Structuring the award in a settlement by use of a special needs trust attorney is highly recommended.

13. *See, e.g.*, Perreira v. Rediger, 778 A.2d 429, 437 (N.J. 2001).

subrogation recovery, as with the Medicaid eligibility trust, requires experienced financial and legal advisors. The topic of repayment, when and if a verdict is reached, should be addressed with the family by the prospective counsel early in the planning of the lawsuit, in writing, and should be documented in the files.

Table of Cases

A

Abrahams v. King St. Nursing Home, Inc., 245 A.D.2d 251 (App. Civ. 2d Dep't 1997), 136 n.28

Adams v. Ashtabula Cnty. Nursing Home, No. 99-CV-193 (Ashtabula Cnty. Ohio Com. Pl. June 15, 1999), 134 n.12

Adam v. Sisters of Bon Secours Nursing Care Ctr., No. 292144, 2011 WL 3903146 (Mich. Ct. App. Sept. 6, 2011), *appeal denied*, 810 N.W.2d 572 (Mich. 2012), 201 n.87

Advocat Inc. v. Sauer, 111 S.W.3d 346 (Ark. 2003), *cert. denied*, 540 U.S. 1012 (2003), 298 n.12, 346 n.36, 372 n.14, 378 n.11

Afamefune v. Suburban Hosp., Inc., 385 Md. 677 (2005), 167 n.158

Alcoy v. Valley Nursing Homes, 630 S.E.2d 301 (Va. 2006), 165 n.145, 166 n.155

Anderson v. Minneapolis, St. P. & S. S. M. Ry. Co., 179 N.W. 45 (1920), 339 n.14, 353 n.16

Anonymous v. Anonymous (L.A. Super. Ct. June 30, 1997), 212 n.33

Asbury Ctr. v. U.S. Dep't of HHS, 77 F. App'x 853 (6th Cir. 2003), 37 n.7, 70 n.8, 111 n.72

Ashcroft v. Iqbal, 556 U.S. 662 (2009), 350–351

Associated Health Sys. v. Jones, 366 S.E.2d 147 (Ga. Ct. App. 1988), 134 n.5, 137 n.34, 158 n.92, 169 n.169

AT&T Mobility LLC v. Concepcion, 131 S. Ct. 1740 (2011), 360 n.9

B

Bailey v. Rose Care Ctr., 817 S.W.2d 412 (Ark. 1991), 129 n.60

Ballard v. Plantation Mgmt. Co., LLC, 2012 WL 992097 (La. Ct. App. 1st Cir. Mar. 23, 2012), 103 n.30

Barbourville Nursing Home v. U.S. Dep't of HHS, 174 F. App'x 932 (6th Cir. 2006), 81 n.38

Barnes v. Andover Vill. Ret. Cmty., 2007 WL 2296459 (Ohio Ct. App. Aug. 10, 2007), 368 n.45, 391 n.10
Barn Hill Care Ctr. v. CMS, Dec. No. 1848 (HHS Departmental Appeals Bd., App. Div., Sept. 24, 2002), 198–199
Barr v. HCF, 2005 WL 3031723, 2005-Ohio-6040 (Ohio Ct. App. Nov. 14, 2005), 368 n.45
Barton v. United States, 2008 WL 872304 (S.D. Miss. Mar. 27, 2008), 313 n.9
Batavia Nursing & Convalescent Ctr. v. Thompson, 129 F. App'x 181 (6th Cir. 2005), 38 n.14
Bebe Med. Ctr. v. Bailey, 913 A.2d 543 (Del. 2006), 120 n.8
Beech Aircraft Co. v. Rainey, 488 U.S. 153 (1988), 292 n.15
Begandy v. Richardson, 134 Misc. 2d 357, 510 N.Y.S.2d 984 (N.Y. Super. 1987), 127 n.49
Bell Atlantic Corp. v. Twombly, 550 U.S. 544 (2007), 350–351
Bentley v. Abbey Nursing Home Inc., 1983 Ohio App. LEXIS 12777 (Ohio Ct. App. 1983), 372 n.13
Benun v. Super. Ct., 20 Cal. Rptr. 3d 26 (Cal. Ct. App. 2d Dist. 2004), 201 n.89
Beverly Enters.-Fla. Inc. v. Spilman, 661 So. 2d 867 (Fla. Dist. Ct. App. 1995), 218 n.68, 344 n.34
Bezark v. Kostner Manor, 172 N.E.2d 424 (Ill. App. Ct. 1961), 142 n.19, 155 n.65, 157 n.87, 158 n.89
Blankfeld v. Richmond Health Care Inc., 902 So. 2d 296 (Fla. Dist. Ct. App. 2005), 367 n.42
Blum v. Sunrise Cmty. Inc., No. 02-10806 CA23 (Miami-Dade Cnty. Fla. Jud. Cir. Ct. 2003), 162 n.120
BMW of N. Am., Inc. v. Gore, 517 U.S. 559 (1996), 177 n.225, 343
Boatwright v. Healthcare Ctr., No. CV-00-1193 (Pulaski Cnty. Ark. Cir. Ct. 2001), 93 n.90
Booty v. Kentwood Manor Nursing Home, 483 So. 2d 634 (La. Ct. App. 1986), 106 n.43, 120 n.10, 121 n.18, 123 n.33
Boston v. 2510 Eagle Inc., No. 97-333 (Leon Cnty. Fla. Cir. Ct. 1999), 85 n.60, 93 n.88
Boudreaux v. Pettaway, 108 So. 3d 486 (Ala. 2012), 341 n.7, 344 n.22

Brashear v. Victoria Gardens, 302 S.W.3d 542 (Tex. App. 2009), 378 n.7

Braud v. Woodland Vill. L.L.C., 54 So. 3d 745 (La. Ct. App. 4th Cir. 2010), *writ denied*, 60 So. 3d 1254 (La. 2011), 202 n.93

Bremenkamp v. Beverly Enters.-Kan., 762 F. Supp. 884 (D. Kan. 1991), 104 n.33, 109 n.61, 111 n.70, 116 n.82

Briarcliff Nursing Home, Inc. v. Turcotte, 894 So. 2d 661 (Ala. 2004), 365 n.33

Briarwood Nursing Ctr. v. CMS, Dec. No. 2115 (HHS Departmental Appeals Bd., App. Div., Sept. 17, 2007), 130 n.64

Brightview Ctr. v. CMS, Dec. No. 2132 (HHS Departmental Appeals Bd., App. Div., Nov. 21, 2007), 130 n.63

Brogdon *ex rel.* Cline v. Nat'l Healthcare Corp., 103 F. Supp. 2d 1322 (N.D. Ga. 2000), 164 n.140, 317 n.29

Brown v. Sun Healthcare Group Inc., 476 F. Supp. 2d 848 (E.D. Tenn. 2007), 164 n.140, 335 n.111, 371 n.6

Brown v. Tift Cnty. Hosp. Auth., 635 S.E.2d 184 (Ga. Ct. App. 2006), 107 n.49, 107 n.51, 110 n.68

Buracynski v. Eyring, 919 S.W.2d 314 (Tenn. 1996), 367 n.38

Burditt v. U.S. Dep't of HHS, 934 F.2d 1362 (5th Cir. 1991), 235 n.11, 330 n.79

Burns v. Metz, 513 N.W.2d 505 (Neb. 1994), 76 n.24, 313 n.10

Busta v. Columbus Hosp. Corp., 916 P.2d 122 (Mont. 1996), 312 n.4, 354 n.17

C

Cal. Ass'n of Health Facilities v. Dep't of Health Servs., 16 Cal. 4th 284, 940 P.2d 323 (1997), 246 n.7

Cannon v. McKendree Vill., Inc., 295 S.W.3d 278 (Tenn. Ct. App. 2008), 107 n.47

Carrasco v. Healthcare & Ret. Corp., No. 02-L-7024 (Cook Cnty. Ill. Cir. Ct. Aug. 11, 2006), 218 n.71

Carter v. SSC Odin Operating Co., 976 N.E.2d 344 (Ill. 2012), 363 n.24

Carter v. Takoda Trails, Case No. C-230329, 2024 Ohio 911 (Ct. App. Mar. 13, 2024), 368 n.46

Caruso v. Pine Manor Nursing Ctr., 538 N.E.2d 722 (Ill. App. Ct. 1989), 219 n.77

Casas v. Paradez, 267 S.W.3d 170 (Tex. App. 2008), 161 n.115, 378 n.9, 378 n.12, 381 n.1, 382 n.4

Caton Ridge Nursing Home v. Califano, 596 F.2d 608 (3d Cir. 1978), 330 n.82

Celotex Corp. v. Catrett, 477 U.S. 317 (1986), 351–352

Centerclair Inc. v. CMS, Dec. No. CR-1747 (HHS Departmental Appeals Bd., Civ. Remedies Div., Mar. 10, 2008), 157 n.86

Christian Care Ctrs., Inc. v. Golenko, 328 S.W.3d 637 (Tex. App.–Dallas 2010), 169 n.169

Coastal Health Servs. Inc. v. Rozier, 335 S.E.2d 712 (Ga. Ct. App. 1985), 165 n.146, 179 n.237

Cockerham v. Lassalle Nursing Home Inc., 930 So. 2d 239 (La. Ct. App. 2006), 215 n.51

Collier v. AMI Inc., 254 So. 2d 170 (La. Ct. App. 1971), 162 n.119

Collins v. Beverly Enters.-Fla., No. 98-433-CA (Taylor Cnty. Fla. Cir. Ct. 2000), 173 n.197

Colwell v. Baker, CV697-1103C (Cape Girardeau Cnty. Mo. Cir. Ct. 1998), 134 n.13

Conley v. Life Care Ctrs. of Am., 236 S.W.3d 713 (2007), 160 n.104, 166 n.150, 321 n.38, 324 n.61, 371 n.8

In re Conservatorship of Gregory, 95 Cal. Rptr. 336 (Cal. Ct. App. 2000), 157 n.85

Convalescent Servs. Inc. v. Schultz, 921 S.W.2d 731 (Tex. App. 1996), 90 n.74, 344 n.32

Corley v. Rosewood Care Ctr., 142 F.3d 1041 (11th Cir. 1998), 331 n.89, 335 n.109

Cornerstone Hosp. of S.E. Ariz. v. Marner, 231 Ariz. 67 (Ariz. Ct. App. 2012), 36 n.2, 374 n.3

Covenant Care v. Super. Ct., 86 P.3d 290 (Cal. 2004), 166 n.156, 177 n.226, 344 n.34

Cox Ret. Props. Inc. v. Johnson, 323 F. App'x 668 (10th Cir. 2009), 45 n.9, 49 n.17

Crawford v. Care Concepts Inc., 625 N.W.2d 876 (Wis. 2001), 179 n.241, 299 n.17
Crestview Parke Care Ctr. v. Thompson, 373 F.3d 743 (2004), 246 n.8
Crockett v. Medicalodges Inc., 799 P.2d 1022 (Kan. 1990), 242 n.21, 321 n.44
Cross Creek Health Care Ctr. v. Health Care Fin. Admin., Dec. No. 1665 (HHS Departmental Appeals Bd., App. Div., July 14, 1998), 137 n.31
Crowne Invs. Inc. v. Reid, 740 So. 2d 400 (Ala. 1999), 214 n.41
Czehowski v. Avery Manor, 2004 WL 5294390 (Mass. Super. Sept. 17, 2004), 95, 108 n.55

D

Daniels v. Twin Oaks Nursing Home, 692 F.2d 1321 (11th Cir. 1983), 120 n.12, 122 n.22, 129 n.57
Daubert v. Merrell-Dow Labs., 509 U.S. 579 (1993), 285 n.11, 352, 353, 371 n.9, 375, 375 n.7
Daughters of Miriam Ctr. v. CMS, Dec. No. CR1357 (HHS Departmental Appeals Bd., Civ. Remedies Div., Sept. 29, 2005), 202
Davis v. Pruitt Corp., 2006 WL 2641137 (Ga. Trial Ct. 2006), 279 n.2
Deerings W. Nursing Ctr. v. Scott, 787 S.W.2d 494 (Tex. App. 1990), 164 n.141, 174 n.204, 175 n.211, 176 n.217
Delaplane v. Beverly, No. 02-CI-01119 (Franklin Cnty. Cir. Ct. Ky. 2006), 250 n.28
Denton v. Super. Ct., 945 P.2d 1283 (Ariz. 1997), 321 n.40
D'Esposito *ex rel.* D'Esposito v. Haym Salomon Home for the Aged, 886 N.Y.S.2d 66 (N.Y. Sup. Ct. 2009), 198 n.65
Devers v. Huntsville Health Servs., 2300 Jud. Cir. Ct. (Huntsville, Ala., June 28, 2002), 229 n.19
Dickhoff v. Green, ___ N.W.2d ___, 2013 WL 2363550 (Minn. Sept. 19, 2013), 322
Diggs v. Susquehanna Ctr., No. 944S1996, 1996 WL 1044797 (Pa. Com. Pl. Dec. 9, 1996), 216 n.54

Diversicare Gen. Partner, Inc. v. Rubio, 185 S.W.3d 842 (Tex. 2005), 165 n.142, 167 n.159, 172, 242 n.20, 325
Doe v. Advisors Healthcare Inc., No. X01CV020170300S, 2005 Conn. Super. LEXIS 1036 (Conn. Super. Ct. Mar. 24, 2005), 160 n.102, 165 n.147, 323 n.54
Doe v. Roe Skilled Nursing Facility, Confidential Docket No. (Orange Cnty. Super. Ct. Cal. July 6, 2012), 102 n.28, 103 n.29
Doe v. Westfall Health Care Ctr., 755 N.Y.S.2d 769 (N.Y. App. Div. 2002), 158 n.93, 163 n.132
Domoroski v. Smithtown Ctr. for Rehab. & Nursing Care, 95 A.D.3d 1165, 945 N.Y.S.2d 345 (N.Y. App. Div. 2d Dep't 2012), 109 n.60
Dove v. Ty Cobb Healthcare Sys., Inc., 699 S.E.2d 355 (Ga. Ct. App. 2010), 203 n.103
Drucker v. Goscar Inc., 184 Neb. 475, 168 N.W.2d 534 (1969), 111 n.71
Dunson v. Blue Ridge Nursing Homes, No. 01A85157-1 (DeKalb Cnty. Ga. Cir. Ct. 2003), 85 n.61, 92 n.85
Dupree v. Plantation Pointe L.P., 892 So. 2d 228 (Miss. 2004), 163 n.129, 171 n.184, 334 n.105, 372 n.10
Dusine v. Golden Shores Convalescent Ctr., 249 So. 2d 40 (Fla. Dist. Ct. App. 1971), 101 n.27, 135 n.22

E

Eichenbaum v. First United Lemberger Ladies Chair, 186 N.Y.S.2d 498 (N.Y. Sup. Ct. 1959), 121 n.19
Elashker v. Med. Liab. Mut. Ins. Co., 847 N.Y.S.2d 268 (N.Y. App. Div. 3d Dep't 2007), 271 n.6, 275 n.23
Emerald Oaks v. Agency for Health Care Admin., 774 So. 2d 737 (Fla. Dist. Ct. App. 2000), 82 n.43, 155 n.72
In re Emerald Shores Health & Rehab. Ctr. v. CMS, Dec. No. CR1385, 229 n.17
Entrekin v. Internal Med. Assoc. of Dothan, P.A., 689 F.3d 1248 (11th Cir. 2012), 365 n.31
In re Epsom Healthcare Ctr., Dec. No. CR1749 (HHS Departmental Appeals Bd. 2008), 105 n.36
Estate of French v. Stratford House, 333 S.W.3d 546 (Tenn. 2011), 238 n.3

Estate of Hary v. Horizon/CMS Healthcare Corp., No. JVR-212802, 1997 WL 831687 (Tarrant Cnty. Tex. Dist. Ct. Nov. 1997), 212 n.27
Estate of Hazleton v. Cain, 950 So. 2d 231 (Miss. Ct. App. 2007), 312 n.1
Estate of West v. Vari-Care Inc., No. CV 91-0617, 1993 WL 631314 (Baldwin Cnty., Ala. Cir. Ct. Nov. 1993), 210 n.18
Est. of Sharp v. Omnicare, Inc., 879 So. 2d 34 (Fla. 5th Dist. App. 2004), 196 n.52
Evergreene Nursing Care Ctr. v. CMS, Dec. No. C-05-386 (HHS Departmental Appeals Bd., Civ. Remedies Div., Aug. 18, 2005), 137 n.35

F

Fal-Meridian, Inc. v. U.S. Dep't of HHS, 604 F.3d 445 (7th Cir. 2010), 320 n.37
Fields v. Senior Citizens Ctr., 528 S.E.2d 573 (La. Ct. App. 1988), 122 n.28
Fine v. Woodside Manor Nursing & Convalescent Home, 830469, 1984 WL 6860 (Ohio Ct. App. 1st Dist. Apr. 18, 1984), 201 n.87
Fink v. Commonwealth (Roanoke Cnty., Va. Cir. Ct. 2005), 169 n.170
First Healthcare Corp. v. Hamilton, 740 So. 2d 1189 (Fla. Dist. Ct. App. 1999), 120 n.5, 128 n.51, 344 n.30
Five Points Health Care Ltd. v. Alberts, 867 So. 2d 520 (Fla. 1st Dist. Ct. App. 2004), 367 n.43
Fleming v. Prince Georges Cnty., 358 A.2d 892 (1976), 195 n.47
Flemming v. Barnwell Nursing Home & Health Facilities, Inc., 15 N.Y.3d 375, 938 N.E.2d 937 (2010), 238 n.2
Fletcher v. Huntington Place Ltd. P'ship, 952 So. 2d 1225 (Fla. 5th Dist. Ct. App. 2007), 365 n.34
Formella v. Ciba-Geigy Corp., 300 N.W.2d 356 (Mich. Ct. App. 1980), 195 n.47
Forum Group at Moran Lake Nursing & Rehab. Ctr., LLC v. Terhune, 733 S.E.2d 808 (Ga. Ct. App. 2012), 109 n.57, 117 n.90
Frakes v. Cardiology Consultants, P.C., 1997 WL 536949 (Tenn. Ct. App. Aug. 29, 1997), 318 n.30

Francis v. Lafon Nursing Home, 840 So. 2d 1281 (La. Ct. App. 2003), 155 n.64, 312 n.3

Franklin Care Ctr. v. CMS, Dec. No. CR1694 (HHS Departmental Appeals Bd., Civ. Remedies Div., Nov. 20, 2007), 168 n.161, 176 n.219

Franklin v. Collins Chapel Connectional Hosp., 696 S.W.2d 16 (Tenn. Ct. App. 1985), 91 n.76, 122 n.21

Franks v. Bowers, No. SC11-1258 (Fla. Sp. Ct. June 20, 2013), 364 n.30

Frye v. United States, 293 F. 1013 (D.C. Cir. 1923), 352, 352 n.12, 353

G

Galen v. Roberts, 525 U.S. 249 (1999), 235 n.11

Garcia v. Seneca Nursing Home, 2011 Ill. App. (1st) 103085, 956 N.E.2d 1005, 353 Ill. Dec. 877 (2011), 114 n.80

Gentry v. Beverly Enters.-Ga., Inc., 714 F. Supp. 2d 1225 (S.D. Ga. 2009), 367 n.41

George Beauvais v. Conn. Subacute Corp. of Waterbury, 2000 WL 1657845 (Conn. Super. Ct. Sept. 19, 2000), 128 n.55

Geters v. Eagle Ins. Co., 834 S.W.2d 49 (Tex. 1992), 347 n.41

Giandana v. Providence Rest Nursing Home, 815 N.Y.S.2d 526 (App. Div. 2006), 109 n.58

Gilmer v. Interstate/Johnson Lane Corp., 500 U.S. 20 (1991), 360 n.10

Goda v. White Cliff Leasing P'ship, No. 2002-917, 2003 WL 22841695 (Pa. Com. Pl. May 21, 2003), 219 n.75

Golden Villa Nursing Home v. Smith, 674 S.W.2d 343 (Tex. App. 1984), 122 n.24

Golden v. Sunrise Assisted Living Mgmt., No. 01-L-012539 (Cook Cnty. Ill. Cir. Ct. July 21, 2005), 206 n.6, 219 n.72

Goliger v. AMS Props., Inc., 19 Cal. Rptr. 3d 819 (Cal. Ct. App. 2d Dist. 2004), 367 n.40

Goodyear v. Care Concepts, 625 N.W.2d 876 (Wis. 2001), 299 n.15

Grace Plaza of Great Neck Inc. v. Elbaum, 588 N.Y.S.2d 853 (App. Div. 1992), *aff'd*, 623 N.E.2d 513 (N.Y. 1993), 51 n.22, 213 n.36

Greenbriar Nursing & Rehab. Ctr. v. U.S. HHS, 686 F.2d 521 (8th Cir. 2012), 198 n.65

Guardianship/Conservatorship of Denton, 190 Ariz. 152, 945 P.2d 1283 (1997), 341 n.9

Guernsey v. Country Living Pers. Care Home, No. 3:CV-04-0423, 2006 U.S. Dist. LEXIS 31450 (M.D. Pa. May 19, 2006), 155 n.66, 164 n.135, 169 n.172, 171 n.188, 177 n.226, 340 n.2

Guffey v. Integrated Health Servs., 1 S.W.3d 509 (Mo. Ct. App. 1999), 122 n.21

Gunn v. Hi-C-Home, 260 Or. 404, 490 P.2d 999 (1971), 111 n.70

H

Hall v. Alden Wentworth Rehab. Ctr. (Cook Cnty. Ill. Cir. Ct. 2007), 93 n.92

Hansen v. State, 928 N.E.2d 653 (Ind. Ct. App. 2010), 57 n.14

Harmony Court v. Leavitt, 188 F. App'x 438 (6th Cir. 2006), 40 n.18, 73 n.10, 84 n.53, 159 n.98

Harris v. Extendicare Homes, Inc., 829 F. Supp. 2d 1023 (W.D. Wash. 2011), 272 n.8

Hayes v. Oakridge Home, No. 89400, 2008 WL 525411 (Ohio Ct. App. Feb. 28, 2008), 367 n.36

Hayward v. Jack's Pharmacy Inc., 115 P.3d 713 (Idaho 2005), 57 n.11, 195 n.45, 198 n.68, 200 n.77, 317 n.29

HCRA of Tex. Inc. v. Johnston, 178 S.W.3d 861 (Tex. App. 2005), 89 n.71, 216 n.62

Healthcare Ctrs. of Tex. v. Rigby, 97 S.W.3d 610 (Tex. App. 2002), 163 n.131

Health & Hospital Corp. v. Talevski, 143 S. Ct. 1444 (2023), 179–180

Hendrix v. Maison Orleans I, L.L.C., 101 So. 3d 1013 (La. App. 4 Cir. 2012), 38 n.15, 325 n.65, 326 n.67

Heritage Healthcare Ctr. v. Agency for Health Care Admin., 746 So. 2d 573 (Fla. Dist. Ct. App. 1999), 82 n.43

Heritage Hous. Dev., Inc. v. Carr, 199 S.W.3d 560 (Tex. App.—Hous. [1st Dist.] 2006), 275 n.22

Hesrkovitz v. Group Health Coop. of Puget Sound, 664 P.2d 474 (Wash. 1983), 322 n.47

Higgins v. Lifecare Ctrs. of Am., 808 N.E.2d 1257 (Mass. App. Ct. 2004), 113 n.77
Hill v. Beverly Enters.-Miss., Inc., 305 F. Supp. 2d 644 (S.D. Miss. 2003), 155 n.68, 273 n.12
Hinlicky v. Dreyfuss, 6 N.Y.3d 636, 848 N.E.2d 1285 (2006), 77 n.26
Hodgdon v. Beatrice D. Weeks Mem'l Hosp., 445 A.2d 1116 (N.H. 1982), 331 n.88
Hohlt v. Complete Health Care, 936 S.W.2d 223 (Mo. Ct. App. 1996), 300 n.18
Hope v. Royal Healthgate Nursing & Rehab. Ctr., A-5072-07T2, 2008 WL 5273084 (N.J. Super. App. Div. Dec. 22, 2008), 165 n.148
Horizon/CMS Healthcare Corp. v. Auld, 34 S.W.2d 887 (Tex. 2000), 344 n.24, 346 n.40, 347
Hout v. City of Mansfield, 550 F. Supp. 2d 701 (N.D. Ohio 2008), 333 n.99
Howell v. NHC Healthcare-Fort Sanders Inc., 109 S.W.2d 731 (Tenn. Ct. App. 2003), 367 n.37
Huls v. Laurel Health Care Co., Case No. 18OT08-0187 (Knox Cnty. Ohio Ct. Com. Pl. June 24, 2022), 93 n.93

I

Integrated Health Care Servs. Inc. v. Lang-Redway, 840 So. 2d 974 (Fla. 2002), 82 n.40, 85 n.58
Ivy Manor Nursing Home v. Brown, 488 P.2d 246 (Colo. Ct. App. 1971), 91 n.77, 122 n.21
Ivy Woods Healthcare & Rehab. Ctr. v. Thompson, 156 F. App'x 775 (6th Cir. 2005), 67 n.2

J

Jaquith Nursing Home v. Yarbrough, 99 So. 3d 745 (La. 2013), 325 n.64
Jennings Guest House v. Gibson, 971 So. 2d 506 (La. Ct. App. 2007), 165 n.149
Johnson *ex rel.* Johnson v. Badger Acq. of Tampa LLC, 983 So. 2d 1175 (Fla. 2d Dist. App. 2008), 191 n.25

Johnson v. Delmar Gardens W., Inc., 335 S.W.3d 83 (Mo. Ct. App. E. Dist. 2011), 274 n.21
Jorgenson v. Vener, 616 N.W.2d 366 (S.D. 2000), 322 n.47
Juhnke v. Evangelical Lutheran Good Samaritan Soc'y, 634 P.2d 1132 (Kan. Ct. App. 1981), 166 n.153, 279 n.3

K

Keaton v. Beverly Enters. Inc., No. CV-2005-282-6 (Ouachita Cnty. Ark. Cir. Ct. 2007), 92 n.83
Kelly v. Bridgeport Health Care Ctr., Inc., 2178 LEXIS (Conn. Super. Ct. Sept. 2, 2010), 129 n.56
Kent v. Cnty. of Hudson, 102 N.J. Super. 208, 245 A.2d 747, *aff'd*, 53 N.J. 546, 251 A.2d 760 (1968), 355 n.22
Kildron v. Shady Oaks Nursing Home, 549 So. 2d 395 (La. Ct. App. 1989), 106 n.46, 312 n.5
Klein v. BIA Hotel Corp., 49 Cal. Rptr. 60 (Cal. Ct. App. 1996), 122 n.27
Klein v. Califano, 586 F.2d 250 (3d Cir. 1978), 336 n.113
Klein v. Mo. Dep't of Health & Senior Servs., 226 S.W.3d 162 (Mo. 2007), 156 n.76, 157 n.80, 162 n.124
K.L. v. Riverside Med. Ctr., 524 N.W.2d 300 (Minn. Ct. App. 1995), 159 n.95, 162 n.125, 168 n.166, 171 n.187, 312 n.6
Kujaswki v. Arbor View Health Care Ctr., 407 N.W.2d 249 (Wis. 1987), 134 n.10, 166 n.154
Kunz v. Little Co. of Mary Hosp. & Health Care Ctrs., 373 Ill. App. 3d 615, 869 N.E.2d 328 (2006), 199 n.71

L

In re Labatt Food Serv. LP, 279 S.W.3d 640 (Tex. 2009), 364 n.27
La. Extended Care Ctrs. v. Miss. Ins. Guar. Ass'n, 87 So. 3d 1030 (Miss. 2012), 378 n.4
Laidlaw v. Andrew Freedman Home, 32 A.D.2d 754, 300 N.Y.S.2d 979 (1969), 106 n.39
Laizure v. Avante at Leesburg Inc., 2013 Fla. LEXIS 249 (Fla. Feb. 14, 2013), 364 n.28

Lake Cnty. Rehab. Ctr. v. Shalala, 854 F. Supp. 1329 (N.D. Ind. 1994), 246 n.9

Lake Mary Health Care v. CMS, Dec. No. 1031 (HHS Departmental Appeals Bd., App. Div., May 14, 2007), 229 n.17

Lakeridge Villa Health Care Ctr. v. Leavitt, 202 F. App'x 903 (6th Cir. 2006), 83 n.52, 134 n.7, 137 n.30

Lama v. Borrs, 16 F.3d 473 (1st Cir. 1994), 62 n.22

Lathan v. Murrah Inc., 174 S.E.2d 269 (Ga. Ct. App. 1970), 110 n.69

In re Lavernia Nursing Facility, 12 S.W.3d 566 (Tex. App. 1999), 175 n.213

Levine v. Rosen, 616 A.2d 623 (Pa. 1992), 301 n.62, 318 n.30

Lexington Ins. Co. v. Educare Cmty. Living Corp., 149 F. App'x 326 (5th Cir. 2005), 178 n.231, 380 n.17

Liberty Commons Nursing & Rehab.-Alamance v. CMS, Dec. No. 2070 (HHS Departmental Appeals Bd., App. Div., Mar. 9, 2007), 129 n.62

Life Care Ctr. Tullahoma v. Sec. of U.S. Dep't of Health & Human Servs., 453 F. App'x 610 (6th Cir. 2011), 200 n.83

Liguori v. Beverly Enters., 762 So. 2d 1069 (Fla. Dist. Ct. App. 2000), 216 n.52

Limbaugh v. Coffee Med. Ctr., 59 S.W.2d 73 (2001), 175 n.214, 241 n.19, 341 n.8, 379 n.13

Living Ctrs. of Tex. v. Penalver, 2010 WL 1708333 (Tex. App. Apr. 28, 2010), 372 n.12

Livingston Care Ctr. v. U.S. Dep't of HHS, 108 F. App'x 350 (6th Cir. 2004), 82 n.41

Lloyd v. Shady Lake Nursing Home, Inc., 92 So. 3d 560 (La. Ct. App. 2d Cir. 2012), 180 n.245

Lohr v. Medtronic Inc., 518 U.S. 470 (1996), 308 n.5

Long v. Brookside Manor, 855 S.W.2d 70 (Tenn. Ct. App. 1994), 176 n.216, 240 n.14, 321 n.38

Love v. CF&H Corp., 89 S.W.2d 68 (Tex. App. 2002), 125 n.40, 128 n.52, 129 n.59

Lowe v. Gen. Motors Corp., 624 F.2d 1373 (5th Cir. 1980), 320 n.33

Lutz v. Brian Ctr. Nursing Care, No. 95-CV-1290 (Catawba Cnty. N.C. Super. Ct. May 27, 1997), 198, 198 n.69, 201, 201 n.85, 210 n.19

M

MacAlpine v. Martin, 205 So. 2d 347 (Fla. Dist. Ct. App. 1967), 111 n.73
Makas v. Hillhaven Inc., 589 F. Supp. 736 (M.D.N.C. 1984), 166 n.151
Manley v. Personacare, 2007 WL 210583, 2007-Ohio-343 (Ohio Ct. App. Jan. 26, 2007), 368 n.44
Maplewood Care, Inc. v. Arnold, 2013 Ill. App. (1st) 120602, 171 n.189
Markowitz v. Helen Homes, 826 So. 2d 256 (Fla. 2002), 209 n.16
Marmet Health Care Ctr., Inc. v. Brown, 132 S. Ct. 1201 (2012), 360 n.9, 362–363, 363 n.21
Marotta v. Whitehall of St. Petersburg, 195 So. 2d 225 (Fla. Dist. Ct. App. 1967), 136 n.27
Marsh v. Bay Convalescent Ctr., No. 93-3758B (Bay Cnty. Fla. Cir. Ct. 1995), 211 n.24, 212 n.34
Mast v. Magpusao, 225 Cal. Rptr. 689 (Cal. Ct. App. 1986), 164 n.139, 179 n.240, 312 n.2, 313 n.8
Matteo v. Geisinger Wyo. Valley Med. Ctr., No 7248-C (Luzerne Cnty. Pa. 1998), 117 n.92
May v. Triple C Convalescent Ctrs., 19 Wash. App. 794, 578 P.2d 541 (1978), 166 n.151, 166 n.152, 375 n.8
McCain v. Beverly Health & Rehab. Servs., 202 WL 1565526 (E.D. Pa. 2002), 317 n.29
McClain v. Mariner Health, Inc., 631 S.E.2d 435 (Ga. Ct. App. 2006), 320 n.34
McCoy v. Alvista Care Home Inc., 391 S.E.2d 419 (Ga. Ct. App. 1999), 122 n.26
McDaniel v. Ong, 724 N.E.2d 38 (Ill. App. Ct. 1999), 171 n.190, 324 n.57
McGillivray v. Rapides Iberia Mgmt. Enters., 493 So. 2d 819 (La. Ct. App. 1986), 121 n.17, 124 n.36, 129 n.61

McLemore *ex rel.* McLemore v. Elizabethton Med. Investors, Ltd. P'ship, 389 S.W.3d 764 (Tenn. Ct. App. 2012), 344, 344 n.23
McMullen v. Ark. Elder Outreach of Little Rock, Inc., 2011 WL 715014 (Ark. App. Mar. 2, 2011), 357 n.29
MeadowWood Nursing Home v. U.S. Dep't of HHS, 364 F.3d 786 (6th Cir. 2004), 69 n.4, 134 n.9, 135 n.23
Mellies v. Nat'l Heritage Inc., 636 P.2d 215 (Kan. Ct. App. 1981), 89 n.69
Miller v. Currie, 50 F.3d 373 (6th Cir. 1995), 334 n.106
Mineo v. Underwriters at Lloyds, London, 2007-0514 (La. App. 4 Cir. Oct. 22, 2008), 325 n.64
Mitchell v. State, 491 So. 2d 596 (Fla. Dist. Ct. App. 1986), 63 n.28
Mitter v. Touro Infirmary, 874 So. 2d 265 (La. Ct. App. 2004), 339 n.1
Montalbano v. Buffman, Inc., 90 So. 3d 503 (La. App. 4 Cir. 2012), 327 n.68
Montgomery Health Care Facility v. Ballard, 565 So. 2d 221 (Ala. 1990), 266 n.12, 376 n.9
Montiel v. City of Los Angeles, 2 F.3d 335 (9th Cir. 1993), 292 n.15
Morgan v. Galilean Health Enters., 977 P.2d 357 (Okla. 1998), 165 n.144, 323 n.52
Morisette v. Terence Cardinal Cooke Health Care Ctr., 797 N.Y.S.2d 856 (Sup. 2005), 200 n.82, 317 n.29
Morris v. Longwood Mgmt. Co., No. BC-310030 (L.A. Cnty. Cal. Super. Ct. 2005), 92 n.81
Morris v. Monterey Yorkshire Nursing Inn, 278 N.E.2d 686 (Ohio Ct. App. 1971), 324 n.60
Morton v. Madison Cnty. Nursing Home Auxiliary, 761 N.E.2d 145 (Ill. 2001), 274 n.20
Moskovitz v. Mt. Sinai Med. Ctr., 69 Ohio St. 3d 638, 635 N.E.2d 331 (1994), 346 n.37
Muccianti v. Willow Creek Care Ctr., No. 625122-7 (Fresno Cnty. Cal. Super. Ct. 2001), 206 n.3, 212
Munson v. Lakewood Quarters Ltd. P'ship, 965 So. 2d 448 (La. Ct. App. 2007), 107 n.52
Murphy *ex rel.* Reliford v. EPI Corp., 2002-CA-002173-MR, 2004 WL 405754 (Ky. Ct. App. Mar. 5, 2004), 171 n.185

Murphy v. Allstate Ins. Co., 295 So. 2d 29 (La. Ct. App. 1974), 120 n.6
Mut. Pharm. Co. v. Bartlett, 570 U.S. 472 (2013), 59 n.19
Myers v. Heritage Enters., Inc., 354 Ill. App. 3d 241, 820 N.E.2d 604 (Ill. App. Ct. 4th Dist. 2004), 107 n.53, 117 n.87

N

Newlin v. Vita Healthcare Grp., Case No. CV-2020-008216 (Delaware Cnty. Pa. Ct. Com. Pl. Dec. 20, 2023), 93 n.95
Niece v. Elmview Group Home, 929 P.2d 420 (Wash. 1997), 158 n.90, 163 n.130, 168 n.160, 169 n.168, 174 n.202
NME Props. Inc. v. Rudich, 840 So. 2d 309 (Fla. App. 2003), 274 n.18
N.X. v. Cabrini Med. Ctr., 765 N.E.2d 844 (N.Y. 2002), 272 n.7

O

O'Bannon v. Town Court Nursing Ctr., 447 U.S. 773 (1980), 329 n.75
Oklahoma v. Thomason, 33 P.3d 930 (Okla. Civ. App. 2001), 299 n.16, 375 n.5
Olson v. Chisholm Trail Living & Rehab. Ctr., No. 98-0-363 (Caldwell Cnty. Tex. Jud. Dist. Ct. 1999), 87 n.67, 92 n.82
Ore & Chem. Corp. v. Stinnes Interoil, Inc., 611 F. Supp. 237 (S.D.N.Y. 1985), 365 n.32
Ostrum v. Manorcare Health Serv., 2007 WL 188132 (E.D. Mich. Jan. 22, 2007), 128 n.54
Oswald v. LeGrand, 453 N.W.2d 634 (Iowa 1990), 333 n.100, 334, 334 n.104
Our Lady of Peace, Inc. v. Morgan, 297 Va. 832, 832 S.E.2d 15 (2019), 172 n.195
Owens v. Coosa Valley Health Care, 890 So. 2d 983 (Ala. 2004), 362 n.19

P

Padgett v. Baxley & Appling Cnty. Hosp. Auth., 741 S.E.2d 193 (Ga. Ct. App. 2013), 107 n.50, 110 n.66
Palermo v. Port of New Orleans, 951 So. 2d 425 (La. Ct. App. 2007), 312 n.4, 354 n.17

Palmer v. Intermed Inc., 270 Ark. 538, 606 S.W.2d 87 (1980), 109 n.62, 110 n.67
Palmer v. S. Ala. Nursing Home, Civ. No. CV-00-2775 (Mobile Cnty. Ala. 2001), 117 n.89
In re Paris Air Crash, 622 F.2d 1325 (9th Cir. 1980), 321 n.43
Parish v. Beverly Enters., CV-1-99-7216CC (Clay Cnty. Ct. Mo. July 2003), 212 n.29
Parker v. Ill. Masonic Warren Barr Pavilion, 299 Ill. App. 3d 495, 701 N.E.2d 190 (1998), 106 n.40, 106 n.42
Parker v. Symphony of Evanston Healthcare, LLC, No. 1-22-0391, 2023 WL 3806800 (Ill. App. June 5, 2023), 66 n.33
Parkview Nursing & Rehab. Ctr. v. Iowa Dep't of Inspections, 2001 WL 726397 (Iowa Ct. App. June 29, 2001), 113 n.76
Pasqua v. Bon Secours N.Y. Health Sys. Inc., 13 Misc. 3d 1036, 827 N.Y.S.2d 548 (N.Y. Sup. Ct. 2006), 116 n.84
Passmore v. Multi-Mgt. Servs., Inc., 810 N.E.2d 1022 (Ind. 2004), 174 n.205
Peay v. Panorama Res-Care, No. 87-CI-701 (Warren Cnty. Ky. Cir. Ct. 1991), 169 n.175
Penny v. Sunbridge Healthcare, No. 02-C-378 (Cass Cnty. Tex. 2003), 105 n.35, 117–118, 118 n.94
People v. Johnson, 595 N.E.2d 1381 (Ill. App. Ct. 1992), 137 n.33, 154 n.60, 156 n.75, 157 n.82
People v. Spence, 648 N.Y.S.2d 636 (App. Div. 1996), 200 n.84
Perreira v. Rediger, 778 A.2d 429 (N.J. 2001), 392 n.13
Perry v. Thomas, 482 U.S. 483 (1987), 360 n.7
Piazza v. Regeis Care Ctr., L.L.C., 852 N.Y.S.2d 53 (N.Y. App. Div. 1st Dep't 2008), 168 n.165
Pineview Manor v. Ohio Dep't of Health, 2003-Ohio-5762, 2003 WL 22434603 (Ohio Ct. App. Oct. 28, 2003), 82 n.44, 83 n.51, 84 n.54
Ping v. Beverly Enters. Inc., 376 S.W.3d 581 (Ky. 2012), 363 n.25
Pitts v. Davis Nursing Ass'n, 2005 WL 2244691, Case 5:05CV00234SWW (E.D. Ark. Sept. 13, 2005), 84 n.57

Pitts v. Wingate at Brighton, Inc., 82 Mass. App. Ct. 285, 972 N.E.2d 74 (Mass. App. Ct. 2012), 112 n.74
Platt v. Palmer, No. 06-CC-04201 (Orange Cnty. Super. Ct. Mar. 27, 2007), 218 n.70
PLIVA, Inc. v. Mensing, 564 U.S. 604 (2011), 59 n.19
Powell v. Parkview Estate Nursing Home, 240 So. 2d 53 (La. Ct. App. 1970), 109 n.60, 122 n.24, 135 n.24
Price v. TLC Health Care, Inc., 2004 OK 8, 85 P.3d 838, 274 n.19
Progressive Preferred Ins. Co. v. Certain Underwriters at Lloyds, 2008 WL 2069404 (Ohio Ct. App. 5/28/2008), 377 n.3

R

Raiteri v. NHC Healthcare Knoxville, E2003-00068-COA-R9-CV, 2003 WL 23094413 (Tenn. Ct. App. Dec. 30, 2003), 367 n.39
Reaux v. Our Lady of Lourdes Hosp., 492 So. 2d 233 (La. Ct. App. 1986), 167 n.158
Reed v. Life Care Ctrs., Case No. 2018-CA-013297-O, 2022 WL 2229485 (Fla. Cir. Ct. Mar. 11, 2022), 93 n.94
Regions Bank & Trust Co. v. Stone Cnty. Skilled Nursing Facility, 49 S.W.3d 107 (Ark. 2001), 163 n.130, 178 n.233
Rehab. Ass'n of Va. v. Kozlowski, 42 F.3d 1444 (4th Cir. 1994), 264 n.6
Reiss v. Stamford Hosp., 205 WL 2009560 (Conn. Super. Ct. Aug. 2, 2005), 128 n.55
Rey v. Park View Nursing Home, Inc., 692 N.Y.S.2d 686 (N.Y. App. Div. 2d Dep't 1999), 270 n.1
Rhodes v. HEB Nursing Home, 8 Elder L.J. 239 (2000), 212 n.28
Richardson v. Abbey Nursing Home, 1983 Westlaw 2867 (Ohio App. 1983), 372 n.11
Richards v. Broadview Heights Harborside Healthcare, 782 N.E.2d 609 (Ohio Ct. App. 2002), 121 n.19
Riegel v. Medtronic, 552 U.S. 312 (2008), 308 n.5
Riley v. Maison Orleans II Inc., 829 So. 2d 479 (La. Ct. App. 2002), 126 n.43, 178 n.229, 379 n.14

Rinaldi v. City View Nursing & Rehab. Ctr., 2005 WL 3215146 (Ohio Ct. App. Dec. 1, 2005), 116 n.81

Rivera v. Brentwood Place Three, No. 00-06777-E (Dallas Cnty. Tex. Jud. Dist. Ct. 2002), 92 n.84

Roberts v. Ohio Permanente Med. Grp., Inc., 668 N.E.2d 480 (Ohio 1996), 322 n.47

Robicheaux v. Adly, 827 So. 2d 429 (La. Ct. App. 3d Cir. 2002), *writ denied*, 836 So. 2d 100 (La. 2003), 194 n.44

Rodebush v. Okla. Nursing Homes Ltd., 867 P.2d 1241 (Okla. 1993), 164 n.133, 174 n.200, 175 n.212, 275 n.24, 344 n.25, 345 n.32

Rodriguez v. Marion Mem'l (Buena Vista Cnty. Ga. Dist. Ct. 2004), 93 n.87, 206 n.4

Rodriguez v. Terence Cardinal Cooke Health Care Ctr., 771 N.Y.S.2d 516 (N.Y. App. Div. 1st Dep't 2004), 168 n.164

Rolling Hills Rehab. Ctr. v. CMS, Dec. No. 2119 (HHS Departmental Appeals Bd., App. Div., Oct. 5, 2007), 162 n.116

Romano *ex rel.* Romano v. Manor Care, Inc., 861 So. 2d 59 (Fla. 4th Dist. Ct. App. 2003), 360 n.3

Roper v. Blumenfeld, 309 N.J. Super. 219, 706 A.2d 1151 (1998), 77 n.27

Rosemont Inc. v. Marshall, 481 So. 2d 1126 (Ala. 1985), 128 n.53, 129 n.58

S

Salas v. Grancare Inc., 22 P.3d 568 (Colo. Ct. App. 2001), 324 n.56, 335 n.109, 336 n.114

Salmon v. Dep't of Pub. Health, 788 A.2d 1199 (Conn. 2002), 163 n.128, 177 n.224

Sandoval v. Summit Care Corp., No. 633197-9 (Fresno Cnty. Cal. Super. Ct. 2003), 84 n.55, 87 n.66, 92 n.86

Sanford v. Castleton Health Care Ctr., LLC, 813 N.E.2d 411 (Ind. Ct. App. 2004), 360 n.6

Satterwhite v. Reilly, 817 So. 2d 407 (La. Ct. App. 2d Cir. 2002), *writ denied*, 825 So. 2d 1193 (La. 2002), 272 n.9, 320 n.34

Sauer v. Advocat Inc., No. crv 2000-5 (Ark. Cir. Ct. 2001), 198 n.62

Saunders v. Beverly Enters., No. 89C-10930 (Marion Cty. Or. filed Mar. 18, 1999), 136 n.26, 216 n.57
Senior Rehab. & Skilled Nursing Ctr. v. U.S. Dep't of HHS, 405 F. App'x 820 (5th Cir. 2010), 49 n.18
Setlock v. Pinebrook Pers. Care, 2012 Pa. Super. LEXIS 3446 (Pa. Super. Ct. Oct. 23, 2012), 364 n.29
Sharp v. Parkview Care Ctr., Inc., 940 So. 2d 724 (La. Ct. App. 2d Cir. 2006), 56 n.7, 238 n.5
Shaw v. BMW Healthcare, Inc., 100 S.W.3d 8 (Tex. App.—Tyler 2002), 195 n.48
Shepard v. Mielke, 877 P.2d 220 (Wash. Ct. App. 1994), 152 n.55, 158 n.91, 159 n.96, 312 n.6
Slobin v. Boasiako, 19 Misc. 3d 1110 (N.Y. Super. Ct. Mar. 18, 2008), 175 n.209, 215 n.45, 216 n.58
Smartt v. NHC, No. 2182 (Warren Cnty., Tenn. Cir. Ct., Feb. 22, 2007), 117 n.88, 274 n.15, 340 n.4
Smith v. Gravois Rest Haven Inc., 662 S.W.2d 880 (Mo. Ct. App. 1983), 106 n.38, 106 n.41
Smith v. Manor Care of Canton, 2006 WL 636975 (Ohio Ct. App. Mar. 13, 2006), 116 n.81
Smith v. Parks Methodist Ret. Vill., No. A-114050 (Ector Cnty. Tex. 2004), 117 n.91
Smith v. Silver Spring-Wheaton Nursing Home, 220 A.2d 574 (Md. 1996), 175 n.208
Somberg v. Fla. Convalescent Ctr. Inc., 779 So. 2d 667 (Fla. App. 2001), 260 n.2
Springhill Nursing Homes, Inc. v. McCurdy, 898 So. 2d 694 (Ala. 2004), 363 n.18
Sprosty v. Pearlview Inc., 106 Ohio App. 3d 679, 666 N.E.2d 1180 (1995), 177 n.222, 243 n.24, 323 n.50, 344 n.31
SSC Odin Operating Co. v. Carter, U.S., No. 12-1015 (petition for review filed Feb. 15, 2013), 363 n.23
State Farm Mut. Auto. Ins. Co. v. Campbell, 538 U.S. 408 (2003), 344 n.35

State v. Boone Ret. Ctr., Inc., 26 S.W.3d 265 (Mo. Ct. App. W.D. 2000), 63 n.28
State v. Brenner, 486 So. 2d 101 (La. 1986), 156 n.79
State v. Janssen, 584 N.W.2d 27 (Neb. Ct. App. 1998), 334 n.107
State v. Oismaiye, 740 A.2d 338 (R.I. 1999), 164 n.231, 178 n.235
State v. Serebin, 350 N.W.2d 65 (Wis. 1984), 62 n.26, 122 n.23, 156 n.77
Stevens v. Axelrod, 162 A.D.2d 1025 (N.Y. App. Div. 1990), 157 n.83, 177 n.223
Stewart v. Renova Health Ctr., No. 05-2005-CA-006508 (Palm Beach Cnty. Fla. Cir. Ct. 2006), 93 n.89
Stiffelman v. Abrams, 655 S.W.2d 522 (Mo. 1983), 165 n.143, 323 n.48, 323 n.52, 371 n.5
Stogsdill v. Healthmark Partners, L.L.C., 377 F.3d 827 (8th Cir. 2004), 62 n.23, 72 n.6, 109 n.63, 325 n.63, 344 n.29, 356 n.23
St. Paul Fire & Marine Ins. Co. v. Alderman, 455 S.E.2d 852 (Ga. Ct. App. 1995), 363 n.15, 379 n.15
St. Paul Fire & Marine Ins. Co. v. Hausman, 604 N.W.2d 908 (Wis. Ct. App. 1999), 379 n.16
Strasel v. Seven Hills, 170 Ohio App. 3d 98, 866 N.E.2d 48 (2007), 334 n.103
Stropes v. Heritage House Children's Ctr., 547 N.E.2d 244 (Ind. 1989), 169 n.167
In re SunBridge Care, Dec. No. 2170 (HHS Departmental Appeals Bd. 2008), 105 n.37
Sunbridge Healthcare Corp. v. Penny, 160 S.W.3d 230 (Tex. App. 2006), 374 n.2, 375 n.6
S. Valley Health Care Ctr. v. Health Care Fin. Admin., 223 F.3d 1221 (10th Cir. 2000), 83 n.50

T

Tait v. W. World Ins. Co., 220 So. 2d 226 (La. Ct. App. 1969), 127 n.48
Tewcyzynski v. Hoffman, No. 1999-29188 (Harris Cnty. Tex. Jud. Dist. Ct. May 12, 2003), 229 n.19
Thibodeaux v. Stonebridge, L.L.C., 873 So. 2d 755 (La. Ct. App. 5 Cir. 2004), 104 n.33, 112 n.75

THI of N.M. at Hobbs Ctr., LLC v. Spradlin, 893 F. Supp. 2d 1172 (D.N.M. 2012), 366 n.35
Tri-County Extended Care Ctr. v. CMS, Dec. No. 2060 (HHS Departmental Appeals Bd., App. Div., Jan. 10, 2007), 82 n.39, 85 n.59
Truehill v. W. Med. Ctr., No. 722908 (Orange Cnty. Cal. Super. Ct. 1996), 211 n.25, 212
Tudor v. Wheatland Nursing L.L.C., 42 Kan. App. 2d 624, 214 P.3d 1217 (Kan. Ct. App. 2009), 107 n.48

U

United States v. Momence Meadows Nursing Ctr., Inc., No. 2 04 C 2289 (CD. Ill. Feb. 8, 2012), 242 n.22
U.S. Fire Ins. Co. v. Scottsdale Ins. Co., 264 S.W.3d 160 (Tex. App. 2009), 378 n.5
U.S. v. Bell, No. 02:04CR0212, 2006 WL 952214 (W.D. Pa. Apr. 12, 2006), 104 n.31, 173 n.198

V

Vandalia Park v. Leavitt, 157 F. App'x 858 (6th Cir. 2005), 142 n.18, 174 n.199, 176 n.221, 297 n.8
Vergara v. Doan, 593 N.E.2d 185 (Ind. 1992), 76 n.24
Virginia S. v. Salt Lake Care Ctr., 741 P.2d 969 (Utah Ct. App. 1987), 122 n.21, 170 n.181

W

Washington v. Nexion Health, 2006 WL 5347044 (La. Trial Ct. 2006), 93 n.91, 279 n.2
Washington v. Wash. Hosp. Ctr., 627 A.2d 177 (D.C. 1990), 318 n.30
Wash. Nursing Ctr., Inc. v. Quem, 442 F. Supp. 23 (S.D. Ill. 1977), 336 n.113
Watts v. Golden Age Nursing Home, 127 Ariz. 255, 619 P.2d 1032 (1980), 104 n.33
Westchester Fire Ins. Co. v. Admiral Ins. Co., 152 S.W.3d 172 (Tex. App. 2004), 380 n.17, 380 n.19

Wilks v. Ave. Care Ctr., No. 95-L-5369 (Cook Cnty. Ill. 1999), 117 n.93
Williams v. Wasserman, 164 F. Supp. 2d 591 (D. Md. 2001), 202 n.94
Windsor Place Nursing & Rehab. Ctr. v. U.S. Dep't of HHS, 649 F.3d 293 (5th Cir. 2011), 67 n.1, 264 n.5
Woodland Vill. Nursing Ctr. v. CMS, Dec. No. CR1367 (HHS Departmental Appeals Bd., Civ. Remedies Div., Nov. 16, 2005), 220
Woodstock Care Ctr. v. HCFA, Dec. No. 1726 (HHS Departmental Appeals Bd., App. Div., May 30, 2000), 157 n.81, 161 n.109, 179 n.239
Woodstock Care Ctr. v. Thompson, 80 F. App'x 962 (6th Cir. 2003), 161 n.108

Y

Yaw v. Dep't of Health Servs., No. 703447, 1993 Conn. Super. LEXIS 1263 (Conn. Super. Ct. May 12, 1993), 163 n.126, 328 n.71

Z

Zeides v. Hebrew Home, 753 N.Y.S.2d 450 (App. Div. 2002), 200 n.81
Zorn v. Life Care Ctrs of Am., 2004 WL 5217647 (S.C. State Ct. 2004), 278 n.1

Index

A

Abuse
- administrator and, 31, 62
- allegations of concealment of, 173–174
- assault in, 146–147, 154, 158–159
- "bad apples" approach to, 147, 149
- battery in, 146–147
- by caregivers, 146–150
- civil liability and, 159
- CMS and state penalties with, 176–177
- confidentiality and, 142 n.20
- criminal aspects of, 154–156
- defending nursing home supervision in, 167–169
- defining, 140
- definitions with, 156–158
- dementia and, 142
- duty of care and, 157–158, 159–161
- economic, by theft or fraud, 334–335
- evidentiary issues with, 178–179
- examples of, 140
- feeding and, 208
- governmental immunity and, 179–180
- Health Care Quality Improvement Act and, 147
- hiring errors and, 174–176
- impulsive, 148–149
- incidence of, 141–142, 145–146
- increase in, 145–146
- intentional, 146–150
- liability for, 150, 152–153, 163–166
- liability insurance and, 177–178
- malpractice and, 166–167
- National Practitioners Data Bank and, 147
- neglect and, 150–152, 157
- ombudsmen programs and, 143–144
- by other residents, 152–154
- overview of, 140–143
- pattern of ignored, 23
- pervasiveness of, 141
- prevention of, 148, 149
- public outrage over, 173

Abuse, *continued*
punitive damages with, 177
reporting of, 45, 142–143, 153, 162, 300
resident behavior as trigger for, 148
responding to, 152–153, 162–163
sexual, 155, 156–157, 169–173
shock over, 173
sources of assaults in, 158–159
of staff by resident, 180–181
supervision errors and, 174–176
by third parties, 152–154
underreporting of, 142–143
understaffing and, 148–149, 154–155
Accounting staff, 64
Accreditation bodies, 37
Activities of daily living (ADLs), as purpose of stay, 24
ADLs. *See* Activities of daily living (ADLs)
Administration
deposition of, 286–287
role of, 62–63
substandard care and, 62–63
in training, 282
as witness, 280–282
Administrative liability, 272–273
Administrator, ownership and, 32
Admissibility, of survey data, 292
Admission(s)
agreements, 233–234
balancing, economics of, 232–233
brochures, 233–234
malpractice and, 51
Medicaid and, 232–233
Medicare and, 232–233
nurses in, 38
rationale for placement and, 231–232
staff and, 63–64
Advance directives. *See* "Right to die"
Advanced practice nurse, role of, 35
Adverse drug interactions, 188–189, 195–196
Adverse effects, 58, 196
Adverse events, with medical devices, 203
Affordable Care Act
management reporting under, 88
nursing home ownership and, 30, 273
Agency for Healthcare Research and Quality (AHRQ), 76
Agreements, admission, 233–234
AHRQ. *See* Agency for Healthcare Research and Quality (AHRQ)
Alarms
bedside, 102
door, 65
for wandering, 127

Allergies, 206
Alteration, of records, 298–299
American Health Lawyers Association (AHLA), 365–366
Antipsychotics
adverse consequences with, 186
excessive use of, 184
inappropriate use of, 184, 186–188
polypharmacy and, 186
Ants, 229
Appeals
of discharge, 236
with falls litigation, 112–113
of surveys, 292–293
Arbitration
award limitations, 365
case for requiring, 360–361
co-equal, 9
costs, 365
criticism of use of, 361–365
defenses against, 366–368
litigation *vs.*, 9–10
overview of, 359–360
procedures, 365–366
Assault, 146–147, 154, 158–159. *See also* Abuse
Assembly of complaint
attorney fee requests and, 243
damages and, 243
elements of due care in, 239–240
elements of due corporate responsibility in, 240–241
elements of knowledge in, 238–239
with feeding issues, 221–222
overview of, 237–238
public defendants and, 241
statute of limitations defenses in, 242
whistleblower claims and, 242
Assisted living facilities, defined, 15
Assistive devices, 304–307
Attorney fee requests, 243
Authentication, of survey data, 292
Autopsy, 260–261

B

Background, 15
Bad-faith litigation, 380
Bankruptcy, 10, 385
Bathing, 228–229
Battery, 146–147. *See also* Abuse
BBP. *See* Bloodborne Pathogens (BBP) standard
Bed rail collapses, 69, 135
Bedside alarms, 102
Beers List, 195
Behavioral and psychological symptoms (BPSD), 186, 187
Billing
inept, 64
overbilling, 64

Bloodborne Pathogens (BBP) standard, 228
BPSD. *See* Behavioral and psychological symptoms (BPSD)
Breach of contract, 335
Brochures, admission, 233–234
Budget, food, 55
Burns, 90–91, 228–229
Byzantine Empire, 19

C

Caps, on damages, 9, 346–347
Care plans, 37–38
  documentation and, 300–301
  wandering and, 124
Causes of action
  abuse and, 146, 149
  in assembly of complaint, 237–238
  breach of contract in, 335
  class actions and, 335–336
  clinical practice guidelines in, 313–318
  economic abuse in, 334–335
  False Claims Act and, 331–333
  fraud in, 334–335
  infliction of emotional distress in, 333–334
  intentional torts in, 327–328
  loss of chance of life in, 322
  malpractice in, 324–327
  misrepresentation in, 331
  negligence in, 312–313
  negligence per se in, 318–321
  overview of, 311–312
  respondeat superior and, 275
  standard of care in, 313–318
  statutory, 323–324
  theft in, 334–335
  wrongful death statutes and, 321
  wrongful discharge in, 329–331
Centers for Medicare and Medicaid Services (CMS), 15
  arbitration and, 360
  dietary services and, 54–55
  Division of Nursing Homes, 225, 226
  guidelines as evidence for standard of care, 76–78
  norms on physician obligations, 47–48
  pressure sores and, 72–73, 74
  staffing levels and, 36–37, 54
Certified nursing assistants (CNAs)
  role of, 35, 36
  training of, 39
Charitable immunity, 357
Charting by exception, 61–62
Choking, 206–207, 209, 210, 213, 214
Choosing Wisely, 187, 197
Class actions, 335–336
Cleanliness, 65
Clients. *See* Plaintiff(s)

Clinical practice guidelines (CPGs), 76–78, 313–318
CMS. *See* Center for Medicare and Medicaid Services (CMS)
CNAs. *See* Certified nursing assistants (CNAs)
Complaint drafting. *See* Assembly of complaint
Complaint surveys, 290
Complexity, of therapy, 16
Compliance
  falls and, 116–117
  minimal, 8
Conditions of Participation, 19, 20
Confidentiality, abuse and, 142 n.20
Consent, informed
  documentation and, 300
  pharmaceuticals and, 194
  restraints and, 40, 50
  tube feeding and, 216
Consumer Product Safety Commission (CPSC), 310
Contractual obligations, 46–47
Contraindications, with drugs, 194
Controls
  federal operational aspects of, 16
  funding and, 18–20
Corporate budget official, ownership and, 31–32
Corporate entities, 246–250
Corporate representatives
  as defendants, 250–251
  deposition of, 287
Corporate responsibility, 240–241
Cost control, 5
  as cause of injury, 64
  drugs and, 58
  litigation and, 7–8
Cost reports, 14
COVID-19 pandemic, ombudsmen complaints and, 144
CPGs. *See* Clinical practice guidelines (CPGs)
CPSC. *See* Consumer Product Safety Commission (CPSC)
Criminal aspects, with abuse, 154–156

D

Damages. *See also* Verdicts
  assembly of complaint and, 243
  bankruptcy and, 385
  calculation of, 338–340
  caps on, 9, 346–347, 381
  death effects and, 341
  elders as having low, 337
  general, 340
  hedonic, 339
  liability allocation and, 340–341
  liens and, 387–388

Damages, *continued*
  Medicaid eligibility and, 347
  multiple defendants and, 269
  noneconomic, 337–338
  with pressure sores, 90
  punitive, 343–346
  punitive, with abuse, 177
  punitive, with pressure sores, 90
  "runaway jury," 378
  special, 337–338
  statutory provisions, 346
  tort reform and, 342–343
  with wandering, 128
Daubert effects, 285–286
Death
  actions after, of plaintiff, 258
  damages and, 341
  documentation and, 296
  with feeding, 207–208
  of plaintiff, 260–261
  with tube feeding, 215–216
  in wandering, 120, 129–130
Defendants
  assembly of complaint and public, 241
  deposition of corporate representatives as, 250–251
  in discovery, ethos favoring, 10
  doctors as, 251–252
  identifying, 29–32, 251
  interconnected corporations and, 246–250
  multiple, 269–276
  naming individual, 270
  overview of, 245–246
  ownership and, 245–246, 247–248
  partial settlements with selected, 384
  with products liability, 252–253
  releases of selected, 384–385
  respondeat superior and, 246, 275–276
  shell companies and, 249–250
Defense(s)
  against arbitration, 366–368
  charitable immunity as, 357
  overview of, 349–353
  related to families, 356
  related to regulators, 356–357
  related to residents, 353–356
  statute of limitations, 242
Definitions, 13–15
Dehydration
  dietitian and, 55
  drugs and, 58
  feeding and, 209–210, 219, 220
  pharmaceuticals and, 58
  pressure sores and, 85, 210
Dementia. *See also* Wandering
  abuse and, 142
  antipsychotic use in, 186
  elopement and, 120–121
  wandering and, 57
Departmental Appeals Board, 21

Deposition
of corporate representatives, 250–251, 287
of management and supervisors, 286–287
Destruction, of records, 298–299
Deterrence, of litigation, 8
Devices, medical, 202–203, 252–253. *See also* Product-related risk
Diabetes, 205–206, 221
Dietary support. *See also* Food concerns
pressure sores and, 75
staffing and, 54–56
Dietitian, 54, 55, 206, 220, 222. *See also* Food concerns
Director of nursing
patient care and, 37–38
role of, 35
Disaster safety, 68
Discharge
appeal of, 236
for change of condition, 64
involuntary, 234–236
for nonpayment, 64
notice of, 234–235
overview of, 231
wrongful, 329–331
Discovery
motions, 369–370
pro-defendant ethos in, 10
Dividing causes, of pressure sores, 82–84
Division of Nursing Homes (DNH), 225, 226
DNR. *See* Do not resuscitate (DNR)
Documentation
advance directives, 300
alteration of, 298–299
assembly for expert review, 297–298
care plans, 300–301
charting by exception in, 61–62
death and, 296
destruction of, 298–299
dietary support and, 56
do not resuscitate, 300
falls and, 104
of food concerns, 205–206
informed consent and, 300
licensure, 301–302
mandatory reports in, 299–300
Medicare Cost Reports in, 302
Office of the Inspector General reports, 302
overview of, 295–297
patient privacy and, 299
of physician decisions, 48
pressure sores and, 73–74, 83, 85
records management in, 62
silence in, 62
staff and, 61–62
survey, 301–302
Document review, 285

Do not resuscitate (DNR), 222, 300. *See also* "Right to die"
Door-exit alarms, 65
Drowning, 228–229
"Drug mentions," 183–184
Drugs. *See* Pharmaceuticals
Duty of care
  abuse and, 157–158, 159–161
  in assembly of complaint, 239–240
  classification of facilities and, 14
  pharmaceuticals and, 198
  restraints and, 138
  wandering and, 119, 130–131

E

Economic abuse by theft or fraud, 334–335
Electrical power, 69
Elopement, 120–121, 124, 127. *See also* Wandering
Emergency Medical Treatment and Active Labor Act (EMTALA), 235, 330
Emergency safety, 68
Emotional distress, 333–334
EMTALA. *See* Emergency Medical Treatment and Active Labor Act (EMTALA)
Enforcement, weakness of, 21
Enteral feeding, 69, 217–218
Errors, medication, 191–192, 200–202
Evacuations, 68
Evidence
  with abuse, 178–179
  decisions on, 375
  demonstrative, 374–375
  with falls, 107–108
  of pressure sores, 88–89
Experts. *See also* Witnesses
  in case evaluation, 280
  Daubert effects with, 285–286
  in document review, 297–298
  falls and, 107
  food concerns and, 214–215
  need for, 279
  nontestifying, 280
  standard of care and, 279
  wandering and, 126

F

FAA. *See* Federal Arbitration Act (FAA)
Facility case-mix ratios, 30
Fact witnesses, 286
Failure to state a claim, 370–371
Failure to thrive, 56
Falls
  appellate level and, 112–113
  assessments for, 98–99
  avoiding, 99–101
  case complexity, 105–107
  case examples, 117–118
  causes of, 96
  costs associated with, 95–96
  documentation and, 104
  drugs and, 58

evaluation of potential litigation with, 113–115
evidence with, 107–108
expert witnesses and, 107
extrinsic factors in, 97–98
incidence of, 96–97
juries and, 110
legal implications of, 107–109
liability for, 106–107
malpractice and, 107
minimum data set and, 98–99
negligence and, 108–111, 115
noncompliance and, 116–117
plaintiff's theory of case with, 115–116
policies and, 116–117
procedures and, 104
proof of causation with, 111–112
resident evaluation for, 101–103
residential products and, 309–310
resource utilization groups and, 99
response to, 104–105
restraints and, 134, 135–136
transportation and, 105
wandering and, 120
False Claims Act (FCA), 41, 64, 242, 331–333
Family representation, 259–260
FCA. *See* False Claims Act (FCA)
FDA. *See* Food and Drug Administration (FDA)
Federal Arbitration Act (FAA), 360, 363
Federal court, removal to, 371
Federal integration of standards, 18
Federal Torts Claims Act, 241
Feeding. *See also* Dietary support; Food concerns
enteral, 69, 217–218
liability with, 218
pump, 215–217
standard of care and, 208, 220
tube, 56, 207, 215–217, 218–219, 222
Feeding assistants, 208–209, 218
Fire safety, 68
"Five Things Physicians and Patients Should Question," 187 n.13, 189
Floods, 68
FOIA. *See* Freedom of Information Act (FOIA)
Food and Drug Administration (FDA)
hazard alerts, 137–138
medical devices and, 203
Food budget, 55
Food concerns
abuse and, 208
acute, 213–214
assembly of case with, 221–222
baseline evaluations with, 222
in chart, 205–206
choking, 206–207, 209, 210, 213, 214

Food concerns, *continued*
chronic, 210–211
dehydration and, 209–210, 219, 220
diabetes and, 221
dietary support and, 54–56, 75
enteral feeding, 69, 217–218
expert testimony with, 214–215
liquid intake, 219
litigation over, 205–209
malnutrition, 206, 221–222
negligence with, 206, 213, 216, 221
nutritional evaluation in, 56, 220–221, 222
pump feeding, 215–217
responsibility for feeding, 217–219
"right to die" and, 212–213, 222
tube feeding, 207, 215–217, 218–219, 222
types of harm from food, 209–210
wasting and, 210–211
weight loss and, 209–211
Fraud, economic abuse by, 334–335
Freedom of Information Act (FOIA), 60
Funding
control through, 18–20
source categories, significance of, 24–25
state-federal, 264

G
GAO. *See* Government Accountability Office (GAO)
Gas lines, 69–70
Generators, backup, 69
Generic drugs, 58–59, 60
Government Accountability Office (GAO), 22
Governmental immunity
abuse and, 179–180
assembly of case and, 241
Guidelines for Environmental Infection Control in Health-Care Facilities, 227

H
HAIs. *See* Hospital- or healthcare-acquired infections (HAIs)
Harm, understaffing as cause of, 53–54
HCQIA. *See* Health Care Quality Improvement Act (HCQIA)
Health Care Quality Improvement Act (HCQIA), 147
Health Insurance Portability and Accountability Act (HIPAA), 179, 297, 374–375
Hedonic damages, 339

HIPAA. *See* Health Insurance Portability and Accountability Act (HIPAA)
Hiring practices, abuse and, 174–176
Hospital- or healthcare-acquired infections (HAIs), 225–227
Hospitals
  nursing homes *vs.*, 13–14
  physicians in, 44

I
Identification, of defendant nursing home owner, 29–32, 251
Immunity
  charitable, 357
  governmental, 179–180, 241
Impeachment and response, 375–376
Improving the Quality of Care in Nursing Homes (Institute of Medicine), 140
Incentives, executive, 64
Incontinence, pressure sores and, 83–84
Indigent patients, 8
Infection(s)
  Bloodborne Pathogens standard, 228
  C. difficile, 93
  citations for, 144
  cleanliness and, 65
  coexisting disease with, 224
  control, 91, 144, 224
  Guidelines for Environmental Infection Control in Health-Care Facilities, 227
  healthcare-acquired, 225–227
  issues, 227–228
  large verdicts in cases of, 92
  liability for, 91, 223–228
  pressure sores and, 72, 73, 84, 86
  rates, measurement of, 225–226
  recognizing, 224
  urinary, 40
  urinary catheters and, 91, 203
Infliction of emotional distress, 333–334
Insects, 229
Insurance
  abuse and, 177–178
  bad-faith litigation and, 380
  beneficial role of, 380
  coverage of nursing home liability cases, 377–379
  group coverage of liability, 269
  liens, 392–393
  life, 260
  long-term care, 5
  policy exclusions, 379
  policy limits, 379–380
  terms, 379
Intake, malpractice and, 51

Intentional torts
in abuse, 149
in causes of action, 327–328
respondeat superior and, 275
workers' compensation and, 180
Interactions, drug, 188–189, 195–196
Interpretive Guidelines, 99–100
Interrogatories, 383
Involuntary discharge, 234–236
IRS Form 990, 31

J
Joint Commission, 37
Juries
falls and, 110
voir dire and, 373–374
wandering and, 123

K
Kidney function, 190
Knowledge, in assembly of complaint, 238–239

L
Laboratory support, 59–60
Law research, state corporation, 273–274
Legal strategies, 9–10
Liability
for abuse, 150, 152–153, 159, 163–166
administrative, 272–273
allocation of, 340–341
for burns, 90–91
civil, for abuse, 159, 163–166
Clinical Practice Guidelines and, 76–78
for falls, 106–107
with feeding, 218
for infections, 91, 223–228
integration with tort, 25–26
for neglect, 71–94, 119–131
nursing, 270–271
with pharmaceuticals, 194
physician, 271–272
of physicians, 43–52
for pressure sores, 75–76, 81–82
products, 252–253
regulation and tort, 22–23
respondeat superior, 275–276
shared, with pharmaceuticals, 192–193
standards of care and, 76–78
wandering and, 127–128
Licensure
documentation, 301–302
ownership and, 30
practice guidelines and, 39–40
state, 265–266
Liens, 387–391, 392–393
Life insurance, 260
Life Safety Code, 68
Limited liability companies (LLCs), 29–30
Liquid intake, 219
Litigation
arbitration *vs.*, 9–10

bad-faith, 380
cost control and, 7–8
costs, 8–9
damage caps as deterrence to, 346–347
deterrence of, 8
fall, evaluation of potential, 113–115
food-related, 205–209
restraint-injury, 135–136
role of, 4
strategies, 9–10
Liver function, 190
LLCs. *See* Limited liability companies (LLCs)
Lobbying, 4–5, 8, 9, 23
Long-term care, defined, 15
Long-term care insurance, 5
Loss of chance of life, 322

M

Maintenance
failures, staff and, 65
safety and, 69–70
Malnutrition, 55, 206, 210, 213, 221–222
Malpractice
abuse and, 166–167
admissions and, 51
as cause of action, 324–327
falls and, 107
hospitals and, 14
intake and, 51
by misprescribing, 193–196
pharmaceuticals and, 192–196
physicians and, 50–51
state law variations with, 324–325
Mandatory reports, 299–300
"Mary Carter" agreements, 270, 384
Mattresses, 75
MDS. *See* Minimum Data Set (MDS)
Medicaid
admissions and, 232–233
Center for Medicare and Medicaid Services (CMS), 15
eligibility, damages and, 347, 392
as funding source, 25
lab testing and, 60
liens and, 387–388, 389
Medicare *vs.*, 19
reductions, 5, 7
Medical device problems, 202–203, 252–253. *See also* Product-related risk
Medical director
contractual obligations of, 46–47
role of, 43–46
Medicare
admissions and, 232–233
Center for Medicare and Medicaid Services (CMS), 15
Cost Report, 302
cost reports, 14

Medicare, *continued*
as funding source, 25
lab testing and, 60
Medicaid *vs.*, 19
morbidity and mortality with, 7
overbilling, 64
Part A, 16, 99
Part B, 16
profit margins and, 86–87
reductions, 7
skilled nursing facilities in, 16
subrogation and, 387–390
Medicare Secondary Payer Recovery Portal, 388
Medication. *See* Pharmaceuticals
Medication management, 185–186, 189–190. *See also* Pharmaceuticals
Minimum Data Set (MDS), 17, 38, 98–99
Misdelivery, of pharmaceuticals, 199
Misrepresentation, in causes of action, 331
Mortality. *See* Death
Motion for failure to state a claim, 370–371
Motion for remittitur, 372
Motion for removal to federal court, 371
Motion for summary judgment, 371

N

National Action Plan to Prevent Healthcare Associated Infections: Roadmap to Elimination (the National Action Plan), 225
National Nursing Home Survey, 76
National Practitioners Data Bank (NPDB), 147
Neglect
abuse and, 150–152, 157
by caregivers, 150–152
defined, 151
liability for, 71–94, 119–131
service providers and, 151
Negligence
burns and, 90–91
in causes of action, 312–313
contributory, 355
with falls, 108–111, 115
with food, 206, 213, 216, 221
infections and, 91
per se, 318–321
with pharmaceuticals, 196–197
pressure sores and, 82–83, 84
regulatory violations in establishment of, 78–80
restraints and, 136
surveys and, 79–80
with tube feeding, 216

understaffing and, 241
wandering and, 121–122, 125, 126–127, 128–129
Nonprofit status, ownership and, 31
NPDB. *See* National Practitioners Data Bank (NPDB)
Nurse practitioner, role of, 35
Nurses
in admissions, 38
liability of, 270–271
role of, 36
as witnesses, 282–283
Nursing care, as purpose of stay, 24
Nursing home(s)
defined, 13
financial power with, 14–15
identification of owners of, 29–32
legal strategies of, 9–10
population of, 19
profit margins and, 86–87
purposes of stay in, 24
revenue, 6
as "victim," 7
Nursing Home Compare (database), 14–15, 88, 227, 296
Nursing Home Reform Act, 15, 20–21, 140
Nursing liability, 270–271
Nutrition. *See* Dietary support; Food concerns

O

OBRA-87. *See* Nursing Home Reform Act
Office of the Inspector General (OIG), reports, 302
Off-label prescriptions, 186, 193, 194
OIG. *See* Office of the Inspector General (OIG)
Older Americans Act, 140, 143
Ombudsman
abuse and, 143–144
roles, 266–267
state oversight and, 266–267
Outrage, public, over abuse, 173
Overbilling, 64
Overdosing, 197–199
Ownership
administrator and, 32
corporate budget official and, 31–32
defendants and, 245–246, 247–248
identification of, 29–32, 251
nonprofit status and, 31
profit and, 30–31
Oxygen lines, 69

P

Peer pressure, plaintiffs and, 257–258
Pest control, 229
Pharmaceuticals
  antipsychotic, 184, 186–188
  Beers List with, 195
  contraindications with, 194
  "drug mentions" and, 183–184
  errors with, 191–192, 200–202
  generic, 58
  inattentive oversight with, 200–202
  interactions with, 188–189, 195–196
  liability with, 194
  likely problems with, in nursing homes, 191–192
  malpractice and, 192–196
  medication management with, 185–186, 189–190
  misdelivery of, 199
  negligence with, 196–197, 199
  off-label use of, 186, 193, 194
  overdosing of, 197–199
  polypharmacy with, 58, 184, 186, 189–190, 196–197
  products liability and, 252–253
  relevant litigation with, 190–191
  as restraints, 57, 123, 133, 199–200
  sales numbers for, 184
  sedative, 57, 123, 197
  shared liability with, 192–193
  side effects with, 185, 193
  standing orders with, 57, 190
  for wandering, 57, 123
Pharmacist, 44–45, 188, 191
Pharmacy support, 56–59
Physical therapists, role of, 36
Physical therapy, 61
Physicians
  admissions and, 51
  care plans and, 37–38
  CMS norms on obligations of, 47–48
  contractual obligations of, 46–47
  as defendants, 251–252
  documentation of decisions of, 48
  in hospitals *vs.* nursing homes, 44
  liabilities of, 43–52, 271–272
  malpractice issues and, 50–51
  medical director and, 43–44
  -patient contact, 46
  pharmacist and, 44–45
  prescriptions and, 49–50, 189–195
  restraints and, 40, 50
  "right to die" claims and, 51–52

role of, 43–52
in supervision of patient care, 48–49
Plaintiff(s)
actions after death of, 258
autopsy with, 260–261
co-morbidities of, 256–257
death of, 260–261
deterioration of mental and physical condition of, 256–257
eggshell plaintiff rule, 257
evaluation of potential, 255–261
family representation and, 259–260
peer pressure with, 257–258
practical issues with, 260
questions for potential, 261
selection, 256
standing and, 259–260
in state wrongful death actions, 258
survey findings utility to, 291–292
testimony issues with, 257
Plaintiff's theory of case, with falls, 115–116
Political aspects, 26–27
Polypharmacy, 58, 184, 186, 189–190, 196–197
Poverty, 25
Prescriptions, physicians and, 49–50
Presentations, 374–375
Pressure sores
CMS and, 72–73, 74
continuous supervision and, 84–85
damages with, 90
defined, 72
dehydration and, 85, 210
dividing causes of, 82–84
documentation and, 73–74, 83, 85
evidence of, 88–89
incidence of, 72
incontinence and, 83–84
infection and, 72, 73, 84, 86
legal issues with, 81–82
liability for, 75–76, 81–82
malnutrition and, 85, 210
negligence and, 82–83, 84
nutrition and, 75
prevention of, 74–75
punitive damages with, 90
regulatory violations and, 78–80
responsibility for, 40
short staffing and, 87–88
stages, 73–74
standard of due care and, 85–87
training and, 86
unavoidable, 74, 81, 83
Preventable errors, in safety, 69
Privacy, documentation and, 299
Private equity firms, 249

Product-related risk
with assistive devices, 304–307
with medical devices, 307–309
overview of, 303–304
reporting of injuries and, 310
with residential products, 309–310
Products liability, 252–253
Profit
Medicare and, 86–87
ownership and, 30–31
Proof of causation, with falls, 111–112
Protective care, as purpose of stay, 24
Provider Enrollment and Chain Ownership System database, 88, 340
Public policy, 5
Pump feeding, 215–217
Purposes of stay, 24

Q

Quality Care for Nursing Home Residents Act, 54 n.1
Quality Indicator Survey (QIS), 79, 79 n.31
Questions, for potential plaintiffs, 261

R

RAI. *See* Resident assessment instrument (RAI)
Rape, 155, 169–173
RAPs. *See* Resident assessment protocols (RAPs)
Record-keeping. *See* Documentation
Records management, 62
Recreational therapy, 61
Registered nurses, role of, 36
Regulation. *See also* State oversight and regulation; Survey
lobbying and, 4
ownership transparency and, 30
pressure ulcers and, 73–74
tort liability and, 22–23
Rehabilitation
as purpose of stay, 24
staffing, 61
Reimbursement rates, with resource utilization groups, 17
Release, of selected defendants, 384–385
Remittitur, 372
Removal, in emergency planning, 68–69
Removal to federal court, 371
Resident(s)
abuse of staff by, 180–181
defenses related to, 353–356
litigation costs to, 8–9
physician contact with, 46
as witness, 288
Resident assessment instrument (RAI), 98
Resident assessment protocols (RAPs), 98, 102
Residential products, risk with, 309–310

Res ipsa loquitur, 121–122, 170
Resource utilization groups (RUGs)
applying measures of, 17–18
falls and, 99
Respondeat superior, 246, 275–276
Responsibilities
allocation of, 39–40
professional, 40–41
Restraints
benefits of, 133–134
chemical, 57, 123, 133, 199–200
examples of, 133
excessive use of, 137
falls and, 134, 135–136
hazard alerts with, 137–138
injuries from, 134–135
litigation with, 135–136
negligence and, 136
norms with, 136–137
overview of, 133–134
physicians and, 50
responsibility for, 40
uses of, 134–135
Revenues, nursing home, 6
"Right to die." *See also* Do not resuscitate (DNR)
feeding and, 212–213, 222
physicians and, 51–52
RUG. *See* Resource utilization groups (RUGs)

S

Safety issues
emergency, 68
evacuations, 68
fire, 68
flooding, 68
maintenance and, 69–70
premises, 67
preventable errors with, 69
removal and, 68–69
stairways, 70
wandering and, 125
Scalding, 228–229
Security, wandering and, 125
Sedation, 57, 123, 197
Self-pay, 5
Senate Select Committee on Aging, 3–4
Service providers, neglect and, 151
Settlements
abuse and, 154
as common, 221
depositions and, 250
effects of, 382–383
facility maintenance and, 69
influences on, 382
"Mary Carter" agreements, 270, 384
Medicaid eligibility and, 347
partial, with selected defendants, 384
products-related risk and, 305
Sexual assault, 155, 156–157, 169–173
Shell companies, 29–30, 249–250
Shock, over abuse, 173
Side effects, with medications, 185, 193

"Significant changes in condition," 38
Silence, in documentation, 62
Skilled nursing facility (SNF)
  applying measures of, 17–18
  in Medicare, 16
Skin ulcers. *See* Pressure sores
SNF. *See* Skilled nursing facility (SNF)
Social Security Act, 54
SOM. *See* State Operations Manual (SOM)
Sophistication, of therapy, 16
Sovereign immunity, 241
Special Focus Facility list, 290–291
Specialized units, support rules of, 65
Staff
  abuse and, 148–149
  accounting, 64
  in admissions, 63–64
  dietary support, 54–56
  in documentation, 61–62
  former, as witnesses, 283–284
  laboratory support, 59–60
  pharmacy support, 56–59
  pressure sores and, 73, 87–88
  rehabilitation, 61
  selection, 64–65
  support, as witnesses, 284–285
  training, 64–65
  turnover, 218, 284
  wandering and, 125–126
  as witnesses, 282–283
Staffing levels, 36–37, 53–54, 148–149, 150–151, 154–155, 241
Stairway accidents, 70
Standard of care
  in assembly of complaint, 239–240
  in causes of action, 313–318
  experts and, 279
  feeding and, 208, 220
  liability and, 76–78
  pharmaceuticals and, 195
  pressure sores and, 85–87
  regulatory violations and, 78–80
Standards, integration of, 18
Standing, 259–260
Standing orders, 57, 190
State corporation law research, 273–274
State integration of standards, 18
State Operations Manual (SOM), 80, 265
State oversight and regulation
  funding and, 264
  ombudsman and, 266–267
  overview of, 263–264
State wrongful death actions, 258
Statute of limitations defenses, 242
Statutory causes of action, 323–324
Subrogation, 387–391
Substandard care
  administrator and, 62–63

pressure sores and, 94
restraints and, 138
wandering and, 131
Summary judgment, 88, 110, 171, 351, 351 n.8, 371
Supervision
abuse and, 174–176
continuous, 84–85
defending, in abuse cases, 167–169
of patient care, by physicians, 48–49
Supervisory nurse, role of, 35
Support rules, of specialized units, 65
Support staff, roles of, 53–66
Survey
admissibility of, 292
appeals of, 292–293
authentication of, as evidence, 292
complaint, 290
findings, 289–291
negligence and, 79–80
patient care and, 38–39
penalties with, 292–293
Quality Indicator Survey, 79, 79 n.31
Special Focus Facility list and, 290–291
standard, 4
use of, 289–293
utility of, to plaintiffs, 291–292

T

Taxation, 7
Testimony issues, with plaintiffs, 257. *See also* Witnesses
Theft, economic abuse by, 334–335
Theft, of drugs, 57
Therapy
in federal controls, 16
in resource utilization groups, 17
Third party
abuse by, 152–154
as beneficiary, in contract law, 60
Training
administrator in, 282
pressure sores and, 86
as responsibility, 39
staff, 64–65
Transfers, within nursing home, 236
Transportation, falls and, 105
Treatment plan, 16
Trial procedure issues, 373–376
Tube feeding, 56, 207, 215–217, 218–219, 222
Turkey, 19

U

Understaffing, 53–54, 148–149, 150–151, 154–155, 241
Urinary catheters, infection and, 91, 203
Urinary infections, responsibility for, 40

V

Verdicts. *See also* Damages
- allocating percentage fault, 383
- bankruptcy and, 385
- against individual actors, 383–384
- interrogatories and, 383

Verdicts, Settlements & Tactics newsletter, 338

Violence, during wandering, 126

Voir dire, 373–374

W

Wandering
- alarms for, 127
- cognitive function and, 124
- complaint framing with, 126–127
- damages with, 128
- defined, 119
- duty of care and, 119, 130–131
- elopement and, 120–121
- exercise and, 61
- expert testimony and, 126
- falls and, 120
- incidence of, 119–120
- jury trials and, 123
- liability and, 127–128
- mortality and, 120, 129–130
- negligence and, 121–122, 125, 126–127, 128–129
- protection in, 122–123
- reasons for, 124
- responses to, 124
- safety and, 125
- security and, 125
- sedation for, 57, 123
- staff and, 125–126
- violence during, 126

Wasting, 210–211

Weight loss, 209–211

Whistleblowers, 41, 242

Witnesses. *See also* Experts
- administrator as, 281–282
- current administrators as, 280–282
- deposition of, 286–287
- document review and, 285
- fact, 286
- former staff as, 283–284
- overview of, 277–279
- preparation of, 285
- resident as, 288
- staff as, 282–283
- support staff as, 284–285

Workers' compensation, 180

Wrongful death actions, 258, 321